Fault Lines After COVID-19

Robert Z. Aliber
Már Gudmundsson • Gylfi Zoega
Editors

Fault Lines After COVID-19

Global Economic Challenges and Opportunities

palgrave
macmillan

Editors
Robert Z. Aliber
Booth School of Business
University of Chicago
Evanston, IL, USA

Már Gudmundsson
Institute of International Affairs
University of Iceland
Reykjavík, Iceland

Gylfi Zoega
Department of Economics
University of Iceland
Reykjavik, Iceland

ISBN 978-3-031-26481-8 ISBN 978-3-031-26482-5 (eBook)
https://doi.org/10.1007/978-3-031-26482-5

This Palgrave Macmillan imprint is published by the registered company Springer Nature Switzerland AG.
The registered company address is: Gewerbestrasse 11, 6330 Cham, Switzerland

Contents

Introduction 1
Robert Z. Aliber, Már Gudmundsson, and Gylfi Zoega

Part I Challenges Ahead 11

What Next for the Post Covid Global Economy: Could Negative Supply Shocks Disrupt Other Fragile Systems? 13
William White

Historical Roots, Cultural Selection and the 'New World Order' 37
Marcus Miller

Part II China 61

President Xi's Perfect Storm 63
Robert Z. Aliber

Growth Without Democracy: Has China's Time of Rapid Growth Come to an End? 81
Thráinn Eggertsson

Denunciations in Autocratic Regimes: How and When Do They Work 97
Tinghua Yu and Stephane Wolton

Dollar Funding Stresses in China 109
Laura E. Kodres, Leslie Sheng Shen, and Darrell Duffie

Part III Ukraine 133

Economic Consequences of Global Tensions 135
Ron Smith

Reconstruction, EU Accession, and Reform of Ukraine 149
Anders Åslund

Different Choices, Divergent Paths: Poland and Ukraine 165
Thorvaldur Gylfason, Eduard Hochreiter, and Tadeusz Kowalski

Russia's Use of the Kosovo Case to Legitimize Military Interventions and Territorial Conquests 185
Valur Ingimundarson

Part IV Central Banking and Financial Integration 199

Relearning Inflation Control in the Post-Covid Era 201
Willem H. Buiter

How the Flows Change When Interest Rates Are Normalized: Risk to Economic and Financial Stability 217
Sigridur Benediktsdottir

Policy Responses in Small Economies to Stability Challenges from Cross-Border Financial Integration 227
Már Gudmundsson

Part V The International Monetary and Financial System 247

The Fed's Swap Lines: Narrow Circle, Broad Effect? 249
Joshua Aizenman

Bond Market Crises and the International Lender of Last Resort 261
Robert N. McCauley

Telegraph to Tether: Challenges in the Global Payments System and the Struggle between Private and Public Interests 279
Catherine R. Schenk

Stablecoins 303
Anne C. Sibert

Part VI Global Warming 315

The Yellow Brick Road to a Decarbonized World Economy 317
Brynhildur Davídsdóttir

Part VII Consequences of the Economic Slowdown 333

The Need for Growth 335
Hian Teck Hoon, Edmund Phelps, and Gylfi Zoega

Correction to: The Need for Growth C1
Hian Teck Hoon, Edmund Phelps, and Gylfi Zoega

Index 347

Notes on Contributors

Joshua Aizenman joined the faculty at University of Southern California (USC) in 2013, where he serves as the Dockson Chair in Economics and International Relations. Joshua also serves as a research associate for the National Bureau of Economic Research. Other affiliations have included teaching and research positions at University of California (UC), Santa Cruz (served as a Presidential Chair of Economics), Dartmouth (served as Champion Professor of International Economics), Hebrew University of Jerusalem, University of Chicago GSB, University of Pennsylvania, and co-editor for the Journal of International Money and Finance (2010–2021). Consulting relationships include the IMF, the World Bank, the Inter-American Development Bank, the Asian Development Bank, and the Federal Reserve Bank of San Francisco.

Robert Z. Aliber joined the faculty of the Graduate School of Business of the University of Chicago in 1965 and left the classroom in 2004. He has written extensively about exchange rates and cross-border investment inflows. While at Chicago he managed the international student exchange programme and developed the Center for Studies in International Finance. He was the founding chair of the Committee for Public Policy Studies, which morphed into the Harris School of Public Policy. He published *The International Money Game* in 1974, and there have been six subsequent editions. Aliber inherited *Manias, Panics, and Crashes* from Charles P. Kindleberger, who brought out the first four editions; Aliber brought out the fifth, sixth, and seventh editions. He was a co-author of *Money, Banking, and the Economy* with James Dusenbery and Thomas Mayer.

Aliber published *The Multinational Paradigm* in 1992. Aliber has written several books on personal finance with the title *Your Money and Your Life*. Aliber has been a visiting scholar at the Federal Reserve Bank of San Francisco, and a visiting professor at the London Graduate School of Business Studies, the Amos Tuck School of Business at Dartmouth College, Williams College, the Free University of Berlin, and Brandeis University. He was a visiting scholar at the Woodrow International Center for Scholars, and at the American Academy of Berlin; he was a Houblon Norman Fellow at the Bank of England. He has been a consultant to the International Monetary Fund, the World Bank, the Board of Governors of the Federal Reserve System, and numerous multinational firms.

Anders Åslund is a senior fellow at the Stockholm Free World Forum and an adjunct professor at Georgetown University. He is a leading specialist on economic policy in Russia, Ukraine, and Eastern Europe. Åslund has served as an economic adviser to the governments of Russia and Ukraine. He is the author of 15 books. He was a professor at the Stockholm School of Economics and the founding director of the Stockholm Institute of Transition Economics. He has worked at five Washington think tanks—the Atlantic Council, the Peterson Institute for International Economics, the Carnegie Endowment for International Peace, the Brookings Institution, and the Kennan Institute for Advanced Russian Studies. He earned his PhD from Oxford University.

Sigridur Benediktsdottir (Sigga) is an Assistant Dean of Undergraduate Education and a senior lecturer at the Jackson School of Global Affairs at Yale University. She teaches courses on international economics, financial stability, and macroprudential policy. Previously she was Director of the Financial Stability Department at the Central Bank of Iceland 2012–2016 and an economist for the US Federal Reserve Board. She was also a voting member of the Danish Systemic Risk Council and one of three appointed to the Parliamentary Special Investigation Commission on the causes of the Icelandic banking collapse in 2008. She received a Bachelor of Science in economics from the University of Iceland in 1995 and a Bachelor of Science in computer science from the same school in 1998. She completed her doctoral degree in economics at Yale in May 2005.

Willem H. Buiter is an independent economic advisor. He was Global Chief Economist at Citigroup and Chief Economist at the European Bank for Reconstruction and Development. He was among the first External

Members of the Monetary Policy Committee of the Bank of England. He has been an assistant professor at Princeton University, a lecturer at the London School of Economics, and a professor at the University of Bristol, the London School of Economics, Yale University, and Cambridge University. He has published in the areas of monetary economics, macroeconomics, public finance, international finance, development economics, and institutional economics. His interests include least-cost disinflation, the economics of freshwater scarcity, and the proper accounting for and management of public sector real commercial assets.

Brynhildur Davídsdóttir is Professor of Environment and Natural Resources within the Department of Economics and the Department of Life and Environmental Sciences at University of Iceland (UoI). Davídsdóttir has 25+ years' experience in teaching, research and consulting with a focus on transitions to low carbon energy systems in different contexts, sustainability assessments in the context of energy with a particular emphasis on social, economic, and environmental benefits, ecosystem services, sustainability indicators, and climate change mitigation and adaptation. In addition to having advised numerous Icelandic governments on climate and energy issues, Davídsdóttir has served on various government-appointed committees linked to energy and the environment. For example, she is the vice Chair of the Icelandic Climate Council and is a member of the Icelandic science committee on climate change impacts and adaptation. She also was a member of the committee tasked with designing future energy policy for Iceland, a policy delivered in 2020. In addition to her academic duties Davídsdóttir is a board member of several Icelandic companies and foundations—for example, he is the chairman of the board of Reykjavik Energy and is on the board of the Arctic Circle Foundation which hosts the largest annual international gathering on the issues of the Arctic.

Darrell Duffie is The Adams Distinguished Professor of Management and Professor of Finance at Stanford Graduate School of Business. He is a fellow and member of the Council of the Econometric Society, a research fellow of the National Bureau of Economic Research, and a fellow of the American Academy of Arts and Sciences. Duffie was the 2009 president of the American Finance Association. In 2014, he chaired the Market Participants Group, charged by the Financial Stability Board with recommending reforms to Libor, Euribor, and other interest rate benchmarks.

Duffie's recent books include *How Big Banks Fail* (2010), *Measuring Corporate Default Risk* (2011), and *Dark Markets* (2012).

Thráinn Eggertsson is Professor Emeritus of Economics at the University of Iceland. During 2011–2019 he was an adjunct professor at Hertie School, Berlin, and in 2005–2010 Global Distinguished Professor of Politics at New York University. Eggertsson served as president of the International Society for New Institutional Economics (now SIOE) 2007–2008, and he co-edited for Cambridge University Press the book series Political Economy of Institutions and Decisions. In the 1980s and 1990s he taught and collaborated with Elinor Ostrom at Indiana University in Bloomington, and Douglass North at Washington University in St. Louis, and Stanford University. His main field of study is comparative economic systems and their basic structure and evolution.

Már Gudmundsson was the Governor of the Central Bank of Iceland from 2009 to 2019. He was the Deputy Head of the Monetary and Economic Department at the Bank for International Settlements (BIS) 2004–2009 and the Chief Economist of the Central Bank of Iceland 1994–2004. He holds an MPhil degree in Economics from the University of Cambridge. He has published several articles in books and economic journals on macroeconomics, monetary policy, exchange rate regimes, financial stability, and pensions and has served on the editorial boards of economic journals in Iceland, at the BIS, and in the UK. After leaving office as governor, he has produced reports for the Icelandic government on the economics of Covid and on pension funds. He has also worked with the South Easat Asian Central Banks Research and Training Centre (SEACEN) in Kuala Lumpur on its project on challenges and options in managing capital flows.

Thorvaldur Gylfason is Professor Emeritus of Economics at the University of Iceland and a research associate at CESifo (Center for Economic Studies) at the University of Munich. A Princeton PhD, he has worked at the International Monetary Fund (IMF) in Washington, D.C., taught at Princeton, edited the *European Economic Review*, consulted for international organizations, and published some 300 papers and 24 books as well as about 1100 newspaper articles plus some 140 songs for voice, piano, and other instruments as well as mixed choir. He was one of 25 representatives in Iceland's Constitutional Council in session from 1 April to 29 July 2011, elected by the nation and appointed by parliament to revise Iceland's constitution.

Eduard Hochreiter is senior research associate of the Vienna Institute for International Economic Studies (wiiw). Previously he was Associate Professor of Economics at the Vienna University of Economics and Business (WU), worked for the International Monetary Fund (IMF), and served as director of the Joint Vienna Institute, for the Oesterreichische Nationalbank (OeNB) in a number of senior economics positions. He served as an alternate member of the Economic and Finance Committee of the EU (EFC) and was on the Executive Board of the Western Economic Association (WEAI), lectured at universities including University of California, Los Angeles (UCLA), the University of Chicago, and Kobe University and published extensively in refereed journals, including the *European Economic* Review on international monetary issues such as European integration and transitional economics.

Hian Teck Hoon is Professor of Economics at the Singapore Management University. He specialises in macroeconomics, international trade, and economic growth. How Singapore managed to grow without being caught in the middle-income trap and understanding what is needed to generate economic prosperity as a mature economy has occupied his mind in recent years. He is author of Economic *Dynamism, Openness, and Inclusion: How Singapore Can Make the Transition from an Era of Catch-up Growth to Life in a Mature Economy* (2019). He is a past Vice-President of the Economic Society of Singapore (2002–04) and co-editor of the *Singapore Economic Review* (2002–20).

Valur Ingimundarson is Professor of Contemporary History at the University of Iceland and Chair of the Board of the EDDA Research Center. He is also an associate of LSE IDEAS and a senior associate fellow at The Royal United Services Institute (RUSI) in London. He holds a PhD in History from Columbia University. He has authored, co-authored, and edited several books and written articles on topics such as contemporary geopolitics and governance; fascism, populism, and nationalism; post-conflict politics in the former Yugoslavia; the politics of justice and memory; Icelandic foreign, security, and Arctic policies; and US-European relations during and after the Cold War. His most recent edited work is *Liberal Disorder, States of Exception, and Populist Politics* (2020).

Laura E. Kodres is the former senior distinguished fellow for the MIT Golub Center for Finance and Policy. Prior to that, she spent 24 years at the IMF, where she was division chief for the Global Financial Stability Division in the Monetary and Capital Markets Department. She previously served at the US Federal Reserve Board and the Commodity Futures Trading Commission and as a finance professor at the Ross School of Business at the University of Michigan. Her research focuses on contagion, macro-financial linkages, methods to measure and mitigate systemic risks and the effectiveness of regulation. She has published in the *American Economic Review*, the *Journal of Finance*, and numerous other financial policy outlets.

Tadeusz Kowalski is Professor of Economics at the Poznan University of Economics and Business, where he received his PhD. He was a member of the Macroeconomic Council of the Ministry of Finance. He has published books and articles on globalization, economic policy, and systemic transformation. He is Editor-in-Chief of *Economics and Business Review*.

Robert N. McCauley is co-author of the 8th edition of the classic *Manias, Panics and Crashes*, including new chapters on the international lender of last resort in the twentieth century and on cryptocurrencies. As a central banker first at the Federal Reserve Bank of New York and then at the Bank for International Settlements in Basel and Hong Kong SAR, he published extensively in international finance. A recent article cast light on the massive dollar obligations in the foreign exchange swap market. He is a non-resident senior fellow at the Global Development Policy Center at Boston University and an associate of the Faculty of History at the University of Oxford.

Marcus Miller After studying philosophy, politics, and economics at Oxford, and seeing Isaiah Berlin in full flow, Marcus Miller went as Henry Fellow to Yale University—with the good fortune to have James Tobin as PhD supervisor. Following stints at LSE and Manchester University, he joined Warwick University Economics Department, with many stimulating colleagues and students, and the occasional inspiration of writing papers with stars like Paul Krugman, Joseph Stiglitz, and John Williamson. Outside interests included co-directing the International Macro programme at CEPR with Willem Buiter and advising the newly formed House of Commons Treasury Committee in reporting on Mrs Thatcher's Monetary Policy. Growing research interest in Russia led to a paper on

Stalin with colleague Jennifer Smith ("In the shadow of the Gulag", *JCE*, 2015).

Edmund S. Phelps is McVickar Professor Emeritus of Political Science and Director of the Center on Capitalism and Society at Columbia University. The 2006 Nobel laureate in Economics, he has written on growth, unemployment theory, recessions, stagnation, inclusion, rewards of employment, indigenous innovation, dynamism, and the good economy. His work can be seen as a lifelong project to put "people as we know them" into economic theory. With *Rewarding Work* (1997) he began to argue that employee engagement, the gratification of succeeding at something, and the experience of flourishing in an unfolding voyage into the unknown are the value added of a genuinely modern society. In *Mass Flourishing* (2013) and *Dynamism* (2020), he argues and tests that broad job satisfaction in a nation requires widespread, indigenous innovating and that depends on the nation's values. His latest book *My Journeys in Economic Theory* is forthcoming from Columbia University Press.

Catherine R. Schenk is Professor of Economic and Social History at University of Oxford and fellow of St. Hilda's College. She has held academic appointments at University of Glasgow, Royal Holloway University of London, and University of Wellington, New Zealand, and has been visiting professor at Nankai University, China, and University of Hong Kong. She has also held visiting positions at the Bank of England, the International Monetary Fund, the Hong Kong Monetary Authority, and the Bank for International Settlements. She is the author of several books and many articles on international financial and monetary relations since 1945. Her European Research Council-funded project analyses the development of the global payments system since 1870.

Leslie Sheng Shen is a financial economist at the Federal Reserve Bank of Boston and a visiting scholar at the Massachusetts Institute of Technology (MIT) Golub Center for Finance and Policy. Her research focuses on international finance, banking, and macroeconomics, covering topics including financial and banking globalization, global financial networks, capital flows, financial regulation, inequality, and household consumption. She has served as an economist at the Federal Reserve Board and was the recipient of the European Central Bank (ECB) 2019 Young Economist Prize. She holds a PhD in Economics from the University of California, Berkeley.

Anne C. Sibert is Professor of Economics at Birkbeck, University of London. She is a Fellow of Centre for Economic Policy Research (CEPR), the European Economic Association, and Center for Economic Studies and IFO Institute for Economic Research (CESIfo). Her main research and policy interests are central bank design, cryptocurrency and stablecoins, intertemporal open economy public finance, financial regulation, economic and political aspects of economic and monetary union in Europe, and the political economy of structural reform. She is a member of the London Times Shadow Monetary Policy Committee. She was an external member of the Monetary Policy Committee of the Central Bank of Iceland, the Panel of Economic and Monetary Experts for the European Parliament's Committee for Economic and Monetary Affairs, and the Council of Economic Advisors to the Opposition Front Bench, UK. She was an associate editor of the *Economic Journal* and *Macroeconomic Dynamics*. She holds a PhD in Economics at Carnegie-Mellon University.

Ron Smith is Professor of Applied Economics at Birkbeck, University of London, where he teaches econometrics, statistics, and forecasting. He has also been a visiting professor at London Business School and the University of Colorado, is the author or editor of 10 books, and has published over 200 papers mainly in applied econometrics, defence economics, and political economy. He is an associate fellow of the Royal United Services Institute. His book *Military Economics: The Interaction of Power and Money*, Palgrave 2009, was shortlisted for the 2010 Duke of Westminster's Medal for Military Literature. He was awarded the 2011 Lewis Fry Richardson Award for contributions to the scientific study of militarized conflict by the European Consortium of Political Research. His latest book is *Defence Acquisition and Procurement: How (Not) to Buy Weapons*, Elements in Defence Economics, 2022.

William White is a senior fellow at the C.D. Howe Institute in Toronto. From 2009 until March 2018, he chaired the Economic and Development Review Committee at the OECD in Paris. Prior to that, he spent 14 years as Economic Adviser at the Bank for International Settlements (BIS) in Basel. Before joining the BIS in 1994, he was the Deputy Governor for international affairs at the Bank of Canada in Ottawa. In addition to publishing widely, White's other activities included membership of the Issing Committee and advising Chancellor Merkel on G-20 issues. White was honoured with the Adam Smith Award in 2016, the highest prize presented annually by the National Association of Business Economists in Washington.

Stephane Wolton is Associate Professor of Political Science at the London School of Economics and Political Science. He holds a PhD in Economics from the University of Chicago. His research focuses on political economy issues in democracies and autocracies. He serves as joint editor-in-chief of the *Quarterly Journal of Political Science*. He is also affiliated to the Center for Economic Policy Research, the Rimini Center for Economic Analysis, and Pericles Center at Bocconi University.

Tinghua Yu is a Lecturer (Assistant Professor) in Economics at Birkbeck, University of London. She holds PhD in Political Science from Columbia University. She uses formal theory and quantitative methods to study the political economy of institutions and development. Her research focuses on political selection, intrinsic motivation, and authoritarian politics.

Gylfi Zoega is Professor of Economics at the University of Iceland and part-time at Birkbeck College, London. He is also a Foreign Member of the Center on Capitalism and Society, Columbia University, and a member of CESifo Munich. He was an external member of the Central Bank of Iceland Monetary Policy Committee from 2009 to 2023 and took part in the analysis of the causes of the financial collapse in Iceland in 2008 as well as in the formulation of monetary policy tools in the years after. He holds a PhD degree in Economics from Columbia University. His research area covers economic growth, unemployment, and lifecycle saving behaviour, including the effect of pension funds on consumption and saving. He co-edited the books *Preludes to the Icelandic Financial Crash* and *The 2008 Global Financial Crisis in Retrospect* with Robert Aliber (Palgrave, 2011 and 2019). His most recent books are *Dynamism* (2020) and *The Great Economic Slowdown* (Palgrave, 2023), both with Edmund Phelps and Hian Teck Hoon.

List of Figures

Historical Roots, Cultural Selection and the 'New World Order'

Fig. 1 Countries that are free, partly free or not free (shading indicates percentages), and electoral democracies (line shows percentage). (Key: Bottom layer: free. Middle layer: partly free. Top layer: not free. Source: Freedom House, 2022) 45
Fig. 2 Historic centralisation of power and current individualism: East versus West. (Source: Roland, 2020) 47
Fig. 3 How evolving powers of state and society can lead towards different forms of government 49
Fig. 4 The options facing Putin as strongman president 53
Fig. 5 USSR/Russian governance 1990–2019: Gorbachev, Yeltsin and Putin 57

Dollar Funding Stresses in China

Fig. 1 Cross-currency bases, including USD/CNY and USD/CNH (**a**) Advanced economies and China and (**b**) Emerging markets 111
Fig. 2 Cross-currency basis Z-scores: Covid versus 2019 112
Fig. 3 Trends in US dollar activities of non-US banks 113
Fig. 4 US dollar funding gaps 116
Fig. 5 FX swap turnover by entities in China (net-gross basis, average daily volume) 120

Different Choices, Divergent Paths: Poland and Ukraine

Fig. 1 GDP per capita and life expectancy. (Statistical sources: World Bank, *World Development Indicators*) 169

Fig. 2 Investment and exports (% of GDP). (Statistical sources: World Bank, *World Development Indicators*) 174
Fig. 3 Export concentration and diversification 1995–2020 (indices from 0 to 1, higher values mean more concentration and less diversification). (Statistical sources: UNCTAD) 175
Fig. 4 Education. (Statistical sources: World Bank, *World Development Indicators*) 176
Fig. 5 Agriculture and manufacturing. (Statistical sources: World Bank, *World Development Indicators*) 176
Fig. 6 Democracy and freedom. (Statistical sources: Center for Systemic Peace and Freedom House) 177
Fig. 7 Rule of law and press freedom. (Statistical sources: World Justice Project and Reporters Without Borders) 178
Fig. 8 Equality and corruption. (World Bank, *World Development Indicators*) 178
Fig. 9 Inflation and unemployment. (World Bank, *World Development Indicators*) 180

The Fed's Swap Lines: Narrow Circle, Broad Effect?

Fig. 1 FEDs swap lines, December 2007–December 2009. (Source: Aizenman et al., 2011) 251
Fig. 2 Cross-currency basis (3-month swaps, basis points) widened during the COVID-19 crisis. (Source: Aizenman et al., 2011) 254
Fig. 3 Many advanced and emerging-market central banks auctioned US dollars during the COVID-19 crisis. (Source: Aizenman et al., 2022). Note: Auctions by major central banks are those conducted by BoE, BoJ, ECB, SNB. Auctions by other CBs with Fed facilities are those conducted by Australia, Denmark, Hong Kong (China), Indonesia, Korea, Mexico, Norway, Singapore, Sweden after the announcement of the Fed swap line or announcement of approval of access to these economies under FIMA. Auctions by other CBs without Fed facilities include those conducted by central banks of Chile, Colombia, Georgia, India, and Indonesia (prior to approval of FIMA access if relevant) 256
Fig. 4 Economies with access to Fed liquidity lines saw smaller decline in US treasury holdings between February and April 2020. (Source: Aizenman et al., 2022) 258

Bond Market Crises and the International Lender of Last Resort

Fig. 1 Emerging market bond prices rise as Fed buys US corporate bonds 273
Fig. 2 Flows into global bond funds recover as Fed buys US corporate bonds 274

Telegraph to Tether: Challenges in the Global Payments System and the Struggle between Private and Public Interests

Fig. 1 Value, volume of message; number of correspondent relations (Index Jan 2011=100) 281
Fig. 2 Index of number of active correspondents (2011=100) 282
Fig. 3 Global payment system. (Note: Payment may or may not go through a national payments system) 283
Fig. 4 Average size of payment, in thousands of USD 287
Fig. 5 SWIFT connections (firms and countries), 1977–2011. (Source: Scott & Zachariadis, 2014: 113) 298

The Need for Growth

Fig. 1 Output per hour and TFP in the current eurozone and the US, 1900–2019. (US dollars 2010 ppp based. Source: Bergeaud et al. (2016), updated.) 342

List of Tables

Historical Roots, Cultural Selection and the 'New World Order'

Table 1 Three eras of political economy post–World War II 39
Table 2 Strongmen leaders in the twenty-first century 41
Table 3 Various perspectives 44

Different Choices, Divergent Paths: Poland and Ukraine

Table 1 Initial conditions and early transition policies 171

Relearning Inflation Control in the Post-Covid Era

Table 1 Taylor rule implied policy rates for four leading central banks 205
Table 2 Monetary base (% of GDP, end-of-period) 210

How the Flows Change When Interest Rates Are Normalized: Risk to Economic and Financial Stability

Table 1 Latin American debt crisis 219

Policy Responses in Small Economies to Stability Challenges from Cross-Border Financial Integration

Table 1 Correlations of long-term government bond rates with US rates and gross external assets and liabilities (international investment positions) relative to GDP 233

The Need for Growth

Table 1 Growth of output, productivity and TFP by decade 340

Introduction

Robert Z. Aliber, Már Gudmundsson, and Gylfi Zoega

The world economy is recovering from the crisis caused by the recent COVID-19 pandemic but the war in Ukraine and heightened geopolitical tensions have created additional negative shocks. The pandemic temporarily shrouded other underlying issues and problems that will come increasingly to the fore, such as global warming, population aging, faltering growth in China, autocratic challenges to democracy, flaws in the international monetary and financial system and high debt levels. In the beginning of September 2022, a group of renowned academics and policy makers gathered in Reykjavik, Iceland, for an event hosted by the Institute of International Affairs of the University of Iceland and discussed these issues. This volume contains a collection of the papers that were presented.

R. Z. Aliber
University of Chicago, Evanston, IL, USA

M. Gudmundsson
Institute of International Affairs, University of Iceland, Reykjavík, Iceland
e-mail: margud@hi.is

G. Zoega (✉)
University of Iceland, Reykjavík, Iceland

Birkbeck, University of London, London, UK
e-mail: gz@hi.is

R. Z. Aliber et al. (eds.), *Fault Lines After COVID-19*,
https://doi.org/10.1007/978-3-031-26482-5_1

The scene is set by the two first chapters that provide a big picture analysis of global economic challenges on the one hand and ominous political developments on the other. William White, the former head of the Monetary and Economic Department of the Bank of International Settlements, who is credited with having flagged some of the financial fragilities that led to the 2008 financial crisis, analyses in the first chapter many problems and dangers facing the world in our economic, political, environmental and public health systems that can spill over from one system to another. He draws attention to the record high levels of debt and the large number of countries in danger of debt distress now when US interest rates are rising. Asset prices, both house prices and stock prices, are also high in many countries with the associated risk of abrupt correction. The ageing of the population in most Western countries is putting pension funds and public health systems under pressure. The future decline in the labour force in the West will cause real wages to rise and investment to increase, which will make the real rate of interest rise. In the nearer term, there are supply-side problems caused by COVID-19 and the war in Ukraine and inflation caused by the expansionary monetary policies used to mitigate the economic effects of the pandemic. There is a risk that the economic fragilities will cause political instability and threaten democracy.

In the second scene setting chapter, Professor Marcus Miller of Warwick University analyses political developments in the West in the past decade, the rise of Trump, Putin and Erdogan with an emphasis on developments within Russia. He splits the post–World War II era into three epochs; the Keynesian one that ended in 1975, the neoliberal one that ended in 2005 and the "era of the strongman" during which "strong" leaders have come to power in countries as diverse as Turkey, India and Hungary, Trump's US and Johnson's UK. He characterizes the "strongman" as having a cult of personality, a contempt for the rule of law, a claim to represent the "people" against the "elite" and nostalgic nationalism. Russia and China have never experienced democracy and freedom—autocracy has deep historical roots—nor reached the "narrow corridor" of Acemoglu and Robinson with its equilibrium between the power of the state and the power of the people, the latter represented by unions, free press and universities. While Gorbachev and Yeltsin increased the power of the people, they overshot the narrow corridor and Russia spiralled into anarchy, which Putin reversed only to bring Russia back into autocracy. Miller ends on the optimistic note that in the competition between the autocracy and liberal democracy, the latter will prevail because in the democracies governance relies on institutions and the rule of law while strongman rule invariably leads to the creation of a personality cult, which rests on fear and coercion leading to megalomania and paranoia. There is an inherent flaw in the rule of the strongman.

The following section is devoted to China. Taken together, the chapters suggest that China might face a rough road ahead when its economy stalls, the population begins to decline and the political grip of the party starts to loosen. This could result in an economic or a political turbulence, or both.

Robert Aliber, Professor Emeritus of the Booth School of Business at the University of Chicago, gives a gloomy prognosis for the Chinese economy. Aliber sees signs that its thirty-years of high growth are coming to an end. China has depleted its reservoir of labour in the countryside, it faces an ageing and a declining population and can no longer count on importing foreign technologies. The overheating in the housing market is threatening macroeconomic stability and the housing bubble is bursting. Nevertheless, the economic performance of the past thirty years is nothing short of miraculous but the economic slowdown was bound to occur as in Japan in the 1990s.

Thráinn Eggertsson, Professor Emeritus at the University of Iceland, shows how the authoritarian regime of Xi Jinping is using technology to both protect the power of the Chinese Communist Party and to attempt to propel China to the world's technology frontier. His policies test the theory that democracy and frontier growth have to go together, that a civic society is needed to constrain the government and economic freedom is needed to liberate the innovators and entrepreneurs. In effect, President Xi is fearful of the "road to freedom" to paraphrase Friedrich Hayek and hopes to preserve his power and frontier growth using digital technology and artificial intelligence. Eggertsson gives a pessimistic prognosis of the future of Xi, that the experiment will fail because unrestrained dictators make fateful mistakes, which they find difficult to correct.

Tinghua Yu of Birkbeck College in London and Stephane Wolton of the London School of Economics describe the methods used by the Chinese authorities to monitor their citizens. They face the choice between offering monetary rewards to people for denouncing their fellow citizens as being disloyal to the party or relying on voluntary denunciations. The authors describe their game-theoretic work, which shows that autocratic authorities that want to monitor citizens have an incentive to organize densely populated cities so that citizens easily discover if others are engaged in anti-government behaviour. In this case, paying for information will generate many and also truthful denunciations.

Laura E. Kodres of MIT, Leslie Sheng Shen from the Boston Fed and Darrell Duffie of Stanford University describe the dollar linkages between China and the rest of the world and the possibility of China needing very significant US dollar funding during periods of stress. There is the danger that in future periods of financial stress, China might find it difficult to quickly find a sufficient quantity of dollar financing to control liquidity stresses on its corporate and financial institutions. There could be adverse effects for the world economy in the form of China defaulting to US or other Western banks and financial distress spreading to other countries with dollar exposures.

The next four chapters cover geopolitical tensions and the situation in Ukraine. The first describes geopolitical shocks and the formulation of policy responses. The next two describe the economic situation in Ukraine, before the war, its current state and future prospects. Both chapters are optimistic about Ukraine's future economic development after the end of hostilities. The last chapter discusses the inherent inconsistencies in Russia's justification for the invasion.

Ron Smith of Birkbeck College, London, writes about geopolitical shocks, such as Russia's invasion of Ukraine or the recent pandemic. They are drawn from low frequency, fat-tailed distributions and difficult to predict. In response to them, financial variables adjust rapidly at high frequencies, economic variables more slowly and institutions very slowly. Smith goes on to discuss how difficult it is to predict such shocks, taking World War I as an example of a completely unanticipated shock. He then discusses the transmission mechanisms of shocks, the economic-strategic interactions such as how the Vietnam war contributed to the collapse of the Bretton Woods system and the adoption of floating exchange rates. The economic-strategic interactions are visible, for example, in the current military rivalry between the US and China centred on the location of semi-conductor production in Taiwan and in the effect of the conflict in Ukraine on the supply of oil and gas. Finally, Smith discusses the policy response and the interplay of economic and strategic issues in policy formulation.

Anders Åslund from the Center for Social and Economic Research has followed developments in Ukraine since its independence. He compares Ukraine and Poland back in 1991 in terms of domestic institutions, economic policy, public understanding and international engagement. While Poland was an independent state with a central bank and a ministry of finance, Ukraine had to build its national institutions from scratch. Poland had a private sector and Ukraine did not. Knowledge of economic policy was limited in Ukraine until the mid-1990s, and the country suffered from hyperinflation and continued state control of the economy. The European Union embraced Poland and gave it access to its market and full membership by 2004. Åslund writes that Ukraine has come a long way in setting up the institutions of a modern economy with moderate inflation and responsible state finances. However, there is endemic corruption. Aslund assesses the destruction wrought by the Russians since the invasion. He then maps a plan of recovery after the war has ended that includes a reconstruction period, a reform period and finally EU accession.

Thorvaldur Gylfason, Professor Emeritus at the University of Iceland, Eduard Hochreiter of the Joint Vienna Institute, and Tadeusz Kowalski of Poznan University of Economics and Business compare the economic history of Ukraine to that of Poland. They emphasize differences in initial conditions between the two countries. While Ukraine had been a part of the Soviet Union, Poland had been a quasi-independent country. Poland had privately run small enterprises and farms at the beginning of the 1990s, while Ukraine had none of this. Poland had more human and social capital. The authors argue that these differences made Poland go for EU membership, full transition to a market economy and democracy while Ukraine was ambivalent towards all three. The consequences can be found in an increasing difference in life expectancy between the countries. Currently, Poland ranks significantly higher in terms of economic freedom, press freedom and quality of public governance and lower in terms of corruption.

Valur Ingimundarson, Professor of History at the University of Iceland, writes about Russia's motives behind the invasion and the political and legal justifications given by its government. The motive is to wage a geopolitical battle with the US and NATO while the official justification is not convincing and full of contradictions. The stated justification is found in NATO's intervention in Kosovo in 1999, which was started without a UN Security Council resolution. There is also the subsequent recognition of Kosovo's independence in 2008. This provided Putin with a legal justification for intervening in Georgia in 2006, taking over Crimea in 2014 and then the invasion of 2022. However, already in Crimea in 2014 Russia went much further than the West had done in Kosovo by absorbing it into the Russian Federation.

Three chapters discuss the challenges faced by central banks in the current environment. Willem Buiter, of the Council of Foreign Relations, sets the stage by taking a critical look at monetary policy in recent years. He finds that central banks in the West have been too slow to respond to rising inflation. Using a Taylor rule to assess the appropriate monetary policy stance, Buiter finds that interest rates of all major central banks are too low, fall short of the neutral rate. Buiter attributes the mistake to cognitive errors interpreting the data and also to a valid fear of financial instability. But he emphasizes fiscal dominance, that governments in the US, the UK and especially in the eurozone rely on money creation to satisfy government's intertemporal budget constrain. In the eurozone, the weaker member states, such as Italy, Greece and Spain, rely on the ECB creating money to fund their budget deficits. Fiscal dominance may also be taking hold in the US and the UK. Buiter concludes that in the fight between independent central banks and a government that cannot pay its debt without inflation, central bank independence cannot survive.

Sigridur Benediktsdottir of Yale University draws lessons from the 1980s, the last time when US interest rates rose rapidly to quell inflation. The higher dollar interest rates, as well as the rising dollar exchange rate, created financial distress in countries that had borrowed in dollars in the 1970s, such as Mexico, Argentina and Chile. During 2022, US interest rates are expected to rise by around 400 basis points and Benediktsdóttir predicts new crises because of the massive expansion in public and private dollar debt in the years since the financial crisis of 2008. Now with both dollar interest rates rising and the appreciation of the dollar, systemic risk threatens to materialize in many countries.

Már Gudmundsson, a former governor of the Central Bank of Iceland, analyses the risks to macroeconomic and financial stability arising from cross-border financial integration in small, open and financially integrated economies. These have two related sources. First, the interaction of a weakened transmission of monetary policy through the interest rate channel, a potentially disorderly exchange rate dynamics, and domestic financial vulnerabilities like currency mismatches. Second, a global financial cycle that is mostly driven by the US and creates synchronized swings in capital flows to small, financially integrated economies unrelated to their domestic conditions. The optimal policy response includes structural reforms—including financial regulations, financial buffers and sound financial supervision—that increase resilience to shocks and the capacity of economies absorb volatile capital flows. For most emerging market economies and some of the smaller and more vulnerable advanced economies there will still be a need for additional stabilization tools and an integrated policy framework around them. These are the tools of macroprudential policy, foreign exchange intervention and capital flow management measures.

The next four chapters address aspects of the international monetary and financial system. Joshua Aizenman, Dockson Chair in Economics and International Relations at the University of Southern California, takes stock of the growing networks of central banks' bilateral swap lines in the past twenty years. He describes how concerns that the financial crisis of 2008 would result in the Great Depression of the twenty-first century induced the Federal Reserve to act as the dollar lender of last resort, extending unprecedented selective swap lines. In the COVID-19 crisis, the Fed provided US dollar liquidity to the global economy by reactivating or enhancing swap arrangements with other central banks, and by establishing a new repo facility. The selectivity of the swap lines during the two crises indicates that countries with significant trade, financial and geopolitical linkages can expect access to ad-hoc swap arrangements on a case-by-case basis, in ways that fit the priorities of major central banks.

Robert McCauley, Boston University, gives an account of how the Fed's buying of last resort in the US bond market in spring 2020 supported the global market for dollar bonds, including those of non-US borrowers. The massive selling of bonds severely strained the working of the US bond market. In response, the Fed opened its discount window to primary dealers, and bid without limit for Treasury bonds. It also took the unprecedented step of using its emergency powers to buy not only short-term paper but also US corporate bonds. This purely domestic buying of last resort stabilized the global market for dollar bonds, reversing investor sales and boosting prices of international dollar bonds.

The chapter by Catherine Schenk, professor at the University of Oxford, is motivated by the recent sanctions imposed on Russia after its invasion of Ukraine, in particular the governments of the US and Europe excluding Russian banks from the global payment system SWIFT. Shenk gives a thorough overview over the history of the international payment system. She tells the story of how the cross-border payment systems has evolved over the longer term and responded to shocks, globalization and technological innovation. The chapter draws on archival records from the USA, UK and Europe to take the long view on understanding the evolution of the underlying plumbing of the international economic system from telegraph to Tether.

Anne Sibert, Birkbeck College, describes the market for stablecoins, the EU regulatory response and the regulatory challenges and issues associate with stablecoins. She finds that there is a case for consumer protection because the ability to exchange a stablecoin for fiat currency is often limited, reserves are not necessarily held in safe and liquid funds, and stablecoin holders can have limited protection in the event of bankruptcy. However, regulation requires multinational regulation since, for example, EU residents can earn interest on stablecoins on non-EU platforms.

We are left with the biggest challenge of them all, manmade climate change. Brynhildur Davídsdóttir, professor at the University of Iceland, describes the prospects for emissions of greenhouse gases and climate change after the Paris accords of 2015. She writes that evidence shows that climate change is taking place and is already having social and economic consequences, for example, increased frequency and intensity of climate and weather extremes. The effects will be most felt in the least developed countries, coastal areas, small islands and also for the species in the Arctic. The increase in greenhouse gas (GHG) emissions continues unabated and in 2019 emissions were 54% higher than emissions in 1990, the global concentration of CO_2 continues to increase. The relationship between economic growth and GHG emissions has not weakened, which shows that further measures are needed. Although GHG emissions are lower in the EU and the US than in 2019, this may be caused by air and marine transport not being included as well as GHG emissions in the production of imported goods in their countries of origin. Davíðsdóttir concludes that immediate action is required to decouple economic growth and GHD emissions, which would have many positive side effects.

The last chapter ends on the optimistic note that a revival of productivity growth in the not-so-distant future would help resolve many of the problems currently faced in the world economy. Edmund Phelps, Hian Teck Hoon and Gylfi Zoega describe some of the consequences of low rates of productivity growth in the West in recent decades. These include a falling equilibrium real rate of interest, sky-high stock prices and an increasingly unequal distribution of wealth, stagnating real wages and political turbulence, in addition to geopolitical tensions. It follows that a resurgent growth of productivity, a return to the post-war golden era, would resolve many of the problems described in this book. Rising output due to higher productivity growth would lower the burden of debt, making it easier to reduce greenhouse gas emissions and increase political stability. The authors propose policy measures to increase productivity growth. These would include eliminating or reducing impediments to growth such as rules and regulations that protect vested interests such as mandatory redundancy payments, tariffs, red tape and industrial subsidies and state contracts awarded on the basis of political connections. Moreover, the economy needs institutions that encourage innovations instead of rent seeking, a healthy financial system and values that emphasize self-reliance, independence and good work ethics. The rule of law and the protections of property rights are essential as is an emphasis on good education. While special interests are more entrenched in some developed countries than others and also the incentives to innovate, there is the hope that current technological breakthroughs such as artificial intelligence will generate a wave of innovations that will raise productivity in the future.

PART I

Challenges Ahead

What Next for the Post Covid Global Economy: Could Negative Supply Shocks Disrupt Other Fragile Systems?

William White

The Nature of the Policy Problem

Successful policymakers first clearly define the objectives they are seeking to achieve. Fortunately, in recent years a consensus seems to have emerged in democratic countries that we want "sustainable and inclusive growth in a free society." Less fortunately, there are still many different views about the appropriate trade-offs between these varied objectives when specific policy suggestions imply more of one good thing (say sustainability) and less of another (say inclusion). Vigorous debates around such issues are underway and seem sure to continue.

What seems less well understood is that success in meeting policy objectives, however ordered, depends on the sustainability of each of a number of underlying systems. Tolstoy famously wrote that "All happy families are the same, but each unhappy family is unhappy in its own way." By this he meant that many conditions must be met simultaneously to ensure

W. White (✉)
C.D. Howe Institute, Toronto, ON, Canada

R. Z. Aliber et al. (eds.), *Fault Lines After COVID-19*,
https://doi.org/10.1007/978-3-031-26482-5_2

happiness in a family. Similarly, instability in any one of our economic, political, environmental or public health systems would prevent us from realizing our broader policy objectives. Worse, a breakdown in any one of these interdependent systems could lead to a breakdown in other systems as well.

Each of these underlying systems is, by nature, a complex adaptive system (CAS).[1] Such systems involve the interaction of many heterogeneous agents (each following simple rules) that are constantly interacting (often with positive feedback loops[2]) and evolving in consequence. Their fundamental properties ("emergent properties") arise from these interactions. By analogy, they are much more like forests than machines. CAS share many characteristics, but the one most pertinent to this volume is that these systems regularly become unstable with probabilities being determined by a Power Law. That is, small instabilities occur much more frequently than larger ones.

Unfortunately, each of the systems just referred to is showing increasing signs of stress and potential instability. Our economic and financial system has already suffered numerous crises in recent years. Our democratic political systems are under increasing attacks from both left and right. Our environment is threatened by population growth and still rising emissions of greenhouse gases. And finally, our public health systems were almost overwhelmed by Covid-19, just one of over 200 zoonotic pathogens identified since the end of World War II. These threats to our health will reoccur and indeed will become more severe in light of climate change.[3]

Against this broader background, the issue dealt with in this chapter is the likelihood that further problems will emerge in our economic and financial system (Section "Could Economic Stability Be Threatened by Negative Supply Shocks?"), and the likelihood that these problems will spill over into the political sphere (Section "Could Political Stability Be Threatened by Economic Instability?").[4] In section "What Policy Measures Might Help Restore Stability?", attention is directed to policies that might help preserve stability in the economic and political spheres. Unfortunately,

[1] For a layman's introduction to this literature, see Ball (2012).

[2] Buchanan (2013).

[3] See Barnes (2022).

[4] Similar papers could be written about each of the twelve direct spillovers (in both directions) possible between four nested systems. Then, of course, consideration would also have to be given to how spillovers could then have spillovers in turn. Complex indeed!

implementing such policies also involves a political process that might or might not be supportive.

Could Economic Stability Be Threatened by Negative Supply Shocks?

Many, perhaps most, of the people who lost their lives during the covid pandemic suffered from comorbidities. That is, they had serious illnesses before being infected. Similarly, the global economy suffers from many initial imbalances, both real and financial, that increase the likelihood of a serious economic downturn should negative supply shocks materialize. The potential effects on the stability of the global financial system and the economy, of tighter monetary policy in response to such shocks, is a particular source of uncertainty.

Indicators of Underlying Fragility

Perhaps the most important concern is that global debt ratios[5] have been rising for decades, and this continued even after the Global Financial Crisis (GFC). Moreover, the rate of increase accelerated sharply with the onset of the pandemic. The Institute of International Finance[6] estimates a ratio of 280% (end of 2008), rising to 321% (2019) and then 360% (peak 2021). Moreover, the quality of that debt has been declining. Corporate debt ratings have been falling, with a growing percentage of new bond issues clustered just above the "junk" level.[7] Further debt downgrades would make many such bonds ineligible for purchase by many institutions. In addition, loans to corporations increasingly involve higher leverage, floating rates and are "covenant light." This implies growing risks as interest rates rise and unusually low recovery rates in the case of corporate bankruptcies. Finally, the IMF estimates[8] that 60% of low-income countries are already "in or at high risk of debt distress," a level that has doubled since 2015. Indeed, UNCTAD became so concerned that, early

[5] Defined as the sum of private (household and corporate) and public debt over GDP.

[6] The Institute of International Finance publishes a regular Global Debt Monitor. See also J. P. Morgan (2022).

[7] *The Economist* magazine (2022) estimates that 58% of investment grade non-financial corporate bonds are rated BBB. As well, 20% of listed US and European companies have an interest coverage ratio of less than two.

[8] Chabert et al. (2022).

in October 2022, it called[9] for the Federal Reserve to stop monetary tightening to alleviate the strain of higher debt service on poorer countries.

Also of concern have been the high valuations given to many assets, the so-called "everything bubble," with equity valuations and record high house prices being of particular concern in many countries. While some of these prices fell throughout the first half of 2022, concerns remained that further falls were warranted. The McKinsey Global Institute[10] noted that the historic link between the growth of net worth and GDP has been broken since around the turn of the millennium due to the sharp increase in asset prices in subsequent years. Moreover, their calculations show that less than 7% of total assets (real and financial) are productive real assets like infrastructure, machinery and equipment, and intangible investments. In short, we are confronted with a massive, inverted pyramid of "measured assets" resting on a tiny fulcrum of "the type of assets that typically drive economic growth."[11]

It is also a fact that investment ratios in many countries have been weak since the onset of the GFC and that the growth rate of total factor productivity has been slowing. Many commentators suggest that ultra-easy monetary policy has contributed to this by sustaining "zombie" companies,[12] encouraging resource misallocations[13] and by supporting valueless mergers and acquisitions.[14] All of these factors imply that, if the historic link between the growth of net worth and GDP is to be restored, it is more likely to be due to a further reduction in asset prices than to a sharp increase in real GDP.

The malfunctioning of financial markets could be another indicator of potential problems. There have been a growing number of "anomalies," where prices fail to adjust to satisfy arbitrage conditions.[15] "Flash crashes," where prices move vastly in excess of what normal distributions would

[9] As reported in the *Financial Times* (2022).

[10] McKinsey Global Institute (2022).

[11] Ibid. p. 10.

[12] See OECD (2017) and Banerjee and Hoffman (2018).

[13] Not least, companies whose business model is focussed, not on medium term profits, but on the use of price subsidies (like Uber) to gain market share and eventual market domination. Evidently, only one of the various firms competing in a given sector can be such a winner.

[14] See Lynn (2010).

[15] See Borio et al. (2016). Perhaps most important, the covered interest parity theorem has been violated almost continuously since 2008.

imply, have also been sharply on the increase. Finally, market liquidity has been declining in many markets for years, with the market in US Treasuries being a recent and notable addition. Indeed, conditions deteriorated so much in September 2019 and March 2020 that the Federal Reserve felt compelled to intervene with massive purchases of bonds and other measures to support prices.

The stability of financial firms has also been questioned. Banks capital requirements have been raised substantially, but from levels that Paul Tucker once called "wafer thin."[16] The question then arises if they have been raised high enough, with many experts expressing serious doubts.[17] Their arguments are supported by noting that banks face new and unprecedented risks: increasingly outdated technological platforms, competition from FinTech firms, cybercrime, climate change and profit margins squeezed by low interest rates.

Similarly, the business model of insurance companies faces threats from climate change, while pension funds fear the effects of aging. Both also suffer from low interest rates on longer-term bonds. In response, both sectors have increased risk taking and leverage in a "search for yield." These are all "known knowns." Even more important are the "known unknowns." Tightened post-GFC regulation, especially of banks, has led to significant structural change within the financial sector. Market finance has gained at the expense of traditional financial intermediaries, with asset management firms and private equity firms becoming increasingly important. How this unregulated shadow-banking sector might react to periods of market stress remains a critical "known unknown."[18] And, finally, the reality of the "unknown unknowns" must also be recognized. Financial instability can cascade outwards from unexpected places.

Supply-Side Shocks to Date and the Policy Reaction

Against this backdrop of growing imbalances and potential financial stress, the global economy by mid-2022 had had to adjust to two significant supply-side shocks: the covid pandemic and the Russian invasion of

[16] Tucker (2018).

[17] For a list, see White (2021) p. 170.

[18] The IMF expressed concern that "open end funds holding illiquid assets while offering daily redemptions can be a key driver of fragility in asset markets." See International Monetary Fund (2022).

Ukraine. The former significantly affected the supply of labour, and the latter contributed to higher commodity prices, especially for food and energy. European producers were also constrained by the limited availability of Russian gas, as Russia responded to NATO sanctions with trade measures of its own. However, in both cases, there was also a negative effect on demand which helped constrain the broader effect on global inflation. If workers stayed home in response to covid (and "lockdowns" of various sorts), consumers also stayed home which had a particularly depressing effect on the demand for services.[19] In the case of higher commodity prices, the consumers of such goods had less income left over to purchase other goods and services. The effect was thus deemed to be "stagflationary"; that is, the commodity shock both lowered growth and raised prices.[20]

The macroeconomic authorities in the advanced economies clearly gave priority to sustaining growth over reducing inflation. In response to the pandemic, government deficits rose sharply in 2020 and 2021, with the US deficit averaging 10.5% of GDP.[21] Monetary policy was also eased sharply, with policy rates reduced to zero in some countries and even below zero in others. As well, major central banks engaged in "Quantitative Easing" leading to unprecedented increases in their balance sheets. The size of the balance sheet of the Federal Reserve alone went from $4 trillion in early 2020 to $9 trillion in mid-2022,[22] almost 23% of GDP. As a result of this joint easing, the growth rate of the money supply also rose sharply,[23] reaching 42% in the US and 21% in the Euro area (end 2019–May 2022).

In retrospect, it seems clear that this policy response was excessively expansionary since core inflation (e.g., food and energy) subsequently began to rise sharply in most advanced countries. By the second half of 2022, overall growth in the CPI (over the past year) was close to 10% in

[19] An important factor working in the opposite direction was the ordering of goods over the internet. This pushed up sharply the ratio of good to services in GDP and created bottlenecks in supply systems for goods worldwide.

[20] This was the common interpretation of the effects of the energy price shocks of the 1970s.

[21] This was three times the pre-pandemic level.

[22] Three earlier rounds of Quantitative Easing, starting in 2008, increased the portfolio by only $3 trillion.

[23] The fiscal authority made expenditures which showed up as increased deposits at commercial banks (money). These expenditures were largely financed by the central bank, whose asset holdings (of government bonds) rose along with their liabilities (reserves held by commercial banks).

many countries, a level not seen since the 1970s, and wage growth was also accelerating.

Early in the pandemic, the authorities underestimated how much supply potential had been reduced by illness and lockdowns, and how much goods prices would rise in response to demand shifts and disruptions to international supply chains. Later on, the authorities erred in suggesting that these shocks would only be "transitory," thus concluding that monetary resistance was unwarranted.[24] Compounding these mistaken assessments of supply-side issues, the authorities failed to foresee the rapidity of the post-pandemic recovery of demand and employment and its effect on inflation. The prevailing wisdom was that Philips curves were flat[25] and that inflationary expectations were well anchored. In retrospect, both assumptions have also proved "wildly incorrect."[26]

As the economic effect of the pandemic eased and fiscal support schemes ended, government deficits began to fall. More importantly, central banks around the world eventually began to tighten monetary policy in response to rising inflation. The size of successive rate increases, and the proportion of the world's central banks participating, were both unusually large.

This aggressive response reflected concerns that a wage-price spiral was already developing, and that by some measures monetary policy was still extremely loose.[27] In effect, the credibility of central banks as inflation fighters was thought to be in the balance. As well, due to the relative tightness of US monetary policy, the effective value of the US dollar also rose to record highs. Since this implied a lower value for other currencies, and higher prices for imports priced in US dollars, other central banks had yet another reason to follow the example of the Federal Reserve. Moreover, the failure of monetary tightening to show quick results, especially in the US, strengthened the argument that further tightening would be necessary near the end of 2022 and into 2023.

In contrast, others argued near the end of 2022 that further tightening should proceed cautiously if at all. Given the normal lags in the effect of monetary tightening on inflation, further effects were in the pipeline. It

[24] The conventional wisdom in central banking circles is that "temporary" increases in aggregate price measures, due to a relative price shift (e.g., higher energy prices), should be ignored by the monetary authorities.

[25] That is, a fall in the level of unemployment would not lead to significantly higher inflation.

[26] See Wheeler and Wilkinson (2022) p. 7.

[27] For example, real ex post short rates in the US were still around –5% in mid-2022.

was also thought possible that simultaneous tightening in many countries would have effects greater than those anticipated by individual central banks. As well, it was noted that supply shocks in the past did not generally lead to wage price spirals[28] and that longer-term inflationary expectations had risen much less than shorter-term expectations. This implied that "real" rates at longer horizons had in fact risen significantly.

More ominously, those advising caution increasingly drew attention to the underlying fragilities described above as well as growing evidence that monetary tightening was already having significant effects on financial variables.[29] While short-term policy rates had risen only about three percentage points in the US, a variety of monetary conditions indicators showed a much greater degree of tightening. Equity market fell sharply through September 2022, while spreads reflecting credit risk and duration risk also widened. The prices of commercial property and houses also declined markedly in many countries, including the US. Credit markets tightened with lower grade credits often finding that credit was simply unavailable. Emerging market borrowers, especially from countries with high sovereign debt ratios, also had financing difficulties. Those who had borrowed in US dollars increasingly faced problems of debt service and liquidity constraints.

Market liquidity also became a problem. In October 2022, against a backdrop of rising policy rates, yields in the UK gilt-edged market spiked sharply. While the trigger was an "imprudent" UK minibudget, the underlying problem was UK defined benefit pension funds unwinding leverage dictated by liability-driven investment strategies. As rates on longer-term gilts rose, pension funds received calls for "margin" which they could meet only by selling assets whose prices were already under pressure.[30] To short circuit this positive feedback mechanism, the Bank of England was forced to intervene to restore order.

Given previous problems in the market for US Treasuries, this incident immediately raised concerns about similar problems associated with leverage in other countries and in other markets. Moreover, since the Bank of

[28] See Bluedorn (2022).

[29] These changes are documented in International Monetary Fund (2022) which notes, "There is a risk of a disorderly tightening of financial conditions that may be amplified by vulnerabilities built over the years." For similar warnings going back over many years, see successive Annual Reports of the BIS and White (2012).

[30] George Geanakoplos drew attention to these kinds of problems decades ago. See Geanakoplos (2010).

England had to *buy* gilts to support financial stability, when it was already committed to *selling* gilts to support the tightening of UK monetary policy, more fundamental questions arose. Could policies directed to reducing potential financial fragility eventually result in higher inflation?

Further Negative Supply-Side Shocks and the Implications for Future Inflation

It must first be recognized that the recent, negative supply shocks to the global economy are likely to have significant effects that linger over time. Moreover, a new and rather different set of negative shocks can also be anticipated. Unlike shocks deemed "stagflationary" in the past, many of these shocks will make investment more attractive and strengthen aggregate demand rather than reduce it. This implies that central banks in the future will face even greater difficulties in keeping inflation under control. In turn, this raises the likelihood and the costs of future economic and financial crises.

All significant downturns have scarring (hysteretic) effects,[31] and the covid pandemic seems especially likely to do so. While supply chain bottlenecks have been mostly overcome, companies have become much more aware of the need to balance resilience against efficiency. In consequence, many old supply structures will have to be written off and replaced with new ones. Further, as long as China continues with its zero covid policy, the reliability of its production processes will be suspect, aggravating the need for change in global supply chains. Labour supply effects also seem likely to be long lasting. The working age dead are no longer in the work force and "long covid" is increasingly mentioned as the probable cause of the recent decline in labour force participation rates in many countries.

While the Russian-Ukrainian war aggravated the price rise of many commodities, it is important to note that prices were rising well before the conflict, perhaps reflecting underlying secular trends. A still rising (if decelerating) global population is putting food security at risk. As well, the future supply of both food and other commodities (like lumber) could be threatened by climate change. The production of metals will also be threatened by low levels of past investment, and the reality that most promising mining sites have already been exploited.

[31] Cerra and Saxena (2017).

The need to confront climate change will impose another negative economic shock, since both mitigation and adaptation will prove costly. Mitigation requires reducing the use of fossil fuels and expanding the use of alternative sources of energy. If the supply of fossil fuels declines (as it has done due to low investment levels) before alternatives can fill the gap, then the price of fossil fuels must rise in the interim. As well, the investments required to provide alternative fuels and the new infrastructure to use them will also put a heavy demand on resources in aggregate.[32] More specifically, a fossil-free future is also likely to be a metal-heavy future, putting extended price pressure on particular commodities.[33] Adaptation will also require heavy investment for relocations, flood barriers, stricter building codes and the like. Finally, in spite of efforts both to mitigate and adapt to climate change, huge losses seem certain to occur regardless.[34] Rebuilding destroyed property and infrastructure will put another heavy strain on global supply capacity.

A recent book by Goodhart and Pradhan (2020) reminds us of yet another emerging supply-side problem. The global supply of people of working age has started to decline. This trend started in Europe and Japan but is now evident in China, Korea and many other countries. Goodhart and Pradhan suggest that the shortage of workers will cause real wages to rise, after many years of stagnation linked to more positive demographic trends. Higher real wages for those working, together with a high marginal propensity to consume (out of income) on the part of pensioners, will support future consumption.[35] With this expectation in mind, companies will invest more to replace more expensive workers. The need for higher investment will be compounded by the need for institutional care for the growing proportion of older people affected by dementia. Goodhart and Pradhan project that real interest rates will have to rise for an extended

[32] The IEA estimates that investments of $6 trillion per year will be needed prior to assure a net zero future. For a broad review of this financing problem, see White (2019).

[33] As for demand, consider the need for the metal-based ingredients in batteries to power EVs and to meet other storage requirements, the need to construct solar and wind facilities as well as the need for new transmission lines for geographically dispersed electricity sources. As for supply, the typical time lag between identifying a deep mine deposit and actual production is around ten years.

[34] See Keen et al. (2021).

[35] This is a controversial insight. Many commentators focus on the fact that pensioners spend absolutely less than working people raising a family.

period to lower aggregate demand to meet aggregate supply and resist inflationary tendencies.

Finally, two other negative supply-side developments could also contribute to higher prices in the future. First, in recent years, zombie companies[36] and companies selling at subsidized prices to gain market share have proliferated in an era of easy financing. Should financing conditions tighten, and these companies disappear, prices will rise directly. Further, growing market concentration in recent years in many jurisdictions will make it easier for other companies to maintain or even raise profit margins. Second, geopolitical tensions, especially between the US and China, are a further significant threat to the efficiencies provided by global supply chains and global competition in pursuing technological progress. Recalling the earlier discussion of complex adaptive systems, and the degree to which the Chinese and American economies are already integrated, the economic damage caused by these developments should not be underestimated.

Negative supply shocks in recent years are already threatening to trigger underlying economic instabilities. Future shocks, possibly more varied and more long lasting, could have even more dangerous economic effects. Both depression (accompanied by deflation) and high inflation are extreme opposite outcomes that are both plausible. In complex, adaptive systems, outcomes arise from feedback processes that are essentially impossible to predict ex ante. However, what we do know is that high debt levels increase economic vulnerability in both good times and bad,[37] and that many countries now have very high levels of both private and public debt. Highly respected economists have in fact given concrete descriptions of the processes through which high *private* sector debt can lead to debt-deflation[38] and how high *public* sector debt can end in hyperinflation.[39] The fact that private sector debt often gets transferred to the public sector

[36] See Acharya et al. (2020) for a discussion of how such companies can both reduce aggregate productivity growth and lower prices. Also, Banerjee and Hoffman (2018).

[37] In tough times, debtors have trouble raising revenues to meet existing debt service requirements. In good times, rates rise, and debt service requirements rise.

[38] The classic description is given by Fisher (1933), based on his experience of the Great Depression of the 1930s. See also Schumpeter (1934).

[39] See Sargent and Wallace (1981) for the theory of how this process might work, and Bernholz (2006) to see how this process has often been observed historically.

would seem to tilt the balance in favour of an eventual inflationary outturn.[40]

Whatever the outcome, some form of serious economic crisis now seems possible and even likely. In the event of such an economic crisis, the effects on other fragile systems might be quite negative. Potentially, there could be a "cascade of tipping points" between systems,[41] similar to the potential cascades that scientists have already identified within the environmental system.[42]

For example, a serious economic crisis might have severe fiscal effects that prevented governments from playing a significant role in pursuing climate change mitigation. Given that greenhouse gases are still rising, not falling towards net zero targets already agreed, global warming might proceed to a point (a tipping point) where the process could not be reversed. Similarly, given a severe economic crisis, public health systems might lack resources to respond to new challenges. At the least, the capacity of the health system to address the backlog of operations and appointments arising from the pandemic would be severely compromised. Should these environmental and public health challenges materialize, they would aggravate the threat to political stability. Indeed, these indirect effects of economic instability on political stability could prove, as or even more, significant than the direct effects discussed below.

Could Political Stability Be Threatened by Economic Instability?

There is a growing literature indicating that financial crises can lead to a sharp decline in voter support for ruling parties, and to a polarization of views around extremes. Funke, Schularik and Trebesch (2015) identify those extremes as being right-wing nationalism and left-wing socialism. Moreover, as Hayek (1944) pointed out in *The Road to Serfdom*, both wings are similar in having little respect for individual freedoms.[43] In the end, these extremes can even unite to form anti-democratic movements like the National Socialists in Germany in the 1930s. There now seems

[40] Reinhart and Rogoff (2009) provide many examples.

[41] A recently introduced term for this is "Global Polycrisis" popularized by historian Adam Tooze. See Lawrence et al. (2022).

[42] See Keen et al. (2021) p. 2.

[43] It is notable that Hayek's book was "Dedicated to the socialists of all parties."

general agreement that support for this movement was encouraged by the economic turmoil in Central Europe that followed World War I; first hyperinflation and then the Great Depression. Today, democracy could also be at risk, given some economic trigger, and of course political turmoil has the clear capacity to aggravate the economic problems in turn.

Indicators of Underlying Fragility

Like an economy, a democratic system is a complex, adaptive system that requires many conditions to be met to ensure its stability.[44] Many of these requirements can be written into laws or constitutions: free and fair elections, one man-one vote, competition for votes based on platforms and a free press, among others. However, other requirements are more subtle and hard to codify: public trust in institutions and decent behaviour on the part of political opponents. In turn, the latter requires respect for others motives and a willingness to show restraint in the exercise of power. A corollary of this complexity is that democratic systems are naturally fragile. The failure to meet even one of the necessary requirements could threaten the stability of the whole system.

Moreover, there is always a tension in democracies between individual freedoms and the public good and these tensions can easily become excessive. On the one hand, James Madison in the Federalist Papers worried that the pursuit of *individual* interests could lead to the formation of factions (parties) that would culminate in "instability, injustice and confusion." An observer of modern-day US politics might add "gridlock" and the failure to address structural problems to Madison's list of concerns. On the other hand, the subordination of individual freedoms to the *public good* could also become excessive. In recent books, Madelaine Albright (2018) and Jason Stanley (2018) have warned that populist causes often tip over into outright fascism.[45] Otherwise put, there can be no guarantee that the "popular will" will always freely choose the democratic way forward.

[44] See, for example, Levitsky and Ziblatt (2018).

[45] I use the word "fascist" in the same way as Albright (2018, p. 11). "To my mind, a Fascist is someone who identifies strongly with and claims to speak for a whole nation or group, is unconcerned with the rights of others, and is willing to use whatever means are necessary—including violence—to achieve his or her goals. There can be no direct lineage or direct comparison with the movements of the 1930s.

If the above comments are essentially theoretical, political fault lines are increasingly evident in practice. In many democratic countries, growing inequality is threatening the legitimacy of the political system. Not only is inequality rising with respect to income and wealth, but it is rising with respect to opportunity. Intergenerational mobility has been falling, particularly in the US and the UK, implying that many parents have quite valid reasons to believe that their children will have more difficult lives than they had. Similarly, in many countries, the proportion of people or households classified as middle class has been declining, a trend decried by political scientists as far back as Aristotle.[46] Stanley (2022, p. 4) summarizes one possible endgame as follows: "For a fascist party to triumph … voters merely have to be persuaded that democracy is no longer serving their interests." For many voters this might now seem to be the case.

The political impact of these trends has been aggravated in recent decades by an amplification process. It begins with the relatively disadvantaged becoming convinced that the rich and other elite elements are consciously gaming the economic system to their own advantage. The conviction that "it's not fair" then triggers an emotional response, of anger and resentment, and a retreat into silos of like-minded people.

In the modern world, this anger is then likely amplified by the "echo chamber" effect of social media.[47] Worse, there are domestic elements in any society who will try to divert that anger into cultural and racial resentment.[48] Finally, there is growing evidence that foreign powers (especially Russia and China) also seek to identify divisive issues in democracies and to aggravate them in order to make their own regimes look better to their own people.[49] While they often use the internet and front organizations to do so, in some cases it appears that laundered money has also been used directly to buy political influence in some countries.[50]

[46] Aristotle in "Politics" states, "It is clear then that the best partnership in a state is the one which operates through the middle people, and also that those states in which the middle element is large … have every chance of having a well-run constitution."

[47] See Haidt (2022).

[48] Stanley (2022) argues that such tactics were first employed by the Klu Klux Klan in the US and only later spread to Europe.

[49] Snyder (2018).

[50] See Cooper (2021) and Bullough (2019).

More Direct Evidence That Democracy Is Under Threat

The last Annual Report of Freedom House (2022) suggests "The global order is at a tipping point." The previous year (2021) marked the sixteenth year in a row in which the number of countries becoming "less free" exceeded the number of countries becoming "more free." Seventy-five percent of the world's population now live in countries that became less free last year. These countries include core democracies such as the US and the UK.

More specifically, there is growing evidence that some of the *codified principles* supporting democracies are under threat. In a number of countries, not least the United States, efforts are under way to restrict the right of "one man, one vote" and also to impede the orderly transfer of power.[51] An objective "free press" is increasingly subordinated to editorial control driven by ideological considerations. *Non-codified* requirements are also under threat. Polls in democratic countries show a continuing decline in "trust in government" to record lows. As for the need to show respect and restraint in dealing with political opponents, this is being increasingly replaced with behaviour more akin to tribal warfare.[52]

If this last problem shows that Madison's concerns about factionalism were valid, there is evidence that concerns about the threat of fascism warrant even more attention. Right-wing nationalist parties have been gaining support in many democratic countries.[53] Moreover, the popular support for "strongmen" has been on the rise, with personalities like Trump, Bolsonaro, Modi and Orban all being (initially at least) freely elected. Resonating with the experience of Hitler and Mussolini, their electoral success was achieved in spite of campaigning actively against the media, elites and even democracy itself.

Closely related, there has been a gradual erosion of Karl Popper's "Open Society" and its replacement by "us versus them" thinking. And if this divides democratic societies at home, it also implies a much-reduced

[51] Stanley (2022) argues that "legal practices historically have enforced and perpetuated unjust hierarchies of value in ways that often go unnoticed." Consider Jim Crow laws in the United States, and more recent laws restricting the rights of convicted prisoners to vote. These laws largely affect prospective black voters in the US. In India, new citizenship laws are designed to discriminate against Muslims who do not have proof of citizenship.

[52] See Levitsky and Zablitt (2018).

[53] The latest example has been the rise of the Sweden Democrats in Sweden. With organizational links back to World War II Nazism, they became the second largest party in Parliament in the elections of September 2022.

appetite for international cooperation[54] and a greater likelihood of international confrontation.[55] Ironically, the growing split between authoritarian regimes and more democratic ones could support the case for "strongmen," people thought capable of providing the strong domestic leadership needed to achieve victory. History teaches us that, in the pursuit of such nationalistic objectives, democratic rights and freedoms are often the first casualties.

What Policy Measures Might Help Restore Stability?

An initial point is that we require an *analytical revolution* in thinking about policy solutions to problems. Policymakers must accept that they are dealing with complex, adaptive systems and that each is nested in other such systems. This has two implications. First, within each system, policy will have both short-term and long-term effects and it is important to consider both.[56] Second, policies designed to stabilize one system might easily destabilize another system. More economic growth to reduce the real burden of debt, at the expense of irremediable climate change, is not obviously a good bargain. Political scientists grasped these concepts decades ago and coined the phrase "wicked problems"[57] in consequence. In contrast, many (most?) macroeconomists use models that are simple, linear, deterministic and based on highly implausible assumptions.[58] Both longer-term (unintended consequences) effects of policies and

[54] The success of the referendum in the UK on "Brexit" is a case in point.

[55] Such a confrontation between the US and China now seems extremely likely. Whether this extends to hostilities between a democratic camp and an authoritarian one (say, China, Russia, North Korea and Iran) remains to be seen.

[56] In contrast to Keynes' view that "In the long run we are all dead" consider von Mises who said, "No very deep knowledge is usually needed for grasping the immediate effects of a measure, but the task of economics is to foretell the remoter effects, and so to allow us to avoid attempts to remedy a present ill by sowing the seeds of a much greater ill for the future."

[57] For example, see Head (2018) for an overview. Head quotes (p. 3) approvingly another political scientist who states, "Every problem interacts with other problems and is therefore part of a system of interrelated problems … a mess … The solution to a mess can seldom be obtained by independently solving each of the problems of which it is composed."

[58] For particularly vitriolic assessments see Buiter (2009) and Romer (2016).

interactions with other systems are generally ignored. While new economic policy frameworks are now being investigated,[59] a paradigm shift has yet to occur.

The principal threat to *economic stability* currently is the overhang of debt, both private and public. Moreover, the contractionary effect of needing to service private sector debts will grow significantly[60] as interest rates rise in the face of rising inflationary pressures. To avoid this process ending in a cascade of disorderly bankruptcies, explicit and orderly debt restructuring is required. Unfortunately, numerous studies from the OECD[61] and the Group of Thirty (2018) indicate that the judicial and administrative mechanisms to do this are sorely lacking and need to be put in place. These shortcomings apply to household and corporate debt, but even more to financial institutions. The "too big to fail" problem has in some countries morphed into a "too big to save" problem. As for sovereign bankruptcies, basic principles still must be agreed at the international level as to when this should occur. A further problem is finding agreement on loss sharing between traditional lenders (like sovereign and international institutions and creditors in advanced economies) and new Chinese creditors whose public/private status is not yet clear.

The sovereign debts of advanced market economies have also risen to record levels (as a proportion of GDP) in recent years, beginning to raise fears of "fiscal dominance."[62] This threatens higher inflation on the one hand, or explicit cuts to expenditures on the other if the former threat is to be averted.[63] The probabilities of both will rise as interest rates go up in

[59] The Institute for New Economic Thinking (INET) was set up by George Soros with this ultimate purpose in mind. A project established in 2010 at the OECD, called New Approaches to Economic Challenges (NAEC), had a similar objective. Both INET and various student groups have been actively trying to change the content of economics courses at universities. See de Muijnck and Tieleman (2021).

[60] This is the Keynesian "paradox of thrift." As everyone cuts expenditures to service debts, overall saving falls.

[61] See, for example, OECD (2016).

[62] When debt levels rise too high, private sector purchasers begin to worry about debt service and repayment. Unwilling to pay higher interest rates, governments increasingly rely on finance from the central bank ("fiscal dominance"). Observation of this practice can send inflationary expectations and interest rates higher still. A currency crisis often emerges. See Sargent and Wallace (1981) and Bernholz (2006), also cited above.

[63] Evidently, expenditure cuts could be avoided through increases in the efficiency of production of government services. Even if pursued with vigour and success, this would take a long time to provide significant results.

response to resource constraints and rising inflation, as described above. Either could lead to social unrest and become a threat to democracy. As well, constrained governments might struggle to make the investments required to stabilize the environment or prepare for future pandemics. In these circumstances, a better alternative might be significant tax increases, targeting consumption in particular. Different countries might choose different taxes, but higher taxes on fossil fuels, property and taxes directly on consumption would generally be favoured. Cuts to tax expenditures, often subsidizing special interests, would also have high priority.

It is important to recognize the ineffectiveness of tighter monetary policy in addressing inflation concerns when fears of fiscal dominance are widespread. Higher interest rates on government debt exacerbate funding problems which can further stoke inflationary fears. Moreover, the likelihood of this happening rises as the duration of the outstanding debt becomes shorter. Unfortunately, programs of Quantitative Easing (QE) in advanced economies have significantly increased that problem as central banks have bought-in longer-term debt and paid for it with newly created overnight money.[64] As well, the same programmes almost ensure that central banks will face operational losses in coming years that will further swell government deficits.[65] In contrast, such fears would be alleviated by tax increases. Moreover, tighter monetary policy could reduce investments that need to be encouraged, not least investments in "green" energy that are highly capital-intensive. In contrast, restrictive fiscal measures could directly target consumption.

The threat to *political stability* in democracies is amplified by feedback effects and complex social processes. These should be identified and resisted, especially the disruptions intended by those (both domestic and foreign) that profit from social unrest and political upheaval. However, the principal and underlying problem seems to be growing inequality, whether of income, wealth or opportunity. Alleviating this will require significant changes in both private practices and public policy.

[64] Another complication has been the growing reliance of some governments (notably the UK) on TIPs for financing. Thus, as rates rise with only lagged effects on inflation, governments are hit by a "double whammy."

[65] An interesting further complication is that, as longer-term interest rates rise, central banks who have done QE will suffer significant mark-to-market losses that will generally far exceed their available capital. Since central bank liabilities are the medium of exchange, they can never go bankrupt and do not need capital. Nevertheless, the optics could help erode confidence.

As to the former, the relative compensation of senior management needs review, as does the issue of share buybacks[66] that often benefit senior management while weakening future corporate profits and resilience. The nascent movement towards replacing shareholders' interests with stakeholders' interests should also be encouraged. As for governments, restoring the trust of average citizens will require legislation promoting equality in various ways. Changing the tax system to make it more progressive, to cut unfair corporate subsidies and to reduce international tax evasion would be desirable, as would measures to restrain corporate lobbying.

Governments must also contemplate higher minimum wages. Training and lifetime learning should be significantly enhanced, and the formal education system reviewed to ensure it meets modern needs. Finally, insolvency laws need to be reviewed and made more debtor-friendly in many countries. Continuing to "bail out bankers" does not increase the government's credibility when it comes to reducing inequality and promoting the "fair" treatment of ordinary citizens.

All of these suggestions to enhance economic and political stability, not least the desirability of raising consumption taxes, will be very hard to sell politically. *Voters* will instinctively resist suggestions that affect their short-term lifestyle, even if their longer-term best interests imply they should do so. The challenge is to convince them that we are transitioning from an "age of abundance" to an "age of scarcity," implying there is simply no alternative to making hard and unpleasant choices. The willingness of most citizens in most democracies to make serious sacrifices in the face of the Covid-19 pandemic gives some cause for optimism. The nationalist sentiments evoked by international conflict might also elicit voter support for putting public policy on a "war-time footing."

However, voters are not the only people who need to be convinced. Measures to alter distribution will be instinctively resisted by the *rich and powerful*. Somehow, they must be convinced that change is in their own best interest. Walter Schiedel (2017) has documented historically how great inequality has always been swept away by one of the Four Horsemen of the Apocalypse. Better then to accept the need to limit such extremes than to resist such limits and lose everything. Of course, even if this logic is accepted, action will not follow if individuals feel they can be free riders in this process.

[66] See Smithers (2019) who argues that the "bonus culture" has many downsides.

The final group that needs to be convinced and engaged are *politicians in democratic countries.* Without such leadership, the convictions of both voters and the powerful are unlikely to be swayed. Today, at least for some politicians, re-election seems to be their central motivating force. Somehow the moral element of leadership must be restored.[67] Politicians must strive to do what is in the public interest, and this is particularly so when there is a constituency for policies that are "dangerously foolish."[68] A denial of the need to face up to the urgency of current economic, political, environmental and public health challenges would seem accurately described using such pejorative terms.

Without greatly renewed efforts, the minimal reforms required to stabilize the economic system in the face of expected supply shocks might not be forthcoming. If this is the case, the future could hold either debt deflation or high and lasting inflation, or both in one order or another. Whatever and whenever the economic shock hits, it also seems unlikely that our democracies will have been reformed to a point that their resiliency has become unquestionable. In such an environment, concerns about the environment and public health might also fall by the wayside. With all this at stake, the arguments for policies to help our economy adapt to a possible new age of scarcity would seem overwhelming. At the least, we need insurance against cascading risks that could prove existential.

References

Acharya, V., Krosignani, M., Eisert, T., & Eufinger, C. (2020). *Zombie credit and (dis)inflation: Evidence from Europe.* Federal Reserve Bank of New York.

Albright, M. (2018). *Fascism: A warning.* New York: Harper Collins.

Ball, P. (2012). *Why society is a complex matter.* Springer.

Banerjee, R., & Hoffman, B. (2018). The rise of zombie firms: Causes and consequences. *BIS Quarterly Bulletin*, 67–78.

Barnes, O. (2022, 28 April) "Climate change poses pandemic threat by acclelerating animal virus spread, study warns". Financial Times.

Bernholz, P. (2006). *Monetary regimes and history: Economic and political relationships.* MPG Books.

[67] For example, in recent years, there has been a truly worrisome degree of support, from within their own parties, for Boris Johnson (in the UK) and Donald Trump (in the US). Both men were well known to have committed immoral and possibly even illegal acts, but their colleagues felt their personal chance of re-election was greater under their leadership.

[68] This is how President Kennedy defined a statesman in his book *Profiles of Courage.*

Bluedorn, J. (2022, October 5). Wage-price spiral risks appear contained despite high inflation. *IMF Blog*.

Borio, C., McCauley, R., McGuire, T., & Sushko, V. (2016). Covered interest parity lost: Understanding the cross currency basis. *BIS Quarterly Review*, 45–64.

Buchanan, M. (2013). *Forecast: What physics, meteorology, and the natural sciences can teach us about economics*. Bloomsbury.

Buiter, W. (2009). The unfortunate uselessness of most 'state of the art' academic monetary economics. blogs.ft.com/mavercom

Bullough, O. (2019). *Moneyland*. Profile Books Ltd.

Cerra, V., & Saxena, S. (2017, November). *Booms, crises and recoveries: A new paradigm of the business cycle and its implications* (IMF Working Paper 250).

Chabert, C., Cerisola, M., & Hakura, D. (2022, April 7). Restructuring debt of poorer nations requires more efficient coordination. *IMF Blog*.

Cooper, S. (2021). *Wilful blindness*. Optimum Publishing International.

de Muijnck, S., & Tieleman, J. (2021). *Economy studies: A guide to rethinking economics education*. Amsterdam University Press.

Fisher, I. (1933). The debt-deflation theory of great depressions. *Econometrica, 1*, 337–357.

Funke, M., Schularick, M., & Trebesch, C. (2015). *Going to extremes: Politics after financial crisis, 1870-2014* (CESifo Working Paper No. 5553).

Geanakoplos, J. (2010). *Solving the present crisis and managing the leverage cycle*. Federal Reserve Bank of New York Policy Review.

Goodhart, C., & Pradhan, M. (2020). *The great demographic reversal*. Palgrave Macmillan.

Group of Thirty. (2018, September). *Managing the next financial crisis*. https://group30.org/publications/detail/2658

Haidt, J. (2022, May). Why the past ten years of American life have been uniquely stupid. *The Atlantic*.

Hayek, F. A. (1944). *The road to serfdom*. London: Routledge.

Head, B. (2018). *Forty years of wicked problems literature: Forging closer links to policy studies*. Policy and Society (Open access) Routledge, Taylor and Francis Group.

International Monetary Fund. (2022, October). Executive summary. *Global Financial Stability Report*.

Keen, S., Lenton, T. M., Godin, A., Yilmaz, D., Grasselli, M., & Garrett, T. J. (2021). *Economists erroneous estimates of damage from climate change*. https://arxiv.org/abs/2108.07847

Lawrence, M., Janzwood, S., & Homer-Dixon, T. (2022, September). *What is a global polycrisis? And how does it different from a systemic crisis* (Discussion Paper 2022-4). Cascade Institute.

Levitsky, S., & Ziblatt, D. (2018). *How democracies die: What history tells us about our future*. Broadway Books.

Lynn, B. C. (2010). *Cornered.* John Wiley and Sons.

McKinsey Global Institute. (2022). *The rise and rise of the global balance sheet.* McKinsey Global Institute.

Morgan, J. P. (2022, July 12). One more giant leap for global debt. *Global Data Watch*, 1–4.

OECD. (2016, March 25). Insolvency regimes and productivity growth: A framework for analysis. *Working Party 1.*

OECD. (2017). *Confronting the zombies: Policies for productivity revival.* OECD Economic Policy Papers.

Reinhart, C., & Rogoff, K. (2009). *This time is different: Eight hundred years of financial folly.* Princeton University Press.

Romer, P. (2016, January 5). *The trouble with macroeconomics.* Commons Memorial Lecture of the Omicron Epsilon Society. https://paulromer.net/the-trouble-with-macro/WP-Trouble.pdf

Sargent, T. J., & Wallace, N. (1981). Some unpleasant monetarist arithmetic. *Federal Reserve Bank of Minneapolis Quarterly Review*, *5*(Fall), 1–17.

Scheidel, W. (2017). *The great leveller: Violence and the history of inequality.* Princeton University Press.

Schumpeter, J. A. (1934). Depressions. Can we learn from past experience? In J. In Schumpeter et al. (Eds.), *The economics of the recovery program* (pp. 3–21). McGraw-Hill.

Smithers, A. (2019). *Productivity and the bonus culture.* Oxford University Press.

Snyder, T. (2018). *The road to unfreedom: Russia, Europe, America.* Crown Publishing Group, Random House.

Stanley, J. (2018). *How fascism works: The politics of us and them.* Random House.

Stanley, J. (2022, October 28). One hundred years of fascism. *Project Syndicate.*

The Economist. (2022, October 1–7). Debt, denial and deleveraging, 53–54.

Tucker, P. (2018, June). *Is the financial system sufficiently resilient?* BIS Annual Conference.

Wheeler, G., & Wilkinson, B. with a foreword by White, W. (2022, July). *How central bank mistakes after 2019 led to inflation* (Research Notes). The New Zealand Initiative.

White, W. (2012). *Ultra-easy monetary policy and the law of unintended consequences* (Working Paper No. 126). Federal Reserve Bank of Dallas Globalisation and Monetary Policy Institute.

White, W. (2019, September 16). How to pay for The Green New Deal. *Forum for a New Economy.*

White, W. (2021). International financial regulation: Why it still falls short. In U. Kortsch (Ed.), *The next money crash and a reconstruction blueprint.* IUniverse Books.

William White is a senior fellow at the C. D. Howe Institute in Toronto. From 2009 until March 2018, he chaired the Economic and Development Review Committee at the OECD in Paris. Prior to that, he spent fourteen years as Economic Adviser at the Bank for International Settlements (BIS) in Basel. Before joining the BIS in 1994, he was the deputy governor for international affairs at the Bank of Canada in Ottawa. In addition to publishing widely, Mr. White's other activities included membership of the Issing Committee, advising Chancellor Merkel on G-20 issues. Mr. White was honoured with the Adam Smith Award in 2016, the highest prize presented annually by the National Association of Business Economists in Washington.

Historical Roots, Cultural Selection and the 'New World Order'

Marcus Miller

Introduction

With their proposal to create a New World Order, the leaders of Russia and China have thrown down the gauntlet by openly challenging the West in a clash of civilisations. But the first shock of arms has pitched brother against brother in the heart of Europe. How to comprehend the origins and implications of these earth-shaking events?

A broad overview of post–World War II developments in the realms of macroeconomics, politics—and geopolitics—is first provided. Then various lenses for viewing these developments are offered—beginning with the once-fashionable forecast of liberal democracy as the 'end of history';

The author is most grateful to Peter Hammond, Andy Krupa, Herakles Polemarchakis, Dennis Novy, Robert Skidelsky and Bill White for their comments and suggestions; to Gerard Roland for making his datafiles available and to Jennifer Smith for help in analysing them.

M. Miller (✉)
University of Warwick, Coventry, West Midlands, UK
e-mail: Marcus.Miller@warwick.ac.uk

R. Z. Aliber et al. (eds.), *Fault Lines After COVID-19*,
https://doi.org/10.1007/978-3-031-26482-5_3

and moving swiftly on to the contrary view that 'deep historical roots' play a decisive role in creating cultural divergence. There follow two perspectives involving competition—either a social struggle *inside* the country concerned, or a more internationalist, cultural struggle *between* countries.

These perspectives are then employed to focus on Russia under President Putin, leaving China for others to discuss.

Three Post-war Eras

In opening his account of the Gallic War, Julius Caesar famously noted that the lands he was invading could be divided into three distinct regions.[1] In like fashion, Gideon Rachman, in his account of global political economy post–World War II, suggests dividing the period into three distinct eras. We follow this lead in Table 1, where key features of political economy in Europe and North America are briefly indicated, along with global geopolitical developments.

The first two periods of thirty years apiece are labelled as 'Keynesian' and 'Neo-liberal', respectively, to mark the prevailing economic orthodoxy of the time. The third period—still ongoing—is a time of crisis which has spurred the worldwide rise of strongmen to positions of power. Further discussion follows.

The First Era (i.e. the Three Decades Following the End of World War II in 1945)

As well as major physical reconstruction after the ravages of conflict, the immediate post-war years saw the creation of welfare states in European countries—and of global institutions, designed to promote a rule-based international order. These included the IMF and World Bank based in Washington, the GATT[2] based in Geneva, and the United Nations in New York.

The hope that wartime alliances would persist into peacetime was soon dashed by the onset of the Cold War, setting Russia at odds with the West. This triggered the organisation of NATO, starting with a dozen members

[1] *Gallia est omnis divisa in partes tres* are the opening words of Caesar's *Commentaries on the Gallic War*.

[2] General Agreement on Tariffs and Trade, later succeeded by the World Trade Organisation.

Table 1 Three eras of political economy post–World War II

Era	*Duration*	*Setting*	*Economics*	*Politics*	*Geopolitics*
1	**1945–1975** (30 years) **'Keynesian era'**	Rule based international economic order (including **IMF, World Bank, GATT**) on US Dollar standard.	Keynesian demand management in *les trentes glorieuses*. But oil price shocks of 1973 lead to **global inflation**	Post-war construction of **Welfare States** in the West.	Allies set up UN in 1945. But **Cold War** starts in 1947; **NATO set up** in 1949. Chairman Mao's experiments fail in China.
2	**1975–2005** (30 years) **'Neo-liberal era'**	Win–win world of globalised capitalism, with **floating exchange rates**	Monetarism; then **inflation targets** (inspired by Milton Friedman, then Robert Lucas)	**Liberal democracy** in ascendance (with Thatcher and Reagan as cheerleaders)	Collapse USSR in 1990; **end of Cold War,** with US as hegemon. Deng sets China on spectacular growth path.
3	**2005–?** (17 years—and counting) **'Era of the Strongman'**	**Global financial crisis** of 2008; **Covid** pandemic of 2020 onwards; Russian invasion of **Ukraine** 2022	Recourse to **unconventional** macro policy measures to cope with crises (e.g. QE and furlough)	Populism and protection. **Democracy in disarray** in US and UK.	Putin and Xi Jinping emerge as strongmen, with plan for New World Order in 2022—leading to **New Cold War?**

Source: Rachman (2022b)

in 1949; and, not long after, it took the world to the edge of nuclear war[3] in the Cuban missile crisis of 1962.

In terms of domestic politics, according to Robert Reich, these years—referred to in France as *les trentes glorieuses*—saw an intellectual shift from concerns of 'political economy' to more universal and scientific 'laws'.[4]

[3] How close, is analysed dispassionately in Dixit et al. (2021).

[4] John Maynard Keynes's *General Theory of Employment, Interest and Money* (1936) dominated American economic policy from the end of World War II until the late 1970s.

> After World War II, under the powerful influence of Keynesian economics, the focus shifted from the field of political economy toward government taxes and transfers as means of both stabilizing the business cycle and helping the poor. Reich (2015, p. xx)

But when the global economy got close to capacity in the early 1970s, the rise in commodity prices—oil in particular—set in motion a widespread wage-price spiral of inflation.

The Second Era (i.e. the Thirty Years Following 1975)

As a consequence, the pragmatism of Samuelson, Solow, and like-minded 'saltwater' economists, yielded pride of place to the 'freshwater' economics of mid-Western universities, inspired by the market fundamentalism of Friedman and Lucas. With Mrs. Thatcher and Ronald Reagan acting as joint cheerleaders, indeed,

> for a brief period of world history, liberal democracy seemed ascendant and unchallenged. After the fall of the Berlin Wall in 1989, the big economic and political questions appeared settled. In economics, the answer was free markets. In politics, the answer was democracy. In geopolitics, America was now the sole superpower. Rachman (2022b, p. 16)

This liberal ascendancy was not to last: for the hubris of capitalist triumphalism met its nemesis in a financial crisis that threatened a repeat of the Great Depression.

The Third Era (Where We Are Now After 2005)

What if the elite in the US and the UK were in the process of consolidating their power and wealth via their market dominance, as alleged by Robert Reich (2015)? And what if Hyman Minsky's prediction of financial market instability were to come true—but those who practised what he described as a Ponzi lending were to be bailed out in order to prevent the collapse of capitalism? Such factors would favour the rise of political strongmen offering to save the people from the self-serving elite. As Robert Reich put it:

> The real question is not whether [Britain and the United States] will move towards a capitalism that works for the many rather than the few. … The question is whether this change will occur through democratic reforms or by means of authoritarian mandates. Reich (2015, p. xiv)

Economic disaster was avoided by timely fiscal intervention together with prolonged Quantitative Easing, but economic recovery was slow. Moreover, the nostrums of governance in the West faced a challenge from statist, top-down control in China, where economic growth proceeded at a spectacular rate.

With democracy in disarray, one country after another yielded control to those Rachman labels strongmen, as listed in Table 2, where Presidents Putin and Erdogan feature as early starters (who have nevertheless remained in power to the time of writing—unlike Boris Johnson and Donald Trump).

What then are the distinctive characteristics of strongman rule? Rachman (2022b, pp. 10–15) lists the following:

- **Cult of the personality.** Thus, for example, in imitation of Mao Zedung, 'Xi Jinping thought' has been put into Chinese constitution, which is rewritten to allow the president more than two terms of office.
- **Contempt for the rule of law**, as challengers are—to put it mildly—denied the opportunity to run for office. Thus Alexei Navalny was

Table 2 Strongmen leaders in the twenty-first century

	Strongman rulers	*Country*	*Since*
1.	Putin	Russia	2000
2	Erdogan	Turkey	2003
3	Xi Jinping	China	2012
4	Modi	India	2014
5	Orban and Kaczynski	Hungary and Poland	2015
6	Johnson	UK	2016
7	Trump	US	2016
8	Duterte	Philippines	2016
9 and 10	MBS and Netanyahu	Saudi Arabia and Israel	2017
11 and 12	Bolsonaro and Amlo	Brazil and Mexico	2018
13	Abiy Ahmed	Ethiopia	2019

Source: Rachman (2022b, pp. vii, viii)

first poisoned then imprisoned at the behest of the Russian president, with his supporters proscribed as agents of a foreign power.

- **Populism**—with claims to represent the 'real people' against the governing elite, as when President Trump promised to just 'Build the Wall!' to check immigration from Mexico.
- **Nostalgic nationalism**—with politics driven by fear, as with Putin's claim that, to meet increasing threats from NATO, the Russian empire must be restored.

Four Perspectives

According to Kantian maxim, 'theories without facts are empty, but facts without theories are blind'. So, to follow our brief factual summary, we appeal to various theories advanced to help explain these facts—beginning, however, with an auspicious precedent.

In a celebrated meeting of the British Association for the Advancement of Science in Oxford in June 1860, two sharply contrasting perspectives of early human history were presented to the waiting throng—some thousand strong! First came Samuel Wilberforce, Bishop of Oxford, adhering faithfully to the writings of the Old Testament; to be promptly countered by Thomas Henry Huxley, the 'bulldog of Darwin', citing the just-published theory of natural selection. When challenged to say whether it was through his grandfather or grandmother that he claimed his simian descent, Huxley replied that, if asked to choose, he would opt for a humble monkey as progenitor rather than a privileged and pompous figure like the bishop. At which point, Robert Fitzroy (Darwin's captain on the famous voyage of *HMS Beagle*) left the rowdy proceedings holding aloft the Bible and crying, 'The Scriptures! The Scriptures!'

Inspired by this example, we examine different perspectives to help understand the historical developments summarised above. The first of these is the bold prediction of Francis Fukuyama, who reckoned that 'Western liberal democracy is the final form of human government'. This claim of a clear path of convergence to a universally acceptable model of governance is surely not one that Darwin would have supported. In *The Descent of Man*, after citing with approval a remark of Walter Bagehot[5] that 'We are apt to look at progress as the normal rule in human society; but history refutes this', he went on to observe that 'The ancients did not

[5] An early supporter of his evolutionary theory of society, Bagehot (1872).

even entertain the idea; nor do the oriental nations at the present day' Darwin (1873, chapter 5, p. 166).

In any case, Fukuyama's confident forecast was famously challenged by Samuel P. Huntington (1993). He proposed instead that, with the end of the Cold War, deep-seated cultural divisions would define future conflict, in what he called a Clash of Civilisations. For a contemporary formulation of such a historical perspective, we turn to research conducted by Gerard Roland (2020). He investigates how current cultural divisions may have their origins in the 'deep historical roots' of founding civilisations—be they statist hierarchies like those of the orient, or individualist, market-driven societies like that of early Mesopotamia, the cradle of Western civilisation.

In place of such cultural determinism, Daron Acemoglu and James Robinson, hereafter designated A & R, have developed a game theoretic perspective where the political structure is viewed as the outcome of a continuing tussle between competing domestic forces—the state versus that of the common people. In *The Narrow Corridor: How Nations Struggle for Liberty*, A & R (2019), the pursuit of liberal democracy is seen as a hazardous enterprise, with 'liberty is as rare as it is fragile, wedged uneasily between tyranny and anarchy'.[6]

But what if it is not so much forces *within* a given society but competition *between* different societies that better describes the forces at work in our history? This was the perspective offered by Charles Darwin himself in the *Descent of Man*, where natural selection determines the evolution of societies in global competition for survival.

For convenience, the four different views to be considered are first listed in Table 3 and then discussed in some more detail.

First Perspective: Fukuyama's Prediction of 'Immaculate Convergence'

In *The End of History?*, published in the summer of 1989, Francis Fukuyama foresaw the coming global triumph of liberal democracy. He wrote:

> What we may be witnessing is not just the end of the Cold War, or the passing of a particular period of post-war history, but the end of history as

[6] Joel Mokyr, cited in Acemoglu (2019).

Table 3 Various perspectives

	Perspective	*Key idea*	*Author(s)*
1.	**'End of History'**	'Western liberal democracy is the final form of human government'	Francis Fukuyama (1989)
2.	**Significance of 'Deep Historical Roots' (DHR)**	Cultural continuity of statism and individualism	Gerard Roland (2020)
3.	**Liberty and justice nurtured in a 'shackled state'**	'Political liberty comes from social struggle of equals'	Daron Acemoglu and James Robinson (2019)
4.	**Darwinian competition of cultures**	Altruism pays international dividends	Charles Darwin (1873); Bowles and Gintis (2011)

> such … that is, the end-point of mankind's ideological evolution and the **universalization of Western liberal democracy** as the final form of human government. Fukuyama (1989, p. 4) Emphasis added

The fall of the Wall of Berlin within the year and the dissolution of the Soviet Union two years later in 1991 appeared to offer dramatic confirmation of his bold prediction—one that was music to the ears of President Reagan and Margaret Thatcher, key leaders of the neo-liberal era.

That Fukuyama's forecast was ultimately set to fail, however, is indicated by surveys collected by Freedom House[7] shown in Fig. 1. To start with, in seeming support of Fukuyama's perspective, the line showing the percentage of 'electoral democracies'[8] in the world rose sharply from 40 to 60 percent over the next decade. That he was riding a wave about to lose impetus, however, is indicated by the subsequent levelling out of this bumpy line and of the fraction of free countries, which peaked at about a half in the early years of this century, before echelons of strongmen listed above came to power.

[7] An NGO that measures the degree of civil liberties and political rights in every nation around the world.

[8] Note, however, that Freedom House's term 'electoral democracy' differs from 'liberal democracy' in that the latter also implies the presence of a substantial array of civil liberties (as enjoyed in free countries).

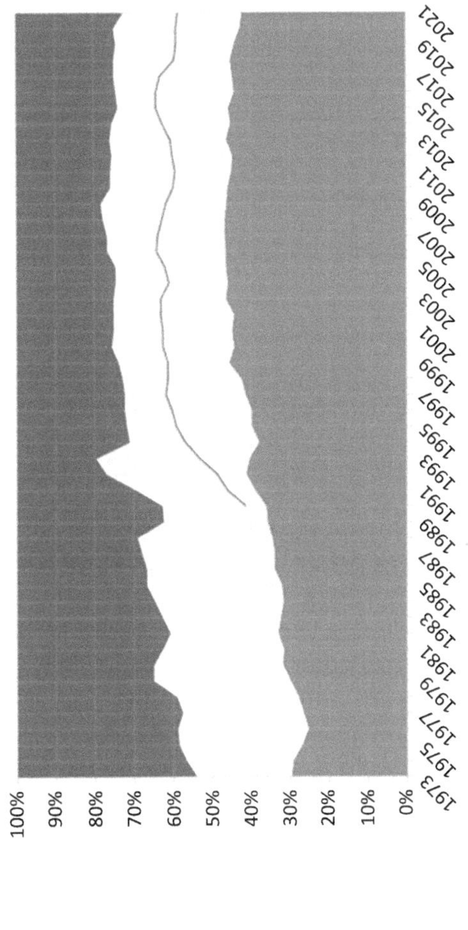

Fig. 1 Countries that are free, partly free or not free (shading indicates percentages), and electoral democracies (line shows percentage). (Key: Bottom layer: free. Middle layer: partly free. Top layer: not free. Source: Freedom House, 2022)

Second Perspective: Gerard Roland's Postulate of Cultural Determinism

Speaking in St. Petersburg in 2017 on the anniversary of the Russian Revolution, Gerard Roland proposed that the contrast between Communism and capitalism was but one chapter of a very long-running saga. In the published paper, entitled 'The deep historical roots of modern culture', this view is elaborated as follows:

> There have been since antiquity two opposed types of institutional systems: one resembling central planning and present in ancient China, ancient Egypt, the Inca Empire and other territorial states, and another one, with strong market institutions [and] protection of property rights, present mostly in city-states, not just in the Mediterranean but throughout the world. … These institutional differences can be seen to be at the root of the two cultural systems in today's world: collectivism versus individualism. Roland (2020, p. 483)

A relevant illustration of this hypothesis (of cultural bifurcation based on Deep Historical Roots, hereafter DHR) is provided in Fig. 2 for a sub-sample of the extensive dataset he has assembled—specifically, China and Russia together with the twelve founding members of the North Atlantic Treaty Organisation. This shows a current measure of each society's individualism (its Hofstede score, on the horizontal) plotted against a measure of power centralization in its founding civilization (as provided in Roland's dataset and kindly made available).

From the downward sloping line of best fit, it is evident that, in this sample, the historical centralisation of power is negatively associated with current individualism, in line with DHR hypothesis. A further striking feature is the contrast it provides between the East (as represented by China and Russia—both situated well above the 45-degree diagonal), and the West (represented by NATO, whose original members, all except for Portugal,[9] lie below).

Could current events be bearing out Roland's idea of enduring cultural types?

[9] Note that the Portugese *Estado Novo* regime was one of the longest-surviving authoritarian states in twentieth-century Europe, lasting from 1933 to 1974, with Antonio de Salazar in charge from its inception until 1968!

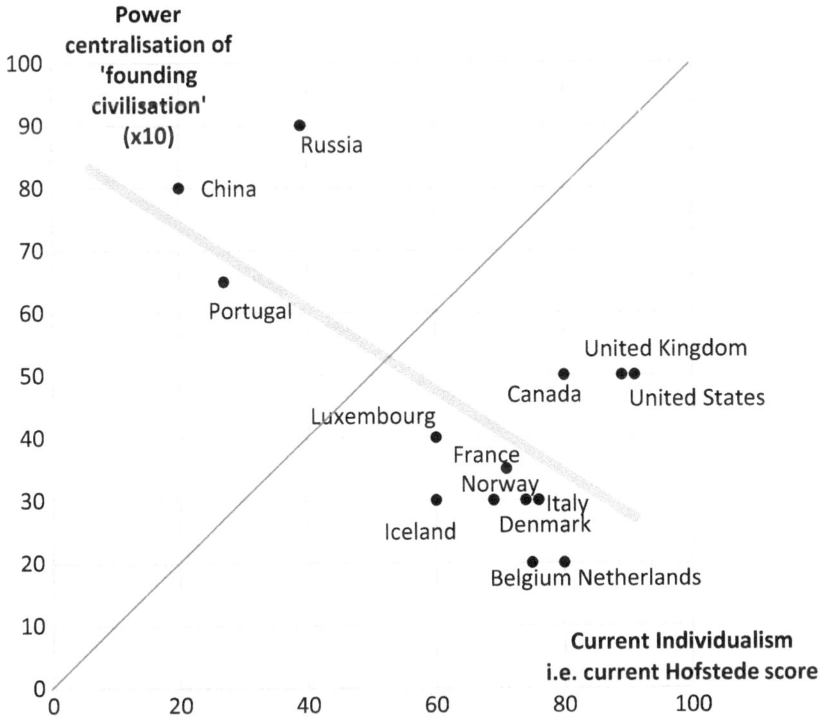

Fig. 2 Historic centralisation of power and current individualism: East versus West. (Source: Roland, 2020)

For, in what Samir Puri (2022, p. 206) calls the 'now legendary bilateral meeting' between Putin and China's President Xi Jinping at the opening ceremony of the Beijing Winter Olympics, on 4 February 2022, the two presidents proposed a New World Order. What this involves was described by Gideon Rachman (2022a) as follows:

> Beijing and Moscow argue that the current world order is characterised by American attempts to impose Western ideas about democracy and human rights on others ... The **new world order** that Russia and China are demanding would instead be based on distinct spheres of influence.
>
> While the Western liberal tradition promotes universal human rights, Russian and Chinese thinkers make the argument that different cultural

traditions and "civilisations" should be allowed to develop in different ways. (Emphasis added.)

In the joint declaration, moreover, China backed Russia's objections to any further expansion of NATO—whose earlier expansion is widely seen as the *casus belli* for Russia's attack on Ukraine that began only three weeks later, as discussed further below.

Third Perspective: Non-cooperative Game Theory

In *The Narrow Corridor: How Nations Struggle for Liberty*, A & R explicitly reject both such ideas of cultural determinism and those of ineluctable progress towards enlightenment. They propose instead a contingent, game-theoretic perspective, where political liberty may—or may not—emerge from social struggle. This approach received the enthusiastic endorsement of Avinash Dixit (2021), a distinguished game theorist,[10] in an extended review which covers the technical details with admirable clarity.

The conflict they describe is between society (the people) and the state, where the latter is represented by elite institutions and leaders. As Acemoglu (2019) explains, however: 'You need this conflict to be balanced. An imbalance is detrimental to liberty. If society is too weak, that leads to despotism. But on the other side, if society is too strong, that results in weak states that are unable to protect their citizens'.

To illustrate how this creates a 'narrow corridor' in which liberty flourishes, they present their approach in a diagram, see Fig. 3, where political outcomes depend on the relative strength or 'power' of the two parties engaged in a dynamic, non-cooperative game—rather like two firms competing to patent a new product or process.

In what is labelled the Narrow Corridor around the diagonal—where the two powers are in approximate balance—liberal democracy prevails and economic growth is encouraged, as indicated by the arrow pointing towards the upper right. Outside this corridor, however, the stronger party is assumed to enjoy increasing returns, while the weaker suffers from a fatal 'discouragement effect'. As a consequence, paths outside the corridor lead to divergent outcomes lying in the segments labelled either S_1

[10] Who, as indicated above, recently analysed the evolving risk of Armageddon in the 1962 nuclear confrontation between the USA and the Soviet Union (Dixit et al., 2021).

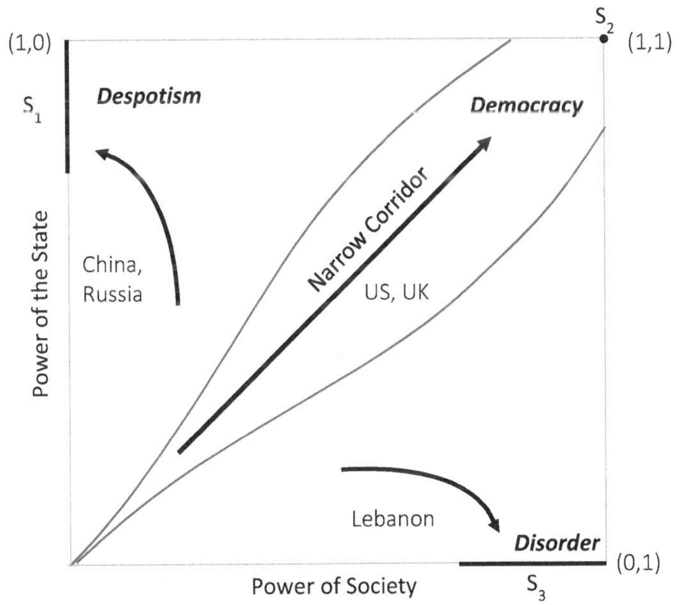

Fig. 3 How evolving powers of state and society can lead towards different forms of government

or S_3, where either Society or the State is ultimately reduced to abject powerlessness.[11]

Here, as for Fukuyama, there are trajectories that lead on to liberty and justice, but there is no guarantee that these will be chosen rather than others leading to Despotism or Disorder. A & R offer a dynamic perspective, with dangerous downsides that lead to highly undesirable long-run steady states.

It is interesting to note that the path for despotic regimes, shown on top left of the figure, seems[12] in accord with Acton's dictum that 'power tends to corrupt, and absolute power corrupts absolutely'.

On the persistence of despotism, indeed, their perspective resembles the DHR view of Roland; for according to Acemoglu (2019), the longer a despotic state exists,

[11] The country names shown, and their location, are as indicated in A & R (2019).

[12] On the assumption that corruption involves reducing the power of society.

> the more self-reinforcing it becomes. … The more it takes root, the more it sets up a hierarchy which is hard to change, and the more it weakens society. … That's why I think dreams of China smoothly converting to a democratic system have been misplaced—[it's had] 2,500 years of state despotism.

An important qualification to this gloomy prospect is noted by Dixit (2021, p. 1355), who observes that: 'A literal interpretation would be that polities are fated to follow whatever destiny their historical condition may entail. But A & R have examples where the initial point can be shifted or manipulated'. Their treatment of the collapse of the Soviet Union—treated as a downward shift in the power of the state[13]—is a key example of how an 'exogenous political shock' can have a major impact by shifting society onto a new path.[14]

Are there shifts or shocks that might rescue society from the depths of despotism, one is tempted to ask? At the conference, William White appealed to cyclical theories of politics—such as those described by the Greek historian Polybius. Our preferred response involves Darwinian competition, as described next.

Fourth Perspective: Darwinian Cultural Competition

A further challenge to cultural determinism comes from the perception that different cultures are engaged in international competition. In *The Descent of Man*, Charles Darwin sketched the role of 'natural selection' in the diffusion of social and moral qualities:

> Selfish and contentious people will not cohere, and without coherence, nothing can be effected. … When two tribes of primeval man came into competition, if one tribe included, other things being equal, a greater number of courageous, sympathetic and faithful members, who were always ready to warn each other of danger, to aid and defend each other, this tribe would succeed best and conquer the other …
>
> A tribe possessing the above qualities in a high degree would spread and be victorious over other tribes; but in the course of time it would be in turn overcome by some other more highly endowed tribe. Thus social and moral

[13] See Fig. 3 in A & R (2019, p. 290).

[14] In his review of *The Narrow Corridor*, James Fenske (2021, p. 10) argues that 'External shocks may matter more than they appear in the book', an important critique explored in the next section.

> qualities would tend slowly to advance and be diffused around the world. Darwin (1981 [1873], pp. 162–3)

This perspective is echoed by Samuel Huntington, who begins his analysis of the 'global politics of civilizations' with the assertion that:

> Civilizations are the ultimate human tribes, and the clash of civilisations is a tribal conflict on a global scale. Huntington (1998, p. 207)

In their wide-ranging study of human reciprocity and its evolution, Bowles and Gintis (2011, pp. 50, 51), after citing Darwin as above, go on to observe that:

> Differential group success plays a central role in the evolution of human behaviours and institutions, members of less successful groups copying the more successful or being eliminated by them. Examples of this process include the peopling of many parts of the world by people of European ancestry and the associated spread of European customs and institutions in the past half millennium, and the spread of agriculture and its associated novel systems of social organization and behaviour from the Middle East to Europe beginning 11 millennia ago.

Empirical evidence of the spread of individualist culture (based on 'genetic closeness' to the USA) has been provided by Gorodnichenko and Roland (2017). This appears to support a dynamic Darwinian view of how culture gets disseminated (i.e. by imitation, migration and/or elimination).

A Focus on Russia[15]

The First Perspective—Fukuyama's Forecast

Russia provides a leading counter-example to Fukuyama's 'doctrine of immaculate convergence' to liberal democracy. As Samir Puri puts it bluntly: 'Putin's Russia is now mounting an open civilizational revolt against Western-led hegemonic uniformity' Puri (2022, p. 252, 253).

[15] An update of an earlier assessment in Miller (2021).

Second—The Role of History

What then of the pervasive power of Deep Historical Roots in explaining its current culture, as illustrated graphically in Fig. 2 above? This appears much closer to the mark. While there have, apparently, been successive efforts in Russian history to move towards liberal democracy, each in turn has failed, as described in Sixsmith (2012) and Figes (2022).

Historian Robert Skidelsky (2022) explains this as follows:

> Because serfdom was abolished only in 1861 and the system of Russian autocracy collapsed only in 1917 (only to be swiftly restored), Russia never experienced the period of bourgeois civilization which, in Europe, established the outlines of the constitutional state. ... Russia was always an empire, never a nation-state. Autocracy is its natural form of rule.

With respect to Ukraine, moreover, it has been argued that:

> Vladimir Putin thinks that Russian-speaking parts of Ukraine belong to a Moscow-centred Slavic civilization state, and that Ukraine as a whole must pledge fealty in perpetuity to Russia. Puri (2022, p. 252)

To enforce this historical perspective, and to check the eastward extension of NATO, Putin has unleashed the dogs of war upon his fellow Slavs.

> With this war, Putin did not want to rebuild the USSR but to reunite the lands of Ancient Rus, the civilization space that Putin feels has been turned against itself by the USA's use of NATO as a vanguard for injecting the nefarious temptations of geopolitical Westernisation into the region. Puri (2022, p. 256)

The Third Perspective—On Life Outside the Narrow Corridor

Writing in 2019, A & R forecast with commendable accuracy what was to come, and their framework provides a convenient canvas for describing the course of events since then. They reckoned that, following the collapse of the USSR:

> Russia was too distant from the corridor. Though the collapse of the despotic Soviet state pushed it in the right direction, it wasn't enough to tame

the Russian state, which just picked up where the Soviet one had left off and reconstituted its despotic control over society. A & R (2019, p. 288)

This was illustrated in their diagram, A & R (2019, p. 290) by a movement leading downwards from where things stood in the USSR (before the collapse in 1990) to where they saw them under Putin in 2019 (still above the Narrow Corridor), as is shown in Fig. 4.[16] To capture the notion of strongman rule in this context, an elliptical shape has added to the figure, lying largely above the Narrow Corridor, with Russia under Putin in 2019 situated therein.

On the question of where Putin was to go from there, Sergei Guriev (2022) referenced the three 'authoritarian options', as defined by Adam Przeworski of Columbia University, that lay open to the

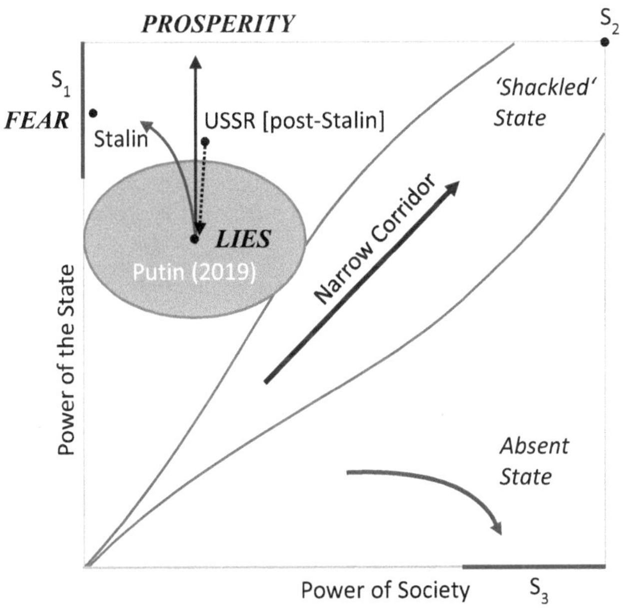

Fig. 4 The options facing Putin as strongman president

[16] This simple downward shift leaves out of account significant interim steps taken by Gorbachev, Yeltsin and Putin himself, which are indicated, albeit briefly, in the Annex.

president—indicated in Fig. 3. These options—and their feasibility—may be described as follows, starting with Economic Prosperity, shown by an upward pointing arrow, and ending with Fear, which involves following the trajectory heading towards Despotism.

Economic Prosperity—the idea of implementing a more efficient autocracy. This option was stifled by increasing centralisation and endemic corruption—as Alexei Navalny bravely showed after he recovered from an attempted poisoning by Russian security services.

Lies—the strategy of staying put, using propaganda to maintain political control without resorting to terror. The façade of fake democracy had worked for a while[17]—but Putin's popularity fell below 60 percent for the first time in April 2020.

Fear—that is, to carry on along a path towards Stalinesqe despotism, as indicated in A & R's analysis. This is what Putin has chosen. Political opposition has been suppressed, with Navalny imprisoned and his Anti-Corruption Foundation (FBK) outlawed, for example; and an invasion of Ukraine—launched, perhaps, in the expectation of boosting the president's popularity as when Crimea was annexed in 2014.

The Fourth Perspective: Cultural Competition

To judge from the extensive list of practitioners in Table 2, the strongman approach pioneered by President Putin has proved attractive elsewhere. So Russian culture has passed an important test for international success.

But Putin's conduct has greatly changed over time. As reported in *Financial Times* in March 2021, for example:

> Over two decades in power, Russia's leader has cast himself first as champion of prosperity and then as anti-western patriot. But now ... he has transformed once more—into brutal strongman. Foy (2021)

And that was written before the invasion of Ukraine—a conflict where Darwin's parable of two warring tribes offers Putin cold comfort.

So will Russia preserve its allure as an exemplar of the NWO? A diplomatic response would be that of Chinese premier Zhou Enlai in 1972

[17]And was to fool outside observers like Guriev and Treisman (2022)—and Miller and Zissimos (2022)!

when asked about the impact of the 1968 student uprising in France: that it is 'too early to say'.

With the advent of nuclear weapons, however, the clash of cultures involves more than issues of moral and social choice for society; there is a real risk of a war to end all wars. But what if the NWO is viewed as a type of cartel? Is there not then the prospect of self-discipline? By waging sudden war to widen Russia's already-vast territorial sway—and threatening nuclear escalation when his battle plans go astray—Putin could be seen as cheating on the terms of a pact of cultural cooperation. If so, as an ex-colonel of People's Liberation Army has put it bluntly, China could intervene 'by simply telling Russia; don't use nuclear weapons, Mr President' (Bo, 2022).

Conclusion: History Matters, but Cultures Evolve—In Competition

With strongman leaders pledging common cause to confront the West with authoritarian rule in a New World Order, the world stands witness to a clash of civilisations. Deep historical roots of absolutism seem to propel both Russia and China towards despotism—along a path that is set to continue if the prognosis provided by Acemoglu and Robinson holds good.

The words of Alexander Dugin, a Russian academic, offer chilling confirmation:

> Huntington was absolutely right and Fukuyama was absolutely wrong. There are civilisations and one of them is Russia. And we had no other way of proving Huntington right than by attacking Ukraine. It's us who started this conflictual situation in order to be heard. Puri (2022, p. 26)

In this context, however, the ideas of Darwin and Bagehot (on natural selection as among societies) must give pause for thought. For what the West seeks to offer is liberal democracy—where governance relies on institutions and the rule of law. What autocracy provides, however, rests perilously on the shoulders of authoritarian leaders, free to change constitutional limits on their power—and to go to war with close neighbours—as the spirit moves.

From this, Rachman (2022b, p. 232,3) derives an important conclusion:

> Strongman rule almost invariably leads to the creation of a personality cult [which] ultimately has to rest on fear and coercion. … Even if their physical health holds up, decades in power can often cause a leader to succumb to megalomania or paranoia … When a strongman loses power, the stability of the entire political system built around him is at risk… . For these reasons, strongman rule is an inherently flawed and unstable form of government. It will ultimately collapse.

Since it is an unstable form of government, then, from the Darwinian viewpoint of natural selection, it should not provide an enduring role model—quite the contrary.

Epilogue[18]

When the history of this clash of civilisations comes to be told, will the vaunted champions of absolutism be fated to be forgotten? like Ozymandias, King of Kings,

> *Whose vast and trunkless legs of stone stand in the desert; And, on the pedestal, these words appear: Look on my Works, ye Mighty, and despair!*

Or could the lofty Statue of Liberty be dethroned from her pedestal at the sea-washed, sunset gates of the New World? no more to cry:

> *Give me your tired, your poor,*
> *Your huddled masses yearning to breathe free.*

Only time will tell.

Annex: On USSR/Russian Governance 1990—2019: Gorbachev, followed by Yeltsin, then Putin

In the text, the broad perspective of Acemoglu and Robinson is shown in Fig. 4 as the modest reduction in the power of the state as between the point labelled USSR [post-Stalin] and that labelled Russia (2019). As indicated here in Fig. 5, however, to reach this point Putin had to reverse the reform efforts of his two immediate predecessors.

[18] With due acknowledgement of lines from 'Ozymandias' by Percy Bysshe Shelly and 'The New Colossus' by Emma Lazarus.

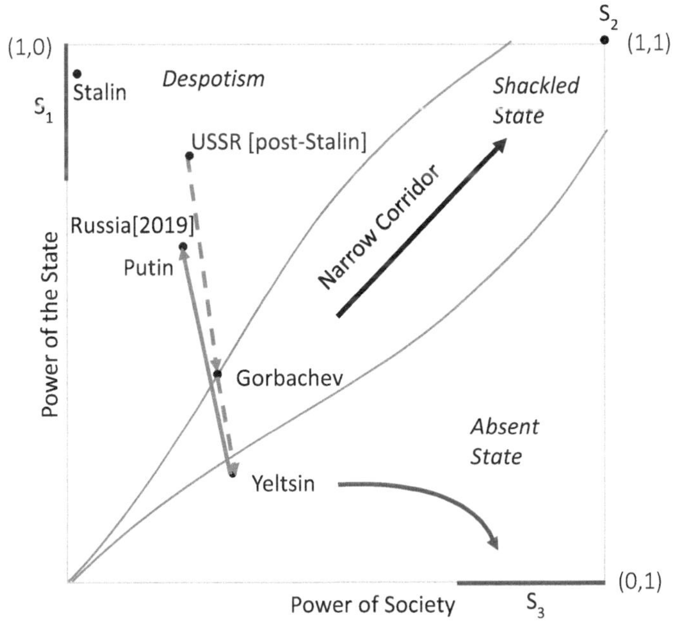

Fig. 5 USSR/Russian governance 1990–2019: Gorbachev, Yeltsin and Putin

First was the attempt by Mikhail Gorbachev as head of state, and finally president of the USSR, to democratise the USSR—by modernising the state (with *perestroika* and *glasnost*) and by ending the monopoly of the Communist Party. Such changes were designed to take the system into the narrow corridor, as indicated—tentatively—in the figure.

Second was the takeover of power by Boris Yeltsin, who had been elected as chairman of the Russian Supreme Soviet, and became president of Russia after the USSR collapsed in 1990. *Ex ante*, things looked promising:

> His platform ... included a radical program of market reform. Democracy, economic reforms—it looked like the Russian despotic state was getting tamed. A & R (2019, p. 285)

But with the Russian elite benefitting enormously from the corrupt privatisation of state assets (the 'loans for shares' scheme in particular), these hopes were dashed. For many, indeed, it seemed that the government, though technically powerful, was failing in the essential task of running the country—as suggested by locating Yeltsin's regime just inside the region of the Absent State in Fig. 4. In any event, he was persuaded to leave his post early, designating Vladimir Putin as his unelected successor.

Including these interim steps indicates that there was considerable instability in how Russia was governed in the 1990s before Putin took over in December 1999—and proceeded to lead Russia back to the point labelled Russia (2019). For what happens next, see main text.

References

Acemoglu, C. (2019). https://news.mit.edu/2019/narrow-corridor-acemoglu-liberty-0924þ

Acemoglu, D., & Robinson, J. (2019). *The narrow corridor: How nations struggle for liberty*. Penguin.

Bagehot, W. (2015 [1872]). *Physics and politics: Or thoughts on the application of the principles of natural selection and inheritance to political society*. Cambridge University Press (e-book collection).

Bo, Z. (2022, October 28). China can use its leverage with Moscow to prevent a nuclear war. *Financial Times*, Friday.

Bowles, S., & Gintis, H. (2011). *A cooperative species: Human reciprocity and its evolution*. Princeton University Press.

Darwin, C. (1981 [1873]). *The descent of man*. Princeton University Press.

Dixit, A. K. (2021). Somewhere in the middle you can survive. *Journal of Economic Literature, 59*(4), 1361–1375.

Dixit, A. K., Skeath, S., & McAdams, D. (2021). Brinkmanship: 'The Cuban missile crisis'. In *Games of strategy* (5th ed., pp. 517–543). Norton.

Fenske, J. (2021). An adaptation of *the narrow corridor. Journal of Public Finance and Public Choice, 36*(1), 1–29.

Figes, O. (2022). *The Story of Russia*. Bloomsbury.

Foy, H. (2021). Putin's Third Act. *Financial Times Magazine* March, 13–14.

Fukuyama, F. (1989). The end of history? *The National Interest, 16*, 3–18.

Gorodnichenko, Y., & Roland, G. (2017). Culture, institutions and the wealth of nations. *Review of Economics and Statistics, 99*(3), 402–416.

Guriev, S. (2022, April 17). Putin's dictatorship is now based on fear rather than spin. *Financial Times.*

Guriev, S., & Treisman, D. (2022). *Spin dictators: The changing face of tyranny in the 21st century*. Princeton University Press.

Huntington, S. P. (1993). The clash of civilizations? *Foreign Affairs, 72*(3), 22–49.
Huntington, S. P. (1998). *The clash of civilizations and the remaking of world order*. Simon and Schuster.
Miller, M. (2021). *Deep historical roots, culture choice and the 'New World Order'* (CEPR Discussion Paper No. 17396).
Miller, M., & Zissimos, B. (2022). Populism and the 'narrow corridor' of liberty and justice. *National Institute Economic Review, 259*(1:The Political Economy of Populism), 31–50.
Puri, S. (2022). *Russia's road to war with Ukraine*. Biteback Publishing.
Rachman, G. (2022a, January 24). The demand for a new global order. *Financial Times*.
Rachman, G. (2022b). *The age of the strongman*. The Bodley Head.
Reich, R. (2015). *Saving Capitalism*. Alfred A. Knopf.
Roland, G. (2020). The deep historical roots of modern culture: A comparative perspective. *Journal of Comparative Economics, 48*, 483–508.
Sixsmith, M. (2012). *Russia: A 1,000-year chronicle of the Wild East*. BBC Books.
Skidelsky, R. (2022, June 14). Russia's path to premodernity. *Project Syndicate*.

Marcus Miller, After studying philosophy, politics and economics at Oxford, and seeing Isaiah Berlin in full flow, Marcus Miller went as Henry Fellow to Yale University—with the good fortune to have James Tobin as his PhD supervisor. Following stints at LSE and Manchester University, he joined Warwick University Economics Department, with its many stimulating colleagues and students, and the occasional opportunity of writing papers with stars like Paul Krugman, Joseph Stiglitz and John Williamson. Outside interests included co-directing the International Macro programme at CEPR with Willem Buiter and advising the newly formed House of Commons Treasury Committee in reporting on Mrs. Thatcher's Monetary Policy. Growing research interest in Russia led to a paper on Stalin with colleague Jennifer Smith ('In the shadow of the Gulag', *JCE*, 2015).

PART II

China

President Xi's Perfect Storm

Robert Z. Aliber

The lockdowns in Shanghai and other Chinese cities that President Xi adopted to prevent the spread of the pandemic has tripped the country's economic growth by interrupting the purchases of apartments. The irony is that the virus that began in Wuhan, the ninth largest city in the country, either in a food market or in a research lab, has triggered a sharp decline in China's rate of economic growth. Suddenly, many of the books and articles about the country's challenge to U.S. hegemony appear outdated. Consider *The Avoidable War*; the title is a refrain on *The Thucydides Challenge*, which presented more than ten examples of a rising power nipping at the heels of the hegemon (Rudd, 2022). Its author developed fluency in Mandarin as a student in China and then became foreign minister and prime minister in Australia; he is head of the Asia Society in New York. "Avoiding the Thucydides Trap" is the last chapter in another new book, *Financial Cold War* (Fok, 2022).

The implicit assumption in these books and articles is that China will continue to achieve an economic growth rate of 4–5 percent a year and its per capita GDP eventually will climb above that in the United States; even now some have suggested that China's GDP is higher than

---

R. Z. Aliber (✉)
University of Chicago, Evanston, IL, USA

R. Z. Aliber et al. (eds.), *Fault Lines After COVID-19*,
https://doi.org/10.1007/978-3-031-26482-5_4

U.S. GDP. Emmanuel Roman, chief executive of Pimco was interviewed in the 16/17 July "Lunch with the FT" column. "As for China, we are far less worried than other people. It's a supertanker. Yes they are locked down, but they can push the accelerator and get to 4.5 percent growth without too many problems" (Russel). Roman focuses on the demand side of growth; he neglects the supply side and that increasingly Chinese household consumers will spend more of their income on services—education, transportation, health care, recreation—and that productivity growth in services in Western economies has rarely exceeded 2 percent.

The irony in applying the Thucydides metaphor is that China is now aging more rapidly than the United States because of the belated impacts of the one-child policy that it adopted in the early 1980s. Its abysmal demographics is only one of the elements that President Xi Jinping now faces in "a perfect storm"; its other elements include a financial implosion as apartment prices cascade downward, the loss of its international competitive advantage to Vietnam and to Bangladesh and to other countries that have much lower wage rates, and the departure of the multinational firms that provided the brand names that made it easy to sell goods produced in China in foreign markets. Moreover, Xi's hostile approach to the country's extraordinarily successful entrepreneurs will encourage tens of thousands of businesswomen and men to move to Singapore, Australia, Canada and the United States. Several hundred million Chinese who aspired to a middle-class lifestyle are likely to become angry because the train they hoped to board will have left the station before they had enough money to buy their tickets.

The 2020 decade for China will be similar to the 1990s in Japan, when its growth rate fell below 1 percent in response to the implosion of the massive asset price bubble that had developed in the second half of the 1980s. Japan had achieved double-digit growth rates in the 1950s and the 1960s; its growth rate then declined to 5 percent in the 1970s. Some of the projections in Tokyo were that Japan would continue to achieve annual growth rates of 4–5 percent and that its per capita income eventually would exceed that in the United States. The market values of Japanese stocks and real estate at the end of the 1980s was six times higher than at the end of the 1970s—and then the financial crash in the 1990s led to a decline in the market values to their 1979 levels. Japan had three recessions in the 1990s as its banks and other financial institutions contracted and failed. All of the structural factors that enabled Japan to achieve a 4 percent growth rate in the 1980s—the high savings rate, the government support of industry, the extraordinary competitiveness of the firms within most industries—were in place in the 1990s. Growth was handicapped by the need to sort through ownership issues after stock prices and real estate prices tumbled and the need developed to scale down indebtedness to sustainable values.

The first section of this note reviews the Andy Warhol Theory of Economic Growth that a country can have the highest rate of economic growth in the world for twenty or thirty years as its unskilled workers move from the farms to the factories—but then its supply of unskilled labor becomes exhausted and its top position is displaced by countries with much lower labor costs (see Aliber, 1991). The decline in China's population and labor force are reviewed in the second section; the ratio of retired workers to the active labor force will increase steadily and inexorably. The crash in China's real estate market is considered in the third section, the sharp decline in the market value of several tens of millions of vacant apartments that were acquired as stores of value is leading to a massive fall in household wealth and a massive erosion of the capital of the banks. The collapse in real estate prices will lead to widespread failure of banks and other financial institutions, the Beijing government will need to recapitalize the banks and the ratio of government indebtedness to GDP suddenly will become the highest in the world. China's period of rapid economic growth began when its per capita income was \$200; its per capita income now is \$12,000 and value added per worker approaches \$40,000 (an hourly wage rate of \$20) means that it will lose share of markets for textiles, shoes, and consumer durables to nearby countries with much lower real wage rates.

The Andy Warhol Theory of Economic Growth

The Andy Warhol theory of economic growth is a riff on his quip that "everyone is famous for fifteen minutes"; every country has twenty or thirty years when it has been or may be at the top of hit parade of the most rapidly growing countries during that period. Great Britain was at the top of hit parade from 1830 to 1870, then its growth rate fell sharply after the construction of its railroads had been completed. The United States moved into the top position on the growth rate hit parade as its population surged from 1870 to 1920 and the continent was "filled in." Germany also was at the top of the hit parade as the city-states in Germany became integrated into a national economy. Japan was in the number one position from 1950 to 1990 in part initially as it recovered from the massive destruction of the Second World War. South Korea achieved an extraordinarily high rate of growth from 1970 to 2000. China has had twenty years of brilliant economic achievements since it joined the World Trade Organization in 2001.

One of the most significant inputs to the high rates of growth in the countries that have been in the number one position on the growth rate hit parade was the movement of young unskilled workers from the farms and villages to the factories and the cities. Worker productivity was much higher in the factories, so the redeployment of labor automatically led to a higher growth rate, even if productivity in each sector remained unchanged. (The redeployment also might lead to an increase in productivity on the farms because of the reduction in the number of individuals at work in the fields and rice paddies). The growth rate in every country slowed when the supply of unskilled labor on its farms had been exhausted. (Germany imported hundreds of thousands of unskilled workers from Turkey after the supply of comparable workers on its farms had been exhausted.)

China's economic data are dodgy. Officials in many of the country's provinces understate the number of individuals that have left for the cities because the money they receive from Beijing is based on headcount. The migration of workers to the cities has ended because there are no longer any young people in the villages (see Roselle & Hell, 2020).

China's Population Dynamics

The decline in the China's growth rate in next few years will be more severe than the fall in Japan's in the 1990s because the country's labor force has started to shrink as a result of the one-child policy adopted in the early 1980s, while Japan's increased for several decades after its asset price bubble imploded. Rudd does not have an intuitive feel for economic data; he wrote (page 117), "China's 2021 census found that the Chinese population grew by only 72 million in 2021 and representing a massive 18 percent drop in the number of newborns from 2020." Neither statement is correct. China's population increased by four million from 2020 to 2021. Its population now will decline by one million a year for each of the next ten or so years. Its labor force will decline even more rapidly because the number of sixty-year-old workers that will retire will be larger than the number of twenty-year-olds that will enter the labor force.

The number of future mothers has declined sharply because of the one-child policy. Each woman in China of child-bearing age has had 1.3

children; because of the strong preference for boys, it is convenient to use the one child assumption when projecting the supply of future mothers. Assuming 100 births in 1980, half were girls. Twenty years later in 2000, each of these fifty girl babies became a mother, about half of these newly-borns were girls. The supply of future mothers in 2020 was 25 percent of the supply in 1980. The implication is that China's population will decline for at least the next forty years because of the sharp reduction in the number of women of child-bearing age.

The one-child policy has been reversed. The inference from the Japanese experience is that the population will continue to fall although at a less rapid rate because the many of the women of child-bearing age in the cities will be content to have one child.

China's population now is slightly more than four times the U.S. population. Twenty years from now, China's population will be twice the U.S. population.

One impact of the one-child policy was to reduce the dependency ratio, the ratio of non-workers to the workers. Now this ratio is flipping because of the aging of the population, the number of retired individuals will increase relative to the number of workers. (If the birth rate increases, the dependency ratio will increase further.) The household saving rate will decline because the number of retired individuals spending down their accumulated savings will be increasing relative to the number of those still at work. (The Japanese experience suggests that this transition led to a modest decline in the savings rate.) The composition of household expenditures will change, less on school books and clothing and more on health care and assisted living facilities for the aged retired.

The Crash in the China Real Estate Market

China has experienced a massive building boom in part to provide accommodation to the several hundred million people who have moved to the cities in the most extended migration ever. In the early 1990s, urban residents were allowed to buy the government-owned units that they lived in for a payment of less than a year's income. Soon after some of these residents sold their recently acquired apartments to the migrants from the countryside, and traded up to newly built apartments.

Ten million new housing units a year have been built in each recent year, spending on these apartments accounted for 10 percent of the country's GDP and construction provided employment for seventy or eighty million workers. Twenty million units have been in the construction pipeline. Moreover, the increase in spending on new apartments is associated with purchases of furniture and appliances and window treatments and led to employment of hundreds of thousands of workers. (See the description of the forthcoming crash in China's housing market in the epilogue to the seventh edition of *Manias, Panics, and Crashes*, Aliber & Kindleberger, 2015.)

The demand for accommodation led to increases in apartment prices that were significantly more rapid than the increases in household income. Households became eager to acquire apartments because the real rate of return from the increase in their prices was so much higher than both the increase in the consumer price level and the return on bank deposits. Property developers competed extensively to buy the land for building sites that urban governments sold in auctions, which had been obtained by displacing farmers. A significant part of the revenues of these governments came from land sales; the governments were responsible for infrastructure spending around the apartment complexes.

Most of the 250 million apartments constructed in the last 30 years have been purchased for accommodation; the buyers have moved into the units or rented them. Perhaps forty to sixty million of the apartments constructed since the early 1990s remain vacant and were purchased as stores of value. The owners did not rent these apartments because the anticipated rate of return was very low compared with the anticipated return from year-to-year price increases.

The adjustments in Japan after the implosion of its asset price bubble in the 1990s provide a useful comparison for prospective developments in China. The market value of Japanese real estate at the end of the 1980s was seven to eight times the country's GDP; the market value of the real estate at the end of the 1990s was 15–20 percent of the market value ten years earlier—perhaps 150 percent of the country's GDP. Japan had to adjust to a massive decline in household wealth. There were only a trivial number of vacant apartments. In contrast, China will have to absorb several tens of millions of vacant apartments that are massively overpriced relative to household incomes. The anecdotal experience is that the market prices, especially in the largest cities were fifteen to twenty times higher than annual household incomes.

The buyers of apartments as stores of value have made massive bets on the greater fool theory—the belief that they will be able to sell the apartments at even higher prices to some other investors. Investor confidence in this momentum has been shattered, potential buyers are taking a "wait and see" attitude, and prices are falling.

The fall in property prices will lead to an immense decline in national financial wealth, which might continue for ten years. Assume that the market value of Chinese real estate peaked at ten times GDP and will decline to two times GDP; the decline in household wealth would then be eight times GDP. By comparison the market value of U.S. housing is slightly higher than GDP; during the home construction boom that preceded the crisis, the market value of residential real estate increased to 150 percent of U.S. GDP.

Apartment owners will incur most of the losses from the fall in apartment prices. The property developers in China are extensively leveraged, and most will tumble into bankruptcy unless the government provides some financial assistance as a way to dampen the losses that the banks and other lenders to the developers will incur. Most of the property developers will be inundated by the massive tide as real estate prices tumble. Evergrande, one of the largest of the developers, has been in the news because it has been late in the payment of interest on its $300 billion plus of indebtedness including $20 billion denominated in the U.S. dollar; the firm had nearly 1000 different projects. The firm might have sold more of these projects to get the cash for its scheduled interest payments, which would have enabled it to avoid the unfavorable publicity for its delayed payments. The most plausible reason that Evergrande did not do so is that the highest prices that any other developer would have been willing to pay was too low; Evergrande would have to recognize an immediate loss and be even deeper in its massive hole. Evergrande probably has had a negative net worth for more than ten years, it has been involved in Ponzi finance and has used the cash from the down payments received from those who bought apartments on Tuesday to pay the construction companies to complete the work on the projects that it had sold on Monday.

One of the major decisions that the Beijing government must make is who will be made "whole" when banks and non-bank financial firms incur massive losses; the government will have to decide where to "draw the line"—will it recapitalize the banks and ensure that none of the depositors receives a haircut (yes, much as in Japan) and allow some near-bank financial institutions to fail with haircuts for their creditors, or will it instead provide a comprehensive umbrella so that none of the creditors incurs a loss. (Probably.) The government will have to decide whether to bailout the creditors of non-financial firms. (Probably not.)

The news several months ago featured the anger of the owners of deposits of banks in rural areas of Henan province who were denied access to their money; in effect, their deposits were frozen because the banks did not have the cash to meet their requests. The first day's news reports were that some plainclothes goons beat up the demonstrators. The next day's story was that the authorities brought in the tanks to put down the demonstrators. China has 9000 tanks, not nearly enough to cope with the unrest as asset prices fall and household wealth evaporates.

There will be frequent versions of this story. Many of the smaller banks are illiquid because the larger banks are skeptical about their solvency, which reflects that property prices are trending down so that the borrowers that were solvent last week will be underwater this week.

The Most Expensive Bailout in History

The Beijing government will incur a massive increase in its own indebtedness as a result of its initiatives to re-capitalize the banks and other financial firms that will fail because of their loan losses as real estate prices tumble. Household spending will fall as a result of the decline in personal wealth, which will lead to bank loan losses to many firms that sell to households. The value of the assets of the Chinese banks are four times the country's GDP, and the value of bank real estate loans are 40 percent of their total loans. If the value of bank loans were to decline by 50 percent, then the government investment in re-capitalizing the banks would be twice the country's GDP. The magic is that the government would obtain the funds to recapitalize the banks by borrowing from the banks, the bank assets would then show loans to the government that would approximate the value of the government ownership of equity of the banks.

The key assumption in estimating the impact of the downward adjustment on apartment prices on government finances is the losses that the banks will incur as the ratio of apartment prices to household income declines from ten times China's GDP to two times its GDP. The decline in the market value of residential real estate would be eight times China's GDP. The projected losses are so huge that they invite skepticism. An anecdotal data point—in the autumn of 2013, I visited the real estate sales office of the "Miami Hills" development project in Beijing, a very upscale project. Apartment prices were about $600 K for a two-bedroom apartment of 90 or 100 square meters; the annual income of the buyers was about $20 K; which meant that the ratio of apartment prices to household incomes was thirty to one. In the last eight years, apartment prices have increased more rapidly than household income, which means the ratio has increased. Ten years ago, there was already chatter of twelve or thirteen "ghost cities."

The assumption is that the decline in the price of residential real estate would be ten times China's GDP. (The decline in the value of U.S. household wealth between 2006 and 2010 was 50 percent of one year's U.S. GDP.) The direct and primary impact of this decline will be on household net worth; the indirect impacts will be on banks and other financial firms that have made loans to property developers and to others who will be negatively impacted by the fall in apartment prices. Household holdings of bank liabilities are three times China's GDP, and the holdings of non-bank financial liabilities are about one year's GDP. The assumption is that the decline in real estate prices will lead to a fall of 50 percent in the value of bank assets and a fall of two-thirds in the value of non-bank financial liabilities. Together the decline in the value of assets of banks and other financial institutions will amount to between two and one half and three years of China's GDP. Households will incur losses on their holdings of the IOUs of non-financial firms.

The Beijing government will follow the Japan playbook and ensure that none of the holders of bank deposits will take a haircut; the banks will be re-capitalized by the sale of most of their loans in default to a new government-owned bank, the "bad bank." Similarly, the government will ensure that the owners of the IOUs of the non-bank financial firms will not take haircuts. The liabilities of this new bank are likely to be two and two-thirds of one year's GDP. The new bank will finance its purchase of these loans in default by borrowing from the main banks, who in effect will swap the loans in default for the IOUs of the new bank. The ratio of government indebtedness to GDP will increase from three quarters of one year's GDP to about three years' GDP.

These ballpark estimates suggest that the losses of the banks will be one year's GDP, which can be viewed as an estimate of the costs to the government of re-capitalizing the banks.

China experienced a collapse of its banks in the 1990s, which led to a good bank-bad bank distinction; a new financial institution—the bad bank—was established to buy the doggy loans. The government obtained the money to pay the banks for their doggy loans by borrowing from the banks; the government then is both the dominant borrower from the banks and the dominant shareholder.

The interest payments of the government to the banks will increase by 2–3 percent of GDP. However, the banks will pay dividends to the government on the shares owned by the government, so this cash flow transaction will tend to be a wash, the dividend payments are likely to be larger than the interest payments.

The bank's holdings of the IOUs will soar by 100–200 percent of China's GDP, a guess is 150 percent of GDP; this ratio now is 73 percent, so it will increase to 223 percent. The interest payments of the government will increase by five or six percentage points of GDP, seemingly a small number but an almost prohibitive percentage increase. The government spending on the military, the infrastructure, and its foreign assistance like the Belt and Road Initiative will be crimped by the increase in interest payments.

Economic Decoupling and the Shrinking of China's International Competitive Advantage

Tensions between Washington and Beijing are leading to economic decoupling. China's rapid economic growth from 1990 to 2020 could not have occurred if it had not been able to increase its exports of manufactured goods at a rapid rate; the foreign exchange that it earned enabled it to pay for the imports of petroleum and foodstuffs and machine tools. China imported very few goods if it produced domestic versions of these goods. China produced many low-end automobiles; it imported a handful of Audis and Porsches. The U.S. market was much the largest for China's exports. Virtually, all of the goods that the United States imported from China displaced goods produced in the United States or similar goods produced in Japan or South Korea. China used much of its export earnings to pay for imports of petroleum, copper, and other raw materials, and machinery, and foodstuffs.

The "gains from trade" were immense, largely because the costs to China of producing many of its imports at home would have been five or even ten times higher than the costs of and at least 90 percent of the gains accrued to China.

The motive for the Chinese initiative is to reduce its dependence on foreigners. The motive for the U.S. initiative is that China could become an unreliable trading partner—when it has a monopoly advantage, it may bleed its customers. Decoupling will lead to a reversal of the gains from trade—and China will incur 70 or 80 percent of these losses. China is a big country, but most of the goods that it imports can only be produced in China at significantly higher cost than if they are imported. How large might these losses be. Again guessing—about 0.2–0.4 percent of GDP; a large number in terms of annual productivity gains.

Now a brief quiz. Make a list of twenty Japanese brand names. Easy, seven to nine automobile companies, two airlines, twenty or thirty electronics firms. One more try: identify ten South Korean brand names. One of the brilliant decisions that Deng Xiaoping made in the early 1980s was to invite American, Japanese, and other foreign multinational firms to manufacture for the foreign markets as well as for the domestic market. China's exports surged. Thirty to 40 percent of the high value-added exports from China are produced in foreign-owned firms, who are leaving because of corruption, political tensions, and cost disadvantages. China's gains from trade will become negative as it seeks to reduce its dependence on imports and as the United States reduces its imports from China. The Chinese firms that continue to export will have to reduce prices to dampen the erosion of their market shares.

China's industrial sector will shrink, and a larger share of the employees will work in the service sector—transportation, education, health care, recreation. China already has reduced its steelmaking capacity, and it seems likely that there will be significant consolidation in the production of automobiles. Productivity in the service sector is below that in the industrial sector, hence just as the growth of the industrial sector and the shrinking of the agricultural sector led to an increase in GDP, so the shift to services will lead to a decline in GDP.

Xi's squeeze on Jack Ma and the other extraordinary Chinese entrepreneurs is in the tradition of the political class—now the princelings the grandchildren of those who were with Mao on the grand march—seeking to extract more of the economic rents from those who have grown businesses because of their insights and risk-taking (see Shum, 2021).

Financial Decoupling—The Impact of the Perfect Storm on China's Trading Partners

The United States and China are now involved in economic and financial decoupling. China's policy is to become dai ichi—number one—in ten major industrial fields. The U.S. government has realized too many supply chains meander through China, and that a hostile government in Beijing could intervene. There is also recognition that China has received much the largest share of the gains from trade, and that the Chinese government is unreliable with respect to its commitments. Many American and other foreign firms have begun to reduce their footprints in China.

Financial decoupling is the close cousin to economic decoupling and involves changes in Chinese holdings of U.S. dollar securities and real assets and U.S. holdings of real assets in China and U.S. loans to Chinese banks, property developers, and various Chinese firms. Some U.S. firms already have begun to sell their Chinese subsidiaries.

The Beijing government has indicated that it would like the yuan to become the dominant reserve currency or otherwise a reserve currency on the par with the U.S. dollar. One aspect of this choice is that various foreign groups would increase their holdings of liabilities denominated in the Chinese yuan. Some foreign groups already have begun to acquire IOUs, mostly as hedges against their yuan liabilities that they acquired when they borrowed from a Chinese lender. One of the current factors that limits the foreign demand for the yuan-denominated securities is that there is little confidence that the foreigners will receive fair treatment in Chinese courts when there is a dispute. The second shortcoming is that there will be a lot of uncertainty about the stability of foreign holdings of Chinese IOUs when the price of the yuan is variable.

The Peoples Bank of China holds $3000 billion of U.S. dollar securities; it is as if each resident of China owns $200 of U.S. dollar securities. The economic slowdown that will follow from the sharp decline in household wealth and spending will lead to much diminished purchases of petroleum and copper and machine tools. China's export earnings will decline because of the departure of the foreign multinationals. Chinese firms will scramble to increase their exports because the domestic market is stagnant; the volume of counterfeiting of brand names will surge. The implication is that China's current account surplus will increase, which will lead to an increase in the price of the yuan. This price is also impacted by the capital account transactions, the foreign multinationals will sell their manufacturing plants and their buildings and repatriate their yuan funds to buy U.S. dollars. Chinese firms and investors that own U.S. and other foreign assets are likely to seek to hold these assets, although they will be under government pressure to repatriate these funds.

The Chinese are obsessed with the international role of the yuan, which in the best of all possible worlds would displace the dollar as the dominant reserve currency. One of the problems is trust and the rule of law. Owners of liquid wealth were shocked when Xi proclaimed himself leader for life. (There is an amusing contrast with President Trump trying to become leader for life, but that has not succeeded, at least not yet.) If the PBOC were to sell some of its U.S. dollar holdings to buy more of its own currency, the price of the yuan would soar. If instead the PBOC were to sell some of its U.S. dollar holdings to buy securities denominated in the Euro, the price of the Euro would increase sharply—the European Central Bank might buy the U.S. dollars that the PBOC would be selling.

The projected sharp slowdown in economic growth in China presents some puzzles about the price of the yuan; the decline in the purchases of petroleum and copper will lead to a reduction in their prices, which will tend to put upward pressure on the price of the yuan. The changes in the price of the currency reflect changes in a small number, which is the difference between total Chinese payments for the purchases of foreign goods, services, and securities, and total Chinese receipts from sale of goods, services, and securities to foreigners. The impact of changes in goods market transactions on the price of the yuan are likely to be dominated by the impact of changes in security market and capital account transactions. American and other foreign firms are likely to be quicker to leave China than Chinese firms are to leave the United States. The U.S. and other foreign firms are likely to leave China, and they will sell their factories and other physical facilities to Chinese firms, which will put downward pressure on the price of the currency.

The slowdown in China will have a dramatic impact on the financial position of the Chinese government. There will be an immediate need to "bail out" failed financial institutions; one of the major problems is where the "line will be drawn"—which institutions will be re-capitalized with government funds or government guarantees, and which will be allowed to fail with haircuts for their various creditors. The pressures on the Beijing government to have a massive tent will be intense because the households that are outside the tent will be angry because of the two-class operation.

There are several "bridges to nowhere" around the world—one is Alaska, another in Japan. Governments want to provide the jobs. China already has a first-world infrastructure of high-speed trains and excellent toll roads. Even though there has been massive construction of new apartments, perhaps half the population live in substandard housing. The Beijing government can provide capital to refinance the failing banks and the provincial governments—that is on the demand side and it can arrange to build hundreds of more "bridges to nowhere." Beijing cannot develop innovations that will lead to significant productivity gains and enhance the country's growth rate. Household demand will veer from manufactured goods to services including education, health care, and tourism, which are unlikely sectors for rapid productivity gains.

When the Japanese economy imploded in the early 1990s, many of its firms had large underutilized productive capacity; the United States allowed its trade deficit with Japan to balloon because the country was a massive unsinkable and friendly aircraft carrier. Chinese firms will seek to grow their exports in response to disappointing expansion of domestic sales. The shortage of Chinese brand names with global recognition means that these firms will compete on the basis of price in the U.S. and other foreign markets.

China may seek to increase its trade surplus as a way to minimize the decline in industrial jobs. China can grow its trade surplus only if some other countries are willing to accept the counterpart increase in their trade deficits. China's demand for copper and other raw materials will fall, so their prices will soften after the end of the imports will decline, and it is likely to adopt measures to divert demand from foreign goods. The Peoples Bank of China will buy U.S. dollars to limit the increases in the price of the yuan. Trade disputes between the United States and China will proliferate.

Conclusion

Chairman Xi faces a perfect storm after China has had more than twenty years of brilliant economic achievements; perhaps 400 million individuals have moved from dirt floors in the villages to clean water in and dirty water out in the cities. China's GDP now is the second highest in the world. China has been at the number one position in the economic growth rate hit parade for several decades. Per capita income has increased from \$200 to \$12,000. A significant of the growth resulted from the redeployment of unskilled labor from the farms to the factories, which often is viewed as the major contributing factor to the surge in productivity. An alternative interpretation is that there was an explosion in the urban labor force as workers who contributed modest amounts to GDP on the farms suddenly blossomed when at work in factories, and the value of their output surged because it was priced on a global scale.

One of the brilliant decisions that Deng Xiao Peng made in the early 1980s was to invite American and other foreign multinationals to China. The massive domestic market seemed like an extraordinarily attractive array of carrots to these firms. Wage rates in China were low. There were established markets in many countries for the products with global brand names that could be made in China at much lower costs.

China has been displaced from its number one position on the economic growth rate hit parade because there are no longer any young people on the farms that might move to the factories and the cities. The 2020 decade in China will resemble the 1990s in Japan, with an extraordinarily sharp decline in its growth rate. Japan had had forty years of extraordinarily high growth, initially playing catch up after the devastation during and after the Second World War. Then there was a massive surge in real estate prices and stock prices in the second half of the 1980s; these prices peaked at the end of 1989 when they were six times those of ten years earlier. Asset prices declined throughout the 1990s, all of the large commercial banks and the government-sponsored lenders required bail outs so their depositors would not receive "haircuts" on their financial assets.

One of the belated impacts of the one-child policy that China adopted in the early 1980s is that its population has peaked; its labor force is shrinking. Each woman then had only one child, of whom half were girls. In turn, each of these girls had one child, and again half were girls. In 2020, the number of women of child-bearing age is one-quarter of the number in 1980. China's population will decline for the next fifty years and it will age during this period.

The aging of the population will have many different impacts on the composition of household demand and on the labor supply. The demand for school classrooms will decline; households will need more health care and the support services for the elderly retired.

China has produced ten million apartment homes during most of the last twenty years, in large part to provide accommodation for those moving to the cities and as stores of value for the savings of millions of middle-class urban residents who were not satisfied with the negative real rates of return on bank deposits. Construction of apartments provided work for seventy to eighty million individuals who might otherwise have stayed on the farms. The prices of these apartments increased more rapidly than the goods price level because the price of the land was increasing. The prices of apartments are extraordinarily high relative to household incomes, perhaps ten to fifteen times higher with large variations among cities; the price to income ratio is fifteen to twenty in the tier one cities—Beijing, Shanghai, Guangzhou, and Chongqing. There may be forty to fifty million vacant apartments that were acquired as stores of value to sell at some future date when prices would be higher; another twenty million apartments are in the construction pipeline (see Green, 2022).

The lockdowns associated with the pandemic delayed purchases of apartment; some of the largest developers have gone bankrupt because the buyers disappeared for months. The view that real estate prices would continue to increase until the end of time has been shattered; some of the major developers have become bankrupt. Evergrande and several of the other large developers have been involved in Ponzi finance; they relied on the cash received as down payments from Wednesday's buyers to pay the construction firms that were completing the building of homes that were promised to Tuesday's buyers. Purchases of apartments have slowed sharply, and prices have been declining. The property developers will need immense amounts of cash to complete the building of the units that are in the construction pipeline; the lenders will be reluctant to provide the money because the prices of apartments will decline.

The sharp decline in spending on new apartments will continue for at least three or four years and perhaps for eight or ten years; one impact is that thirty or forty million individuals who previously had been involved in construction will need work. The revenues of the local governments from the land sales to the developers will plummet—and while money spent building out the infrastructure around new apartment complexes will decline, the fall in revenues of the local governments from land sales will be larger, which will intensify the deficits of the local governments. The banks and other financial firms will incur massive losses on their loans to property developers. Household net worth will decline sharply.

The financial implosion will lead to a massive increase in the indebtedness of the Chinese government; the ratio of government indebtedness to GDP now approaches 75 percent; this ratio could quickly approach 300 percent.

The Xi government has been leaning on the entrepreneurs, which will slow innovation. The United States and other Western countries have benefited greatly from the thousands of Chinese who came to study and then entered the labor force.

Part of the great success of China developed from its rapid integration into the global economy; a ballpark estimate is that China received 90 percent of the gains from the increase in its bilateral trade with the United

States. The implication is that China's share of the reduction of the gains from trade also will be large. China's rapid export growth after 1980 was facilitated because 40 or 50 percent of its exports were sourced by foreign-owned multinationals that had recognized brand names. China will have to grow more of its own brand names (although Chinese firms could buy foreign firms for their brand names and distribution networks, as Geeley did with Volvo).

China has a major incipient excess supply problem; its domestic saving will increase even as the domestic investment will decline. During the period of rapid economic growth, China had a current account surplus that at times amounted to more than 5 percent of its GDP. China is the only country that has grown rapidly that has had a large and persistent current account surplus, virtually every other country that has been at the top of the growth rate hit parade has had a current account deficit and has borrowed abroad to finance part of its investment. Moreover, during the last ten years, about 10 percent of Chinese savings have been absorbed in the construction of urban housing, ten million new apartments have been built for each of the last twenty years. Most of these apartments have been absorbed by the tens of millions of individuals that have moved from farms and villages to the factories and cities and needed accommodation. Every apartment has been acquired as a store of value; a significant number have remained vacant because the anticipated rental income has been so modest relative to the anticipated price appreciation.

China will need some major adjustments to absorb its excess savings. Moreover, household savings are likely to increase as prices of apartments and other assets decline and households seek to rebuild wealth. In the past, excess savings has been absorbed by the current account surplus, apartment construction, and infrastructure. China's current account surplus is likely to decline because the United States and some other industrial countries will limit their trade deficits with China. (China may increase its trade surplus by additional transfers under its Belt and Road Initiative, but most foreign countries will be reluctant to increase their indebtedness.) Apartment construction is likely to absorb smaller amounts of savings as long as there remain several tens of millions of vacant apartments. China already has a first-class infrastructure of high-speed railroads and toll roads and airports; most are underutilized because the fares are too high.

China's growth rate is likely to decline to 1 percent a year as a result of supply-side and demand-side factors. The dominant factor on the supply side is that the migration from the countryside to the cities now is over.

References

Aliber, R. Z. (1991). *The multinational paradigm*. The MIT Press.

Aliber, R. Z., & Kindleberger, C. P. (2015). *Manias, panics, and crashes* (7th ed.). Palgrave Macmillan.

Fok, J. A. (2022). *Financial cold war: A view of Sino-US relations from the financial markets*. John Wiley and Sons Ltd.

Green, R. (2022, October 28). China property dream turns to nightmare. *TSLombard*.

Rozelle, S., & Hell, H. (2020). *Invisible China: How the urban rural divide threatens China's rise*. University of Chicago Press.

Rudd, K. (2022). *The avoidable war*. Public Affairs.

Shum, D. (2021). *Red Roulette: An Insider's Story of Wealth, Power, Corruption, and Vengeance in Today's China*. Scribner, New York, London, Toronto, Sydney and New Delhi.

Robert Z. Aliber joined the faculty of the Graduate School of Business of the University of Chicago in 1965 and left the classroom in 2004. He has written extensively about exchange rates and cross-border investment inflows. While at Chicago he managed the international student exchange program and developed the Center for Studies in International Finance. He was the founding chair of the Committee for Public Policy Studies, which morphed into the Harris School of Public Policy. He published *The International Money Game* in 1974, there have been six subsequent editions. Aliber inherited *Manias, Panics, and Crashes* from Charles P. Kindleberger, who brought out the first four editions; Aliber brought out the fifth, sixth, and seventh editions. He was a co-author of *Money, Banking, and the Economy* with James Dusenbery and Thomas Mayer. Aliber published *The Multinational Paradigm* in 1992. He has written several books on personal finance with the title *Your Money and Your Life*. He has been a visiting scholar at the Federal Reserve Bank of San Francisco, and a visiting professor at the London Graduate School of Business Studies, the Amos Tuck School of Business at Dartmouth College, Williams College, the Free University of Berlin, and Brandeis University. He was a visiting scholar at the Woodrow International Center for Scholars, and at the American Academy of Berlin; he was a Houblon Norman fellow at the Bank of England. He has been a consultant to the International Monetary Fund, the World Bank, the Board of Governors of the Federal Reserve System, and numerous multinational firms.

Growth Without Democracy: Has China's Time of Rapid Growth Come to an End?

Thráinn Eggertsson

Why Did China Change Course Early in the Twenty-First Century?

In the late 1970s, after Mao Zedong's dreadful social experiments, *The Great Leap Forward*, 1958–1962, and the *Cultural Revolution*, 1966–1976, China was a poor agricultural country in disarray. In the late 1970s, local communities, often in outlying regions, made spontaneous attempts to improve the organization in agriculture. The experiments preserved central management while permitting private incentives: Once the farmers had met their production quotas at the planned price, they were allowed to sell additional produce at the market price (Eggertsson, 2005, pp. 163–67). President Deng Xiaoping, 1978–1989, encouraged these experiments, which spread through the agricultural economy and into industry where private firms gradually emerged and coexisted with state-owned enterprises. Deng Xiaoping went further, he opened China to the world economy, initially by creating special economic zones and opening

T. Eggertsson (✉)
University of Iceland, Reykjavík, Iceland
e-mail: thrainn@hi.is

R. Z. Aliber et al. (eds.), *Fault Lines After COVID-19*,
https://doi.org/10.1007/978-3-031-26482-5_5

coastal cities (Coase & Wang, 2012). The role of state-owned enterprises became smaller; private enterprises now account for about 60% of GDP. The socialist market economy with Chinese characteristics, to borrow an official term, did exceptionally well from 1980 to 2010. The GDP grew at an annual rate of about 10%, lifting 700–800 million people out of extreme poverty. China became a leading force in world trade after joining the World Trade Organization in 2001. It is still a middle-income country with about 20% of the US per capita income.

China's 30 years of rapid growth confounded many economists who believed that the country lacked a necessary institution for growth: formal exclusive property rights (Clarke, 2003). Most economists agree now that the Chinese growth miracle did not refute the rights hypothesis. In the absence of conventional legal property rights, China initially relied on private ordering or informal economic property rights based on social norms and enforcement by powerful local bosses (Qian, 2000; Ellickson, 2016). Over time, Chinese formal property rights and contract law came to resemble Western legal institutions, although the Chinese legal system, both in form and practice, ultimately serves the Chinese Communist Party (CCP); China has rule by law, not rule of law.

In the last 10–15 years, the Chinese economy has taken a turn for the worse. From 2008 to the present, total factor productivity growth (here after, productivity growth) in China has averaged around 1.5% and recently fallen to 1%, even to zero by some accounts (Brandt et al., 2020; Rajah & Leng, 2022). The evidence indicates that flawed market institutions are partly to blame. The survival rate of inefficient enterprises has risen, and there are few signs of resources moving from inefficient to efficient enterprises (Brandt et al., 2020, pp. 8–11). Low-productivity growth is not fully reflected in figures for GDP growth because China has increasingly used capital accumulation to drive economic growth, investing heavily in real estate and infrastructure. Reckless investment strategies have trebled China's incremental capital-output ratio; compared to a few years ago, three times more capital is now required to produce an additional unit of output (Brandt et al., 2020, p. 15).

There are other issues. The transfer of workers from low-productivity agriculture to high-productivity manufacturing has ground to a halt; the so-called Lewis turning point has been reached. Recently, workers have begun to move out of manufacturing into the service sector, which has lower productivity. There is evidence that market forces have weakened, allowing inefficient enterprises to survive, as already mentioned. Reforms of inefficient state-owned enterprises are not undertaken, or they fail. Undesirable side effects of economic growth are abundant, especially pollution, wasteful use of natural resources, and inequality. Incomes are much lower in agricultural regions than in urban areas, and inequality within urban areas is high. In 2019, China's Gini coefficient, which measures inequality, was 0.418 but the average for the OECD countries was 0.318 (OECD, 2022, p. 8). Corruption is rampant, including judicial corruption and public sector bribery (OECD, 2022, p. 12). Opportunism and disobedience are common, extending to the CCP. Extreme demographic problems are on the horizon, including a large drop in the working-age population, and rapid aging of the nation. Recent strife and conflicts with Western powers have raised doubts in China about relying on imported technology, food, and energy. In 2018, China entered a trade war with the US. In 2022, Western sanctions on Russia as punishment for their Ukraine invasion raised concerns in China that the West might have a similar response to a Chinese invasion of Taiwan. The CCP has not forgotten that access to foreign markets and imported technology, often embodied in direct foreign investment, helped create their growth miracle.

In 2012, when many of the problems listed were already on the horizon, the CCP selected Xi Jinping as head of the party. Xi, who belongs to a radical party faction that is guided by the thoughts of Mao and Lenin (and recently the thoughts of Xi himself), has restored Mao's one-man rule, and aims for a "Great Rejuvenation of the Chinese Nation" by 2049 (Xia, 2022). The following section discusses the road taken by Xi Jinping.

President Xi Jinping's New Strategy

President Xi has two priorities: to preserve CCP rule over China and to rekindle China's growth miracle. Similarly, Xi's strategies have two roots: the politics of Marx and Lenin and a utopian dream about the power of advanced twenty-first-century digital technology. Below I first discuss Xi's ideas for the political system and then his plans for the economy.

New Political Institutions and Policy

Many economists believe that autocratic regimes are unable to reach the global productivity frontier and become high-income countries, because sooner or later lack of democratic institutions holds them back. I refer to these ideas as the dictator's dilemma hypothesis or the democracy constraint and examine them in more detail in a later section. President Xi, who desires both frontier growth and dictatorship, intends to use advanced digital technologies to override the dictator's dilemma. China's past growth miracle relied on informal property rights to bypass the property rights paradox. Now Xi plans to escape the democracy constraint by relying on cyber control of society and cyber-guided entrepreneurship, aided by a tremendous fall in agency and transaction costs under the new technologies.

Since coming to power, President Xi has steadily moved the Chinese political system towards greater central control. He has assumed absolute power instead of relying on collective leadership, brought back Mao's cult of personality, removed the paramount leader's term limit, and rewritten China's history; "Xi Jinping Thought on Socialism with Chinese Characteristics for a New Era" has been incorporated into the constitutions of the CCP and the People's Republic.

Xi's ability to control some 1400 million souls depends on the loyalty and effectiveness of the 97 million members of the CCP. The party branches out to monitor all levels of China's governmental, economic, social, and military organizations. In 2012, when Xi took power, access to unprecedented wealth, major social changes, and new lifestyles had undermined party discipline. The CCP was corrupt, divided into factions, with disobedience spreading among the cadres, reminiscent of a disorderly Mafia organization (Xia, 2022). President Xi hurried to reform the party and strengthen his personal control. He has purged corrupt leaders at all levels, including top figures, but focused on political opponents, replacing them with his supporters. Misconduct has not disappeared, but Xi uses the prevalence of graft to hold his coalition together, threatening potential defectors with charges of corruption. He has neutralized unfriendly factions in the party, gaining virtually full control of its upper reaches. His purges have also involved the armed forces and private sector oligarchs.

Xi has also upgraded the CCP's inefficient internal system for monitoring its own members, a necessary step before intensifying party surveillance of society. A new internal monitoring system is now in place (Fewsmith, 2019), and the party has, for instance, resurrected a dormant rule that requires its cadres to form party cells in their organizations and places of work, when three or more members belong to the same unit. These party cells clamour for more influence. Private companies are now required to include a party cell before they can be listed on domestic stock exchanges. China's wealthy high-technology oligarchs have roused Xi's ire. Their internet apps and platform conglomerates, world fame and fortune, and Western commercialism did not fit in with Xi's new socialist era. In 2021, he slashed their finances, limited the sector's future expansion, and cast a shadow on the tycoons.

The rapid rise of internet technology surprised many dictators and their censors; for a few years they left the new media mostly alone. China was an exception. Already in 1996, the party began building the Great Firewall, a complex system of control that isolates the Chinese online community—one thousand million individuals—from the outside internet world, and monitors and censors the domestic internet. Internet surveillance is only partly automatic, the system employs millions of censors, including an army of contractors that intervene in online discussions to support the CCP viewpoint (Eggertsson, 2019).

The so-called social credit system is the crown jewel in Xi's treasure chest. The system is designed to monitor, measure, and influence the behaviour of all citizens and organizations. The idea of nationwide social credit rating is inspired by financial institutions that evaluate their customers for creditworthiness, except that the social credit project measures populations, not customers of an organization; it considers all types of behaviour; it relies on state power (Devereaux & Peng, 2020). To rate human behaviour, the CCP uses standards ranging from social norms, laws, and regulations to idiosyncratic requirements of the party. A low social credit score brings shame to the recipient, and limits access to valued goods and service; a high score yields various benefits. Positive and negative scores are supposed to influence behaviour in a desirable direction. The data for the social credit system come from direct observations of citizens and from various data banks. Direct observations include data from facial recognition cameras, DNA samples, and people's internet behaviour. The data banks contain public and private sector data, including criminal, commercial, health, financial, and tax records (Creemers, 2018; Devereaux & Peng, 2020). The social credit system was introduced in 2014, the completion of a nationwide system set for 2020, but in 2022 the system was not ready. As is customary, different versions of the new system are being tested in various parts of China. The CCP hopes that artificial intelligence algorithms, using data from the social credit system, will be able to forecast new behavioural trends and emerging social movements, and discover ways to change behaviour and stop or reverse undesirable developments. The new intrusive digital technologies advance rapidly. Street cameras can identify a jaywalker, register the offense in data banks, and even publish the offender's name on billboards. China has become a leading developer of advanced surveillance technologies and sells surveillance instruments to dictators worldwide (Freedom House, 2018, p. 8).

Alongside the social credit system, the CCP uses monitoring technology all around, for instance, to manage the public sector. In its war on pollution, the party has substituted real-time monitoring of pollution for reports made by local officials, who have strong incentives to maximize economic growth and underreport pollution. In a comprehensive regression study, Greenstone et al. (2020) find that automated monitoring significantly improved the quality of the data, raising by 35% reported levels of pollution. China has gone further than any other country in applying artificial intelligence to its courts of law. "More recently, courts across the country have initiated experiments to integrate AI into adjudication by introducing software that reviews evidence, suggests outcomes, checks the consistency of judgments, and makes recommendations on how to judge cases" (Stern et al., 2021, p. 518). China's purpose by creating smart courts is to raise efficiency in the judiciary and to solidify CCP power. Stern et al. (2021) examine the feasibility and wisdom of smart courts, finding that lack of efficient and reliable data, and weak AI algorithms are serious bottlenecks.

The CCP now uses digital technologies and traditional methods of surveillance to enter all levels of Chinese life, down to the village. In the late 1980s and 1990s, when about 80% of the Chinese lived in rural areas, rather than appointing the village chairman, the CCP allowed many villages to elect their chairman. Local democracy lasted until the early 2000s when elected village governments gradually lost their autonomy. Martinez-Bravo et al. (2022), in a careful empirical study, explain this anomalous behaviour of the CCP as a practical response to high-agency costs and resource constraints. In the 1980s and 1990s, the party had limited resources to effectively monitor villages. Often, it was more cost-effective to let the villagers elect and monitor their leaders, under the supervision of county officials. In the affluent twenty-first century, the party has removed these vestiges of democratic rights. The CCP has become a wealthy possessor of new communication and monitoring technologies that have reduced the cost of central control, and the need for decentralization. Yet, many observers believe that relatively weak central control and considerable autonomy of villages, cities, and provinces released local energy and creativity, which encouraged spontaneous experiments that propelled China's growth miracle. It is not obvious that low-agency costs benefit a dictator who is aiming for frontier economic growth.

New Economic Institutions and Policy

To achieve his other major objective, to restore sustained economic growth, President Xi must raise productivity growth. Moreover, confrontations with the West force him to rely mostly on new domestic technologies. To meet these challenges, Xi plans a Chinese Industrial Revolution and hopes to reach the global productivity frontier in one or two decades. In the critical field of artificial intelligence, for instance, the detailed 2017 *New Generation Artificial Intelligence Development Plan*by the State Council (see, Webster et al., 2017 for full English translation) has China reaching world levels in some AI fields by 2025 and becoming the world's primary AI innovation centre in 2030. China's industrial masterplan from 2015, *Made in China 2025*, "targets virtually all high-tech industries that strongly contribute to economic growth in advanced economies: automotive, aviation, machinery, robotics, high-tech maritime and railway equipment, energy-saving vehicles, medical devices and information technology to name only a few" (Wübbeke et al., 2016, p. 6).

Inland cities that the recent hi-tech boom in coastal regions left behind are the site for the new industrial revolution. The new location will require inland migration of skilled workers (The Economist, April 16, 2022b). President Xi has shifted the focus of his industrial revolution from, what he calls, "soft digital technology," used by the consumer internet industries to applications of "hard digital technology" that will be used to upgrade the means of production. Multitudes of new inland research and development start-ups will produce productivity-enhancing digital intermediate goods that embody new technologies such as AI, Big Data analysis, and robotics.

Mr. Xi's tight timing of his enormous project requires China to set up at lightning speed a vast number of start-ups and seed firms. The scheme is a unique instance of top-down entrepreneurship with the state guiding the project choices of venture capital (The Economist, June 27, 2022a). By favouring specific technologies and projects through state-controlled or state-guided investment funds, the authorities send clear signals to private venture capital. A ministry may select specific projects and enterprises for financial support, and local governments provide cheap land for start-ups. In this environment, private venture capitalists and private enterprises are likely to follow state guidance rather than their business instincts. In Xi's words, gone are the days of "disorderly expansion of capital" with excessive flow of funds into soft digital technology, real estate, and financial speculation abroad—much of which was authorized by Xi in the early days of his presidency.

The Long-Term Outlook

Although the long-term economic outlook for China depends on several factors, two issues are of critical importance: (a) the relevance of the democracy constraint under cyber dictatorship, and (b) the availability of inputs and new technologies—the proximate sources of growth. I begin by discussing the dictator's dilemma and ideas underlying the hypothesis and go on to consider whether a dictator can use digital technology to override the democracy constraint. The section's second half puts economics of institutions aside and examines China's economic prospects in terms of productivity growth and available factors of production.

The Dictator's Dilemma and Cyber Dictatorship

Economists have long speculated about the relationship between democracy and economic growth: whether autocracies can grow beyond mid-level prosperity. Joseph Schumpeter (1942) saw democracy as a necessary condition for sustained economic growth. In formal Schumpeter growth models, Aghion and Durlauf (2009) make democracy a necessary condition for frontier growth. Effective limits on state power have a key role in the work of Douglass North (1990) and his co-authors (North et al., 2009) on historical roots of sustained growth. Acemoglu and Robinson (2019) examine the link between democracy and institutional equilibrium, using a model that includes a political system and an economic system. In the model, institutional equilibrium exists only when *both* systems are open or closed. An open economic system has market competition with free entry. An open political system has political competition and free elections. Institutional disequilibrium prevails when one system is open and the other is closed, because social forces pull the country either towards double closure or double openness. China's current political forces are likely to pull the country back into double closure, according to Acemoglu and Robinson (2019, p. 25).

In the empirical literature, norms of trust and other civic virtues are the cement of society and necessary for long-term economic progress. In a well-known study, Putnam, and co-authors (1994) ask why Italy's administrative regions have widely different rates of economic growth, although, since 1970, the regional governments' de jure institutions are the same. Putnam et al. (1994) conclude that regional variation in participation by citizens in civic society organizations explains regional differences in civic virtues, good governance, and prosperity. Historically, the Middle East was an advanced region, but in the modern era it has fallen behind Western Europe in terms of economic growth and development. Kuran (2004) argues that economic underdevelopment in the Middle East is related to institutional stagnation, including failure to develop free civic society organizations.

The literature emphasizes that free civic society is both a source of civic virtues and a layer between state and society that protects citizens from arbitrary exploitation by the state. Sustained economic growth requires a high-capacity state to tax and provide infrastructure and public services, and simultaneously a strong state that does not abuse its citizens (Acemoglu & Robinson, 2019). Interactions between free civic society and the state create mutual trust and make it possible for free individuals and a strong state to coexist. Civic society is a fusion of myriad organizations, such as labour unions, business groups, political associations, religious groups, professional organizations, and neighbourhood associations. If given free rein, civic organizations destabilize dictatorships, and free entry and private enterprise have the same effect. Dictators stay in power by rewarding elite supporters with exclusive access to valuable resources and industries. Political power rests on economic power; dictators who open the economic system undermine their power (Bueno de Mesquita et al., 2003). China's 1980–2012 growth miracle and gradual opening of the economic system have slowly corrupted the CCP and weakened its hold on power. Xi sees the danger but believes that twenty-first-century information and communication technology will solve the dictator's dilemma. His faith in the new technology recalls twentieth-century beliefs that the computer would rescue central planning in the USSR by rapidly calculating the optimum allocation of resources. The question now is whether the Chinese social credit system can create civic virtues, and whether CCP has the capacity to encourage and lead serendipitous scientific creativity and entrepreneurship.

The greatest source of danger under unbridled dictatorship is the dictator's freedom to make ruinous social experiments. Mao Zedong had his Great Leap Forward and the Cultural Revolution and President Xi has also made revolutionary leaps: He began his rule with plans for quickening China's program of liberalization, but soon reversed course; he initiated a monumental housing project that crashed; he originated the global Belt and Road Initiative, which recalls Lenin's (1917) *Imperialism, the Highest Stage of Capitalism*; he has given priority to confrontation with the West, when China's economy faces crisis and needs foreign markets and technologies; he has tested extreme cyber oppression and mind control technologies in the restless Xinjiang region; he has mulishly followed a reckless zero-COVID policy; he is planning to guide China in the next 10–15 years to world leadership of major twenty-first-century technologies.

The CCP is a little more than 100 years old; the party was founded in 1921. Mancur Olson (1982), writing about the rise and decline of nations, argues that organizations gradually learn to protect themselves and to profit by manipulating their administrative territory. The benefits of rent-seeking often give organizations an incentive to resist reforms until destructive external events intervene and make it possible for reformers to begin anew. The gradual decline of the Communist Party of the old USSR, along with the regime's economic and government organizations, is common knowledge. The CCP, and their system with Chinese characteristics, may already be on the same path, a trail that does not lead to industrial revolutions.

Growth Theory and Proximate Causes of Growth

In economics, growth theory studies the proximate causes of economic growth, rather than the role of social institutions and political economy. Recent statistical forecasts of China's future economic growth often seem to assume that past growth trends will continue, or that China will repeat the economic success of South Korea and Taiwan, which currently have per capita incomes about three times higher than China (Lin, 2017). Both countries entered their rapid growth phase in the early 1960s, some 20 years ahead of China. Rajah and Leng (2022, pp. 11–12) find that recent estimates of China's annual GDP growth over the next two or three decades tend to average 4.5–5%. Some estimates even reach 7%, but low estimates are rare. Rajah and Leng (2022, pp. 50–57) emphasize that small variation in China's future growth has geopolitical implications. If the Chinese economy grows at an average annual rate of 5%, by 2050 it is twice the estimated size of the US economy, and three times larger, if the high estimates are used. However, with annual growth of 2.5%, China does not dominate the world by mid-century; its economy is then about 20% larger than the US, with per capita income about half the US figure.

Scholars sometimes justify their high estimates for China's future growth by arguing that China's leaders have always responded to temporary economic setbacks with a volley of pro-market reforms (Brandt, 2020, pp. 18–22; Sasaki, 2021). It is also argued that China is free from the democracy constraint because the economy is far from the global productivity frontier (Brandt, 2020,18). The first argument overlooks that, under Xi, China has responded to slow growth by recentralizing the economy and increasing party control. Moreover, it is not clear that pro-market reforms are effective after decades of CCP dictatorship. The argument about China being far from the frontier ignores current uncertainty about China's future access to foreign technology, and Xi's plans to make China in 10–15 years a world technology leader. Finally, highly inefficient institutions often bring economic stagnation long before autocracies come close to the global frontier.

The decades ahead are less growth-friendly for China than the last 40 years, as Rajah and Leng (2022) examine in detail. Consider the labour market. The supply of cheap labour from agriculture to manufacturing has dried up, which did not happen in South Korea and Taiwan when their per capita incomes were growing from about 20% to 50% of the US level. Moreover, unlike its two neighbours, China is now seriously concerned about future food security and aims at becoming self-sufficient in key food products, which limits transfers of labour out of agriculture.

From 1975 to 2010, China's working-age population almost doubled, and a rising labour force participation made total hours of work grow even faster. Now, China faces a major population crisis (OECD, 2019; OECD, 2022; Rajah & Leng, 2022, pp. 17–20). The country's working-age population has shrunk since 2015. By 2040, the size of the potential workforce will have fallen by 100 million individuals, and by 220 million in 2050. China's overall population, which peaks in 2022 (and is expected to fall below 800 million in 2100), is aging rapidly (Olcott, 2022). The median age of the Chinese was 25 years in 1990 but rises to 48 years in 2040. Birth rates in China had begun to fall before the one-child policy was introduced in 1980, and the fall has continued after the regime abolished the policy in 2015. These demographic developments will slow economic growth, shrink family networks that provide informal social security, and raise the cost of caring for the elderly (Olcott, 2022). When per capita incomes in South Korea and Taiwan were rising from 20% to 50% of the US level, their working-age populations did not shrink (Rajah & Leng, 2022, pp. 17–20). Finally, South Korea and Taiwan did not face constraints on Western technology and markets as China is likely to face.

With China's productivity growing at 1% or less in the 2010s, the regime achieved economic growth primary through capital accumulation. In the 2020s and onward, China will not be able to enjoy rapid economic growth by adding more capital to a falling number of workers. High and rapidly rising marginal capital-output ratio, along with serious debt problems will prevent a repeat of the 2010s solution. Productivity growth will determine or constrain China's economic future. Economists can only guess at future productivity growth. My favourite guess is that by Rajah and Leng (2022). They extrapolate China's past productivity growth but give China's trend line the negative slope of the lines for South Korea and Taiwan in the decades after they had reached China's 2019 income per capita, which was in 1980 and 1975, respectively. At each point in time, the per capita incomes of the three countries are expressed as fractions of US per capita income. In years when actual figures for all three countries are available, China's productivity growth, at a comparable level of development, is substantially below that of South Korea and Taiwan. Rajah and Leng (2022) include various economic factors in their estimate of China's economic growth but do not consider political issues. They predict that the Chinese economy will grow at an average rate of 2.5% from 2019 to 2049, with the economy growing faster in the early years. Sharma (2022) also predicts 2.5% future growth for China, calling it an optimistic estimate.

Conclusion

A 2.5% growth rate for China's GDP in 2019–2050 is a respectable performance, not another economic miracle. The forecast assumes sound economic policies and political stability, which is not self-evident. The centenarian Chinese Communist Party has arrived at a fork in the road and faces the unhappy choice between greater political and economic liberalization, which lifts the economy but destroys the party, and stronger party control, which sinks the economy. In China, conflicting forces pull and push the system in opposite directions. President Xi now dominates the CCP and pushes the Chinese system back towards double closure of polity and economy. Xi understands that the status quo is an untenable disequilibrium of economic stagnation, political corruption, and lack of civic virtues, but he refuses to choose between economic prosperity and party control. Instead, he is building a third road that leads to total party control and to a Chinese Industrial Revolution. The third road, built on digital surveillance and cyber dictatorship, is a utopian fantasy, like the old USSR dream that the rise of the computer would spawn optimum central planning. When China wakes from its cyber dream, one hopes the Chinese will find a peaceful solution to their internal contradictions.

References

Acemoglu, D., & Robinson, J. A. (2019). Rents and economic development: The perspective of *Why Nations Fail. Public Choice, 181*(1–2), 13–28.

Aghion, P., & Durlauf, S. (2009). *From growth theory to policy design* (Working Paper No. 57). World Bank: Commission on Growth and Development.

Brandt, L., Litwack, J., Mileva, E., Wang, L., Zang, Y., & Zhao, L. (2020). *China's productivity slowdown and future growth potential* (Policy Research Working Paper 9298). World Bank: Macroeconomics, Trade and Investment Global Practice.

Bueno de Mesquita, B., Smith, A., Siverson, R. M., & Morrow, J. D. (2003). *The logical of political survival.* The MIT Press.

Clarke, D. C. (2003). Economic development and the rights hypothesis: The China problem. *American Journal of Comparative Law, 51*, 89–112.

Coase, R. H., & Wang, N. (2012). *How China became capitalist.* Palgrave Macmillan.

Creemers, R. (2018, May 9). *China's social credit system: An evolving practice of control.* Available at https://papers.ssrn.com/sol3/papers.cfm?abstract_id=3175792

Devereaux, A., & Peng, L. (2020). Give us a little social credit: To design or to discover personal ratings in the era of big data. *Journal of Institutional Economics, 16*, 369–387.

Eggertsson, T. (2005). *Imperfect institutions. Possibilities and limits of reform.* University of Michigan Press.

Eggertsson, T. (2019). *Governance in the 21st century: The trend toward digital dictatorship.* Keynote address, WOW 6, Indiana University.

Ellickson, R. C. (2016). When civil society uses an iron fist: The roles of private associations in rulemaking and adjudication. *American Law and Economics Review, 18*, 237–273.

Fewsmith, J. (2019). Reviving Leninism and National Rejuvenation: Can tighter cadre control produce better governance? In *Party watch annual report 2019* (pp. 5–12). Center for Advanced China Research.

Freedom House. (2018). *Freedom on the net 2018. The rise of digital authoritarianism.* https://freedomhouse.org/report/freedom-net/2018/rise-digital-authoritarianism. Accessed 29 Oct 2022.

Greenstone, M., He, G., Jia, R., & Liu, T. (2020). Can technology solve the principal-agent problem? Evidence from China's war on pollution. *American Economic Review: Insights, 4*(1), 54–70.

Kuran, T. (2004). Why the Middle East is economically underdeveloped: Historical mechanisms of institutional stagnation. *Journal of Economic Perspectives, 18*(3), 71–90.

Lenin, V. I. (2011 [1917]). *Imperialism, the highest stage of capitalism.* Martino Fine Books.

Lin, J. Y. (2017, December 1). The economics of China's new era. *Project Syndicate.* https://www.project-syndicate.org/onpoint/the-economics-of-china-s-new-era-by-justin-yifu-lin-2017-12. Accessed 29 Oct 2022.

Martinez-Bravo, Monica, Gerard Padró i Miquel, Nancy Qian, and Yang Yao. 2022. "The Rise and Fall of Local Elections in China." American Economic Review, 112 (9): 2921–58.

North, D. C. (1990). *Institutions, institutional change and economic performance.* Cambridge University Press.

North, D., Wallis, J. J., & Weingast, B. R. (2009). *Violence and social orders. A conceptual framework for interpreting recorded human history.* Cambridge University Press.

OECD. (2019). *OECD economic surveys: China 2022.* OECD Publishing.

OECD. (2022). *OECD economic surveys: China 2022.* OECD Publishing.

Olcott, E. (2022, October 3). China's demographic crisis looms over Xi Jinping's third term. *Financial Times.*

Olson, M. (1982). *The rise and decline of nations: Economic growth, stagflation, and social rigidities.* Yale University Press.

Putnam, R. D., Leonardi, T., & Nanetti, R. Y. (1994). *Making democracy work: Civic traditions in modern Italy.* Princeton University Press.

Qian, Y. (2000). The institutional foundations of China's market transition. In B. Pleskovic & J. Stiglitz (Eds.), *Proceedings of the World Bank's annual conference on development economics, 1999* (pp. 289–310). World Bank.

Rajah, R., & Leng, A. (2022). *Revising down the rise of China.* Lowy Institute Publication.

Sasaki, T., Sakata, T. Mukoyama, Y., & Yoshino, K. (2021). *China's long-term growth potential: Can productivity convergence be sustained?* (Working Paper Series: No. 21-E-7). Bank of Japan.

Schumpeter, J. A. (1942). *Capitalism, socialism and democracy*. Harper & Brothers.

Sharma, R. (2022, October 24). China's economy will not overtake the US until 2060, if ever. Opinion. *Financial Times*.

Stern, R. E., Liebman, B. L., Roberts, M., & Wang, A. Z. (2021). Automating fairness? Artificial intelligence in the Chinese Court. *Columbia Journal of Transnational Law*, 515–553.

The Economist. (2022a, June 27). The rise of China's VC-industries. *The Economist*, 2022 edition.

The Economist. (2022b, April 16). Xi Jinping's bold plan for China's next phase of innovation. *The Economist*, 2022 edition.

Webster, G., Creemers, R., Kania, E., & Triolo, P. (2017). *Full translation: China's 'New Generation Artificial Intelligence Plan'*. Publication of Digichina, Stanford Cyber Policy Center.

Wübbeke, J., Meissner, M. Zenglein, M. J., Ives, J., & Conrad, B. (2016). *Made in China 2025*. The making of high-tech superpower and consequences for industrial countries (Papers on China No. 2-2016). Mercator Institute for Chinese Studies.

Xia, C. (2022). The weakness of Xi Jinping: How Hubris and Paranoia threatens China's future. *Foreign Affairs*.

Thráinn Eggertsson is Professor Emeritus of Economics at the University of Iceland. During 2011–2019, he was adjunct professor at Hertie School, Berlin, and in 2005–2010 global distinguished professor of politics at New York University. Eggertsson served as president of the International Society for New Institutional Economics (now SIOE) 2007–2008, and he co-edited for Cambridge University Press the book series Political Economy of Institutions and Decisions. In the 1980s and 1990s, he taught and collaborated with Elinor Ostrom at Indiana University in Bloomington, and Douglass North at Washington University in St. Louis, and Stanford University. His main field of study is comparative economic systems, their basic structure, and evolution.

Denunciations in Autocratic Regimes: How and When Do They Work

Tinghua Yu and Stephane Wolton

If you stroll around central Beijing, you may see cartoon posters telling a love story between a foreign visitor and a state employee. It all starts well. A young man, the foreigner, meets a young woman, the state employee, at a dinner with friends. They start dating. One day, the young man asks his new girlfriend for a favour. A bit reluctantly, she agrees and provides the information her boyfriend needs. This is the start of the tragedy. The foreign visitor is revealed to be a spy. In the end of the story, the state employee regrets her action and admits her involuntary crime to the state police. These posters are part of a campaign that serves as a call for vigilance, vigilance against the risk of foreign infiltration. The campaign asks citizens to do their part and to denounce suspicious approaches by foreign agents, hiding under the cover of loving or love-seeking gentlemen.

T. Yu (✉)
Birkbeck College, University of London, London, UK
e-mail: t.yu@bbk.ac.uk

S. Wolton
London School of Economics and Political Science, London, UK
e-mail: s.wolton@lse.ac.uk

R. Z. Aliber et al. (eds.), *Fault Lines After COVID-19*,
https://doi.org/10.1007/978-3-031-26482-5_6

Vigilance and voluntary denunciations do not appear to be enough, however. In June 2022, the Chinese state announced a new policy that offers cash rewards of up to 100,000 yuan (£12,000) for providing tipoffs about suspected foreign spies and national security breaches (The Guardian, 8 June 2022). According to the ministry of state security, "the formulation of the measures is conducive to fully mobilizing the enthusiasm of the general public to support and assist in national security work, widely rallying the hearts, morale, wisdom, and strength of the people".

Every regime in the world uses denunciations. In the West, for example, citizens are constantly reminded to report actions suggesting the onset of a terrorist attack. "See it, say it, sorted" repeatedly says the London tube speaker, "If you see something, say something", urges posters in the subway in New York City. Yet, denunciations play a specific role in autocratic regimes where they become a prominent part of the police state. By actively promoting the participation of citizens into the police state, authorities accomplish two goals. They root out potential enemies and they create a new type of citizens, accomplice to the regime (ex) actions (Weiner & Rahi-Tamm, 2012). As summarized in Lampert (1985: 183), "[Truth-seekers] represent a world of thorough and cold-blooded state control. The whistle-blowers are the totalitarians of the piece, spying on their colleagues and fellow workers and setting themselves up as agents for the prying eyes of the state".

Denunciations have been widely used during Nazi Germany, Stalin's USSR, the German Democratic Republic and Maoist China. In this last case, denunciation campaigns were carried out over decades to mobilize the masses to accuse the "class enemies". The class enemies would be humiliated and tortured in public at "denunciation rallies". This tradition of using denunciations persists nowadays. On top of the example described above, during the Shanghai lockdown in Spring 2022, as part of China's effort to sustain its zero Covid policy, citizens and the management of apartment blocks were encouraged to report their neighbours who might have contracted Covid to the authorities (Reuters, 18 April 2022). As one of the residents in these apartment blocks put it, "they felt invested with the most important mission of their life, being able to play doctor, policeman and judge at the same time".

But how do denunciations work? In an important book, Patrick Bergemann (2019) describes two models of denunciation: the coercion model and the volunteer model. In the coercion model, the regime uses monetary incentives to encourage citizens to report on each other. This is the reward system put into place by the Communist regime in China last summer. In the volunteer regime, citizens only get moral rewards for performing their "duties". The two models lead to different implications. The coercion model yields a high number of denunciations, but many are of little interest to the regime. The volunteer model, Bergemann argues, provides a small number of denunciations, but of higher informativeness.

Yet, Bergemann's useful classification is not the end of the matter. An autocratic regime has to make a choice between the coercion or the volunteer model. This choice depends on what the authorities expect to learn in one compared to the other model. What the regime learns, in turn, is a result of the strategic adaptation of the citizens to the different incentives offered by the authorities. In other words, we need a deeper understanding of how citizens act in the different environments designed by the police state.

A Theoretical Approach to Denunciation

Yu and Wolton (2022) offer a theory to think about the different type of denunciation models a regime can use. The theory is built on a certain number of premises we summarize here. All these features are necessarily simplifications of the real world. They are not meant to capture all aspects of realities. Instead, we seek to eliminate some details to focus on the most important trade-offs citizens and autocrats encounter. All theories are built on ideal types.

We consider a society formed of three different groups. A proportion of citizens is congruent and shares the regime's objectives. Another share of citizens is neutral and just want to get on with their lives without being bothered. The remaining of society consists of non-congruent individuals. These are the "enemies" the regime seeks to root out. In their daily interactions, citizens receive some information about others at work or home. Some of these pieces of information suggest but do not prove that an individual is non-congruent. Others are indicative that an individual is a "good" citizen (where "good" should be understood from the authorities' perspective, same for bad). Citizens can then denounce some of their peers to the authority. Those denunciations do not contain hard evidence. They are statements about others' behaviour, which may or may not have been observed. They can be truthful and report suspicious actions or be false and simple statements against some individuals due to animus, not due to the willingness to uncover some bad types.

The incentives to denounce are distinct for each member of society. Congruent individuals always denounce suspect behaviour and nothing else. Neutral citizens need to receive some small material reward to start denouncing. Non-congruent individuals' first objective is to avoid being caught and, if they have to denounce someone, they would prefer not to denounce individuals who share their preferences.

The regime gathers all denunciations and must decide how to act on it. Historical evidence suggests that the regime never take denunciations at face value. Rather, the authorities use denunciations to decide whom to investigate before making any decisions (Fitzpatrick, 1999; Harrison, 2015). In other words, denunciations are falsifiable. The police or any other regime agents can use two pieces of information when deciding whether to open an inquiry. The first is quite obviously the dossier against an individual: the number of denunciations they have received against them. The second is the action of the individual themselves: has (s)he denounced anyone or did (s)he prefer to remain silent? The act of denouncing, like the refusal to denounce, can serve as an indication of compliance in a well-organized police state.

Denunciation in the Volunteer Model

The volunteer model, you will recall, presupposes that denunciators do not receive any material reward for their actions. Denunciation becomes a moral act. Congruent individuals are unaffected by the presence of encouragement and so denounce anyone they suspect to be non-congruent with the regime. Neutral citizens, who do not oppose the regime nor share its preferences, remain silent in this model. They do not have incentives to become a part of the system of policing society. This leaves non-congruent citizens. How should they behave? The reasoning here becomes a bit subtler.

Suppose individuals who are not congruent with the regime remain silent. As a result, only congruent individuals denounce other members of society. This means that the autocrat has no incentive to investigate a citizen who denounces other members of society. Even if this citizen is herself or himself denounced by others, this must be by mistake since her(his) reporting on others reveal that (s)he shares the autocrat's preferences. Given the autocrats' and their police's reaction to denunciations, non-congruent individuals have strong incentives to imitate congruent citizens by starting to denounce other members of the society. That is, our initial assumption that non-congruent citizens are silent is not consistent with the incentives those citizens face given the autocrat's reactions to denunciations. This means that silence cannot be an optimal strategy for non-congruent individuals.

Let's take the opposite view. Let's now assume that all non-congruent citizens denounce other individuals. We now have two groups who engage in denunciation: congruent individuals who receive damaging information on other members of society and all non-congruent citizens who do so to look good in the regime's eyes. But do the latter accomplish their objective in this case? Not really. If all non-congruent individuals denounce, all the citizens who do not send a report to the police must be either congruent or neutral. Those are not the targets of the regime. Therefore, the police have no incentive to investigate citizens who do not denounce even if they receive some information against them. As a result, non-congruent individuals, anticipating the authorities' reactions, now have the incentive to stay silent. In other words, always denouncing cannot be an optimal strategy.

So, what can it be? It cannot be that all non-congruent citizens remain silent or that all non-congruent citizens denounce. There must be a balance. Some engage in denunciations and others do not. The precise proportion is a matter of circumstances. It is more important to stress the implications of this finding. When non-congruent citizens denounce other members of society, they do it for safety reasons, to avoid the eyes of the police falling on them. Since they prefer **not** denouncing those who share their anti-regime sentiments, they will denounce individuals least likely to be non-congruent. They base their denunciations on their personal animus against some individuals, potentially hoping to get them investigated. As such, a volunteer model is not immune to false denunciations.

To summarize, the volunteer model leads to relatively few denunciations: the congruent citizens when they have relevant information and the non-congruent individuals when they imitate the congruent ones. The latter do not denounce those they know share their anti-regime sentiments, but some other members of the society. As such, the volunteer model is characterized by a relatively low number of denunciations, with little information gathering (many citizens who possess information do not transmit it to the authorities) and a few false denunciations.

Denunciations in the Coercion Model

In the coercion model, the authorities actively reward denunciations. When the tip, in the end, proves to be correct, the denunciator gets some material benefits. We can think of different levels of reward. For the sake of shortness, we focus on the case when the benefits are large enough to induce non-congruent citizens to report on the "enemy" of the regime.

The coercion model changes the reporting strategies of the different types of individuals present in society. Congruent citizens, as before, do the authorities' bidding and only report suspicious members of society. Neutral individuals now fully enter the system of denunciation. Their goal is to get the reward promised by the authority. They report suspicious individuals, but not only. Even absent relevant information, they have an incentive just to try their luck and denounce someone in the hope that this person turns out to be non-congruent. All neutral citizens always denounce, sometimes truthfully, sometimes falsely. Non-congruent individuals, in turn, also adjust their behaviour. When they have information about a possible opponent, they turn on her/him and report her/him to the regime's police. When they do not have information, they denounce someone in order to not look suspicious, just as before.

In the coercion model, the denunciation regime is now in full swing. Denunciations are numerous, coming from all quarters of society, with everyone spying on each other. The benefit? All relevant information is transmitted to the regime. The cost? The regime has to dig out these pieces of information among a mass of false denunciations.

Coercion or Volunteer Model?

With these findings in mind, we are now in a better position to assess the factors determining an authoritarian regime's choice of one model of denunciation over the other. The conclusions above illustrate a possible trade-off for the police state. On the one hand, the volunteer model leads to relatively few true and false denunciations, true in the sense of revealing suspicious behaviour and false in the sense of accusing someone for other reasons than those expected by the regime, as noted above. On the other hand, the coercion model yields many true and many false denunciations.

Hence, most states face a trade-off between the number of denunciations and their informativeness. When informativeness matters, states go for the volunteer model. This is a preferred option when the state police have a low capacity to screen true denunciations from false denunciations. The volunteer model should, therefore, be adopted in the early stage of a regime, especially in countries with low state capacity. It may not be too surprising that the Russian monarchy went for the volunteer model just after the Romanov took power in 1613 (Bergemann 2019, Chapter 3). If the state police have a high capacity, the state then cares about receiving as much information as possible. The screening of information is not so much of an issue. The coercion model then dominates the volunteer model. Historically, the coercion model seems to have been chosen by many totalitarian regimes in the twentieth century (Nazi Germany or Stalin's USSR) as they took full advantage of the strength of their secret police. Kozlov (1996), for example, highlights how the NKVD, Stalin's secret police, could give, at the very minimum, a cursory look at all the denunciations the authorities received.

Note that we wrote above that most states face a trade-off, but not all states. Indeed, our analysis reveals one particular case when the coercion model leads to a high number of denunciations that also happen to be very informative. This situation arises when the likelihood that one individual's suspicious behaviour is detected by at least one other citizen is relatively high. In this case, many of the numerous denunciations received by the authorities are truthful. In the coercive model, every individual has the incentive to report useful information to the regime whenever they uncover it to maximize their chance of getting the reward promised by the authorities. Non-congruent individuals and neutral citizens lie and falsely denounce only if they do not have anything helpful to report. As the chances of detecting suspicious behaviour become high, the likelihood of false denunciations automatically decreases. The regime obtains the best of both worlds: a large number of denunciations with highly informative content.

This last paragraph implies that authoritarian regimes may want to do more than simply pick the coercion or volunteer model. An authoritarian regime may also want to organize the whole society so that it becomes easy for everyone to observe everybody else. In the next section, we describe a few features of life in a communist regime that can be understood as facilitating information gathering on other members of the society.

A Community for Denunciations

In Stalin's USSR, a private flat was a luxury. Most citizens, for many years, lived in communal apartments. The communal dining hall, the room where many slept together, were not places where one could relax; they were places of constant vigilance, vigilance against yourself (no slip was properly permitted) and vigilance against others (who were they really inviting to their place). Many subjects, especially politics, became taboos. People took the habit of whispering. Children were to be informed on a strict need-to-know basis of fear that their tongues would slip. Figes (2007, Chapter 3) captures this environment where everyone was a suspect to others, a possible denunciator or a suspicious individual, often at the same time. The Soviet communal apartment can be viewed as a system facilitating information gathering and, therefore, valuable denunciations.

A private apartment is not a guarantee of safety. The buildings can still be arranged so as to maximize the chances that individuals can spy on each other. This is the case in China. The denunciation campaign during the Covid-19 lockdown in Shanghai highlighted the role of apartment blocks. A typical apartment block consists of apartment buildings ranging from several to hundreds, with a wall surrounding these buildings with several entrances to the apartment block. The origin of gated communities in today's China dates back to the urbanization process that started with the founding of the People's Republic of China. Prior to the economic reform in 1978, a highly centralized planned economy dominated this process. The work unit (*danwei*), which included state-owned enterprises or other service institutions such as health care, education or research, was the principal entity for both production and distribution in the planned economy. Combining housing, workplace and the provision of social services, the work unit model integrated working and living spaces in close territorial proximity. Members of a work unit resided and worked within gated compounds, fostering a dense network of interpersonal relationships where individuals naturally possessed a significant amount of information about one another. The apartment blocks today where so many people live in Shanghai and other cities in China are the heir of the *danwei*. If one agrees with our theory, these types of gated residential compounds serve more than just productive functions. These settlement patterns in urban China can be viewed as a system to facilitate information gathering and, therefore, useful denunciations.

Life in the countryside is also spent under the watch of others. The USSR is well remembered for its kolkhoz and sovkhoz. These forms of communes, where rural citizens had to pass most of their lives due to the existence of internal passports, were also meant to allow every member to know each other, probably too well. In China, the founding of the People's Republic of China didn't change much of the settlement patterns in rural China. The traditional living conditions of kinship families have been preserved. Large clans founded villages in the first place. Over time, smaller clans migrated into the villages. Most villages nowadays often contain one or two lineages together with four or five loosely defined surname groups. Households within a clan often live closely and frequently interact with one another. Many clans have annual rituals and ceremonies where members come together. They also have lineage halls which serve as a focal point for members to socialize. Like other living quarters, the organization of settlements in the countryside is again meant to facilitate information gathering and, therefore, valuable denunciations.

Our claim here is not that every aspect of life in communist China or USSR should be understood through the prism of our theory. Instead, our theoretical approach highlights additional benefits to the regime from how society's living conditions were organized. These positive externalities for the authorities, we believe, were well understood by the regime which saw no loss in turning citizens against each other.

Conclusion

Denunciations are a critical part of the police state in authoritarian regimes. Historians have reported how they have shaped life in Nazi Germany, USSR, communist China, or even earlier during the Inquisition. Our work offers one of the first formalizations of denunciations in autocracies. We build on the idea that citizens have some information about other members of society and must decide whether to report it to the regime. Some individuals, which we have labelled as congruent, happily play the role assigned to them and report to the police all the suspicious activities they observe. Others, which we refer to as neutral, need to be motivated. Finally, the targets of the regime, those we have called non-congruent, try to avoid falling under the watchful eyes of the authorities. All denunciations are falsifiable in the sense that they do not contain verifiable information, just an indication, true or false, that something is aloof, and the regime must decide which of them to investigate.

We compare two models of denunciations following Bergemann (2019): the volunteer and the coercion models. In the volunteer model, citizens who denounce others receive no reward. This model is associated with a relatively small number of denunciations, as neutral individuals remain silent, and a few false denunciations as only non-congruent citizens sometimes denounce. In the coercion model, citizens receive some benefits for tips that lead to the discovery of non-congruent members of society. This model yields a large number of denunciations, as all individuals report to the police, but also many false denunciations as neutral citizens make reports even when they do not uncover suspicious activities. In general, the autocratic authorities in choosing between volunteering or coercion face a trade-off between the number of denunciations they receive and the informativeness of the reports sent by citizens. We also note that no such trade-off appears when the likelihood of uncovering suspicious actions is high: the coercion model leads to a higher number of denunciations that are more informative than in the volunteer model. Many features of life under communist China or the USSR can then be better understood in this light. Apartments, building blocks and even rural settlements were built in order to allow the gathering of information by citizens on other inhabitants. They were meant, among other things, to facilitate a system of denunciations.

Denunciations, while systematized in authoritarian regimes, are not the monopoly of autocracies. Democracies, as we alluded in the introduction, use them as well. What is the difference between denunciations in democracies and in autocracies? To conclude this chapter, we would like to offer some conjectures. We do not see the main distinction to reside in the use of the volunteer rather than the coercion model. Indeed, democratic authorities often use systems of rewards. Texas recently promised $10,000 to anyone successfully suing a medical practitioner who carries out abortions (The Texas Tribune, Sept. 10 2021). The HM Revenues and Customs in the United Kingdom and the Federal Internal Revenue Services in the United States of America offer rewards for anyone whistleblowing tax fraud. Material benefits are provided to citizens who make denunciations in democracies.

Rather, we see two important differences that radically change how whistleblowing is carried out. The first regards the consequences of failing to denounce someone. Democratic systems do not track who denounces and who does not. Nobody has an incentive to falsely report on a member of society to protect herself or himself against the secret police. To see this, consider the cost of not reporting an abandoned bag in an airport. There is none. Denunciations do not make anyone look good; they are rather looked upon frowningly (to be a snitch is a pejorative label). The second difference is in the philosophy of government. To summarize it very broadly, in democracies, everything which is not forbidden is allowed, whereas everything which is not allowed is forbidden in autocracies. This implies that the range of suspicious activities is much more extensive in autocracies than in democracies. The meaning of non-congruence is also completely different. In other words, the likelihood of detecting unwanted actions and the willingness to uncover "enemies of the state" are both much lower in democracies than in autocracies. Denunciations are marginal in democratic systems because the state does not want to spy on all its citizens. It is only when everyone is a potential enemy of the regime that denunciations become a system of governance and all citizens may become agents of the regime.

References

Bergemann, P. (2019). *Judge Thy Neighbor: Denunciations in the Spanish inquisition, Romanov Russia, and Nazi Germany*. Columbia University Press.

Figes, O. (2007). *The whisperers: Private life in Stalin's Russia*. Palgrave Macmillan.

Fitzpatrick, S. (1999). *Everyday Stalinism: Ordinary life in extraordinary times: Soviet Russia in the 1930s*. Oxford University Press.

Harrison, M. (2015). *One day we will live without fear: Everyday lives under the soviet police state*. Hoover Institution Press.

Kozlov, V. A. (1996). Denunciation and its functions in soviet governance: A study of denunciations and their bureaucratic handling from soviet police archives, 1944-1953. *The Journal of Modern History, 68*(4), 867–898.

Lampert, N. (1985). *Whistle-blowing in the Soviet Union: Complaints and abuses under state socialism*. Springer.

The Guardian. (2022, June 8). China offers citizens cash and 'spiritual rewards' for spying tipoffs. Last accessed: 13 November 2022.

The Reuters. (2022, April 18). COVID-shaming pits neighbor against neighbor in locked-down Shanghai.

The Texas Tribune. (2021, September 10). We annotated Texas' near-total abortion ban. Here's what the law says about enforcement. Last accessed: 13 November 2022.

Weiner, A., & Rahi-Tamm, A. (2012). Getting to know you: The Soviet surveillance system, 1939–57. *Kritika: Explorations in Russian and Eurasian History, 13*(1), 5–45.

Yu, T., & Wolton, S. (2022). *A theory of denunciations* (Working paper).

Dollar Funding Stresses in China

Laura E. Kodres, Leslie Sheng Shen, and Darrell Duffie

The need for US dollar funding during the financial stresses in mid-March 2020, as the COVID pandemic news shocked markets, was evident in a number of countries. Notably, however, China's dollar liquidity needs received little attention. Given China's significant economic and financial linkages to the United States and the rest of the world, financial instability there could have implications for the global economy. Hence, it is useful to develop a deeper understanding of the dollar liquidity needs of Chinese banks and non-financial corporations and to probe whether existing avenues of dollar funding for banks and other firms in China are sufficient in times of stress. This is our objective.

L. E. Kodres
MIT Golub Center for Finance and Policy, Cambridge, MA, USA

L. S. Shen (✉)
MIT Golub Center for Finance and Policy, Cambridge, MA, USA

Federal Reserve Bank of Boston, Boston, MA, USA

D. Duffie
Stanford University, Stanford, CA, USA
e-mail: duffie@stanford.edu

R. Z. Aliber et al. (eds.), *Fault Lines After COVID-19*,
https://doi.org/10.1007/978-3-031-26482-5_7

Warning Signs: Evidence of Dollar Funding Stress in March 2020

Dollar funding stresses abroad are instantly observable through the cross-currency basis (CCB) between the dollar and foreign currencies. For a given currency, this basis is the difference between the interest rate for borrowing dollars directly and the interest rate for borrowing dollars synthetically by combining a foreign currency borrowing with foreign exchange (FX) derivatives. If funding markets are efficient, arbitrage between these two alternative methods for borrowing dollars keeps the basis near zero. When access to dollar funding is stressed, however, the magnitude of a cross-currency basis, relative to the dollar, can become significantly negative because of the balance-sheet constraints of potential arbitrageur banks (Du et al., 2018; Avdjiev et al., 2020; Correa et al., 2020).

For example, in mid-March 2020, the basis between the US dollar and the Korean won became quite negative. Korean banks that had difficulty obtaining dollar funding resorted to borrowing won and converting their won loans into dollar funding with FX derivatives. They were willing to pay synthetic dollar funding costs far above dollar borrowing rates available to global banks with more direct access to dollar funding. The magnitude of the USD/KRW basis was reduced when the Bank of Korea held its first US dollar auction at the end of March following the establishment by the Federal Reserve of a temporary dollar liquidity swap line with the Bank of Korea in mid-March. The Bank of Korea then conducted regular dollar auctions that allowed commercial banks in Korea to source dollar funding at considerably lower interest rates than otherwise available on wholesale markets, though the Bank of Korea's dollar funding rates were still above typical prevailing market rates in non-stressed conditions. This facility expired as of December 31, 2021.

The USD/CNY and USD/CNH bases also became quite negative in March 2020, as shown in Fig. 1, tripling in magnitude to about 110 basis points. (CNY refers to renminbi deposits in onshore Chinese banks, while CNH refers to renminbi deposits in Hong Kong banks.) Compared with a set of advanced economies and emerging market countries whose banks also had large US dollar debt exposures, China was among the countries with the largest negative cross-currency bases in March 2020. The bases for USD/CNY and USD/CNH in March 2020 were more than four standard deviations below their 2019 means, lower than that of any other major foreign currency, as shown in Fig. 2. This is clear evidence that Chinese banks

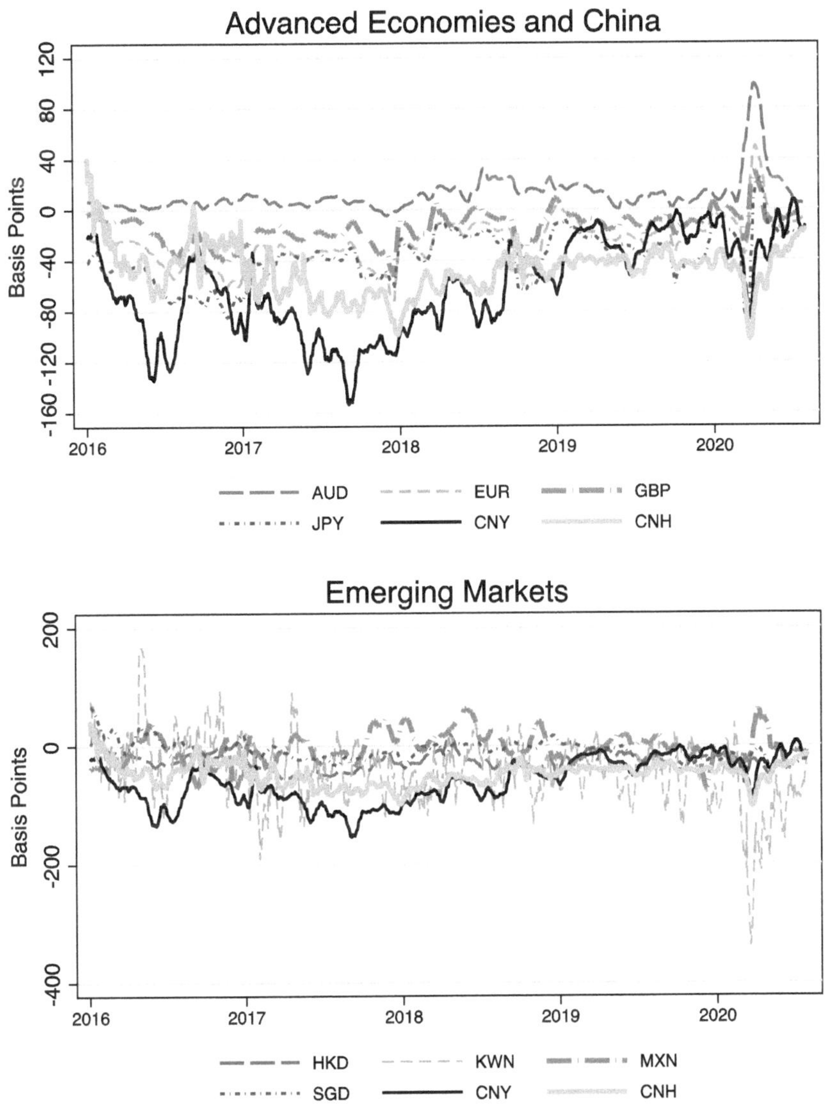

Source: Bloomberg. The figure plots the 10-day moving averages of the three-month Libor-based cross-currency basis.

Fig. 1 Cross-currency bases, including USD/CNY and USD/CNH (**a**) Advanced economies and China and (**b**) Emerging markets

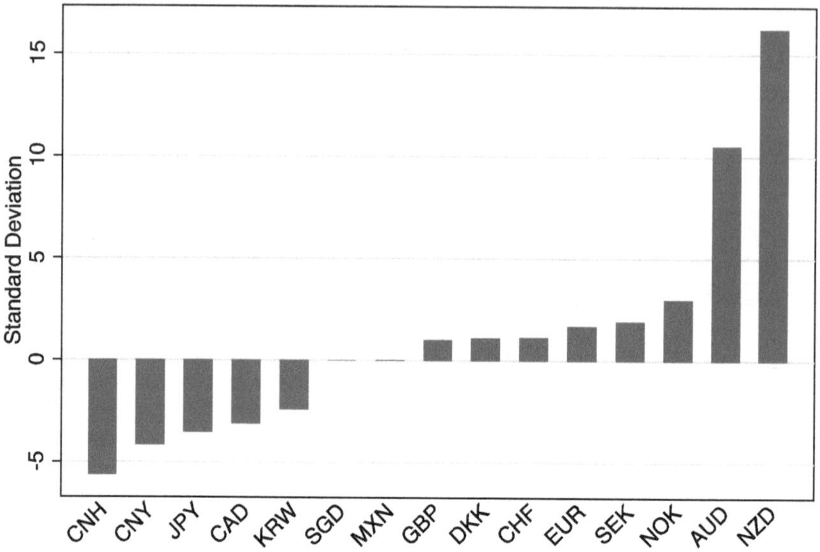

Source: Bloomberg. The figure plots the standard deviations of the three-month Libor-based cross-currency basis during March 17-31, 2020, from the 2019 average.

Fig. 2 Cross-currency basis Z-scores: Covid versus 2019

had significant difficulty obtaining dollar funding at interest rates prevalent in "normal" times. Evidently, China was not an exception with respect to the widening of cross-currency bases, as many dollar-dependent markets, most notably Japan and the euro area, experienced the same form of stress.

As financial market conditions improved alongside the rapid policy responses by central banks around the world, the difficulty of obtaining dollar funding subsided, and cross-currency bases between the US dollar and currencies of some countries with access to the dollar swap lines not only reverted to pre-March levels but even turned positive, suggesting that countries with adequate sources of dollars became dollar providers. This could have benefitted countries, such as China, that had no dollar swap lines, and is consistent with the fact that the USD/CNY and USD/CNH bases did eventually recover, albeit more slowly than some other cross-currency bases.

A cross-currency basis is only one of the available indicators of market stress in dollar funding markets. We next review how dollar borrowing has grown in China's financial and non-financial sectors.

The Extent of China's Dollar-Denominated Debt

Heavy global reliance on dollar-denominated debt has been a phenomenon for some time. Non-US banks commonly issue short-term dollar liabilities and did so even before the run-up to the Global Financial Crisis. Many non-financial firms in foreign countries also finance some of their activities in dollars. The dollar liabilities of non-US banks have now surpassed their 2007 level, as shown in Fig. 3, reproduced from IMF (2019). Aldasoro et al. (2020b) and the IMF (2019) point to the increased extent of dollar borrowing by foreign entities, including non-US banks, non-bank financial institutions, and operating companies. The outstanding quantity of dollar-denominated international debt securities and cross-border loans is 26 percent of global GDP and is 50 percent of outstanding debt securities in all currencies (CGFS, 2020). Factors that support global reliance on dollar funding include complementarity between dollar trade invoicing and the dollar as a safe haven (Gopinath & Stein, 2021), a preference among global investors for dollar-denominated fixed-income assets (Maggiori et al., 2020), and an independent central bank, the Federal Reserve.

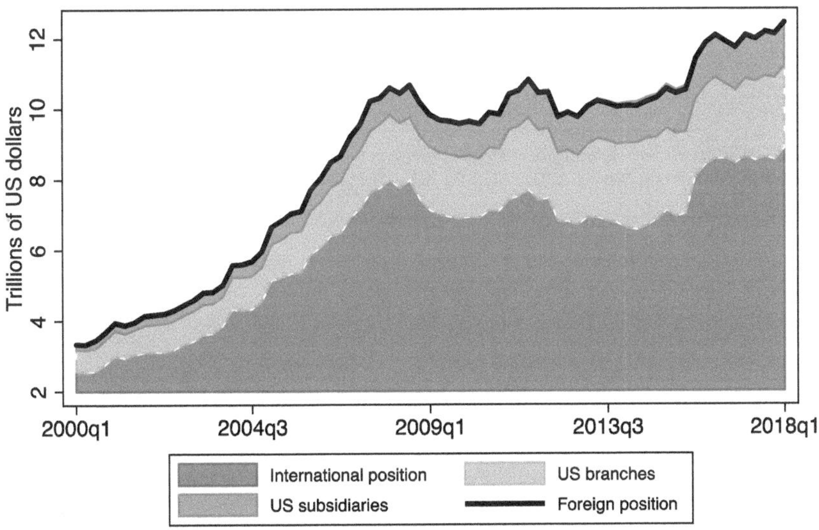

Source: BIS Locational Banking Statistics and IMF Global Financial Stability Report (2019). Foreign position consistents of international position as defined by the BIS plus the positions in US branches and subsidiaries.

Fig. 3 Trends in US dollar activities of non-US banks

China's dollar-denominated debt is primarily issued by its banks, corporations, and local government financing vehicles (LGFVs). The latter two categories are often lumped together (CGFS, 2020).[1] Before providing a rough sense of the magnitudes of dollar borrowing by Chinese entities, we emphasize the incompleteness of the available data. For example, the currency denomination of debt issued by Chinese entities is often not reported or is reported inconsistently. Maturity information is typically difficult to find.

The Dollar Exposures of China's Banks

The Chinese banking system is the largest in the world, with total assets[2] in Q1 2021 of about 330 trillion RMB, or about 325 percent of GDP, which is also high by global standards. Although much of the domestic activities of Chinese banks are denominated in renminbi, the largest banks are highly active abroad and rely most heavily on the US dollar for their foreign borrowing and lending. Banks dominate the Chinese financial system, holding over two-thirds of its assets. They are highly interconnected with other parts of China's financial system and real economy.[3]

According to publicly available BIS banking data, as of Q3 2021, internationally active reporting banks in China (which include a small proportion of non-Chinese banks with affiliates in China) have cross-border liabilities amounting to $1563 billion, of which $586 billion (or 37 percent) is dollar-denominated.[4] However, these same banks have $1057 billion in cross-border dollar-denominated assets, implying a large dollar funding gap. The BIS data cover total cross-border assets and liabilities in a given currency without a sub-breakdown for maturity. According to

[1] Local government financing vehicles (LGFVs) are semi-independent arms of subnational governments used to raise money for local governments to develop infrastructure projects. Since subnational governments are not permitted to borrow without central government approval, LGFVs have been a common "off-budget" solution—borrowing money that could be paid off by selling land near the infrastructure project, which was expected to appreciate by the time the debt was due.

[2] Source: China Banking and Insurance Regulatory Commission.

[3] Source: IMF (2017).

[4] See BIS Locational Banking Statistics, Table A5. https://stats.bis.org/statx/srs/table/a5?c=CN & f=pdf

public BIS data,[5] the on-balance sheet dollar funding gap of $471 billion represents about 20 percent of China's total external debt.

Typically, a dollar funding gap is associated with a reliance on short-term dollar liabilities to fund long-term dollar assets, representing a potential source of financial instability (Aldasoro et al., 2020b; International Monetary Fund, 2019; Iida et al., 2018; McGuire & von Peter, 2009). China's bank supervisors monitor mismatches between assets and liabilities in major foreign currencies.[6] Chinese banks likely cover some of their large dollar funding gap with derivatives such as currency forwards and swaps. The total of direct dollar liabilities and synthetic dollar liabilities achieved in derivatives markets represents a significant rollover risk that becomes apparent during stress periods through an elevated cross-currency basis, as occurred in March 2020.

Comparing with funding gaps in other countries, publicly available BIS data suggest that the dollar funding gap for China's banks is relatively large, in line with those of Japanese and Canadian BIS-reporting banks and is increasing. Banks in countries with negative gaps, such as those of Australia, France, and the United Kingdom, as well as US banks themselves, would in principle be able to provide dollar funding to China's banks. Figure 4 shows the dollar funding gaps by country, relying on publicly available BIS data. However, data for most countries include local positions (domestic lending and borrowing in US dollars), whereas China does not report these domestic exposures to the BIS. Moreover, the publicly available BIS data do not include bilateral relationships among reporting entities on a national basis (including the extent to which Chinese banks lend to each other in dollars within China), which could affect the overall reported quantities for China. Based on confidential underlying data, the analysis of Aldasoro et al. (2020b) shows that combined funding gap of the four largest Chinese banks moved from positive to negative from 2016 to 2018, which suggests they had more dollar liabilities than dollar assets—a situation that could be present even now. This piece of evidence, taken together with the publicly available BIS data, implies that these four banks could help to fund the (larger) funding gaps of the other

[5] Again, see BIS Locational Banking Statistics, Table A5.

[6] The Liquidity Risk Rules, Article 40 requires CBIRC to regularly analyze and monitor the liquidity risk of banks and the banking system from the perspective of liquidity risk profile in significant currencies. Additionally, Article 44 requires the CBIRC to decide whether to monitor the liquidity risk in each significant currency individually, according to the size of foreign exchange business, mismatches in currencies, and market influence of banks. (IMF Financial Sector Assessment Program, Basel Core Principles Assessment, p. 211.)

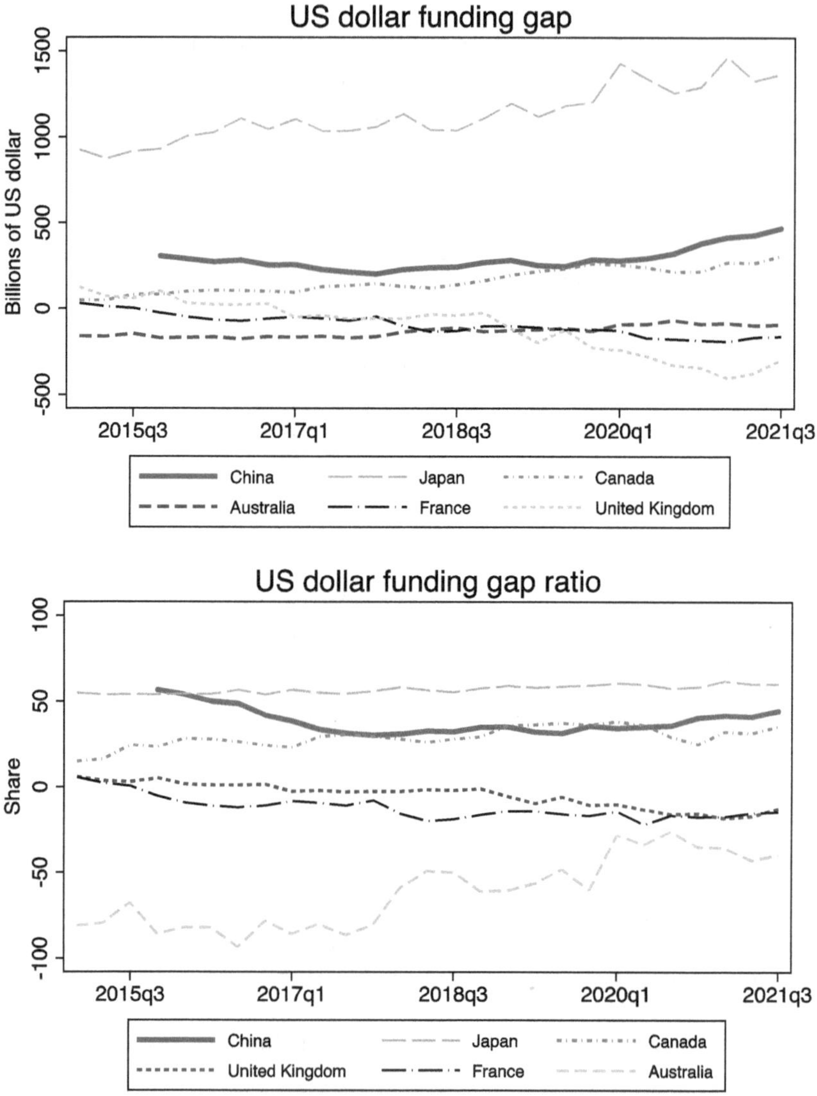

Source: BIS Locational Banking Statistics. US dollar funding gap ratio is defined as the difference between USD assets and USD liabilities, expressed as a ratio of USD assets.

Fig. 4 US dollar funding gaps

Chinese banks. It is possible, however, that the public BIS data provide an inaccurate portrayal of net Chinese bank exposures or both.[7]

BIS debt securities statistics cover debt issued by Chinese banks, in terms of both outstanding amounts and net flows. International debt outstanding issued by Chinese banks amounted to $80.8 billion out of the $229.6 billion total international debt outstanding as of Q2 2021, some 35 percent. Of the international debt outstanding, $63.5 billion (79 percent) is dollar-denominated. Of the total bank debt, the original maturity over one year (of the amount outstanding) was 93 percent. Without more maturity information, we are unable to deduce the exact extent of liquidity or rollover risk, but the dollar proportions indicate that these risks could be large. The average maturity of bank debt tends to be relatively short in comparison with other non-bank corporate debt.

Chinese banks also have dollar liquidity and credit exposures through their lending to borrowers in countries involved in the Belt and Road Initiative (BRI). Horn et al. (2021) estimate that around 75 percent of BRI loans are denominated in US dollars and are provided by China's development banks and four largest commercial banks, which are predominantly state-owned. Updated Aid Data suggest that between 2000 and 2017, $1.6 trillion of dollar-denominated loans and grants (in 2017 constant dollars) were provided to BRI countries—90.6 percent of the total (Malik et al., 2021). These Chinese lenders typically require the borrower to deposit the loan proceeds in the lender's bank. Because of this, the balance sheets of these Chinese banks may not accurately reflect the associated net credit and liquidity exposures. However, since the four large commercial Chinese banks have more than enough liabilities to cover their assets, they appear to avoid the problem of needing to roll over their liabilities. These liabilities could potentially be in the form of stable dollar deposits since they are connected to the long-term infrastructure projects of their borrowers rather than runnable short-term debt. Unfortunately, neither the maturity nor creditor composition of the liabilities is evident in the reports. On the other hand, the balance sheet of one of the largest foreign currency lenders, the China Development Bank, a government-owned entity, *does* appear to have significant dollar (net) exposures, amounting to $100 billion in 2020, according to its annual report. The takeaway is that the liquidity risk may be somewhat less for the four commercial BRI-reporting banks, though it is impossible to precisely gauge

[7] See footnote 5 from Aldasoro et al. (2020b).

the liquidity risk from public data. (There is also likely to be some credit risk associated with the currency risk facing BRI borrowers.)

The Dollar Exposures of China's Non-financial Firms

At the end of 2019, Chinese non-financial firms had $590 billion in outstanding US dollar-denominated bonds, accounting for about 36 percent of all dollar bonds issued by emerging market economies (CGFS, 2020). Forty percent, or $236 billion, is attributed to bonds issued by Chinese property developers and LGFVs, entities that have no natural dollar-based revenues (CGFS, 2020). This suggests a mismatch that would often need to be hedged in FX derivatives markets or rolled over. The $590 billion in outstanding offshore bond issues of Chinese corporations (including LGFVs) accounted for approximately 29 percent of China's total external debt of $2.1 trillion at the time.[8]

In 2020, it was estimated that between 2019 through 2024, a total of $488 billion US dollar bonds issued by Chinese firms were to be extinguished or rolled over with new funding (CGFS, 2020). Among the most stressed of the associated borrowers are property developers, who have been hit by regulatory leverage constraints.[9] As of November 2021, they were facing around $41.5 billion in US dollar liabilities maturing in 2022 alone (Bloomberg).[10] Defaults on dollar-denominated debt in the fall of 2021 by Evergrande, the largest property developer in China, suggest that rollovers may be difficult if lenders observe further weaknesses in this sector.

In sum, non-financial Chinese corporates have a large proportion of the outstanding dollar bonds issued internationally from emerging-market countries. The dollar amounts of these bonds are large. Moreover, a large proportion of these bonds have relatively short maturities (requiring rollover by 2024) and are obligations of entities that have no natural source of dollar income.

[8] Source: World Bank, Joint External Debt Hub.

[9] On February 28, 2021, for example, the *Financial Times*(FT) reported the default of a $530 million bond issued by China Fortune Land Development. Specifically, the FT reported that "The Chinese government outlined a plan in August [2020] aimed at reducing leverage according to three metrics—the so-called three red lines. Analysts have suggested the guidelines are directly affecting primarily the 12 biggest developers."

[10] Estimated from Bloomberg News, "China's Developers Face $1.3 Billion in December Bond Payments, November 28, 2021.

While the information that we have provided about dollar-based exposures of Chinese entities is far from complete, we believe that the available data imply that China has significant dollar exposures that could strain the ability of Chinese banks and corporations to source sufficient dollar fund ing during a period of stress.

China's US Dollar Exposures Are Growing

Although we are unable to obtain an all-in picture of dollar funding exposures in China, given the incomplete available information, the trend toward greater US dollar borrowing and lending by Chinese entities is unmistakable. Moreover, this increase in dollar exposures has been faster in China than in the rest of the world. China is special, in this way, partly because of the faster growth in demand for credit by Chinese firms, relative to the rest of the world, and partly because of the expansion of the Belt and Road Initiative, under which lending in dollars is preferred by both China's lenders and by BRI borrowers.

Further evidence of China's growing use of dollar funding is the expanding reliance of Chinese entities on foreign exchange swaps. The increased use of derivatives, and especially foreign exchange swaps (which underlie the cross-currency basis), is evident from the data on derivatives turnover in BIS Triennial Surveys. Figure 5 shows increasing net notional volumes of trade of FX swaps by entities in China.[11]

Spillovers from China

Dollar funding stress in China could spill over to the rest of the world through several channels. A lack of funding in US dollars for Chinese non-financial corporates and financial intermediaries could result in difficulties in the ability of these firms to roll over dollar-denominated debt, potentially causing them to default to their lenders, which include US banks and banks to which US banks have exposure. In turn, defaults or distress of Chinese non-financial corporates or financial-sector firms could lead to concerns that other similarly positioned institutions, both in China and in other countries with dollar exposures, would also default.

[11] China is only 2.6 percent of all FX swap turnover as of 2019. The proportion of dollar-based FX swaps in the global FX swaps market is 90 percent: for China it is 99 percent.

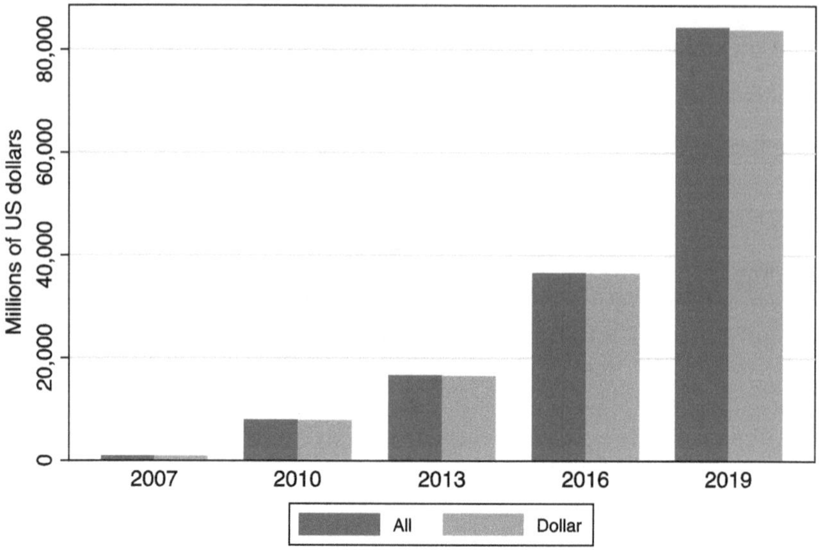

Source: BIS Triennial Central Bank Survey of Foreign Exchange and Over-the-counter (OTC) Derivatives Markets.

Fig. 5 FX swap turnover by entities in China (net-gross basis, average daily volume)

A recent example is contagion risk from the debt troubles of China Evergrande, a large Chinese real estate developer. Such financial disruptions can (and have) caused dollar-denominated corporate credit spreads to widen, affecting other asset classes, including those of US-based high-yield debt. For instance, the rising default risk of Evergrande induced significant widenings of bond spreads in connected countries in Asia and in the US high-yield bond market.[12] Aside from detrimental effects on the cost of debt financing, dollar funding stress in China could induce fire sales of dollar-denominated assets such as US Treasuries and a contraction

[12] The weaknesses discovered in Evergrande, a Chinese real estate developer, on September 14, 2021 and its default on its dollar-denominated debt caused debt yield spreads to increase by 9.5 percent in South East Asian debt markets and by 3.9 percent on US high-yield debt. For instance, correlation between the EM Asian corporate bond index and the US high-yield index increased from -0.13 from January 1, 2021 to September 14, 2021 to 0.57 during the period of distress in September. Source: ICE-BofA Indices.

in the quantity of credit in some countries in which Chinese banks are active lenders. These financial stresses could trigger or exacerbate a regional or global recession, among other knock-on impacts to the economies of many connected countries. Surges in sales of US Treasuries can also cause dysfunctionality in the secondary market for Treasuries, as occurred in March–April 2020 after the World Health Organization declared COVID to be global pandemic.

China's direct financial linkages with the rest of the world have increased in recent years, even though they are more limited than what would be implied by the size of its economy, in large part due to its gradual approach to a loosening of capital controls. Among the advanced economies, Japan and the European Union have the greatest financial exposure to China. Direct linkages between China and the United States have been growing, as US mutual fund exposures to China have increased through both equity and debt.[13] With such increased investor exposure to Chinese financial markets, investors in global bond and equity mutual funds could experience a relatively rapid decline in their wealth after a fall in Chinese debt and equity prices. Another link, in the opposite direction, is the significant amount of US Treasuries held in China's foreign exchange reserves.

Despite the nascent direct linkages, the transmission of financial shocks to date has been experienced through changes in market sentiment and the repricing of risks. For instance, in August 2015 and January 2016, rapid declines in the Chinese stock market of 26.7 percent and 18.8 percent were felt in the United States, with declines in the S & P 500 over the same period of 7.7 percent and 8.8 percent, respectively. Recent estimates by the OECD researchers Pain and Rusticelli (2022) suggest that a slowdown in China induced by stresses in the property development sector would affect global equity markets, partly over uncertainty surrounding financial conditions, and cause a repricing of risks. The OECD global economic model suggests that the largest financial impact would fall on Japan, followed by the United States and then the European Union. Perhaps surprisingly, their model suggests that the financial impact for the United States would be higher than the trade and supply shock components. Generalized contagion through global financial markets could also impact countries that maintain hubs for financial markets of all types. For instance,

[13] Of the top-ten Exchange Traded Fund flow recipients in 2021, iSHARES Core MSCI Emerging Market EFT, has large equity exposures to greater China—26 percent to Hong Kong, 15 percent to Taiwan, and 5 percent to mainland China—adding up to 46 percent.

London, New York, Singapore and Hong Kong Special Administrative Region (SAR) account for 75 percent of all OTC foreign exchange transactions in 2019.[14]

Shocks to the Chinese real economy (the world's second largest) could also find their way to a number of advanced and emerging market countries. Japan and Southeast Asia would likely suffer the most given their strong trade and supply chain links with China. The United States, however, would not be immune, given that China is its largest trading partner—larger than either Mexico or Canada. US imports from China amounted to $435.5 billion in 2020—about 18.6 percent of total US imports—and these imports are invoiced and financed predominantly in US dollars.[15] Difficulties in obtaining dollar liquidity for Chinese importers could result in supply-chain delays and disruptions, including a need for importers to find other suppliers, disrupting consumer goods and other intermediate inputs sourced from China.

Potential Solutions to a Lack of US Dollar Funding for China

While there are many motivations for issuing dollar-denominated debt, as noted in Sec. II, excessive build-ups of dollar funding to Chinese corporations and financial institutions are concerning whenever stressful conditions ensue. Recognizing its institutions' large and growing exposures to US dollars, Chinese authorities have taken mitigating measures, but their effectiveness remains unclear, especially in the near term. There are several existing avenues through which China could obtain US dollar funding on short notice; however, the reliability of these avenues is uncertain.

Actions by Chinese Authorities

Chinese banks are generally required to maintain mostly balanced positions of foreign currency-denominated assets and liabilities (including off-balance sheet derivatives positions). However, even if overall exposures are close to zero, maturity mismatches, whereby short-term dollar liabilities need to be rolled over, are problematic. The new Basel III requirements

[14] The BIS Triennial Central Bank Survey of Foreign Exchange and Over-the-counter (OTC) Derivatives Markets in 2019. Table D11.6.

[15] IMF's Direction of Trade Statistics.

(specifically, the Net Stable Funding Ratio) attempt to limit excessively risky maturity mismatches in each currency. Although China has officially implemented this standard to counter excessive mismatch risk, maturity mismatches are an integral part of a typical bank's business model.

Aside from regulations aimed at domestic banks, Chinese authorities are increasingly restricting debt issuance by non-financial corporations in the property sector and by LGFVs.[16] Lowering overall debt issuance of non-financial corporations and LGFVs could reduce dollar exposures, but only if dollar-denominated debt is reduced proportionately. Regulations now state that new loans are not to be used to rollover existing debt, so liquidity issues may arise before overall debt levels fall to less risky levels.[17] A proposed nationwide property tax on homeownership may help wean local governments from land transfer fees and help reduce the impetus for LGFVs to issue debt on behalf of local governments.[18] However, few countries have accomplished the goal of insulating their non-financial corporations from the risks of foreign-currency-denominated debt, in part due to incentives to move funding activities abroad to circumvent such rules. Nonetheless, China's ability to control large portions of its economy may provide it with the tools to do so.

China's Foreign Exchange Reserves

An often-used measure of a country's ability to withstand liquidity stress is the quantity of its official foreign exchange reserves. The amount of dollar-denominated reserves held by China's State Administration of Foreign Exchange (SAFE), an entity within the People's Bank of China (PBOC), is a closely guarded secret. As of the end of August 2022, SAFE

[16] The "three red lines" for property companies refer to the regulations of the financing and debt levels of property developers, including (1) liability-to-asset ratio (excluding advance receipts) of less than 70 percent, (2) net debt-to-equity ratio of less than 100 percent, and (3) cash-to-short-term debt ratio of more than 100 percent. Authorities have limited local governments' ability to raise off-balance-sheet financing to backstop local government-owned entities (IMF 2021). In July 2021, the authorities ordered banks and insurers to refrain from providing fresh liquidity to LGFV platforms that enjoy implicit guarantees from local governments.

[17] See Ministry of Finance statement "Notice on Issuing the Operational Guidelines for Adjusting the Use of Local Government Special Bonds" at http://yss.mof.gov.cn/zhuantilanmu/dfzgl/zcfg/202111/t20211110_3764807.htm

[18] Huang, T, "China's looming property crisis threatens economic stability," Petersen Institute, January 12, 2022.

reported total foreign exchange reserves of $3.055 trillion (down from $3.8 trillion in 2013), which is a four-year low. Still, SAFE has the world's largest foreign exchange reserves, nearly $1.8 trillion dollars more than Japan's reserves, the world's second largest. IMF data show that, in aggregate, 59.2 percent of all central banks' FX reserves are dollar-denominated. If this percentage is applied to China, then a rough estimate of $1.8 trillion of US dollar-denominated assets would have been available as of August 2022 as a potential source of liquidity, assuming that in a stressful event SAFE would have been willing to sell or obtain dollar financing from these assets (perhaps through the Fed's FIMA Repo Facility, discussed below) and assuming that these dollar assets are not already encumbered.

As another way to estimate China's holdings of US dollar bonds, the US Treasury Department's Treasury International Capital (TIC) System publishes data covering the holdings of various US dollar-denominated securities by country, including total holdings of long-term securities (US Treasuries, Agencies,[19] debt, and equities). As of June 2022, Chinese private and official sector investors (which include SAFE) together held $1.5 trillion of these long-term US securities, of which $0.97 trillion are long-term US Treasuries and $244 billion are US Agency securities.

In principle, if China's banks or corporates were to experience dollar funding stresses, SAFE could sell or finance some of its dollar-denominated assets, so that the PBOC could lend the dollar proceeds to China's banks, which could in turn lend dollars to firms in China. In the month of March 2020, the quantity of Treasuries owned by foreign official sector owners that were custodied by the Federal Reserve Bank of New York fell by slightly over $100 billion, suggesting that some central banks liquidated their Treasuries, perhaps in part to alleviate dollar stresses in their banking systems. TIC data show that China's total holdings of US Treasuries declined by only $20 billion between February and April 2020, indirectly suggesting that SAFE was not much of a source of dollar funding relief, at least via these holdings. Dollar assets are presumably held by China's official sector and banks outside the United States, so it is possible that China provided dollar liquidity obtained from these other locations.

Although funding relief was not apparent in the turmoil of 2020, more recent developments suggest otherwise. Between January and July 2022, while the renminbi fell against the US dollar by around 6 percent, which

[19] These include bonds issued by Freddie Mac, Fannie Mae, and Ginnie Mae.

has made it increasingly expensive for Chinese property developers to meet their dollar obligations, China's holdings of US Treasuries dropped by $98 billion (9.2 percent).[20] This might suggest the indirect use of FX reserves. Chinese authorities have also used other tactics to allow banks to provide dollar funding to property developers, including a lowering of the foreign exchange reserve ratio from 9 percent in May 2022 to 6 percent in September 2022 and managing a slow but steady alteration of the official fixing of the midpoint of the USD/CNY FX range. These actions suggest that some gradual, mostly indirect, interventions have been implemented to slow the depreciation of the renminbi and soften the blow to property developers without directly parting with FX reserves.

FX reserves serve other purposes, including the management of exchange rates and the need to pay for imports. In the past, SAFE has been willing to part with foreign exchange reserves for various purposes. In recent years, SAFE has reduced the degree to which it uses its reserves to support the price of the renminbi. The number of months of import coverage is a common benchmark of FX reserve sufficiency. As of the end of 2021, SAFE reserves covered 13.3 months of China's imports, which would be considered adequate by international standards. On the other hand, relative to broad money (M2), SAFE's FX reserves are below a generic safety threshold of the IMF. This measure considers how reserves could be used to cover a domestic banking deposit outflow from China. Taking into account China's use of capital flow measures, including limitations on capital outflows, the IMF judges its reserves to be adequate.

It is far from obvious that China would wish to suddenly liquidate a large amount of its dollar-denominated official reserves to cover a stressful dollar funding gap in China's banking and corporate sector. A significant rapid sale of dollar assets would cause price-impact losses, reducing both the proceeds of the sale as well as the mark-to-market valuation of the remaining reserves. Indeed, the lack of functionality of the US Treasury market during the March 2020 "dash for cash" suggests a very real risk that liquidation of US Treasury holdings could be detrimental to large holders' balance sheets.[21] Moreover, the associated reduction in dollar-denominated FX reserves would leave China more exposed to future stresses.

[20] As of September 20, the renminbi was down 10.6 percent against the US dollar.
[21] See G30 Working Group on Treasury Market Liquidity (2021).

The FIMA Repo Facility

Rather than liquidating US Treasuries outright when domestic borrowers, including banks, face stressed conditions for the acquisition of dollars, a central bank could potentially obtain dollar financing in exchange for its Treasuries through the Fed's new repurchase agreement facility for foreign and international monetary authorities, the FIMA Repo Facility. Using this facility, a central bank with a custodial account at the Federal Reserve Bank of New York can obtain repo financing for securities held in its custodial account. The interest rate for this facility is 25 basis points, as of April 2022, with a per-counterparty limit of $60 billion. The identities of account holders are confidential. Access to this facility is at the discretion of the Fed, which has the right to approve or deny requests when they are made.[22] Assuming that the PBOC has such an account, it could post its Treasuries and Agencies as collateral and obtain US dollar funding, which could be on-lent to banks in China.

To date, the *FIMA Repo* Facility, which was established as a temporary facility on March 31, 2020, before becoming a standing facility on July 27, 2021, has not been drawn on significantly. In the spring of 2020, the largest use of FIMA occurred during the week of May 13, with an uptake of *$1.4 billion, followed by two other uses (in the weeks ending July 1, 2020, and September 30, 2020, of about $1 billion each)*. This facility did not play a significant dollar funding role during the crucial March–May 2020 period of dollar funding stress, perhaps because the stresses in market conditions were already dissipating by the time that FIMA was set up. Nevertheless, the FIMA Repo Facility potentially can be an effective avenue for providing dollar funding to the PBOC, and thus to China's banks, during a dollar liquidity crunch.

Other Countries' Swap Lines

Another potential avenue for dollar funding is through Chinese banks with affiliates in other countries that have more abundant dollar funding, including through Fed central bank swap lines. Central banks with unlimited Fed swap lines include the ECB and those of Canada, Japan, Switzerland, and

[22] See https://www.federalreserve.gov/newsevents/pressreleases/fima-repo-facility-faqs.htm and https://www.federalreserve.gov/monetarypolicy/files/FOMC_StandingFIMARepoResolution.pdf

the United Kingdom, although Canada has not used the facility.[23] The central banks of these countries would need to accept the credit risk of the Chinese bank affiliates in their jurisdictions if they were to supply dollar funding to them. The short-term debt ratings of the four largest Chinese banks are all P-1, F1+, and A-1 from Moody's, Fitch, and S & P, respectively. We believe that it's natural to view these four giants, mostly state-owned banks, as "too big to fail," and also too affiliated with the government of China to be allowed to fail, except in the most extreme scenarios. Most central banks of countries that can provide local dollar funding explicitly state that they would only lend swap-related dollars to banks that are licensed in their countries or that have formal accounts with the respective central banks. Several Chinese commercial and wholesale banks have this central-bank access, through which dollar funding could be provided.

Chiang Mai Initiative Multilateralization

After the Asian Crisis of 1998, the ASEAN+3 countries' Chiang Mai Initiative provided for a common swap pool, the Chiang Mai Initiative Multilateralization (CMIM). Conceptually, this pool is meant to be drawn when any member country has insufficient foreign exchange reserves to support its currency or to meet capital outflows.[24] Japan and China are the largest contributors of FX reserves to CMIM, with much lower amounts committed by the other ASEAN+3 countries. A likely implication is that Japan and China would be the suppliers of liquidity for the other countries. The facility has been sized with this in mind, at only $240 billion. However, with Japan and China each having much greater US dollar funding needs than the other members combined (see Fig. 4), at this point it would be difficult for this facility to fulfil its formal mandate to provide reserves for any member country. Indeed, some of the other member

[23]See Goldberg et al. (2012), Bahaj & Reis (2020a, b), and McCauley & Schenk (2020) for overviews and analyses of central bank swap lines. See Goldberg and Ravazzolo (2021) for an evaluation of the effectiveness of the Fed swap lines during the stress period of 2020. See Aldasoro et al. (2020a) for an analysis of the link between these swap lines and global bank flows.

[24]The CMIM has been further reinforced since 2014: (i) the size has been doubled to USD240 billion; (ii) the IMF de-linked portion has been raised to 30 percent of each member's quota; (iii) the maturity and supporting period has been extended; and (iv) a crisis prevention facility by the name of CMIM Precautionary Line (CMIM-PL) has been introduced.

countries in the region who could have used the CMIM in March 2020 preferred to tap the IMF's liquidity facility rather than use the CMIM facility, which has yet to be accessed.

Avenues Through Hong Kong SAR

As the financial center closest to mainland China, Hong Kong SAR has served as a conduit for financial flows into and out of mainland China. Although the Hong Kong Monetary Authority (HKMA) does not have a dedicated swap line with the Fed, it has facilitated dollar flows between international financial markets and China through its dollar swap facility and could potentially keep some amount of dollars flowing into China. On July 30, 2021, the HKMA decided to convert its existing temporary US Dollar Liquidity Facility into a standing arrangement, following the announcement that the Fed converted its temporary FIMA Repo Facility into a standing arrangement on July 28, 2021. The HKMA offers a collateralized dollar liquidity facility of $10 billion to its licensed banks, which include several mainland Chinese banks, on the same terms as the FIMA Repo Facility.[25] The HKMA maintains the discretion to scale back or deny bids of the licensed banks.

The Ability to Post Chinese Bonds as Collateral Internationally

Owners of bonds issued by entities in China could in principle obtain secured dollar financing by posting those bonds internationally as collateral. Currently, however, international central securities depositories do not have arrangements that would allow this. In April 2021, BNY Mellon announced that its triparty platform now accepts Chinese bonds as collateral, when pledged through Hong Kong's Bond Connect.[26] In a separate report,[27] the CEO of BNY Mellon Government Securities stated that

[25] Details about the extension and functioning of HKMA's collateralized dollar liquidity facility can be found at https://www.hkma.gov.hk/eng/news-and-media/press-releases/2021/07/20210730-3/

[26] BNY Mellon (2021) wrote: "In the first trade, which printed last week, a broker-dealer client was able to collateralize Chinese government securities through BNY Mellon's triparty solution. Under the transaction, BNY Mellon accessed the client's bonds, which were under custody at HSBC, and reflected the assets in BNY Mellon triparty, enabling the client to use the collateral for financing and other purposes."

[27] See "Chinese govies step closer to collateral acceptability," *Findesk*, July 7, 2021.

"The Chinese bond market is now the second largest in the world, with overseas investors balances of Chinese assets ever growing. Providing a solution supporting assets to be used as collateral within the secondary market is critical in enabling liquidity, enhancing financial stability and reducing funding risk."

Although bonds denominated in CNY would typically be assigned a substantial haircut, an increasing ability to pledge China bonds globally would, nevertheless, open the door to a substantial new potential source of dollar funding for banks, asset managers, or securities dealers in China that hold unencumbered high-quality CNY-denominated bonds, such as Chinese government securities.

Conclusion

We have documented that China's potential needs for US dollar funding during periods of stress are large. China's use of relatively short-term dollar funding has been increasing and seems likely to continue to grow. In March 2020, pandemic-induced turmoil in global dollar funding markets, as reflected in violations of covered interest parity, afflicted a number of countries relying on large dollar rollovers. The dislocations in dollar funding for Chinese financial institutions seem to have been large, judging from the data that we have presented from the cross-currency bases for USD/CNY and USD/CNH.

During future periods of stress in dollar funding markets, China might have difficulty in quickly sourcing a sufficient quantity of dollar financing to control liquidity stresses on its financial institutions and corporate sector, which could lead to global spillovers.

After noting some of the solutions that the Chinese authorities are attempting to implement to mitigate dollar exposures, we documented some avenues for dollar funding to Chinese entities during stress periods. Among these, the FIMA Repo facility (to the extent available to the PBOC) may turn out to be effective, in terms of size and immediacy, assuming that China's FX reserves include a large quantity of US government securities that are custodied at the Federal Reserve Bank of New York. FIMA and central bank swap lines are partial substitutes for each other—neither is likely to cover all needs, and both offer significant potential dollar funding to central banks facing a dollar funding stress event.

In any case, there is a risk of disruption to dollar funding markets arising from a potentially large and sudden need for China's banks and corporates to roll over dollar-denominated debts. Absent a means of rapidly and efficiently dealing with these large dollar funding stresses, the adverse impacts on China's financial stability and economic growth could be substantial and could spill over to the rest of the world.

References

Aldasoro, I., Cabanilla, C., Disyatat, P., Ehlers, T., McGuire, P., & von Peter, G. (2020a). Central bank swap lines and cross border bank flows. *BIS Bulletin,* Number 34, December.

Aldasoro, I., Ehlers, T., McGuire, P., & von Peter, G. (2020b). Global banks' dollar funding needs and central bank swap lines. *BIS Bulletin,* Number 27, July.

Avdjiev, S, Eren, E., & McGuire, P. (2020). Dollar funding costs during the Covid-19 crisis through the lens of the FX swap market. *BIS Bulletin*, Number 1.

Bahaj, S., & Reis, R. (2020a). Central bank swap lines during the Covid-19 pandemic. *Covid Economics, 2*, 1–12.

Bahaj, S., & Reis, R. (2020b). Central bank swap lines: Evidence on the effect of the lender of last resort. The Review of Economic Studies. Forthcoming.

BNY Mellon. (2021). BNY Mellon Triparty Now Accepts Chinese Bonds as Collateral, Press release, April 12, 2021.

Committee on the Global Financial System (CGFS). 2020. US dollar funding: an international perspective. CGFS Papers Number 65.

Correa, R., Du, W., & Liao, G. (2020). *U.S. banks and global liquidity* (Working Paper). Federal Reserve Board and University of Chicago.

Du, W., Tepper, A., & Verdelhan, A. (2018). Deviations from covered interest rate parity. *The Journal of Finance, 73*(3), 915–957.

G30 Working Group on Treasury Market Liquidity (2021). U.S. treasury markets: steps toward increased resilience, Group of 30, Washington, DC, July.

Goldberg, L., & Ravazzolo, F. (2021). *The Fed's international dollar liquidity facilities: New evidence on effects.* Federal Reserve Bank of New York, Staff Reports No. 997, December.

Goldberg, L., Kennedy, C., & Miu, J. (2011). *Central bank dollar swap lines and overseas dollar funding costs.* Economic Policy Review, Federal Reserve Bank of New York, 3–20.

Gopinath, G., & Stein, J. (2021). Banking, trade and the making of a dominant currency. *The Quarterly Journal of Economics, 136*(2), 783–830.

Horn, S., Reinhart, C., & Trebesch, C. (2021). China's overseas lending. *Journal of International Economics, 133*(November), 103539.

Iida, T., Takeshi, K., & Sudo, N. (2018). Deviations from covered interest rate parity and the Dollar funding of global Bank. *International Journal of Central Banking, 14*(4), 275–325.

International Monetary Fund (IMF). (2017). People's Republic of China: Financial System Stability Assessment, December 2017, IMF Country Report No 17/358, Washington, DC.

International Monetary Fund (IMF). (2019). Banks' dollar funding: A source of vulnerability. In Chapter 5 in the *Global financial stability report*. Washington DC.

International Monetary Fund (IMF). (2021). Global Financial Stability Overview: A Delicate Balance, Chapter 1 in the *Global Financial Stability Report*, Washington DC.

Maggiori, M., Neiman, B., & Schreger, J. (2020). International currencies and capital allocation. *Journal of Political Economy, 128*(6), 2019–2066.

Malik, A., Parks, B., Russell, B., Lin, J., Walsh, K., Solomon, K., Zhang, S., Elston, T., & Goodman, S. (2021). *Banking on the Belt and Road: Insights from a new global dataset of 13,427 Chinese development projects*. AidData at William & Mary.

McCauley, R., & Schenk, C. (2020, April). *Central bank swaps then and now: Swaps and dollar liquidity in the 1960s* (BIS working paper 851).

McGuire, P., & von Peter, G. (2009, March). The US dollar shortage in global banking. *BIS Quarterly Review*, 47–63.

Pain, N., & Rusticelli, E. (2022, January 14). A sharp slowdown in China's property markets would damp global growth. *Ecoscope*, OECD.

Laura Kodres is a private consultant and affiliated with the Golub Center for Finance and Policy at the Sloan School of Management, Massachusetts Institute of Technology. Leslie Sheng Shen is a Senior Financial Economist at the Federal Reserve Bank of Boston and a visiting scholar at the Golub Center for Finance and Policy at the Sloan School of Management, Massachusetts Institute of Technology. Darrell Duffie is the Adams Distinguished Professor of Management and Professor of Finance at the Graduate School of Business, Stanford University, CDI Research Fellow, and Resident Scholar at the Federal Reserve Bank of New York. The views expressed here are strictly those of the authors and do not necessarily represent the views of the Federal Reserve Bank of Boston, the Federal Reserve Bank of New York, or the Federal Reserve System. We are grateful for conversations with Adolfo Barajas, Sally Davies, Patrick Hess, Patrick McGuire, Li Lian Ong, Swapan-Kumar Pradhan, Goetz von Peter, Manmohan Singh, Tao Sun, and Jason Wu.

PART III

Ukraine

Economic Consequences of Global Tensions

Ron Smith

Introduction

There are many sources of global tensions and this chapter will focus on geopolitical shocks, such as Russia's February 2022 invasion of Ukraine, with its implications for energy and commodity markets, and China's August 2022 military exercises around Taiwan, with its implications for semiconductor production. Such shocks feed into long-standing rivalries and security concerns, while the responses to the shocks can amplify their effects on finance, trade, military expenditures and other economic variables. Other sources of global tensions include pandemics, made more likely by environmental disruption, and natural disasters, made more likely by climate change. These geopolitical tensions interact with other challenges, such as demography, migration, financial fragility, and deglobalisation, making it more difficult to achieve the international cooperation required to respond effectively to them.

Macroeconomic consequences are often analysed by identifying a shock, establishing a transmission mechanism by which it impacts a set of crucial variables, and specifying a policy response function. This structure

R. Smith (✉)
Birkbeck, University of London, London, UK
e-mail: r.smith@bbk.ac.uk

R. Z. Aliber et al. (eds.), *Fault Lines After COVID-19*,
https://doi.org/10.1007/978-3-031-26482-5_8

is used to estimate impulse response functions that describe how the shock diffuses through the system over time. This chapter uses a qualitative version of this structure to discuss the economic impact of geopolitical shocks. Big geopolitical shocks, like earthquakes, tend to be drawn from a low-frequency, fat-tailed distributions, following power laws. Like earthquakes, which also follow power laws, big geopolitical shocks are difficult to predict. Different elements of the system adjust differently. Financial variables adjust rapidly at high frequency, economic variables more slowly, and institutions very slowly. All three sets of variables are subject to structural breaks and responses to shocks are unlikely to be constant over time. I discuss the shocks and their predictability, the transmission mechanism, how the economic and security systems interact and how that interaction is managed.

Shocks: Identifying and Quantifying Global Tensions

I treat global tensions as being geopolitical risks. The Federal Reserve Geopolitical Risk Index, Caldara and Iacoviello (2022), defines "geopolitical risk as the threat, realization, and escalation of adverse events associated with wars, terrorism, and any tensions among states and political actors that affect the peaceful course of international relations." They add a footnote, "The term 'risk' is a bit of a misnomer, since it includes both the threat and the realization of adverse events."

In addition to Ukraine and Taiwan, current examples of tensions are the more general hostility of the US and EU to Russia and China over various issues; Middle East conflicts, such as those in Syria, Lebanon, Palestine, Yemen and Libya; Islamic insurgency in the Sahel and East Africa; regional antagonisms like Iran and Saudi Arabia; North and South Korea, India and Pakistan. Some are acute and some are chronic: antagonisms like those between Greece and Turkey can simmer quietly for a while then boil over. Balkans' hostilities, like that between Serbia and Kosovo, continue. The outside world has mixed feelings on many of these hostilities, for instance, within the EU, Spain, Slovakia, Cyprus, Romania, and Greece still do not recognise Kosovo for various different reasons. Alliances and antagonisms can be non-transitive as in the India-Russia-China triangle, where India and China are enemies, but Russia tries to be a friend of both, though neither India nor China endorsed the Ukraine invasion.

Armed conflicts are a major source of global tensions and there are many data sources on conflict. The 2021 update of the Uppsala Conflict Data Program (UCDP) data on organised violence reveals that at least 119,000 people died as a result of organised violence in 2021.[1] This is an increase of 46 percent compared to the year before and the highest figure since 2015, driven by Afghanistan, Ethiopia and Yemen. UCDP recorded 54 state-based conflicts in 2021, a decrease by two compared to the previous year. Prior to the invasion of Ukraine, most of these were far from Europe and while their local impact was great their global impact was small.

The biggest geopolitical shock would be a major, possibly nuclear, war. Judging the probability of such an event is difficult. The Bulletin of the Atomic Scientists Doomsday Clock is set at 100 seconds to midnight. The record of command, control and maintenance of nuclear weapons during the Cold War is not reassuring about our ability to avoid accidental, unauthorised or inadvertent use in times of tension. Schlosser (2013) provides an account of a sequence of near misses that suggest that the world was very lucky to avoid disaster.

Pinker (2012) argues that the world is becoming less violent, but with respect to major wars, it seems to be the case that we cannot know. The classic statistical work on the frequency and severity of major inter-state wars was done by Lewis Fry Richardson in the 1940s, who showed that their frequency follows a Poisson distribution and their severity, like that of earthquakes, follows a power law.[2] Clauset (2020) discusses Richardson's contribution and confirms his findings with later data and a power law exponent around 1.5. The difficulty is that for a stationary power law of this form, 75 years without a really big war is not a guarantee that a big one will not arrive soon. Just as 75 years without a really big earthquake in California is not a guarantee that a big one will not arrive soon.[3] The Tohoku earthquake and Tsunami that hit the Fukushima nuclear reactor in 2011 was the most powerful that had ever hit Japan, but that is characteristic of power law distributions.

[1] The number of deaths from organised violence is small relative to deaths from unorganised interpersonal violence like homicide and more people kill themselves than are killed by others.

[2] In a power law, the probability of an event greater than a particular size beyond some threshold is given by the size to the power of the negative of an exponent. They occur in many contexts.

[3] Barro and Jin (2011) examine the size distribution of rare macroeconomic disasters which also follows a power law, but with a larger exponent.

One might argue that the process generating big wars is not stationary and that the interactions of capitalism, globalisation, prosperity and democracy make peace more likely. Friedman (1999) argued that "No two countries that both had McDonald's had fought a war against each other since each got its McDonald's." The argument was that in a country rich enough to support McDonald's, its people lose interest in fighting wars. It was not long before Russia disproved Friedman's theory—first with its 2008 invasion of Georgia, then with its 2014 invasion of Ukraine. Following Russia's 2022 invasion of Ukraine, McDonald's closed its 850 franchises in Russia.[4] The fact that the world was highly globalised in 1914 before World War I should also have cast doubt on the theory. Norman Angell had written *The Great Illusion* in 1910 arguing that interdependence had made war futile.

There are more indirect indicators of geopolitical tensions than wars. Financial markets are certainly sensitive to political events. Robert Engle's Volatility Laboratory uses financial market prices as the basis of an indicator of geopolitical risks.[5] Geopolitical risks cause innovations to volatility over a very wide class of assets, which are highly correlated across countries. They look at days when there was a large common shock to volatility across countries and try to identify the origin of the shock. Often the origin is political, though sometimes it is difficult to identify the origin precisely. Their website compares it to other measures: the Blackrock geopolitical risk index; the Economic Policy Uncertainty Index and the Fed Geopolitical Risk Index. These others are all text-based measures, based on sources like newspapers or brokers reports.

The top five of the GEOVOL events at the end of July 2022 were March 9, 2020: Covid, all of Italy is locked down. Saudi Arabia/Russia oil price war; June 24, 2016: Brexit; September 17, 2001: market reopens after 9/11; February 27, 2007: rumours of a Chinese crackdown on market speculation. Alan Greenspan warns of possible impending recession. Dick Cheney assassination attempt. Drop in durable goods orders: August 24, 2015. Flash crash, Chinese Black Monday. The day Russia invaded Ukraine, February 24, 2022, does not appear on list though it started to

[4] Like Iceland, which managed to survive without McDonald's which were closed in October 2009 after the financial crisis, Russia replaced the chain with a local substitute.

[5] https://vlab.stern.nyu.edu/georisk/GEORISK.COUNTRY-GD.GEOVOL

increase, peaking about March 14 before subsiding. Since it is an innovation measure, there may be a large risk that is already embodied in expectations. This raises a question about how well events are predicted.

Predicting Shocks

It can be hard to predict shocks. Even if you could predict the geopolitical shocks, you do not know how the markets will interpret the shock and hence how economic variables, like the oil price, will react to them.

Forecasting continuous variables like the oil price is different from forecasting events. Tetlock and Gardner (2015) argue that there are some super-forecasters who are not "experts" but can give good probabilistic answers to questions about events. The examples they give on page 2 of their 2015 book are "Will Russia officially annex additional Ukrainian territory in the next three months?" and "In the next year, will any country withdraw from the eurozone?" However, somebody has to ask the right questions and those two questions were posed after Russia had invaded the Ukraine in 2014 and there had been a eurozone debt crisis. Nobody, except perhaps writers of dystopian fiction, can ask questions about the "black swans" that appear out of a blue sky.

Even if the "what" is predictable—there will be another earthquake in California and another pandemic—the "when" is not. Furthermore, the economic system is so interdependent that it is very difficult to predict how the shock will impact. In the shorter term, there is a tendency to under-estimate the possibility and size of the shocks: few anticipated the pandemic and lockdown, the 2022 invasion of Ukraine, or inflation over 10 percent in the UK and elsewhere in that year. In the longer term, it is common to over-estimate the impact, by not taking account of how much adjustment and substitution is possible. Life goes on as it did during the pandemic lockdown with people working from home. Oil prices and the rouble bounced after the Ukraine invasion. Economies adjust to sanctions, as Iran shows. An example where life does not go on is large-scale famines. But these are often a manifestation of state failure, as Sen showed with the Bengal Famine of 1943.

This raises the question: how good are financial market expectations? During the nineteenth century, bond yields were very sensitive to geopolitical tensions. Ferguson (2006, p. 81) says, "Once again it is remarkable that the biggest short-run jumps in yields occurred on dates that mean more to the political historian than to the economic historian." However, the biggest geopolitical event, World War I, was completely unanticipated.

Archduke Franz Ferdinand was assassinated at Sarajevo on June 28. Ferguson (2006, p. 98) says, "It was not until 22 July—more than three weeks after the Sarajevo assassinations—that the possibility of a European political crisis was first mentioned as a potential source of financial instability in the financial pages of *The Times.* A plausible inference is that continental markets were anticipating the belligerent tone of the Austrian ultimatum to Serbia, published on 23 July, which demanded official cooperation with an Austrian inquiry into the Sarajevo assassinations. This was the signal to investors that war was a real danger." Austria declared war on Serbia on July 28, markets closed on July 31. Britain entered the war on August 4.

Ferguson (2006, p. 102) says, "Like an earthquake on a densely populated fault line, its victims had long known that it was a possibility, and how dire its consequences would be; but its timing remained impossible to predict, and therefore beyond the realm of normal risk assessment."

Similarly, Keynes did not believe that there would be a war and made various investments just before the war on that basis. Like Keynes, we could be surprised by a major war in the near future.

Transmission Mechanisms: Economic Strategic Interactions

Geopolitical tensions have effects on trade, financial systems and military expenditures which then impact the rest of the economy and feed back into the geopolitical conflicts. Similarly, economic shocks have geopolitical effects. The relative dominance of the economic base and the political superstructure changes over time. In the 1990s there was concern about *The Retreat of the State*, the title of Strange (1996) and how states had handed power to the multinational firm in the interests of creating wealth. There was a perception that while states had competed for power as a means to wealth, increasingly they competed for wealth as a means to power but maintaining domestic rather than international power. While this may have been true during the optimistic phase following the end of the Cold War, it seems less true now when leaders like Xi Jingpin and Vladimir Putin seem willing to sacrifice wealth for power. Xi and Putin treat their own oligarchs and entrepreneurs harshly to re-establish state powers, but other states are also reasserting sovereignty.

The US can assert extra-territorial power, cutting Russian Banks from SWIFT and freezing Russian reserves because of the pervasive use of the dollar. US extra-territorial restrictions on where equipment can be sold prompted many arms manufacturers to design US components out of their systems.[6] Use of the power of the dollar caused many Central Banks to try to diversify their foreign exchange reserves and establish bilateral currency swaps. Even when there is no extra-territorial control, large states can establish standards. The EU can establish global regulations because it is such a large market and mean that it is efficient for firms to adopt regulations like GDPR elsewhere. Californian regulations often have the same effect among US states.

There are often unintended consequences of actions in one sphere on the other. The vengeful politicians at Versailles in 1918 did not anticipate *The Economic Consequences of the Peace* that Keynes predicted in his Polemic. The financial consequences of expenditure on the Vietnam War was one cause of the Nixon Shock of August 1971. These measures led to the collapse of a dollar standard linked to gold, the destruction of the Bretton Woods Systems and the move to floating exchange rates. The 1971 crisis prompted much speculation about the end of the systemic dominance of the US and the dollar. Despite major structural changes in the intervening half century, that dominance was maintained, and speculation persists about loss of US leadership and a reduced role for the dollar.

When John Connally implemented the 1971 Nixon Shock, he famously told a group of European finance ministers that the dollar "is our currency, but your problem." Other examples where domestic economic policy changes in one country appear geopolitical elsewhere are the US monetary tightening that provoked debt crises in emerging markets in the early 1980s and German monetary tightening that drove the UK out of the ERM.

Relatively few people study the global economic-strategic interactions,[7] though the gap left by the academic division of labour between economists and international relations specialists has been partly filled by the sub-specialism in international relations of International Political Economy

[6]Though not Russian ones. Russian equipment recovered in Ukraine was heavily dependent US components, showing both their ability to circumvent export controls and their inability to produce high-technology items, Byrne et al. (2022).

[7]Economists, like Daniel Ellsberg and Thomas Schelling, have studied specific questions of military strategy, often at RAND where both worked.

(IPE): international economics done by non-economists. The group who has studied the interaction most closely are economic historians. Although he did not use the term "hegemon," the book by Kindleberger (1973) on the *World in Depression 1929–1939* was the source of hegemonic stability theory which played a central role in IPE and which we return to below.

The economic historians looking at these interactions are often slightly apologetic. Findlay and O'Rourke (2007, xviii) say,

> A feature of the book that may strike some economists as odd or surprising, but will seem entirely commonplace to historians, is its sustained emphasis on conflict, violence and geopolitics. ... As we point out below, the greatest expansions of world trade have tended to come not from the bloodless tatonnement of some fictional Walrasian auctioneer but from the barrel of a maxim gun, the edge of a scimitar, or the ferocity of nomadic horsemen. ... For much of our period the pattern of trade can *only* be understood as being the outcome of some military or political equilibrium between contending powers. The dependence of trade on war and peace eventually became so obvious to us that it is reflected in the title of this volume.

The volume is called *Power and Plenty.*

They point out that economists often forget that "the pattern of trade can *only* be understood as being the outcome of some military or political equilibrium between contending powers."[8]

Today a major force on the pattern of trade is the military and political equilibrium between the US and China which shapes the battles over the location of semi-conductor production, and whether governments can use Huawei electronics in fifth-generation mobile networks.

It is not just in trade that economics and security interact. Bordo and James (2022), also economic historians, discuss the "trilemmas" that arise from the interactions between the security tensions associated with globalisation, sovereignty and democracy and the economic tensions between free capital movements, independent monetary policy and control of exchange rates. They examine the implications of these interactions for international order and financial stability and note that fixed exchange rate systems, like the Gold Standard, Bretton Woods, or the euro, require a high degree of political coordination, which may be difficult to maintain.

[8] Smith (2009) analyses the interaction of power and money from a defence economics perspective.

Policy Responses

One might be tempted to ask who is responsible for tracking the consequences of one sphere for the other and managing the interactions. Often the answer is no one. There is what is called "separate tracking" of economic and strategic issues, both nationally and internationally. The members of the defence and foreign policy elite that handle international strategic affairs are quite distinct from those that handle international economic affairs. The separate tracks have different languages, preconceptions and concerns. The difference in perceptions is illustrated by attitudes to the Soviet Union in the mid-1980s. Economics conferences described a collapsing "basket case" with falling life expectancy and falling productivity. Military conferences described an incredibly capable expansionist power that the West had to arm against.

There are some politicians who have operated in both spheres and been well informed about each of them. But they have tended to be constrained by their roles whether strategic or economic. As political scientists say: where you stand on an issue depends on where you sit. George Shultz is an example. He had served in the Marines in World War II; got a PhD in economics from MIT, where he also taught; was Dean of the University of Chicago School of Business; served on the Council of Economic Advisors; was first director of the Office of Management and Budget. After the Nixon Shock, he followed John Connally as US Secretary of the Treasury from 1972 to 1974. After a spell in business at Bechtel, Shultz served as Secretary of State under Reagan from 1982 to 1989 and, according to Wikipedia, relied primarily on the Foreign Service to formulate and implement Reagan's foreign policy. He emphasised professional over political credentials in the process and the Foreign Service responded in kind by giving Shultz its "complete support," making him one of the most popular Secretaries since Dean Acheson.

In our model of the interaction, we need a policy response function that describes how foreign policy responds to economic events and economic policy responds to geopolitical events. The policy response function in macroeconomic models is often a Taylor rule that specified how the Central Bank should adjust the policy rate of interest in response to inflation and the output gap. Taylor himself operated in both spheres serving as Under Secretary of the Treasury for International Affairs, 2001–2005, when he had to assemble a coalition to freeze terrorist assets, plan the financial reconstruction in Afghanistan and develop a new Iraqi currency without Saddam's image. All are described in his book *Global Financial Warriors* (Taylor, 2007). Early in the book (p. xxiii), he says: "Financial Issues have always been a third pillar of foreign policy, along with political and military issues. Over two thousand years ago Thucydides wrote how 'The Athenians,' needing money for a siege, 'sent out twelve ships to collect money from their allies, with Lysicles and four others in command.' In the modern age of globalization the role of finance in foreign policy is even more important, and it is growing rapidly."

One very successful example of using economic means for strategic ends is the Cooperative Threat Reduction program initiated by the Nunn-Lugar Act of 1991. Nunn, a Democrat, and Lugar, a Republican, were both US Senators, and the Act provided money and personnel to decommission Soviet weapons of mass destruction. In particular, it funded the dismantling of the nuclear weapons in Ukraine, Kazakhstan and Belarus and their relocation back to Russia. It made a major contribution to the decision by those three states to give up nuclear weapons. While some in Ukraine now regret that decision, the world would probably have been a more dangerous place in the intervening years has those three states had nuclear weapons.

After World War II there was an effort to develop global public goods, institutions and laws to create what is often called the "rules-based international order" in both the economic and the strategic sphere. In both spheres there is currently talk of the collapse of that order.

This rules-based international order is a world of coordinating organisations, clubs. There are the well-known ones like the EU, IMF, NATO, UN, WB, WHO, WTO and various international courts. But there are many specialised ones like the multilateral export control regimes (Australia Group for chemical and biological weapons; Missile Technology Control Regime; Nuclear Suppliers Group; Wassenaar arrangement for conventional weapons) and the Internet Engineering Technical Forum (IETF). They have various rules about who can join the club and various ways of making decisions: one person one vote (weighted by population); one dollar one vote; one country one vote, UN General Assembly unanimity required P5, consensus like the export control regimes or humming which the IETF uses.[9] Often, countries will only join a club if they have veto powers, but this is not a problem when the organisations are established,

[9] See the description and discussion in Tett (2021).

because then there are common interests. Over time interests diverge and the veto power can cripple the organisation.

Global public goods are also provided by hegemonic powers. They do it in their own interests but have what Olson (1982) described as an encompassing interest. The hegemonic power wants the system to prosper because it will benefit from that prosperity. Britain maintained freedom of the seas in the nineteenth century and the US defended Europe in the second half of the twentieth century, for their own reasons, but other nations could free ride on the externality. Strange (1996, p. 195) notes that these two examples, the UK in the nineteenth century and the US after World War II, resulted from an accidental coincidence of national and systemic interests which could be translated into hegemonic leadership. She argued that there is no reason to imagine that they would always coincide and, as Kindleberger (1973) showed, they did not during the inter-war period, when Britain was unable, and the US was unwilling to provide the required leadership.

Matthijs (2022) contrasts the benign US leadership during the global financial crisis of 2008–2009 with the German coercive rules-based leadership during the subsequent euro crisis of 2010–2013. He considers "why the US *did* and Germany *did not* define its interest as providing the systems with public goods—a market for distress goods, long-term countercyclical lending, lender of last resort facilities and macroeconomic policy coordination—during their respective crises." He attributes the difference to Washington and Berlin reading Kindleberger in quite different ways: the US emphasising the importance of a flexible response to crisis, the Germans the importance of maintaining the rules.

Hegemony may eventually be contradictory, because of the costs and risks involved. Kennedy (1988) describing *The Rise and Fall of the Great Powers* emphasised how wealth creates power and power destroys wealth through the overstretch it generates. Great power transitions are dangerous. Graham Allison coined the term "Thucydides's Trap" to describe the dangers of war when a revisionist rising power, like China, threatens to displace an incumbent Great Power, like the US. In his account of the Peloponnesian War Thucydides said "What made war inevitable was the rise of Athens and the fear it inspired in Sparta." Allison (2017) asks whether the US and China can escape Thucydides's Trap. Some historians have questioned the reality of the trap, pointing to peaceful transitions.

China does not seem to perceive a coincidence of national and systemic interests. It complains about the hegemonic role of the dollar but is unwilling to risk losing control by allowing free movement of capital abroad that would be required were it to create a global currency. It uses its economic power erratically and not necessarily in what many would consider to be its longer-term interests. It has not really mastered the use of soft power, despite the potential provided by companies like TikTok and the large amount of money distributed through the Belt and Road Initiative.

A major global function is debt management which requires coordination and transparency in rescheduling debt in the wake of default. Many emerging markets have heavy debt loads, often denominated in dollars, and are either in danger of default or have done so, like Sri Lanka, whose April 2022 default was its first ever. China is a major creditor of Sri Lanka. It is also the world's largest bilateral lender mainly to developing countries, through a variety of channels. Normally rescheduling is handled by multilateral debt negotiations, through Paris Clubs of Official creditors or London Clubs of Private creditors, perhaps in conjunction with the IMF. Clarity about the nature and extent of the indebtedness is central, so the creditors can judge what restructuring is feasible and how any haircut can be distributed fairly. But despite being a large lender China is neither a member of the Clubs nor being transparent about how much is owed on what terms.

Conclusion

The interaction between geopolitics and economics, power and money, is inevitably problematic. Usually the problems are chronic, simmering conflicts in the overlap. Occasionally, as of the time of writing in the autumn of 2022, the problems become acute. When the problems do become acute, people search for standards of comparison which will help them provide a framework to understand what is happening and hopefully to predict. History may not repeat itself, but it can rhyme. To provide a framework for thinking about today, people tend to ask whether today is like a particular time in the past? Popular choices are currently: the 1970s (inflation and oil shocks); 1948 (a new cold war with barriers between blocs); 1930s (the rise of populism and growing tensions); 1918 (recovery from pandemic); 1914 (the unexpected global war).

References

Allison, G. (2017). *Destined for war: Can America and China escape Thucydides's Trap?* Houghton Mifflin Harcourt.

Barro, R. J., & Tao, J. (2011). On the size distribution of macroeconomic disasters. *Econometrica, 79*(5), 1567–1589.

Bordo, M. D., & James, H. (2022). *Trapped in the trilemma: When security trumps economics* (NBER working paper no. 30506).

Byrne, J., Somerville, G., Byrne, J., Watling, J., Reynolds, N., & Baker, J. (2022). *Silicon lifeline; the western electronics at the heart of Russia's military machine*. Royal United Services Institute for Defence and Security Studies, August.

Caldara, D., & Iacoviello, M. (2022). *Measuring geopolitical risk, international finance discussion papers 1222r1*. Board of Governors of the Federal Reserve System.

Clauset, A. (2020). On the frequency and severity of interstate wars, ch.10. In N. Petter (Ed.), *Lewis fry Richardson: His intellectual legacy and influence in the social sciences* (pp. 113–127). Cham Switzerland.

Ferguson, N. (2006). Political risk and the international bond market between the 1848 revolution and the outbreak of the first world war. *Economic History Review, LIX*(1), 70–112.

Findlay, R., & O'Rourke, K. H. (2007). *Power and plenty: Trade, war, and the world economy in the second millennium*. Princeton University Press.

Friedman, T. L. (1999). *The Lexus and the olive tree*. Anchor Books.

Kennedy, P. (1988). *The rise and fall of the great powers: Economic change and military conflict from 1500 to 2000*. Unwin Hyman.

Kindleberger, C. P. (1973). *The world in depression 1929–1939*. University of California Press.

Matthijs, M. (2022). Hegemonic leadership is what states make of it: Reading Kindleberger in Washington and Berlin. *Review of International Political Economy, 29*(2), 371–398.

Olson, M. (1982). *The rise and decline of nations*. Yale University Press.

Pinker, S. (2012). *The better angels of our nature*. Penguin.

Schlosser, E. (2013). *Command and control*. Penguin.

Smith, R. P. (2009). *Military economics: The interaction of power and money*. Palgrave.

Strange, S. (1996). *The retreat of the state: The diffusion of power in the world economy*. Cambridge University Press.

Tetlock, P., & Gardner, D. (2015). *Superforecasting: The art and science of prediction*. Random House Books.

Tett, G. (2021). *Anthro-vision: How anthropology can explain business and life*. Random House Books.

Taylor, J. B. (2007). *Global financial warriors: The untold story of international finance in the post-9/11 world*. Norton.

Reconstruction, EU Accession, and Reform of Ukraine

Anders Åslund

Introduction

Ukraine has developed greatly since it became independent on August 24, 1991. Its development has not been easy, because in Soviet times it suffered badly from repression and isolation, which has taken time to overcome, but Ukraine's democratic and economic institutions have evolved successfully.

I visited Kyiv the week before the Moscow August 1991 coup to evaluate the opportunities for economic reform, meeting with all the leading economic policy makers. I was shocked. At that time, the superficial verdict was that Poland and Ukraine were similar, reflected in an optimistic report by Deutsche Bank. They were so in size, location, and economic structure. Both had many mines, steelworks, machine building as well as agriculture. Their level of education was also very similar. Therefore, they could take off in parallel. No conclusion could be more flawed. The qualitative conditions were completely different.

A. Åslund (✉)
Georgetown University, Washington, DC, USA

R. Z. Aliber et al. (eds.), *Fault Lines After COVID-19*,
https://doi.org/10.1007/978-3-031-26482-5_9

Four differences stood out: domestic institutions, economic policy, public understanding, and international engagement.

Poland was an independent state with all relevant national institutions, such as a central bank and a ministry of finance, while Ukraine had to build most national institutions from scratch. Although Poland had a socialist economy, it had a large private sector and all institutions for its regulation, relevant state institutions, and functioning courts. Ukraine as a newly independent state had to build all these institutions anew with minimal knowledge.

Poland had a corps of free market economist reformers gathered around its great reform leader Leszek Balcerowicz, who launched an early and comprehensive market reform and macroeconomic stabilization as soon as they could, while Ukraine had few significant market economic reformers in 1991 and they were not given high positions. The Ukrainian decision-makers did not have even elementary knowledge of how to proceed with economic policy until 1994. Meanwhile, Ukraine suffered from horrendous hyperinflation, continued Soviet state regulation, and minimal privatization.

Poland had the necessary human capital for a systemic change, many intellectuals and officials who spoke English and participated in the Western discussions, while few official Ukrainians spoke English and those who did were usually KGB agents. Millions of Poles had spent months abroad in the West in the 1980s as tourists, students, or temporary workers. Being there, they had learned how the West worked, and they were happy to transfer that knowledge to their home country.

Poland had re-joined the International Monetary Fund and the World Bank in 1986. Therefore, the IMF was ready to support Poland from the outset of its reforms in 1989. Finally, the West thought it was worth supporting Poland financially, so it provided the country with sufficient funds from the outset of its reforms in January 1990, and the European Union opened its market to Poland early on and accepted it as a candidate and member in 2004.

Today, Ukraine has caught up qualitatively in all these regards. Since 1991 it has held regular democratic elections for president, parliament, and local authorities. It has repeatedly gone through democratic change of power and has proven itself as an established democracy with a multi-party system, free media, and the freedom of assembly.

Since 1992, Ukraine has established fruitful cooperation with the IMF, the World Bank, and the European Bank for Reconstruction and

Development. Together with them, Ukraine has built a strong central bank, ministry of finance and fiscal service, which before the war had led to orderly state finances, low inflation, and a relatively stable floating exchange rate based on inflation targeting. The Ukrainian nation has become integrated with the West.[1]

Ukraine has numerous qualified professionals of all kinds. Tens of thousands of Ukrainians have been educated abroad and spent long time there. They speak good English and other foreign languages, and they have learned how the West works. Preconditions matter. Today, Ukraine is united as a nation and ready for a breakthrough. It has caught up with and probably overtaken Poland in these important qualitative regards.

Yet, because of many years of serious economic distortions, such as multiple prices for basic commodities such as gas, a small elite enriched itself through rent seeking in symbiosis with top government officials. This corruption requires additional measures.

Russia's Aims and Destruction

Since its independence in 1991, Ukraine has declared itself neutral, endeavouring to maintain good relations with both Russia and the West. In 1994, it agreed to give up its numerous nuclear arms—to Russia, in an agreement with the United States, the United Kingdom, and Russia. All the signatories offered Ukraine "security assurances," which turned out to be of no value. The Ukrainians felt cheated. In 1997, Ukraine concluded a far-reaching friendship treaty with Russia, and it leased the important naval base in Sevastopol to Russia for twenty years. Russia was persistently Ukraine's largest trading partner by far. Russia's gas trade with Ukraine was the main source of large-scale corruption in Ukraine.

In spite of very close and friendly bilateral relations, Putin launched a war against Ukraine in February 2014 and another in February 2022. He has denied the existence of Ukraine as an independent state or nation and claims that Russians and Ukrainians are one people.[2] This had little to do with Ukraine's aspirations to develop closer relations with the European Union, and NATO accession was not even on the agenda. Instead, Russian President Vladimir Putin aspired to wars with Ukraine to boast his popu-

[1] Åslund, Anders, *How Ukraine Became a Market Economy and Democracy*, Peterson Institute for International Economics, Washington, DC, 2009.

[2] Putin, Vladimir V. 2014b. Direct Line with Vladimir Putin, April 17, www.kremlin.ru

larity rating. Ukraine's problem was that it was non-aligned so it stood on its own against Russia. In March 2014, Putin annexed Crimea with force, and his popularity rating in Russia surged to 88 percent, according to the independent Levada Center. His current war in Ukraine led to a new peak in his popularity rating of 83 percent.[3]

Putin has been remarkably disinterested in the Russian costs of the war. Russia has been badly hit by Western sanctions, and GDP appears likely to decline by 4 percent in 2022. The Russian government does not publish its military losses, but the Ukrainian government claims that Russia has lost 70,000 soldiers and thousands of tanks and armoured vehicles. Most of the Russian armed forces have been destroyed, but the war goes on with newly mobilized resources.

Ukraine has suffered enormously from Russia's ruthless and unjustified aggression and it is suffering ever more. In 2014, Russia seized 7 percent of Ukraine's territory and caused it a loss of 17 percent of its GDP, since it occupied part of the highly industrial eastern Donbass region. Since the war is continuing, it is uncertain how large the damage will be, but it will be horrendous.[4]

As of October 2022, Russia occupies 19 percent of Ukraine's territory, in the south and the east (Crimea, almost the whole of Luhansk oblast, half of Donetsk oblast, much of Zaporizhe oblast, and most of Kherson oblast). Currently, Russia is trying to hold on to its concurred territories, while Ukraine attempts to take back Kherson oblast. Intermittently, Russia sends missiles from submarines in the Black Sea, Belarus, and Russia against any part of Ukraine. These Russian attacks primarily directed against civilian targets and the infrastructure in the whole of Ukraine are highly disruptive.

The Ukrainian material and human losses from the Russian aggression are enormous. Both the Ukrainian government and the private Kyiv School of Economics maintain databases of the country's material losses. They have as yet recorded losses of more than $120 billion. But this is based on original cost. With realistic assessment of the reconstruction cost, the amount is likely to double to $200 billion. Most of the losses are

[3]Levada Center, Approval of Institutions, Ratings of Politicians, September 14, 2022. https://www.levada.ru/en/2022/09/14/approval-of-institutions-ratings-of-politicians/

[4]Anders Åslund, Anders, "Kremlin Aggression in Ukraine: The Price Tag," Report, Atlantic Council, Washington, DC, March 2018.

buildings and infrastructure. The cities of Mariupol and Chernyhiv have been devastated.

The Russians have killed tens of thousands of civilian Ukrainians and presumably three times as many have been injured. After Libyan officers planted a bomb on an airplane that blew up over Lockerbie in Scotland in 1998, Libya eventually agreed to pay $2.7 billion in compensation to the 270 victims' families, that is, $10 million per victim. If Russia has killed 50,000 Ukrainians, it would have to pay $500 billion by the same standard.

To this comes the current Russian devastation of the Ukrainian economy. After nine months, Ukraine's GDP had fallen by 35 percent, which is likely to be the loss for the whole of 2022. Ukraine's electricity consumption has declined by about 35 percent since the Russian assault in February, and in the short-term electricity consumption is a good proxy of GDP. Since Ukraine's 2021 GDP was $200 billion, that would mean a loss of Ukraine of $70 billion in 2022. Nobody is predicting a fast recovery of the Ukrainian economy and we don't know as yet how large a share of it that Russia is likely to keep, making it impossible to predict Ukraine's total losses.

In August 2022, the World Bank published the most detailed assessments of Ukraine's damaged and needs. It assessed the total damages as of June 1, 2022, at $97 billion, the total losses at $252 billion, and the total needs at $349 billion.[5] The World Bank numbers appear to reflect a broad consensus.

Russia's war has also caused major movements of population. In the last Soviet census in 1989, Ukraine had 52 million inhabitants. As elsewhere in Eastern Europe, the population has declined because of substantial emigration and low birth rates as everywhere else in Europe. There is no authoritative tally, but before the war in 2014 Ukraine had at most 44 million inhabitants, and 5–6 million of them spent substantial time abroad, primarily in Europe.

In February–March 2014, Russia conquered Crimea with a population of 2.3 million. The territory of its two quasi-states in Donetsk and Luhansk oblast had barely 5 million inhabitants before the war of 2014. Of those, 1.7 million fled to Ukraine and probably 0.8 million to Russia, leaving about 2.5 million inhabitants, to a large extent old-age pensioners.

[5] World Bank, "Ukraine: Rapid Damage and Needs Assessment," Washington, DC: World Bank, August 2022, p. 14.

After Russia's attack on February 24, 2022, the already dramatic demographic situation became truly dramatic. No less than 11 million people have fled to the EU, while almost as many Ukrainians, probably 7 million, are internally displaced. More than half of the refugees, about 6 million, appear to have returned. The main recipient country is Poland, where 3.5 million Ukrainians stayed at some time. Other major recipients of Ukrainian refugees have been the other Central European countries and Germany. Fortunately, all countries have received Ukrainian refugees with open arms, as most Europeans have greatly sympathized with their hardship and cause.

Initially, most refugees appear to have found private housing, but these conditions are largely temporary. Over time, the hosts welcome is likely to wear out. Given that most of the refugees are women, children, and old-age pensioners, uncommonly many of them are likely to return to their homeland to reunite with their men. Many refugees have already returned to the western and central parts of Ukraine. Yet, the longer the war lasts the more refugees are likely to stay abroad, and the greater the tensions and costs will be.

Ukraine Needs Reconstruction, Reform, and EU Accession

When this war finally ends, Ukraine faces three giant tasks—reconstruction of the war damage, EU accession, and completion of its structural reforms. It would be advantageous to combine these three tasks, while before the war has ended all interested parties need to provide Ukraine with as much support as they can without the delay of excessive coordination.

The Ukrainian people have bravely stood up in defence of their nation and they have done so with impressive success, astounding the world. Russia's assault on Ukraine has convinced the Ukrainian nation that Russia is not ready to pursue peaceful cooperation with Ukraine but desires its elimination. Therefore, they no longer desire to be non-aligned. The European Union has drawn the same conclusion. Today, a large Ukrainian majority wants their country to become a full member of the EU and NATO, and the EU has been greatly impressed by the Ukrainians' commitment to European values. Realizing that Ukraine is a full-fledged

European country, the EU welcomes Ukraine. Ukraine and the EU have come to the same conclusion. They have made a clear choice: They aspire to far-reaching integration.

Ukraine is a European country and Article 49 of the Treaties of the European Union states unequivocally: "Any European State which respects the values referred to in Article 2 and is committed to promoting them may apply to become a member of the Union."

Article 2 spells out standard democratic values and the rule of law: "The Union is founded on the values of respect for human dignity, freedom, democracy, equality, the rule of law and respect for human rights, including the rights of persons belonging to minorities. These values are common to the Member States in a society in which pluralism, non-discrimination, tolerance, justice, solidarity and equality between women and men prevail."

Between 2007 and 2011, the EU and Ukraine leisurely negotiated an extensive Association Agreement, including a Deep and Comprehensive Free Trade Area (DCFTA). They signed it on March 21 and June 27, 2014. Ukraine has adopted broad-based reforms in line with this Agreement.[6] The DCFTA came into force in 2017. In the same year, the EU granted Ukrainians visa freedom, which was greatly welcomed by the Ukrainian population.

In June 2022, the EU took the next big step, deciding to offer Ukraine membership perspective and to become a candidate for EU membership. The European Commission offered a brief preliminary assessment. The political assessment was very short, but positive: "Overall, as regards the political criteria, Ukraine is well advanced in reaching the stability of institutions guaranteeing democracy, the rule of law, human rights and respect for and protection of minorities." The Commission delved a bit further on the economic criteria, raising more concerns, while still passing a positive verdict:

> Concerning the economic criteria, Ukraine has continued its strong macroeconomic record, demonstrating a noteworthy resilience with macroeconomic and financial stability ensured also after Russia's invasion in February 2022. This reflects not only a very strong political determination, but also

[6] European Union, "ASSOCIATION AGREEMENT between the European Union and its member states, of the one part, and Ukraine," *Official Journal of the European Union*, May 29, 2014.

> relatively well-functioning institutions. At the same time, ambitious structural reforms to remove corruption, reduce the State footprint and the persistent influence of oligarchs, strengthen private property rights and enhance labour market flexibility need to continue in Ukraine to improve the functioning of its market economy. The capacity of the country to cope with the competitive pressure in the EU will depend crucially on how post-war investments in Ukraine are designed and sequenced in order to upgrade its physical capital, improve educational outcomes and spur innovation.[7]

While the Commission and the Council accepted Ukraine as an EU candidate, it did so on seven conditions, and the Commission will monitor Ukraine's progress in fulfilling these steps and report on them, together with a detailed assessment of the country, by the end of 2022. They are abridged:

- To enact and implement legislation on a selection procedure for judges of the Constitutional Court of Ukraine;
- to finalize the integrity vetting of the candidates for the High Council of Justice members by the Ethics Council and the selection of candidate to establish the High Qualification Commission of Judges of Ukraine;
- to further strengthen the fight against corruption;
- to complete the appointment of a new head of the Specialized Anti-Corruption Prosecutor's Office; to ensure that anti-money laundering legislation is in compliance with the standards of the Financial Action Task Force (FATF); to adopt an overarching strategic plan for the reform of the entire law enforcement sector as part of Ukraine's security environment;
- to implement the Anti-Oligarch law to limit the excessive influence of oligarchs in economic, political, and public life;
- to tackle the influence of vested interests by adopting a media law that aligns Ukraine's legislation with the EU audio-visual media services directive and empowers the independent media regulator; and
- to finalize the reform of the legal framework for national minorities.[8]

[7] European Commission, "Opinion on the EU membership application by Ukraine," Brussels, June 17, 2022, p. 2.

[8] European Commission, "Opinion on the EU membership application by Ukraine," Brussels, June 17, 2022, p. 2.

This is a concrete list of measures with minimal budgetary cost, rendering it easy for the Commission to assess Ukraine's progress. Tellingly, the four first EU conditions are legal, while the three others are democratic principles. The economic reforms have proceeded further.

For the EU, the ensuing step is to start membership negotiations. This is a lengthy process because it involves substantial institutional reforms to the benefit of the Ukrainian nation, but it is important to start it early on.

Financing

First of all, Ukraine needs to rebuild after the destruction caused by the Russian invasion. This requires substantial financing. Ideally, Russia should be forced to pay war reparations for all the damage it has caused in Ukraine, but the West and international financial institutions also need to make substantial contributions. Hopefully, Ukraine's further development will also attract major private investment.

In April 2022, eight economists from the respected Centre for Economic Policy Research (CEPR) put out a substantial and useful report "A Blueprint for the Reconstruction of Ukraine."[9] Their report on Ukraine's reconstruction distinguished between three stages of reconstruction:

> "A. Emergency response (akin to the response to a natural disaster hitting a country).
> B. Rapid restoration of critical infrastructure and services.
> C. Laying foundations for future growth and modernization.
> Each of these stages has different objectives and requirements. The emergency response is a set of measures usually taken after major natural disasters. The second stage aims to revive the basic functions of the economy and the government. The third stage is meant to put the country on a rapid, sustained growth trajectory."[10]

At the Ukraine Recovery Conference in Lugano, July 4–5, 2022, the Ukrainian government presented a rather detailed and very ambitious reconstruction plan for 2022–2032, asking for a total of about $750

[9] Torbjörn Becker et al. "A Blueprint for the Reconstruction of Ukraine," Centre for European Policy Research (CEPR), April 6, 2022.

[10] Torbjörn Becker et al. "A Blueprint for the Reconstruction of Ukraine," Centre for European Policy Research (CEPR), April 6, 2022.

billion for a decade, an enormous amount. Sensibly and in the same fashion as the CEPR, the Ukrainian government divided this period into three phases: emergency funding for 2022 (and now also for 2023), reconstruction for 2023–2025, and the development phase for 2026–2032.[11] Another Ukraine Recovery Conference was held in Berlin on October 25, 2022.

It makes sense to divide Ukraine's recovery into three phases. In the first emergency phase of 2022 and as long as the war lasts in 2023, little coordination is possible. The important thing is that Ukraine receives as much humanitarian and military assistance as possible and as fast as possible. That is best done by individual countries and international organizations on an ad hoc basis.

The second phase, the three years 2023–2025, should be very different. The amounts required are vast, which means that substantial coordination, transparency, and good governance are vital. Unless the governance is not sufficiently good, the funds are not likely to be granted. At this stage, private investments are unlikely, so the financing need to come from governments or intergovernmental organizations.

The third phase, 2026–2032, should also be quite different. Then, Ukraine should do its utmost to attract foreign private financing. That will only be possible if Ukraine has caried out substantial judicial reforms to improve its business environment. The West should facilitate investment in Ukraine by offering beneficial political risk insurance.

At the end of 2021, Ukraine had public debts of 49 percent of GDP, but in 2021 the GDP was $200 billion, and it is likely to fall to about $135 billion in 2022, while the public debt has increased. Dragon Capital expects it to reach 85 percent of GDP at the end of 2022, which is hardly sustainable.[12] Therefore, it is important that Ukraine primarily receives grants and not loans for its recovery financing. Hence, it is vital that Ukraine receives grants rather than credits. The United States has understood that and almost all its assistance to Ukraine consists of grants. The EU macro-financial assistance, on the contrary, comprises only credits, though the EU members bilateral assistance is primarily grants.

[11] Ukraine's National Recovery Council, Ukraine's National Recovery Plan, Lugano July 2022, https://www.urc2022.com/urc2022-recovery-plan

[12] Dragon Capital, *The Dragon Daily*, Kyiv, October 3, 2022. Cf Antezza, Arianna, et al. "The Ukrainian Support Tracker," Kiel Institute for the World Economy, Working Paper, August 2022.

Unfortunately, only half of these funds are forthcoming. According to the Ukrainian brokerage Dragon Capital, by September 30, a total of $35.3 billion had been pledged, but only $19.6 billion had been disbursed to Ukraine. The dominant donor is the US, which has already disbursed $8.5 billion and it has committed $1.5 billion for each of the remaining months of 2022. The big problem is the European Union. Until the end of September, the EU had only disbursed $2.8 billion.[13] It disbursed $2 billion more in October. Individual EU members have contributed another $2 billion. Thus, the EU and its members have so far given the Ukrainian government budget support of $6.8 billion this year or about half of the US support.[14]

Last May, the EU committed €9 billion in macro-financial assistance, but out of these funds it has only disbursed €3 billion. Hopefully, the EU can free up €3 billion more in November and December, but this is after a substantial delay and presumably €3 billion will not be disbursed at all. This is impermissibly slow in a crisis.[15]

For 2023, both Ukraine and international partners expect a financing gap of the state budget of about $38 billion. At present, both the United States and the EU intend to provide financing of $1.5 billion a month each, but there is an obvious danger that both will be delayed with their financing.

In the absence of external financing, the Ukrainian government has no choice but to turn to monetary financing, that is, the National Bank of Ukraine prints money for the government, which inevitably drives up inflation. In August, inflation had risen to 23.8 percent, and it rose to 24.6 percent in September.

This is not tenable. In a recent article in Bloomberg, Niall Fergusson pointed out that Ukraine's army is winning but its economy is losing because of insufficient EU financial support. He warned of hyperinflation, and so do I. A report by the Centre for Economic Policy Research recommends that the government raise tax revenue and sell domestic debt rather

[13] EU Neighbors East, "EU Releases its First Tranche of $1 billion Macro-Financial Assistance for Ukraine," August 1, 2022, https://euneighbourseast.eu/news/latest-news/eu-releases-first-tranche-of-new-e1-billion-macro-financial-assistance-for-ukraine/

[14] Dragon Capital, *The Dragon Daily*, Kyiv, October 3, 2022.

[15] Dragon Capital, *The Dragon Daily*, Kyiv, October 3, 2022.

than monetize it through the central bank, but I doubt that is feasible during the war.[16]

The ultimate Western aim today is that Ukraine wins the war both militarily and economically. The military expenditures cannot be cut. The other public expenditures have been slimmed down to an utter minimum, and you cannot really raise tax expenditures in the middle of a hot war. Hyperinflation is all too common in or after wars. At the end of communism, most of the formerly communist countries were hit by hyperinflation, defined as at least 50 percent inflation a month. Hyperinflation inevitably undermines all public trust in the state and usually results in authoritarian rule, as we have seen in the former Soviet Union.

President Vladimir Putin no longer claims to pursue his war against only Ukraine but against "the collective West." Thus, it is our common Western duty to at least keep the Ukrainian afloat during the war. In the short term, this can only be done through more Western contributions to the Ukrainian budget. Reforms and alternative financial manoeuvres can only be considered after the war.

Something must be done! We cannot allow Ukraine to fail financially for no fault of its own because the EU is too preoccupied with its bureaucratic rules. The best solution, which I have advocated, would be that the seven Western countries that hold the $316 billion of frozen reserves of the Central Bank of Russia confiscate them and use them for Russia's war reparations to Ukraine.[17] Canada has already adopted such a law but it has not collected any Russian funds as yet.

The EU offered substantial grants to its members in compensation for Covid-19 damages and it could do so with far smaller means to Ukraine. An alternative method is to demand compulsory subscription from its members as the EU did in 2016 in order to finance its migration agreement with Turkey. If there is an EU will, there are many means.

[16] Becker, T. B. Eichengreen, Y. Gorodnichenko, S. Guriev, S. Johnson, T. Mylovanov, K. Rogoff, and B. Weder di Mauro, Macroeconomic policies for wartime Ukraine, Centre for European Policy Research (CEPR), 12 August 2022.

[17] Hufbauer, Gary Clyde and Jeffrey J. Schott, "The United States Should Seize Russian Assets for Ukraine's Reconstruction," Peterson Institute for International Economics, April 21, 2022; Robert B. Zoellick, "Russian Cash Can Keep Ukraine Alive This Winter," *Wall Street Journal*, October 26, 2022.

How to Organize the Reconstruction

At present, there is much talk about a Marshall Plan for Ukraine, which appears appropriate given the size of the undertaking and the financing needed.[18]

A first requirement is that since the funds required are large, it is vital that an independent international authority is set up to manage these funds in a transparent fashion because Ukraine's foremost problems have been corruption and insecure private property rights. This authority needs to have a decisive Western majority. Otherwise, Western countries will refuse to provide funding.

A second requirement is sensible coordination of Ukraine's reconstruction, reform, and EU accession. The reconstruction of private homes and enterprises as well as the properties of local authorities could be organized as insurance claims and thus be decentralized. Ukraine will need a completely new infrastructure that is focusing on European rather than Russian integration. It needs to be modern and green. That requires central government planning. Finally, Ukraine requires reforms to fulfil its EU accession criteria and the widely held views of necessary reforms.

A third requirement is that the reconstruction authority becomes fast and effective so that it does not become a slow bureaucracy.

Various ideas have been put forward. The driving force in the Western support for Ukraine appears to have become the highly informal G-7. It needs some administration. The European Union has offered to set up such an administration in Brussels, but independently from the European Commission that may become too slow and bureaucratic. A moot point is to what extent EU accession and reconstruction will be coordinated.[19]

Our hope is that Ukraine, and the collective West, will combine and cooperate in these three processes: reconstruction, EU accession, and the completion of Ukraine's reforms. While we hope that the EU will be able

[18] Kubilius, Andrius, "Ukraine: Our Next Steps," Vilnius, July 6, 2022. https://elpnariai.lt/en/a-kubilius-ukraine-our-next-steps/

[19] Becker, T, B Eichengreen, Y Gorodnichenko, S Guriev, S Johnson, T Mylovanov, K Rogoff and B Weder di Mauro. A Blueprint for the Reconstruction of Ukraine, Centre for European Policy Research (CEPR), April 6, 2022; Philip Zelikow, Philip and Simon Johnson, "How Ukraine Can Build Back Better," *Foreign Affairs*, April 19, 2022; Ronja Ganster, Jacob Kirkegaard, Thomas Kleine Brockhoff, and Bruce Stokes, Designing Ukraine's Recovery in the Spirit of the Marshall Plan, Washington, DC: German Marshall Fund, September 2022.

to take a lead in this process, it is important that the United States, the United Kingdom, Canada, Japan, and other democratic countries participate. Since this is a major long-term project, we must get it right.

Structural Reforms

At present, the Ukrainian government does not have any clear economic ideology.[20] All recent governments have embraced sound macroeconomic policies as reflected in the National Bank of Ukraine (NBU), the Ministry of Finance, and the State Fiscal Service. This has meant a limited budget deficit, limited public debt, low inflation thanks to inflation targeting, floating exchange rate, increasingly broader tax bases and reasonably low tax rates, and a far-reaching computerization of the tax system.

Yet, a few major steps need to be taken to get the Ukrainian state and economy working effectively. First, the functioning of the state administration needs to be faster and simpler. Second and most important, the rule of law needs to be established to that private property rights become credibly. Third, the government needs to combat corruption more effectively. Fourth, Ukraine has a market economy, but the market reforms need to be completed. Fifth, Ukraine has still far too many state-owned enterprises that are neither innovative nor productive. Most of them should be sold off as fast as possible. Finally, corporate governance of the remaining state-owned enterprises needs to be reinforced.

Economic freedom has not been much appreciated by any government. Some relaxation of outmoded Soviet regulations has occurred, but too little and too slowly. All too often, the economic thinking of the government and parliament lapses into a Soviet state-oriented thinking, typically suggesting that a new state agency or company be established to resolve one problem or the other, or that the government should subsidize certain enterprises or activities. Price controls have persisted far too often, and the government maintains all kinds of restrictions and regulations that cannot be understood. In wartime, it is understandable that various regulations have been imposed, but also before the war the many government interventions have been characterized by voluntarism rather than any principles.

[20] This section draws on European Commission, "Commission Opinion on Ukraine's application for membership of the European Union," Brussels, June 17, 2022; My view: Anders Åslund, Anders, *Ukraine: What Went Wrong and How to Fix It*, Washington: Peterson Institute for International Economics, 2015.

Many, but not all, new EU members have excelled with eminent growth rates soon after they became members. In the 1990s, Ireland and Poland were the stars. In the 2000s, Estonia, Latvia, and Lithuania stood out. In recent years, Romania has excelled. These countries have shown that countries can sustain growth rates of 7–8 percent a year during a decade or more. But it does not come automatically. Other countries have failed. In hindsight the reasons are clear. They have not carried out a proper reform of their state administration or secured the rule of law. They have pursued conservative fiscal and monetary policies and not allowed public expenditure to grow larger than the economy could bear, and they have privatized state enterprises.

If Ukraine is to succeed, it needs to draw the right lessons from these many examples. It has already carried out many reforms, but much remains to be done. First of all, Ukraine needs to render its state administration more efficient. Second, it must impose the rule of law and effective anti-corruption agencies. Third, the market needs to be opened up with a sound competition policy. Fourth, a far-reaching privatization is needed. Fifth, sound corporate governance needs to be imposed on the remaining large state companies.

Interestingly, in July 2022, First Deputy Prime Minister and Minister of Economy Yuliya Svyrydenko published an article advocating for "the philosophy of the free step." She sensibly called for 7 percent growth a year for the next decade by cutting the tax burden from 45 percent of GDP to 30 percent of GDP, by radically liberalizing the economy, and by imposing the rule of law.[21] This was a clear policy advice in line with what has worked in the recent winners in the EU, but it remains to be seen what policy will win.

Conclusion

Russia's war of aggression against Ukraine has had many important consequences. The big negative effect is of course massive destruction and the loss of tens of thousands of lives and the uprooting of millions of refugees and internally displaced people.

[21] Julija Svyrydenko, "Kakuyu ekonomiku my stroim? (Vad för slags ekonomi bygger vi)?" *Ukrainskaya pravda*, July 8, 2022.

Yet, the war has also had positive effects. Ukrainians are proud of their nation's impressive victories in the war against Russia. The Ukrainian nation has become more united than ever and identified with Europe and the West as never before.

The Ukrainian nation and the West will face three joint tasks when the war is hopefully over: Reconstruction, EU accession, and completion of Ukraine's structural reforms. This requires plenty of funding and good organization that will be important topics in the future years. It will be very difficult if not impossible to finance Ukraine's reconstruction unless Russia is being forced to pay substantial war reparations. The best way of securing such financing is to seize and confiscate the $300 billion of Russian Central Bank currency reserves held in the West.

Different Choices, Divergent Paths: Poland and Ukraine

Thorvaldur Gylfason, Eduard Hochreiter, and Tadeusz Kowalski

In three earlier papers, two of us compared economic developments in each of the three Baltic countries (Estonia, Latvia, and Lithuania) with developments in three regional peers (Georgia, Croatia, and Belarus).[1] The results we reported were broadly similar across the three comparisons: the Baltic economies grew more rapidly than those of their peers during the first 20–30 years of their transition to a market economy. As was to be expected from the theory of economic growth, the Baltics grew more

The authors thank Anders Åslund, Mario Holzner, Kateryna Romanchuk, Robert Stehrer, and Richard J. Sweeney for their comments on earlier versions of this material.

[1] Gylfason and Hochreiter (2009, 2011, 2022).

T. Gylfason (✉)
University of Iceland, Reykjavík, Iceland

CESifo, Munich, Germany
e-mail: gylfason@hi.is

R. Z. Aliber et al. (eds.), *Fault Lines After COVID-19*,
https://doi.org/10.1007/978-3-031-26482-5_10

rapidly because they placed more emphasis on investment, education, and trade as well as on good governance and institutions inspired by the European perspective, that is, their determination to join the European Union at the earliest possible opportunity.

In this paper, we undertake a similar comparison of economic developments in Poland and Ukraine since the collapse of communism in Central and Eastern Europe (CEE), seeking to understand how and why Poland charged so far ahead of Ukraine. Among other things, we want to understand the extent to which observed growth differentials can be traced to increased efficiency in the use of capital and other resources (intensive growth) rather than to simple accumulation of capital (extensive growth).

History and Initial Conditions

Sharing a long border of 535 km, Poland and Ukraine have long and closely related histories. For more than two centuries the lands of western Ukraine were a part of the Polish-Lithuanian Commonwealth. At the end of the eighteenth century, the Commonwealth ceased to exist after three consecutive partitions. Prussia annexed its western part. Its eastern territory, including Ukrainian lands, became a part of the Russian Empire. The south-eastern part, Galicia, inhabited mainly by people who would define themselves as Ukrainians, found itself under Habsburg Austria's reign (Snyder, 2003).

For over 123 years, the multicultural peoples of the former Polish-Lithuanian Commonwealth lived under three different governance cultures. Prussia and Russia had military and bureaucratic foundations (Thompson, 1939). The modern German Reich, established by Bismarck in 1871, soon transformed itself into a well-organized and governed key European industrial superpower. In contrast, imperial Russia continued its autocratic system, heavily relying on comparative advantages based on natural resources and a rather late and regionally and sectorally uneven process of industrialization.

E. Hochreiter
wiiw—The Vienna Institute for International Economic Studies, Vienna, Austria

T. Kowalski
Poznan University of Economics and Business, Poznań, Poland

The Austrian Empire and later Austria-Hungary was a diversified multicultural state with relatively high regional freedom of administration, a large agricultural sector and also a rather late industrialization spurt. Galicia itself remained a source of agricultural products as well as an area with nascent oil and gas extraction. The Russian Empire and the German Reich followed Russification and Germanisation policies, respectively. The scope and depth of the past imprint—that is, path dependence—in the Polish and Ukrainian lands was a function of their time under these governance cultures and institutions.

The outcome of World War I (WWI) greatly changed the map of Europe. In 1918, like several other European counties, Poland was recreated in its former territories and became an independent state until Nazi Germany and Soviet Russia's invasion and partition in 1939. The western and parts of the south-western Ukrainian lands returned to the re-emerged Polish state after 123 years. The rest of Ukrainian lands continued to be controlled by Russia, which replaced the tsarist autocracy with a Soviet dictatorship after the Bolshevik revolution.

After World War II (WWII), Poland's borders were redefined by the Allies. Its territory in the east was reduced, and Poland was shifted to the west. Ukrainian lands became formally integrated under the label of the Ukrainian Soviet Socialist Republic. The republic continued to be a part of a centralistic, single-party controlled Soviet Union deprived of market allocation mechanisms and the principles of the rule of law and civic liberties. In 1945–1989 Poland was a part of Soviet-controlled CEE. The Soviet model was imposed on Poland, but the country, in all respects, enjoyed relatively more leeway than many Soviet satellite regimes in CEE. In economic terms, what mattered most was the preservation of private ownership, including 70% of the arable land, the private small business sector, and international academic and cultural relations, including greater freedom of thought and speech. These circumstances made it possible in Poland to build human and social capital. Individuals could climb the ladder outside the state and party ranks. Such specific conditions and the politically progressive Catholic hierarchy at that time were vital for developing a partly independent intellectual climate. To the extent possible, Poland became a CEE leader in at least partly opposing the Soviet-imposed oppressive model of inefficient state-directed central planning.

Any comparative study of the transformation of Poland and Ukraine needs to consider their historical heritage. In the twentieth century up to 1991, only western Ukraine had an inter-war episode of a market economy and democracy. That period was shared with Poland. After WWII, Ukraine and Poland (up to 1989) functioned under distinct Soviet models.

All told, there emerged stark differences between the two countries, specifically their different approaches towards

(a) The EU versus Russia—in that Poland decided to join the EU as quickly as possible and did so in 2004 while Ukraine vacillated between conflicting plans to cooperate with the EU and Russia, culminating in the Maidan Revolution of 2014, followed by a Russian invasion later in 2014 and again in 2022.
(b) Full versus incomplete transition to market economy—in that Poland developed quickly into a full-fledged market economy while Ukraine's transition has been less complete and more volatile and remains work in progress.
(c) Democracy versus anocracy—in that Poland became a full-fledged democracy while Ukraine suffered setbacks and cannot yet be viewed as an unfettered democracy.

After regaining independence during 1989–1991, the shape of the trajectory of per capita GDP was qualitatively similar across the CEE region. In each country, the trajectory was shaped like a sickle but still with large quantitative differences. Due to its close economic ties to Russia, Ukraine suffered the largest fall during the collapse, even deeper than Russia, while the output decline in Poland as well as in the CEE region, including the Baltics, was much smaller (Fig. 1a). Ukraine is unique in that its per capita GDP in 2021 had not yet been restored to its initial level in 1990.

Sources do not agree on the initial levels of per capita GDP at PPP in the two countries. The World Bank reports that per capita GDP was 45% higher in Ukraine than in Poland in 1990 (World Bank WDI 2022, see Fig. 1).[2] Poland's experiment with shock therapy as described by Sachs (1993) produced the shortest and mildest but still painful transformation recession among CEE countries. Poland has enjoyed stable growth since 1992, resulting in a more than threefold rise in real per capita GDP at

[2] Kowalski (2013) reports that they were about the same in 1989.

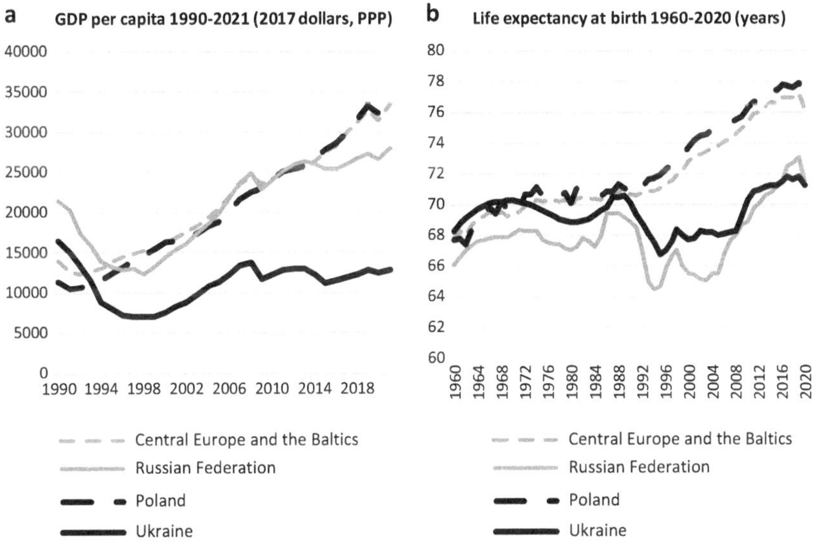

Fig. 1 GDP per capita and life expectancy. (Statistical sources: World Bank, *World Development Indicators*)

PPP. By contrast, Ukraine's economy has been stagnant or rather in decline since 1990.[3]

Economic indicators tell only part of the story. Figure 1b presents a corresponding comparison of life expectancy at birth; it was similar in Poland and Ukraine in 1960 as well as 1990. In Poland, life expectancy declined by a year after 1989 compared with a decline of almost four years in Ukraine, a difference that has persisted as Poland's life expectancy exceeded that of Ukraine by more than five years in 2020—76.5 years in Poland versus 71 years in Ukraine. The point of this comparison is that key economic and social developments tend to go hand in hand. The figures on life expectancy are not subject to the same concerns about accuracy as the data on GDP.

Since 1990, due to emigration, Poland's population has been stagnant at 38 million. From 1990 to 2021, Ukraine lost about 15% of her population to emigration, from 52 million in 1990 to 44 million in 2021.

[3] The reliability of these comparisons is in doubt, however, due to concerns about the quality of especially the Ukrainian data.

The importance of the initial position of the two countries around 1990 goes far beyond the level of per capita GDP. Whether or not per capita GDP was similar in the two countries at that time, their initial conditions were quite different in many ways (Åslund, 2015, Ch. 1). Millions of Poles had visited western Europe as tourists or temporary workers during the 1980s and many spoke English, so they knew the West in 1990 and how it functioned and they wanted Poland to become more like the West, while hardly any Ukrainians had the same experience. In Ukraine, hardly anybody spoke English or had any Western education. By 1990, Poland had for the most part freed itself from Russia and adopted the rule of law, but Ukraine had not. Poland gained competent leaders, including a liberal economic group around Leszek Balcerowicz, who had knowledge of the structure and functioning of the market economies of the West and had worked for years on ways to change the economic system, but Ukraine did not. In Ukraine, put bluntly, nobody had a clear clue of what kind of market economy to strive for.

As an old independent state, Poland had all relevant state institutions as well as relevant though outdated laws to regulate its relatively large private sector. Ukraine had none of this. Poland had some rule of law, Ukraine did not. Ukraine had to break out of the unruly rouble zone, suffering disastrous hyperinflation, while Poland had just a bout of it. In short, Poland was ready for new conditions, but Ukraine was not. Poland enjoyed all the international support it needed, both financial and trade access, Ukraine did not. Ukraine became independent in a compromise between the old nomenklatura, which wanted to escape radical reforms à la russe, and western Ukrainian nationalists who just wanted independence. These differences explain some of the differences catalogued in Table 1.

Tinbergen (1955) distinguished two kinds of economic policy, qualitative and quantitative. Any successfully launched systemic transformation requires the design and implementation of a qualitative economic policy first. It must adjust the existing institutions and set up a framework of new institutions overhauling the old structures accountable for unfavourable initial conditions. A well-designed and implemented qualitative policy is only a necessary condition for the departure from the initial doldrums. It must be accompanied by a bold and consistent quantitative economic policy to achieve a new path of sustainable development. Comparative analyses of cases of economic transformation, apart from the technicalities of both kinds of policies, need to consider the external and internal conditions. They set up boundaries of socially and politically feasible solutions.

Table 1 Initial conditions and early transition policies

Specification	*Ukraine*	*Poland*
Programme launch	Nov. 1994	Jan. 1990
Monetary and fiscal policy	Restrictive	Restrictive
Incomes policy	Mild	Restrictive
Exchange rate policy	Devaluation	Devaluation
Nominal anchor	Managed floating rate	Fixed exchange rate and wage control
Real anchor	Money supply and interest rate	Interest rate
Internal convertibility (for companies)	Yes	Yes
Internal convertibility (for households)	Restricted	Yes
External convertibility	Very restricted	Restricted
Main privatization method	Coupon	Direct
Date of starting privatization	1995	1990
Launch of stock exchange	1991	1991
Lowest level of GDP in year	1998	1991
Scale of decrease (1989=100)	36.6	82.2
Population in 1990 (million)	51.9	38.1

Source: Kowalski and Shachmurove (2018)

At the outset of politically feasible economic transformation, no theory was ready to be implemented. So, Poland's first cabinet, voted in by a new semi-freely elected parliament, had no choice but to experiment with an overhaul of the old system with a new one based on market principles. In 1989, the reformers did not have to create a new legal environment from scratch because some laws enacted before WWII were still valid. The overhaul of the legal framework was vital for the liberalization of the economy, the creation of a new financial system, and privatization, which became a foundation for the new socio-economic system. In other CEE countries, particularly those under prolonged Soviet dominance like Ukraine, introducing a modern legal system based on the protection of property rights and freedom of entrepreneurship was a significant hurdle. Ukraine, launching its major reforms almost five years after Poland, was a latecomer and could base its transformation on experience of the pioneers. Yet, due to the initial gap and lack of expertise, this task needed much time, slowing transition, and contributed to some flaws, for example, in the process and outcome of privatization.

The transition varied across CEE because the process of rejecting state socialism differed from country to country. The long-lasting process of rejecting single-party rule started in Poland in 1956. Later, a series of protests (1968, 1970, 1976, 1980–1981) resulted in the establishment of the independent trade union 'Solidarity' movement, which, at its peak, claimed over 10 million members. The economy became a battlefield of the powers wishing to preserve the one-party rule and the democratic opposition representing revolted consumers. In 1989, the accrued social and political conflicts could finally be resolved in Round Table Talks. The transformation in Ukraine was ignited by the implosion of the Soviet Union and was controlled by the progressive members of the then-Ukrainian parliament.

In Poland, the economic situation at the end of 1989 was highly unfavourable. Hyperinflation and supply shortages had to be addressed first by the stabilization policy package introduced in January 1990.

Polish stabilization policy, based on fiscal, monetary, and exchange rate policies, aimed at overcoming internal and external disequilibria. The internal disequilibrium was represented by hyperinflation and supply shortages. The external disequilibrium was reflected in the lack of foreign reserves, a massive gap between official and black-market exchange rates, and inability to service foreign debt. Hard budget constraints, control of wage rates, attractive interest rates on Polish zloty deposits, and a steep devaluation of the zloty were implemented (see Table 1). After the mildest and shortest transformation recession among all CEE countries, this policy package put the economy on a new path of development. Fiscal, monetary, and exchange rate policies were fine-tuned in the following years. What mattered very much was that all changes implemented in the domain of qualitative policy were consistent with the EU *Acqui Communautaire*.[4]

The Ukrainian economy was deeply integrated with the rest of the USSR. It started to deteriorate in the wake of disturbances stemming from the collapse of the centrally planned economy, disturbances that a market-based system could not immediately replace. Ukraine's fiscal, monetary, and exchange rate policies followed the path of Poland's and some other early reformers, but they were hampered by deficiencies in qualitative policy and, in particular, the method and practice of privatization, which in Ukraine led to the concentration of ownership and power. The oligarchs influenced both the design and the implementation of industrial

[4] Already in 1991, Poland declared its intention to join the EU.

and fiscal policy as well as the banking system. The similarity of Ukrainian quantitative policy was apparent; what mattered was the unfinished qualitative framework of economic policy and the burden of value chains and economic ties with the Russian Federation, which failed to create a modern state of the law with functional markets and democratic institutions. Moreover, Russia's constant interference in Ukrainian internal affairs worsened the Ukrainian situation, culminating in Russia's annexation of Crimea and eastern strips of Ukraine in 2014. The years 2014–2022 were marked by Ukrainian efforts to improve its institutions and the functioning of markets despite adverse domestic and external economic conditions.

General Methodological Framework and Determinants of Growth

The study of systemic transformation in CEE around 1990 needs a broad theoretical and methodological context as developed by the new institutional literature. For our comparative study, the concepts of path dependence and Schumpeterian creative destruction are particularly useful for understanding the qualitative dimension of systemic transformation.

What can the theory of economic growth tell us about the reasons for the substantial differences in economic developments in Poland and Ukraine? Recall that these differences are highlighted by the threefold difference in per capita GDP and five-year difference in life expectancy. Our aim is to compare some key determinants of growth, using economic and social indicators side by side. We attempt to disentangle efficiency and accumulation and to combine path dependence and the role and scope of creative destruction, to ask what they can tell us about Poland and Ukraine since 1990. We realize that, to answer our question, statistics will not do. We also need stories to put meat on the skeleton we want to present.

We begin with investment, trade, and education.

A. Investment, Trade, and Education

Investment matters for growth. Both countries invested about 21% of GDP on average during 1990–2021, a figure that is equal to the OECD average of recent decades, but far less than is needed in the two countries under review. Poland's investment ratio was less volatile while that of Ukraine declined over time (Fig. 2a). Net FDI inflows in both countries

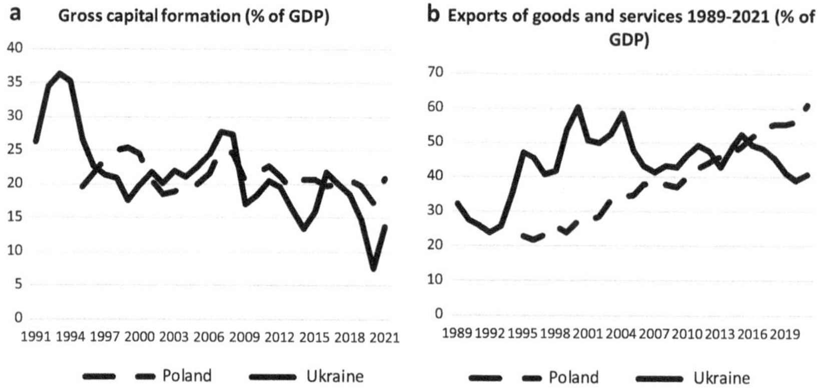

Fig. 2 Investment and exports (% of GDP). (Statistical sources: World Bank, *World Development Indicators*)

fluctuated widely and amounted to a bit less than 3% of GDP on average 1990–2020, a bit more in Poland than in Ukraine (not shown).

Poland's exports amounted to 39% of GDP on average 1995–2021 compared with 47% in Ukraine. Poland's export ratio grew steadily after 1995 while that of Ukraine was stagnant (Fig. 2b). About three quarters of Poland's exports go to Germany and other EU countries, while China is Ukraine's largest foreign trade partner, followed by Germany, Poland, and Russia. Import restrictions were phased out in Poland as required by EU membership, while Ukraine retains significant restrictions, including some remnants of currency control (not shown). Ukraine's trade faces many other hurdles, including frequent legal disputes concerning the determination of customs value. Poland's trade and investment were encouraged by its EU and NATO membership in 2004 and 1999.

Exports from Poland are less concentrated and more diversified than exports from Ukraine (Fig. 3). This matters because economic diversification as an insurance strategy against macroeconomic risk is good for growth (Gylfason, 2017). Less concentration means more competition among exporters and greater diversification implies more pluralism among trade partners. Competition and pluralism are good for growth.

Concerning education, the evolution of net secondary school enrolment favours Poland, not Ukraine (Fig. 4a). School life expectancy is

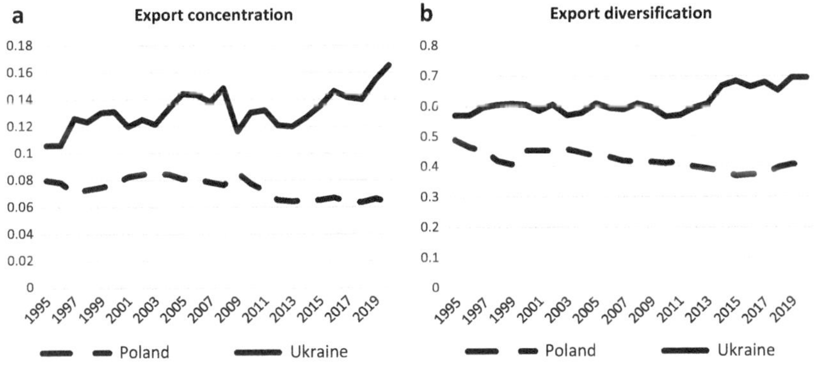

Fig. 3 Export concentration and diversification 1995–2020 (indices from 0 to 1, higher values mean more concentration and less diversification). (Statistical sources: UNCTAD)

16 years in Poland against 15 years in Ukraine.[5] On the other hand, Ukraine has more students enrolled at the university level (Fig. 4b), but both levels and composition of education matter. Natkhov and Polishchuk (2019) report a much higher ratio of law students to science students in Ukraine than in Poland, presumably a reflection of excessive rent seeking in Ukraine at the expense of science.

B. Industrial Structure

The share of agriculture in GDP has declined sharply in both countries (Fig. 5a); from 25% in 1991 to 11% in 2021 in Ukraine, a major exporter of wheat, and from 6% in 1995 to 2% in 2021 in Poland, slightly above the EU average.[6] Meanwhile, the share of manufactures in exports grew from 60% to 80% during 1992–2021 in Poland but declined from 66% to 43% in Ukraine during 1996–2021 (Fig. 5b).

C. Democracy and Governance

Both countries have a complex relationship with democracy even if the Polity IV project, the industry standard for democracy metrics, has

[5] Source: UNESCO, http://data.un.org/Data.aspx?d=UNESCO&f=series%3ASLE_1T6

[6] Both countries are net exporters of food and agricultural products.

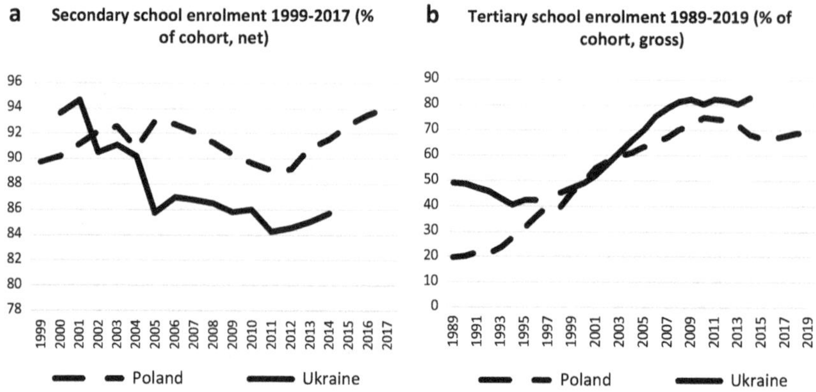

Fig. 4 Education. (Statistical sources: World Bank, *World Development Indicators*)

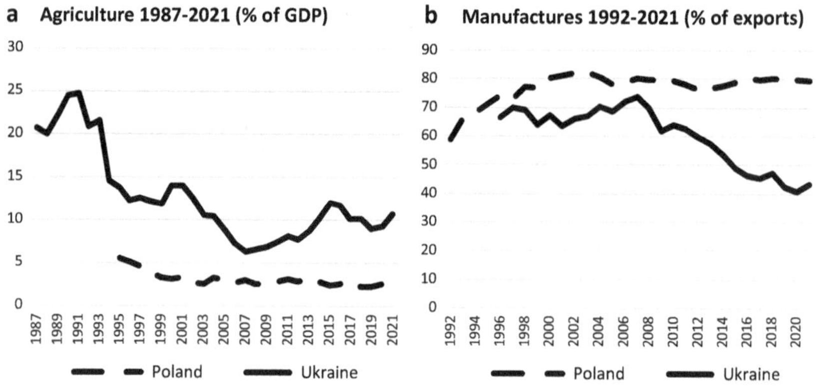

Fig. 5 Agriculture and manufacturing. (Statistical sources: World Bank, *World Development Indicators*)

awarded Poland a full score of 10 since 2002 on a scale from -10 to 10 (Fig. 6a). Other related and relevant metrics include the following:

(a) Freedom House awards Poland a democracy score of 81 out of 100 in 2022, down from 93 in 2016, while Ukraine scores 61, virtually unchanged from 2012 (Fig. 6b).

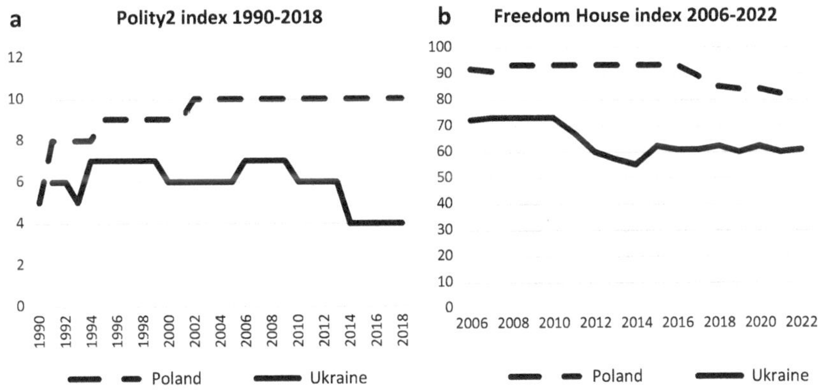

Fig. 6 Democracy and freedom. (Statistical sources: Center for Systemic Peace and Freedom House)

(b) The Heritage Foundation ranks economic freedom in Poland 39th among 177 countries compared with Ukraine's rank of 130 (not shown).[7]
(c) The World Justice Project awards Poland a higher score than Ukraine for the rule of law (Fig. 7a).[8]
(d) Reporters Without Borders award Poland a higher ranking than Ukraine for press freedom (Fig. 7b).[9]
(e) The World Bank assigns Poland higher scores for public governance than Ukraine by an increasing overall margin (not shown).[10]
(f) Poland is less egalitarian than Ukraine (Fig. 8a).[11]
(g) Transparency International considers Poland less corrupt than Ukraine, registering small gains in Ukraine since 2013 and losses in Poland since 2015 (Fig. 8b).

[7] Heritage Foundation, https://www.heritage.org/index/ranking

[8] World Justice Project, https://worldjusticeproject.org/our-work/research-and-data/wjp-rule-law-index-2021

[9] Reporters without borders, https://rsf.org/en/index

[10] World Bank, *World Development Indicators* 2022.

[11] Most data for Ukraine, particularly regarding the first years of transformation, must be interpreted cautiously. During 1992–2019, Ukraine's Gini index as reported by the World Bank was on average similar as in Sweden (27), well below Germany (30), Poland (33), the UK (38), and the USA (41).

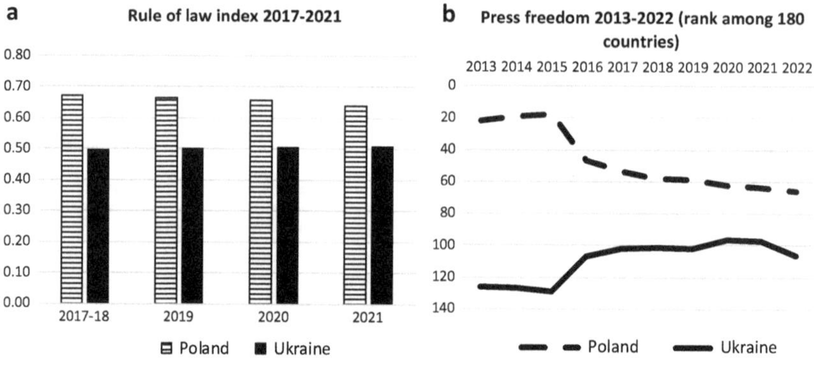

Fig. 7 Rule of law and press freedom. (Statistical sources: World Justice Project and Reporters Without Borders)

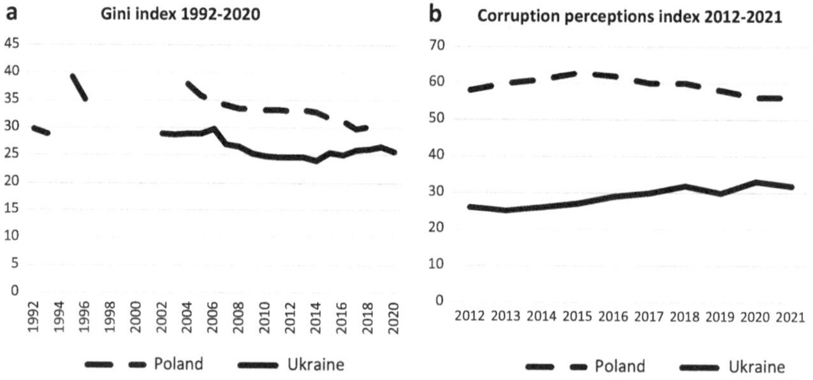

Fig. 8 Equality and corruption. (World Bank, *World Development Indicators*)

Let us offer a few further comments on some of these charts.

Beginning with Fig. 7a, both countries face significant challenges concerning the rule of law. In Poland, the government has been credibly accused of failing since the 2015 elections to adhere to European and Polish constitutional law, thus creating a conflict, at home as well as vis-à-vis the EU, which remains unresolved. In Ukraine, reorganization of the military, the Ministry of Finance, and the Central Bank have brought those institutions outside the sphere of influence of the old elites, which in the past earned Ukraine a reputation for pervasive corruption. In the judicial system, however, much remains to be done.[12]

As shown in Fig. 7b, Poland enjoys much freer press than Ukraine, where mass media from the onset of systemic transformation became dependent on the money of oligarchs, who were interested in establishing their influence in the state apparatus, either by their own direct participation in state governance or indirectly through their representatives. The press and other media became a major tool in this respect. In Poland, the first independent national newspaper, *Gazeta Wyborcza*, was launched in 1989 to support the Solidarity movement in its participation in the first semi-free election. It still exists and has the highest circulation of all newspapers (both print and digital) in Poland. Despite the lead position of GW, the press market is rather fragmented. Recently, a set of regional newspapers was bought by the state-controlled oil company Orlen S.A. The regional titles got new chief editors and became partisan. Despite these developments, the press in Poland remains efficient and free.

Like the rule of law and press freedom, good governance is good for growth as Olson et al. (2000) and many others have argued. Poland scored higher than Ukraine in each of the four categories of governance reported by the World Bank in 2010 and 2020 (not shown). As already mentioned, after the 2015 election the government introduced a series of institutional changes breaching independence and focused on the structure and governance of the judicial system. The changes were against the *Acquis Communautaire* and were opposed by a vast majority of rank-and-file judges (Sweeney, 2018; Kowalski, 2021). Poland is less egalitarian than Ukraine (Fig. 8a). This matters because equality tends to go along with growth as well as with several other ingredients of social capital—democracy, transparency, trust, the rule of law, and low corruption (Fig. 8b)—that are also good for growth (Berg & Ostry, 2017).

When deserved, trust is good for growth, both popular trust in institutions and the trust that citizens have in one another. Trust is an important ingredient of social capital, viewed as the glue that keeps society functioning smoothly and cohesively, without corrosive strife. Poland was included

[12] With regard to Ukraine's application for EU accession, the European Commission has made seven key recommendations, six of which concern judicial reform and corruption prevention Source: Commission Opinion on Ukraine's application for membership of the European Union, 17 June 2022, https://neighbourhood-enlargement.ec.europa.eu/opinion-ukraines-application-membership-european-union_en. The European Council, on 23 June 2022, granted candidate status to Ukraine.

in five of the seven waves of measurements taken by the World Values Survey since 1990 and Ukraine was included in four.[13] Among the questions asked in the surveys is whether respondents think that most people can be trusted or whether they think they need to be careful in their dealings with others. Poland in 1994 is the sole instance of trust outweighing distrust in either country.

D. Monetary and Fiscal Policy

After an initial bout of hyperinflation as communism collapsed, both countries managed to bring inflation down (Fig. 9a). Poland reduced inflation to low single-digit figures from 2001 onward.[14] Ukraine had greater difficulties, registering 13% annual inflation on average 1997–2021 compared with 4% in Poland. Both countries imposed fiscal and monetary restraint, coupled with massive currency depreciation. However, Poland was more consistent and started earlier, in January 1990 compared with November 1994 in Ukraine (recall Table 1).

Fig. 9 Inflation and unemployment. (World Bank, *World Development Indicators*)

[13] Source: World Values Survey, https://www.worldvaluessurvey.org/wvs.jsp

[14] Following the pandemic and war in Ukraine, Poland records one of the highest inflation rates in CEE in 2022.

Up to 2016 consecutive Polish governments pursued rather conservative fiscal policies regardless of their political orientation. Such an attitude stemmed from the recent history of hyperinflation and the determination to prepare the economy for EU membership. Overcoming inflation would not be possible without a conservative and independent central bank. In Central Europe, Poland was one of the pioneers of prudent fiscal policy (Green et al., 2001). It was also reflected in the new Constitution of 1997, which envisaged rules protecting the country from breaching the 60% threshold of public debt to GDP.

Along with other CEE countries, Poland established a politically and functionally independent central bank (Hochreiter & Kowalski, 2000). Its position was guaranteed in the 1997 constitution as well. Meanwhile, the Ukrainian economy suffered from the implosion of the Russian economy and struggled to establish its own currency. The institutional framework for fiscal and monetary policy was not fully developed. In the first years of independence and after 1994, Ukraine's central bank directly financed parts of public sector borrowing requirements. Therefore, its inflation reflected both real economic challenges and institutional deficiencies. The IMF's financial development index for Poland exceeds that for Ukraine (not shown).

E. Labour

Poland had higher and more volatile unemployment than Ukraine during 1992–2001, or 11% versus 9% of the labour force on average, but still managed to bring unemployment down from 20% of the labour force in 2002 to 3% in 2021, an impressive feat (Fig. 9b). Relatively low unemployment in Ukraine is partly due to stalled restructuring in Ukrainian manufacturing and mining. As already emphasized, both main sectors of the economy were controlled by oligarchs who were able to shape legislation in such a way that they continued to extract profits without much effort to modernize their sectors.[15]

[15] Several Ukrainian enterprises switched to part-time work, which official statistics recorded as full employment.

Conclusion

Investment, exports, and education are important pillars of economic growth around the world. In Poland and Ukraine, investment in machinery and equipment relative to GDP has been roughly the same since 1989, while Poland had more extensive and diversified exports and fewer import restrictions. Poland developed education, which shows up in one extra year of school life expectancy, 16 years in Poland compared with 15 years in Ukraine. While Ukraine vacillated between cooperation with the EU versus Russia and was invaded by Russia in 2014 and again in 2022, Poland was strongly motivated by the EU perspective, which materialized in 2004. It encouraged political and economic integration, including liberalized trade, access to the single European market, flows of capital, restructuring of the economic system, privatization of state assets, and the construction of market-friendly institutions to EU specifications as well as membership in NATO. While all this was going on in Poland, across the border, Ukraine was hampered by political divisions, corruption, poor governance, halting democracy, and haphazard human rights. Ukraine's success in its fight for survival might also have a deep and sustained positive impact on institutions and economic structures.

References

Åslund, A. (2015). *Ukraine: What went wrong and how to fix it.* Peterson Institute for International Economics.

Berg, A., & Ostry, J. D. (2017). Inequality and unsustainable growth: Two sides of the same coin? *IMF Economic Review, 65*(4), 792–815.

Green, C. J., Holmes, M. J., & Kowalski, T. (2001). Poland: A successful transition to budget sustainability? *Emerging Markets Review, 2*(2), 161–183. https://doi.org/10.1016/S1566-0141(01)00015-2

Gylfason, T. (2017). From double diversification to efficiency and growth. *Comparative Economic Studies, 59*(2), 149–168.

Gylfason, T., & Hochreiter, E. (2009). Growing apart? A tale of two republics: Estonia and Georgia. *European Journal of Political Economy, 25*(3), 355–370.

Gylfason, T., & Hochreiter, E. (2011). Growing together: Croatia and Latvia. *Comparative Economic Studies, 53*(2), 165–197.

Gylfason, T., & Hochreiter, E. (2022). To grow or not to grow: Belarus and Lithuania. *Comparative Economic Studies.* https://doi.org/10.1057/s41294-022-00188-1

Hochreiter, E., & Kowalski, T. (2000). Central banks in European emerging market economies in the 1990s. *Banca Nazionale del Lavoro Quarterly Review, 53*(212), 45–75.

Kowalski, T. (2013). *Globalization and transformation in central European countries: The case of Poland*. Poznan University of Economics Press.

Kowalski, T. (2021). The post-2015 institutional shock in Poland: Some empirical findings. *CESifo Forum, 22*(01), 43–48.

Kowalski, T., & Shachmurove, Y. (2018). Economic development in Poland and Ukraine: The case of foreign trade. *Interdisciplinary Journal of Economics and Business Law, 7*(2), 35–61.

Natkhov, T., & Polishchuk, L. (2019). Quality of institutions and the allocation of talent: Cross-national evidence. *Kyklos, 72*(4), 527–569.

Olson, M., Sarna, N., & Anand, V. (2000). Governance and growth: A simple hypothesis explaining cross-country differences in productivity growth. *Public Choice, 102*(3), 341–364.

Sachs, J. (1993). *Poland's jump to the market economy*. The MIT Press.

Snyder, T. (2003). *The Reconstruction of Nations: Poland, Ukraine, Lithuania, Belarus, 1569–1999*. Yale University Press.

Sweeney, R. J. (2018). Constitutional conflicts in the European Union: Court packing in Poland versus the United States. *Economics and Business Review, 4*(18), 3–29.

Thompson, D. (1939). The problem child of Europe. *Foreign Affairs*, 18–389. https://www.foreignaffairs.com/articles/germany/1940-04-01/problem-child-europe. Accessed 20 Feb 2022.

Tinbergen, J. (1955). *Economic policy: Principles and design*. North-Holland.

World Bank WDI, (2022). World Development Indicators. https://data.worldbank.org/

World Values Survey. (2021). See http://www.worldvaluessurvey.org/WVSContents.jsp

Russia's Use of the Kosovo Case to Legitimize Military Interventions and Territorial Conquests

Valur Ingimundarson

While Russia has offered a mixture of rationalizations for its 2022 invasion of Ukraine, including "denazification," "demilitarization"[1] or the "return of Russian lands,"[2] it has consistently clung to a core political and legal justification for engaging in military interventions and border changes in post-Soviet states. It refers to the "Kosovo precedent" or NATO's 1999 military intervention against Serbia—without a UN Security Council backing—and the West's subsequent recognition of Kosovo's indepen-

[1] "Address by the President of the Russian Federation," President of Russia website, February 24, 2022, accessed October 25, 2022, http://en.kremlin.ru/events/president/news/67843

[2] "[Vladimir Putin's] Meeting with young entrepreneurs, engineers and scientists," President of Russia website, June 9, 2022, accessed October 15, 2022, http://en.kremlin.ru/events/president/news/68606

V. Ingimundarson (✉)
University of Iceland, Reykjavik, Iceland
e-mail: vi@hi.is

R. Z. Aliber et al. (eds.), *Fault Lines After COVID-19*,
https://doi.org/10.1007/978-3-031-26482-5_11

dence in 2008. Russia's interpretation does not only apply to the use of force itself, which it has usually justified in pre-emptive as well as preventive terms—to deter or stop "ethnic cleansing" and "acts of genocide"—but also to the conferring of state recognition on contested territories in Georgia and Ukraine, such as Abkhazia and South Ossetia in 2008, Crimea in 2014, and Donetsk, Luhansk, Kherson, and Zaporizhzhia in 2022. The Kosovo case is part of a broader Russian anti-Western narrative, centring on U.S. efforts to preserve a post-Cold War unipolar order through a variety of unilateral actions designed to weaken Russia. It includes military interventions in the former Yugoslavia, Iraq and, later, in Libya as well as NATO's eastward expansion, with the prospective additions of Georgia and Ukraine.[3]

In this chapter, I discuss how Russia has used Western support for Kosovo to instrumentalize contested international norms for geopolitical and territorial aggrandizements. To further its foreign policy aims in Georgia and Ukraine, Russia has sought to do two things: first, to assert its power and authority over what it considers its own "spheres of influence," variously dubbed, in euphemistic terms, as "post-Soviet space," "near-abroad," or "regions of Russian privileged interest"[4]; and second, to compete geopolitically with the West through mimicry or by framing its own actions as mirror images of Western ones.[5] To combine these separate, if interlinked motives for armed intervention, the creation of new states and the annexation of territories, the Russians have turned concepts such as "genocide," "self-determination," and "sovereignty" into signifiers without fixed legal or political meanings. These terms are constantly being reconfigured, reinterpreted, and reframed to fit each circumstance without the need to establish consistency or inner logic. Thus, paradoxically, even if Russia still refers to the Kosovo War as a breach of international law and sticks to its opposition to Kosovo's independence, it relies on both examples to justify its own military interventions and territorial revisions in post-Soviet states.

[3] See, for example, Fyodor Liyanov, "Putin's Foreign Policy: The Quest to Restore Russia's Rightful Place," *Foreign Affairs* 95 (May–June 2016): 30–37.

[4] See Andrei Kazantsev, Sergei Lebedev, and Svetlana Medvedeva, "Russia's Policies in the Post-Soviet Space: Between Constructive Relations and Fighting the New Cold War," *Russian Politics*, 6, no. 4 (2021): 503–530.

[5] See Vasile Rotaru and Miruna Troncotă, "Continuity and change in instrumentalizing 'The Precedent.' How Russia uses Kosovo to legitimize the annexation of Crimea," *Southeast European and Black Sea Studies*, 17, no. 3 (2017): 325–345.

Framing the Kosovo Case

NATO rationalized the 1999 air war against Serbia on humanitarian grounds, that is, to put an end to ethnic cleansing operations against the majority Albanian population in Kosovo. Subsequently, most Western states supported the solution proposed, in 2007, by the Finnish UN's Special Representative for the future status of Kosovo, Martti Ahtisaari, for "supervised independence" of the entity, which had been under direct UN rule since the conclusion of the war.[6] When Russia and Serbia rejected the plan, the West backed Kosovo's unilateral declaration of independence in 2008. Prior to Kosovo's separation, Russia had consistently advocated against the right to unilateral secession and refused to recognize territorial changes in disputed areas. It pointed out that the Yugoslav ethno-federal system was modelled on the constitution of the Soviet Union,[7] which, in theory, accorded secession rights only to republics but not to autonomous units. Thus, even if Russia was partly responsible for maintaining the "frozen conflicts" in Abkhazia, South Ossetia, Transnistria, and Nagorno-Karabakh, it refused to recognize any of these separatist territories as independent.[8] Needless to say, other political explanations also played a role.[9] Russia was able to maintain its preponderant influence in "post-Soviet space" as a power broker in these unrecognized territories or independent states like Georgia, Moldova, Armenia, and Azerbaijan. Similarly, Russia wanted to cultivate its intimate historical relations with Serbia through its support on the Kosovo question.

The Western legal case for Kosovo's independence could be faulted for being legally and politically ambivalent. Kosovo was seen as a special case, sui generis, rooted in the violent disintegration of the former Yugoslavia,

[6] "Report of the Special Envoy of the Secretary-General on Kosovo's future status," UN Security Council, March 26, 2007, accessed October 15, 2022, https://digitallibrary.un.org/record/595358?ln=fr

[7] See Pavel K. Baev, "Russia's stance against secessions: From Chechnya to Kosovo," *International Peacekeeping,* 6, no. 3 (1999): 73–94; Baev, "The 'Kosovo Precedent' and Russian-Georgian Relations," PONARS Eurasia Policy Memo, No. 5 (March 2008), accessed October 15, 2022, https://www.ponarseurasia.org/wp-content/uploads/attachments/pepm_005.pdf

[8] On frozen conflicts, see, for example, Anton Bebler (ed.), *"Frozen conflicts" in Europe* (Opladen, Berlin, Toronto: Barbara Budrich Publishers, 2015).

[9] See Tero Lundstedt, "Inherited National Questions: The Soviet Legacy in Russia's International Law Doctrine on Self-determination," *Nordic Journal of International Law* 89, no. 1 (2020), 38–66.

which did not apply elsewhere. Before Serbian President Slobodan Milosevic's decision to deprive Kosovo—through extra-constitutional means—of its autonomy in 1989, it had been part of the rotating collective presidency of Yugoslavia, which gave it an elevated constitutional status on par with the six republics.[10] In addition, strengthening their case for self-determination, the two million Kosovo Albanians, who made up 90% of the population, had their own language, culture, and history, with the Serbian minority constituting only 5%. Yet, secession rights of the former republics of Yugoslavia did not include Kosovo because it was classified as a Serbian province.

Hence, there were only two ways to rationalize Kosovo's divorce from Serbia. First, it was argued, as Ahtisaari did, that after a sustained period of UN rule, during which Serbia's sovereignty was suspended, Kosovo's final status had to take the form of sovereignty; it was "unrealistic" to contemplate Kosovo's return to Serbia, for it would provoke a violent reaction by the Albanians. It was also contended that Kosovo's position was constitutionally weaker as part of Serbia than it had been under the Yugoslav ethno-federal system, which made it more vulnerable to Serbian repression. Second, a remedial legal argument was put forward: that Serbia had forfeited its right to rule over Kosovo because of its abysmal human rights record.[11] Indeed, many of the around 100 states that have so far recognized Kosovo's independence referred to victim-centred arguments, often colonial in nature, which were based on the notion that Serbia had lost moral authority to rule the territory.[12]

The counterargument was that the Kosovo case could hardly be interpreted as being unique in this regard because some other independence movements could claim that they had been subjected to gross human rights violations. Yet, given the changed realities on the ground—with a strong U.S. and NATO presence in Kosovo—the Serbs realized that there was no chance of evoking the status quo ante. Hence, in 2007, they were prepared to accept continued UN administration of Kosovo for 20 years as well as extensive Kosovo Albanian autonomy rights to retain formal

[10] The republics within Yugoslavia were: Serbia, Croatia, Slovenia, Macedonia, Montenegro, and Bosnia.

[11] "Report of the Special Envoy of the Secretary-General on Kosovo's future status."

[12] See, for example, Grace Bolton and Gezim Visoka, *Recognizing Kosovo's independence: Remedial secession or earned sovereignty?* Occasional Paper No. 11/10 (Oxford: Oxford University Press, 2019).

control over it. To the Albanians this sounded like institutionalizing a neo-colonial rule under UN auspices, which they firmly rejected.[13]

Russia's Intervention in Georgia

Russia's abrupt decision to abandon its long-standing policy on secession after the Georgian crisis erupted in August 2008 was justified by referring to Western acceptance of Kosovo's declaration of independence six months earlier. According to the new interpretation, former autonomous units in "post-Soviet space" could have a right to secede based on the "Kosovo precedent," especially, if not exclusively, on the grounds of remedial secession.[14] What prompted it was Georgia's failed invasion of South Ossetia, leading to a Russian military intervention. Shortly thereafter, Russia recognized both breakaway Georgian provinces of Abkhazia and South Ossetia, with populations of 230,000 and 50,000, respectively, as independent states. Russia accused Georgia of having breached the UN charter, with the aim, in President Dmitry Medvedev's words, of taking over South Ossetia "at the price of exterminating a whole people"—and preparing the same fate for Abkhazia, which was mostly spared in the 2008 conflict.

Even if its whole argument for intervention and recognition was based on the Kosovo case, Russia initially sought to distance itself from it in an uneasy attempt to accommodate the new policy with the old. It cited its historical mediating and peacekeeping roles in the conflict since the disintegration of the Soviet Union and its respect for Georgia's territorial integrity, even after Kosovo's declaration of independence. Russia's discourse soon, however, became fully aligned with its policy reversal; it contained ample references to UN "responsibility to protect" norms developed after the wars in Rwanda and in the former Yugoslavia, where international collective action was justified to protect populations against "ethnic cleansing," "war crimes," and "genocide."[15] Engaging in mimetic

[13] See Valur Ingimundarson, "The Politics of Memory and the Reconstruction of Albanian National Identity in Postwar Kosovo," *History and Memory*, 19, no. 1 (2007): 95–123.

[14] On the concept of remedial secession, see Jure Vidmar, "Remedial Secession in International Law: Theory and (Lack of) Practice," *St Antony's International Review*, 6, no. 1 (2010): 37–56.

[15] See Don Hubert and Ariela Blätter, "The Responsibility to Protect as International Crimes Prevention," *Global Responsibility to Protect* 4, no. 1 (2012): 38, 47–48; Emma McClean, "The Responsibility to Protect: The Role of International Human Rights Law," *Journal of Conflict & Security Law*, 13, no. 1 (2008), 125; Rama Mani and Thomas G. Weiss, "R2P's Missing Link, Culture," *Global Responsibility to Protect*, 3, no. 4 (2011), 454–455.

geopolitics, the Russians argued that if Kosovo was a unique case, South Ossetia and Abkhazia were also sui generis. To counter the accusation that Russia was pursuing a double standard because it refused to recognize Kosovo's independence, the Georgian human rights situation was described as being far more serious, spanning over 17 years during which ethnic cleansing and genocidal actions took place.[16]

Such an argument may have squared with Russia's new-found enthusiasm for "humanitarian warfare" after abandoning the principle of territorial integrity of states. But given Russia's patronage of the secessionist regions,[17] it raised the question of why the Russians had not intervened earlier to stop a genocide. There was, in fact, nothing that suggested that the Abkhaz and South Ossetian ethnic populations were facing an existential threat. The South Ossetians were the ones who had initiated the skirmishes, which prompted Georgian retaliation in August 2008. Georgia's failed attempt to bring the South Ossetians to heel by invading the territory in attempt to reclaim it gave the Russians the perfect pretext to intervene.

Russia's policy change on secession has, of course, to be seen as part of a broader goal to exert political influence in Georgia and Ukraine, reverse their Western orientation, and prevent them from joining NATO. Thus, Russia was not only determined to teach the Georgians a lesson, which it claimed was borrowed from a Western playbook, but also to deter U.S. geopolitical ambitions in the former Soviet republics. At the Bucharest summit in April 2008, NATO had stated that Georgia and Ukraine would eventually become members of the alliance.[18] France and Germany had vetoed a fast-track membership route for the countries because they feared that it would be seen as a provocation by Russia. But to sooth the United States, which was pushing for NATO's expansion, the open-ended wording of the statement on Georgia and Ukraine, containing no timetable,

[16] Gearóid Ó Tuathail, "Russia's Kosovo: A Critical Geopolitics of the August 2008 War over South Ossetia," *Eurasian Geography and Economics*, 49, no. 6 (2013), 697.

[17] See Andre W. M. Gerrits and Max Bader, "Russian patronage over Abkhazia and South Ossetia: implications for conflict resolution," *East European Politics*, 32, no. 3 (2016): 297–313.

[18] "Bucharest Summit Declaration Issued by the Heads of State and Government participating in the meeting of the North Atlantic Council in Bucharest on 3 April 2008," accessed October 25, 2022, https://www.nato.int/cps/en/natolive/official_texts_8443.htm

suggested a far more realistic prospect for accession than was the case. Finally, Russia was aware that any Western encroachments in this region would spoil its own efforts to facilitate the integration of former Soviet states into a political and economic bloc modelled on the EU. One such institutional body was the Eurasian Economic Union (EEU), made up of Russia, Belarus, and Kazakhstan, which Putin described—rather loftily—as being a supranational association capable or becoming one of the poles in the modern world.[19]

While de facto separate, Abkhazia and South Ossetia depend politically and economically on Russia and have failed to gain international recognition.[20] Thus, in contrast to Kosovo, only four states have done so: Venezuela, Syria, Nicaragua, and Nauru. This shows that Russia's argument for secession based on this precedent without any involvement of the state it formally belonged to, Georgia, was viewed with scepticism. Hardly viable as a state, South Ossetia never professed any desire to remain independent, a stance that has also much to do with the fact that North Ossetia is part of the Russian Federation. Following the Russian invasion of Ukraine, it declared that it would schedule a referendum on its integration with Russia in the summer of 2022; while it subsequently withdrew its plan pending further discussion with Russia, its goal of eventually becoming part of Russia has not changed.[21] Abkhazia, which is economically stronger, has shown no such interest, while continuing to rule out any constitutional ties with Georgia. The Abkhazians, however, are deeply reliant on Russia for external representation, with those of its citizens who do not have Russian passports being, in effect, stateless.

[19] "Putin's power play jeopardizes Eurasian Union plans," Deutsche Welle, March 15, 2014, accessed October 25, 2022, https://www.dw.com/en/putins-power-play-jeopardizes-eurasian-union-plans/a-17493164

[20] See David S. Siroky, Milos Popovic, and Nikola Mirilovic, "Unilateral secession, international recognition, and great power contestation," *Journal of Peace Research*, 58, no. 5 (2021): 1049–1067.

[21] "Georgian breakaway territory suspends announced referendum on joining Russia – decree," Reuters, May 30, 2022, accessed October 25, 2022, https://www.reuters.com/world/europe/georgian-breakaway-territory-suspends-announced-referendum-joining-russia-decree-2022-05-30/

Using Ukraine as a Case for Territorial Revisions

After its 2014 occupation of Crimea—in the wake of the downfall of the pro-Russian government in Ukraine—Russia acted in a far bolder fashion than in Georgia. It did not only want to grant Crimea independence but also to absorb it quickly into the Russian Federation. In Crimea's proclamation of independence, the right was reserved for applying to Russia for the inclusion of the territory as a separate subject. The proclamation itself was clearly modelled on Kosovo's declaration of independence,[22] but there was one sharp departure. Kosovo's constitution explicitly states that it "shall have no territorial claims against, and shall seek no union with, any State or part of any State."[23] What this really meant was that Kosovo was prohibited from joining Albania, which Western states believed could lead to regional instability.

Russia's decision to recognize Crimea as an independent state was rationalized by referring to the 2010 judgement of the International Court of Justice (ICJ) that Kosovo's independence declaration did not violate international law. While it may be argued that the ruling did not preclude such a legal interpretation, it was, in fact, more narrowly framed. It specifically focused on Kosovo within the context of UN Security Council Resolution 1244, which was adopted after the Kosovo War and which created the temporary exceptional legal regime that superseded the Serbian legal order in Kosovo. The failure to come to a negotiated settlement on Kosovo's future status, as required by the resolution, paved the way for a unilateral decision on independence.

Thus, in the case of Crimea, Russia continued to use the Kosovo precedent, but tweaked its meaning to fit different circumstances. The ICJ, in fact, stated unequivocally that "declarations of independence are illegal when connected with the unlawful use of force," which could be said to have applied in Russia's case.[24] As if realizing that it needed stronger

[22] See Juan Francisco Escudero Espinosa (ed.), *Self-Determination and Humanitarian Secession in International Law of a Globalized World. Kosovo v. Crimea* (Cham, Switzerland: Springer, 2017).

[23] "Kosovo's Constitution of 2008 with Amendments through 2016," The Constitute Project, April 27, 2022, accessed October 25, 2022, https://www.constituteproject.org/constitution/Kosovo_2016.pdf?lang=en

[24] International Court of Justice, "Reports of judgments, advisory opinions and orders accordance with international law of the unilateral declaration of independence in respect of Kosovo advisory opinion of 22 July 2010," 437–438, accessed October 25, 2022, https://www.icj-cij.org/public/files/case-related/141/141-20100722-ADV-01-00-EN.pdf

arguments to justify its annexation policy, Russia also referred to historical rights and to the correction of historical wrongs: that Crimea had belonged to Russia for centuries until it was illegally transferred to Ukraine in the 1950s. Such a claim may have buttressed support for incorporating Crimea into the Russian Federation, but it had no basis in international law.[25] And given Ukraine's strong opposition to the Crimean annexation, only about 15 states have recognized it—some of them formally and others informally through supporting statements.

The Crimean intervention was a dress rehearsal for Russia's 2022 war against Ukraine. The day before the invasion, Russia recognized the independence of Donetsk and Luhansk in the Donbas region. Using the same methods as in Abkhazia and South Ossetia, Russia claimed that the decision had been made on humanitarian grounds to protect civilians, including Russian ones, facing what it termed the "threat of direct physical annihilation by the Ukrainian government," whose military actions in the Donbas were "nothing short of a genocide against Ukraine's own people."[26] As was the case in Georgia, there was nothing to support this claim. While it is estimated that the civil conflict in the region had cost over 2000 civilian lives from August 2014 until February 2022, the vast majority of which occurred in 2014–2015, it could not by any means be squared with the definition of a genocide as an attempt to annihilate systematically a group of people. In April 2022, Putin justified Russia's recognition of the "republics of Donbass" by referring to the independence of Kosovo. And, as the Russians did with respect to Crimea, he also mentioned the ICJ ruling on Kosovo: that in exercising the right to self-determination, there was no obligation to apply for permission to declare independence to the central government or that of Ukraine.[27]

After the invasion of Ukraine, Russia's goal of territorial aggrandizement became far more explicit. To be sure, the Russians had to abandon their original war objective of staging a "regime change" and of imposing

[25] "Address by the President of the Russian Federation [on Crimea]," March 18, 2014, accessed October 15, 2022, http://en.kremlin.ru/events/president/news/20603

[26] "Russian Foreign Ministry statement on recognising the independence of the Donetsk and Lugansk people's republics," February 23, 2022, accessed October 25, 2022, https://russiaeu.ru/printpage/en/node/7353

[27] "Putin cites precedent of Kosovo in explaining recognition of DPR, LPR," TASS, April 26, 2022, accessed October 15, 2022, https://tass.com/politics/1443661?utm_source=google.com & utm_medium=organic & utm_campaign=google.com & utm_referrer=google.com

a direct rule over the whole of Ukraine. But they are still committed to the late September 2022 decision—made after show referendums—to annex the eastern provinces of Luhansk and Donetsk and well as the southern ones of Kherson and Zaporizhzhia from Ukraine. Earlier, the Russians had prepared the groundwork by referring to Kosovo. In mid-May 2022, former President Medvedev and current Deputy Chairman of Russia's Security Council, put it, sarcastically, this way: "[O]ur country doesn't care about G7's non-recognition of the new borders [of Ukraine]; what matters is the true will of the people living there. Do not forget the Kosovo precedent, our Western friends."[28] Putin went further in dividing states into true sovereign states, which had to fulfil strict "military-political" and "technological-social" criteria to qualify as such, and "colonies," which are unable to make sovereign decisions.[29] It is possible that the ICJ's rejection of the legality of declarations of independence when connected directly with military force may have played a role in Russia's decision to recognize the independence of Donetsk and Luhansk before attacking Ukraine. In Kherson and Zaporizhzhia, however, the use of referendums instead of unilateral declarations may have been an attempt to give added legitimacy to the independence claims made in the name of those two regions.

Yet, Russia's formal evocation of the ICJ opinion on unilateral declaration of independence—to justify the rights of the people of "Donbass and the south of Ukraine" to self-determination and to join Russia following the referendums in Kherson and Zaporizhzhia[30]—only weakened its legal case. The referenda, which were organized under military administration—with handpicked international observers and the exclusion of international organizations—lacked credibility and legitimacy. An occupation by a foreign power, even if it is dressed up in legal terms as an "invitation" does not grant permanent sovereignty in the territory. For that reason, there was no legal case for holding referendums about independence or annexation. What is more, Russia only partially controlled the territories of the regions it annexed. Only two states, Syria and North Korea, which

[28] "Russia doesn't care if G7 recognizes new Ukrainian borders — Medvedev," TASS, May 14, 2022, accessed October 25, 2022, https://tass.com/world/1451025

[29] "[Vladimir Putin's] Meeting with young entrepreneurs, engineers and scientists."

[30] "Russian Foreign Ministry's statement on the referendums in the DPR, LPR, Kherson and Zaporozhye regions," September 28, 2022, accessed October 25, 2022, https://russiaeu.ru/en/news/russian-foreign-ministrys-statement-referendums-dpr-lpr-kherson-and-zaporozhye-regions

are especially close to Russia, have recognized the territorial conquests of Kherson and Zaporizhzhia. There will be a strong incentive to refrain from doing so, not only because states are usually reluctant to recognize independence claims that are contested by the territorial state in question but also because border changes were, in this case, engineered by military force as a prelude to annexation.

It is clear that Russia has abandoned any pretence of making newly proclaimed states viable as separate entities. Having, in 2023, withdrawn its recognition of Moldova's sovereignty over Transnistria, Russia is poised to recognize its proxy region as an independent state, which could signal a willingness to annex it at a future date. No matter how the Ukrainian war ends, enforced border changes have been made part of a Russian discourse that has jettisoned territorial integrity in favour of self-determination. Yet, as practiced by Russia, it is not a universal legal doctrine but a highly selective one. While it refers to the Kosovo case, the Russians only apply it to post-Soviet states with Russian-speaking minorities.

Conclusion

Russia has relied so extensively on the Kosovo trajectory that it has even used it justify an act that has nothing to do with it, such as the incorporation of Crimea into the Russian Federation as well as the attempt to do the same with other southern and eastern Ukrainian territories. This raises the question of how unique the Kosovo experience really is and to what degree it has been used as a precedent in other situations. The failed Western intervention in Libya was steeped in humanitarian warfare rhetoric and secession movements, such as that in Catalonia, have mentioned Kosovo's path to statehood. Yet, Kosovo did not become a key reference point in either case. That no claim to statehood has been supported by more states gives some validity to the argument that Kosovo is, indeed, a different case. As noted, just a few states have followed in the footsteps of Russia and recognized the secession of Abkhazia, South Ossetia, Crimea, Donetsk, Luhansk, Kherson, Zaporizhzhia, or their absorption into the Russian Federation.

Kosovo's independence is, however, still contested because of the example could set for other secessionist movements. And the West's rhetoric on the territorial integration of states has become, in many ways, similar to that of Russia prior to Ukrainian crisis. Kosovo is not a universally recognized state and is not a member of key international organizations, such as the United Nations. In addition, five EU member states still refuse to recognize its sovereignty for self-interested political reasons, involving real or imagined secessionist threats in their own countries or neighbouring ones. Romania does not want to do anything that could embolden the Russians in Transnistria and undermine Moldova, a stance that has much saliency within the context of the war in Ukraine; Slovakia is worried about potential nationalist stirrings of its Hungarian minority; Greece and Cyprus are thinking of the unrecognized Turkish state claim in Northern Cyprus, and Spain is worried about strengthening Catalan and Bask separatism.

Russia's post-2008 policy reversal on territorial integrity has not pleased Serbia, which has refused to recognize the independence of the "states" Russia has created in the former Soviet Union since it would undermine its continued claim to Kosovo. Paradoxically, Russia's legal stance invites autonomous regions within Russia itself such as Chechnya, where a strong remedial case could be made to demand secession rights on the basis of self-determination. In short, Russia is trying to have it both ways. Its instrumental use of the Kosovo case has served the purpose of providing a political cover—dressed up as a legal one—for Russia's efforts to reassert its authority in those countries that belonged to the Soviet Union and to engage through mimicry in a geopolitical competition with the West. Thus, contested terms associated with intervention or secession have not only assumed contradictory meanings in the Russian official vocabulary; they have also been turned into a ritual political means to justify expansionist military ends.

References

Address by the President of the Russian Federation. President of Russia website, February 24, 2022. Accessed October 25, 2022. http://en.kremlin.ru/events/president/news/67843

Address by the President of the Russian Federation [on Crimea]. March 18, 2014. Accessed October 15, 2022. http://en.kremlin.ru/events/president/news/20603

Baev, P. K. (1999). Russia's stance against secessions: From Chechnya to Kosovo. *International Peacekeeping, 6*(3), 73–94.

Baev, P. K. (2022). *The 'Kosovo Precedent' and Russian-Georgian relations.* PONARS Eurasia Policy Memo, No. 5 (March 2008). https://www.ponarseurasia.org/wp-content/uploads/attachments/pepm_005.pdf. Accessed Oct 15, 2022.

Bebler, A. (Ed.). (2015). *"Frozen conflicts" in Europe*. Barbara Budrich Publishers.

Bolton, G., & Visoka, G. (2019). *Recognizing Kosovo's independence: Remedial secession or earned sovereignty?* (Occasional Paper No. 11/10). Oxford University Press.

Bucharest Summit Declaration Issued by the Heads of State and Government participating in the meeting of the North Atlantic Council in Bucharest on 3 April 2008. https://www.nato.int/cps/en/natolive/official_texts_8443.htm. Accessed Oct 25, 2022.

Espinosa, J. F. E. (Ed.). (2017). *Self-determination and humanitarian secession in international law of a globalized world. Kosovo v. Crimea*. Springer.

Gerrits, A. W. M., & Bader, M. (2012). Russian patronage over Abkhazia and South Ossetia: implications for conflict resolution. *East European Politics, 32*(3), 297–313.

Hubert, D., & Blätter, A. (2012). The responsibility to protect as international crimes prevention. *Global Responsibility to Protect, 4*(1), 33–66.

Ingimundarson, V. (2007). The politics of memory and the reconstruction of Albanian national identity in Postwar Kosovo. *History and Memory, 19*(1), 95–123.

International Court of Justice. Reports of judgments, advisory opinions and orders accordance with international law of the unilateral declaration of independence in respect of Kosovo advisory opinion of 22 July 2010, 403–453. https://www.icj-cij.org/public/files/case-related/141/141-20100722-ADV-01-00-EN.pdf. Accessed Oct 25, 2022.

Kazantsev, A., Lebedev, S., & Medvedeva, S. (2021). Russia's policies in the Post-Soviet space: Between constructive relations and fighting the New Cold War. *Russian Politics, 6*(4), 503–530.

Kosovo's Constitution of 2008 with Amendments through 2016. The Constitute Project, April 27, 2022. https://www.constituteproject.org/constitution/Kosovo_2016.pdf?lang=en. Accessed 25 Oct 2022.

Liyanov, F. (2016). Putin's foreign policy: The quest to restore Russia's rightful place. *Foreign Affairs, 95*(May–June), 30–37.

Lundstedt, T. (2020). Inherited national questions: The Soviet legacy in Russia's international law doctrine on self-determination. *Nordic Journal of International Law, 89*(1), 38–66.

Mani, R., & Weiss, T. G. (2011). R2P's missing link, culture. *Global Responsibility to Protect, 3*(4), 451–472.

McClean, E. (2008). The responsibility to protect: The role of international human rights law. *Journal of Conflict & Security Law, 13*(1), 123–152.

[Vladimir Putin's] Meeting with young entrepreneurs, engineers and scientists. President of Russia website, June 9, 2022. http://en.kremlin.ru/events/president/news/68606. Accessed Oct 15, 2022.

Putin cites precedent of Kosovo in explaining recognition of DPR, LPR. TASS, April 26, 2022. https://tass.com/politics/1443661?utm_source=google.com & utm_medium=organic & utm_campaign=google.com & utm_referrer=google.com. Accessed Oct 15, 2022.

Putin's power play jeopardizes Eurasian Union plans. Deutsche Welle, March 15, 2014. https://www.dw.com/en/putins-power-play-jeopardizes-eurasian-union-plans/a-17493164. Accessed Oct 25, 2022.

Report of the special envoy of the secretary-general on Kosovo's future status. UN Security Council, March 26, 2007. https://digitallibrary.un.org/record/595358?ln=fr. Accessed Oct 17, 2022.

Rotaru, V., & Troncotă, M. (2017). Continuity and change in instrumentalizing 'The Precedent.' How Russia uses Kosovo to legitimize the annexation of Crimea. *Southeast European and Black Sea Studies, 17*(3), 325–345.

Russia doesn't care if G7 recognizes new Ukrainian borders—Medvedev. TASS, May 14, 2022. https://tass.com/world/1451025. Accessed Oct 25, 2022.

Russian Foreign Ministry statement on recognising the independence of the Donetsk and Lugansk people's republics. February 23, 2022. https://russiaeu.ru/printpage/en/node/7353. Accessed Oct 25, 2022.

Russian Foreign Ministry's statement on the referendums in the DPR, LPR, Kherson and Zaporozhye regions, September 28, 2022. https://russiaeu.ru/en/news/russian-foreign-ministrys-statement-referendums-dpr-lpr-kherson-and-zaporozhye-regions. Accessed Oct 25, 2022.

Siroky, D. S., Popovic, M., & Mirilovic, N. (2021). Unilateral secession, international recognition, and great power contestation. *Journal of Peace Research, 58*(5), 1049–1067.

Tuathail, G. Ó. (2013). Russia's Kosovo: A critical geopolitics of the August 2008 War over South Ossetia. *Eurasian Geography and Economics, 49*(6), 670–705.

Vidmar, J. (2010). Remedial secession in international law: Theory and (lack of) practice. *St Antony's International Review, 6*(1), 37–56.

PART IV

Central Banking and Financial Integration

Relearning Inflation Control in the Post-Covid Era

Willem H. Buiter

Introduction

Central banks have to relearn the art of inflation control in almost all advanced economies (AEs). Controlling inflation today is technically daunting because some of the main drivers of inflation are unlike anything experienced since the oil price shocks of the 1970s. In some countries central banks face the further political challenge of avoiding fiscal dominance or even outright fiscal capture. They have to reconcile operational independence in the pursuit of price stability with the central bank's inescapable role as a fiscal and financial agent of the state.

Rediscovering Inflation Control

Central banks today are facing an array of supply shocks and combined supply and demand shocks. Some are sudden, dramatic, and (one hopes) temporary. This includes Covid, the war in Ukraine and supply chain disruptions triggered by extreme weather events. Others have been building

W. H. Buiter (✉)
Council on Foreign Relations, New York, NY, USA

R. Z. Aliber et al. (eds.), *Fault Lines After COVID-19*,
https://doi.org/10.1007/978-3-031-26482-5_12

up for years, sometimes decades, and are gradual and long-lasting or secular. This includes demographics (ageing populations), deglobalization, climate change, man-made environmental degradation resulting in freshwater scarcity and threats to biodiversity.

In Q2, 2021, AE central banks other than the Bank of Japan (BoJ), suddenly and unexpectedly transitioned from three post-Volcker decades of mostly low and often below-target inflation to what is now a year and a half of materially above-target inflation, reminiscent of the 1970s and early 1980s. The initial characterization by the leading AE central banks of these inflation target overshoots as temporary or transitory was not completely without merit. The statistical "base effect" of very low inflation in the last three quarters of 2020 contributed to higher year-on-year (YoY) inflation rates in the corresponding quarters of 2021. The most important acute inflationary shocks were the labour supply reductions and supply chain disruptions caused by the Covid pandemic and, since February 24, 2022, the disruption of key commodity markets caused by Russia's invasion of Ukraine and the trade and financial sanctions triggered by it. These adverse supply shocks were in part transitory. The major monetary and fiscal stimuli provided at the start of the pandemic could also be viewed as likely mostly temporary. It is time, however, to recognize that the "temporary and transitory" narrative only tells part of the inflation story.

First, there are lasting supply side effects from the Covid pandemic. Covid-related excess mortality is one factor in most countries other than the People's Republic of China (PRC). In the PRC, the continued stringent lockdown measures associated with the zero-Covid policy hurt the supply side of Chinese economy and disrupt global supply chains.

For the US, the empirical evidence is supportive of the view that the labour market is tight, and that mismatch unemployment and other forms of frictional and structural unemployment have increased as a result of the pandemic.[1] The fact that real wages have declined during 2021 and the first half of 2022 by most metrics may appear inconsistent with labour market tightness. I rather view this as a reflection of the underestimation of future price inflation by the parties in the wage negotiations reflected in the recent wage inflation indices.

[1] See, for example, the data on the labour force participation rate, the employment-population ratio, job openings, unfilled job vacancies, the number unemployed, the quit rate, and the rate of layoffs and discharges.

Other secular, enduring potential drivers of higher inflationary pressures through a lower path of potential output include deglobalization driven by rising geopolitical tensions, a growing shift from just-in-time to just-in-case management of supply chains, global warming/climate change and the private and public responses to it, and demographics (see Goodhart and Pradhan (2020)).

The evidence thus far on how leading AE central banks are making the transition from the low inflation era to the post-Covid world of higher underlying inflationary pressures is not encouraging. In the US, headline CPI inflation was 8.3% in August (YoY, unadjusted), slightly down from 8.5% in July 2022 and 9.1% in June 2022 (a 40-year high). Core CPI inflation (excluding food and energy) was 6.3% in August 2022, up from 5.9% in July 2022, but slightly below the 6.5% peak in March 2022. The Personal Consumption Expenditures (PCE) Price Index rose 6.3% YoY in July 2022, down from 6.8% in June 2022, with the Fed's preferred indicator, the core PCE Price Index rising 4.6% in July 2022, slightly down from 4.8% in June and a peak of 5.2% in March 2022. Even allowing for the Fed's (unfortunate) adoption of a flexible average inflation targeting (FAIT) framework, the duration and magnitude of the inflation target overshoot are excessive.[2] In the euro area, headline HICP inflation rose from 8.9% YoY in July 2022 to 9.1% in August, with core HICP inflation rising from 4.0% in July to 4.3% in August. UK headline CPI inflation slowed modestly to 9.9% YoY in August 2022 from a peak of 10.1% in July, with core CPI inflation rising slightly from 6.2% in July 2022 to 6.3% in August. Japan's headline CPI inflation rate hit 3.0% YoY in August 2022, the highest level since September 2014, with core CPI inflation rising to 2.8%, the highest level since October 2014.

Advanced economy inflation has not been this high for decades. What would be especially worrying from the perspective of getting inflation back down to its target level without going through a possibly protracted period of weak economic activity, with output below potential, that is, a recession, would be evidence that inflation expectations are rising. Here the news is more positive. In the US, the Fed of New York's Survey of Consumer Expectations, short-term (one-year) inflation expectations fell to 5.7% in August 2022 after reaching a series high of 6.8% in June 2022. Medium-term (three-year) inflation expectations declined from 3.2% in July to 2.8% in August. Long-run inflation expectations in the US do not

[2] See Buiter (2021b) about the undesirability of FAIT.

appear to have become "unanchored." The 5-year, 5-year forward inflation expectation rate stood at 2.31% on September 2022 after peaking at 2.59% on April 22, 2022. The 10-year breakeven inflation rate stands at 2.33% on September 27, 2022—less than one percentage point above its pre-Covid level. The survey-based 1-year inflation expectation of the University of Michigan was 4.6% in September 2022; 5-year expected inflation was 2.8%.

If inflation is well above target and likely to remain there in the short and medium term, why are policy rates in all AEs except the US below the neutral rate and deeply negative in real terms (including the US)? On September 21, 2022, the Fed engaged in its third consecutive 75 bps increase in the Federal funds rate target range, bringing it to 3.00–3.25%. The European Central Bank's (ECB's) interest rate on the main refinancing operations was raised on September 8, 2022, by 0.75% to 1.25%. The Bank of England's (BoE) Bank Rate was raised by 0.50% on September 22, 2022, to 2.25%. As of September 22, 2022, the Bank of Japan's (BoJ) short-term policy rate remains at -0.10% and the target rate for the 10-year JGB at 0.00%.

Estimates of the neutral real interest rate have come down markedly since the Great Financial Crisis (GFC) that started in the second half of 2007. The original Taylor Rule paper (Taylor (1993)) assumed a value of 2% for the US neutral real interest rate. I will (conservatively) assume a neutral real policy rate of 0.5% for all four AEs just mentioned. With a common target rate of inflation of 2%, the common neutral nominal policy rate is 2.5%, which means that of the four AE central banks, only the Fed is in the restrictive monetary policy range in late September 2022, with the BoE knocking timidly at the door.

The Taylor Rule

The Taylor Rule provides a useful benchmark for what the level of the policy rate should be in a "flexible inflation targeting" or dual mandate framework although it should not be applied mechanically, as it ignores financial stability considerations.

Charles Goodhart noted in February 2022 Goodhart (2022), that using the Taylor Rule Taylor (1993) as a rule of thumb for setting the policy rate, the nominal policy rate in the US should be in excess of 6%, and somewhere around 5% in the UK. In December 2021, I had reached a similar conclusion for the US Buiter (2021c). My December 2021 version of the Taylor Rule implied a Federal Funds target rate of 6.5%. In August 2021, Taylor (2021) had used his rule to generate a Federal Funds target rate of 5.0%. The static version of the Taylor rule is given below:

$$i = r^N + \hat{\pi} + \alpha\left(\pi - \hat{\pi}\right) + \beta \text{gap}$$

where i is the nominal policy rate, r^N is the short neutral real rate of interest (assumed to equal 0.5%), π is the actual rate of inflation, $\hat{\pi}$ is the target rate of inflation (assumed to equal 2.00%) and gap is the percentage difference between actual real GDP and potential real GDP.

I set α, the responsiveness of the policy rate to the deviation of actual inflation from target inflation, at 1.5, consistent with the original Taylor rule. When $\alpha > 1$, a higher rate of inflation will call for a higher *real* policy rate. As regards the responsiveness of the policy rate to the output gap, I will set $\beta = 0.5$, the figure used in Taylor's original formulation and in Taylor (2021), but below the 1.0 value used in Taylor (1999), Bernanke (2015) and others.

To complete the Taylor rule exercise, I would set the actual inflation rate in the Taylor rule (conservatively) at the level of the core inflation rate (for the US the core PCE deflator inflation rate). I assume that the US and the Eurozone are at full employment (early September 2022) and that there are small (1%) negative output gaps in the UK and Japan. The results of my Taylor rule exercise are given in Table 1. Even the BoJ is behind the curve.

The BoE has the largest gap (6.20%) between the actual value of the policy rate (2.25%) and the Taylor rule implied policy rate. In addition to Covid-19 and Russia's war on Ukraine, Brexit has adversely impacted the supply side of the UK economy.

Table 1 Taylor rule implied policy rates for four leading central banks

			$\alpha = 1.5$	$\beta = 0.5$
	i (%)	R^N (%)	$\pi - \hat{\pi}$ (%)	*gap* (%)
Fed	6.40	2.50	2.60	0.00
ECB	5.95	2.50	2.30	0.00
BoE	8.45	2.50	4.30	-1.00
BoJ	3.20	2.50	0.80	-1.00

I do not propose that the Fed move its policy rate to 6.40% at the next FOMC meeting, let alone that the Bank of England set its policy rate at 8.45% at the next MPC meeting. Although the Taylor Rule provides a useful benchmark for the pursuit of maximum employment and stable prices and for flexible inflation targeting under conditions of financial stability, the likely adverse impact of a mechanical application of the Taylor Rule on financial stability, in the US and globally—notably for emerging markets and developing economies (EMDEs)—argues in favour of gradualism, say steps of 75 or 100 bps at each regular rate setting meeting until the Taylor rule interest rate levels in the second column of Table 1 have been reached.

The exercise convinces me that the Fed, like the ECB and the BoE—and even the BoJ—remain far behind the inflation curve. Policy rates should right now (in September 2022) exceed the neutral rate for all four central banks—materially so for the first three. It is time to recognize the painful reality that a sustained reduction in the underlying inflation rate is likely to require a period when aggregate demand and actual output are below potential output—a recession.

Some additional monetary policy tightening is implied by the ending of quantitative easing (asset purchases) and, in the US, the reduction in the size of the Fed balance sheet by $95bn per month phased in over a period of three months starting in June 2022. The tightening involved is modest. The Fed's balance sheet reached $8937 bn at the end of March 2022. With a monthly runoff of $95bn it would take just over four years to get it back to its early March 2020 size of $4242 bn, and just over seven years to regain the $905 bn level it stood at in early September 2008. The Fed's decision to continue to implement an "ample reserves" regime makes it likely that the size of the Fed's balance sheet may not even shrink to the early March 2020 level. In the UK, the BoE decided on September 28 temporarily to resume monetized purchases of gilts to restore order and market liquidity in gilt markets shaken badly by the fiscally unsustainable "mini-budget" of September 23. This makes sense from the perspective of the central bank as market maker of last resort, but further complicates the achievement of the inflation target.

Why Are the Fed, the ECB, the BoE, and Even the BoJ so Far Behind the Inflation Curve?

How come the Fed, the ECB, and the Bank of England stuck to the "transitory and temporary" inflation story when—even before the outbreak of Russia's invasion of Ukraine—it was clear that it was wrong? I believe that the delay in and underwhelming magnitude of the monetary policy response to the surge in inflation can be accounted for in part by cognitive errors interpreting data and identifying transmission mechanisms. But that is not the complete story. I believe that fear of triggering financial instability impeded and continues to impede a more aggressive monetary and financial policy response to the manifest inflationary threat. Lastly, I believe that, at least in the euro area, but possibly also in the UK, fear of complicating the funding of fiscal deficits and adding to the interest burden of servicing the public debt motivated continued asset purchases and policy rate restraint.

The Inescapable Fiscal Dimension of Central Bank Activity, Fiscal Dominance, and Fiscal Capture

Fiscal dominance is present when the central bank is forced to set its policy rates, fund the government, and engage in monetary issuance in ways that are incompatible with the pursuit of price stability.

Central banks purchase government debt for a variety of reasons. Even when the policy rates are not constrained by the effective lower bound (ELB), government securities are routinely purchased or repoed in open market operations that need not be sterilized. When central bank policy rates are at the ELB, central bank asset purchases have been part of the quantitative easing (QE) and qualitative easing that, together with forward guidance and yield curve control, make up the more limited ELB-constrained monetary policy arsenal. QE asset purchases typically are not sterilized—they are monetized. Central banks also undertake asset purchases, including sovereign debt purchases, in the pursuit of their financial stability mandate. As market maker of last resort (MMLR) they engage in outright purchases of financial instruments to restore market liquidity in systemically important financial markets. According to Fleming and Ruela (2020), between March 15 and March 31, 2020, the Fed purchased $775 billion in Treasury securities and $291 billion in agency MBS. Garbade and Keane (2020) report cumulative Fed purchases between March 13 and July 31, 2020, amounting to $1.77 trillion of Treasuries and $892 billion of agency MBS. From September 28, 2022, the BoE initiated 13 days of MMLR gilt purchases, adding up to £65 billion. It also delayed selling down its £838 billion government bond holdings. Finally, central banks engage in (typically monetized) sovereign debt purchases to finance government deficits. This need not pose a threat to the central bank's price stability mandate. In a growing economy with low and stable inflation, the demand for central bank money will grow modestly. A limited quantum of non-inflationary central bank monetary financing of the government deficit is therefore, in general, feasible. But it can easily get out of hand when the central bank loses its independence.

The central bank is beneficially owned by the government, through the national fiscal authority—typically the Treasury Department or Ministry of Finance of the central government. The formal ownership structures are varied, and at times unusual and confusing, but the state is the ultimate claimant on the profits of the central bank.[3] The magnitude of the profit transfers of the central bank to the government can be significant. In 2021, the Federal Reserve System remitted an estimated $107.4 billion to the US Treasury (0.47% of GDP)—an amount only exceeded by the $117.0 billion transferred in 2015.

Meaningful public debt sustainability analysis (DSA) considers the assets, liabilities, current and anticipated future primary surpluses of the consolidated general government and central bank, henceforth the "state." The debt that matters for fiscal-financial sustainability—the solvency—of the state is the ***non-monetary*** debt of the consolidated general government and central bank.

[3] In the US, each of the 12 Reserve Banks is separately incorporated with a 9-member board of directors. Commercial banks that are members of the Federal Reserve System must hold (non-tradable) stock in their District's Reserve Bank. These "stocks" are rather like non-voting preference shares. The Federal Reserve Board of Governors funds its operations by assessing the 12 Federal Reserve Banks. The Fed is quite explicit that "The Federal Reserve System is not "owned" by anyone." The Board of Governors is an agency of the US Federal Government and reports to and is directly accountable to the US Congress. The Reserve Banks are legally required to transfer net earnings to the US Treasury, after paying for the expenses of the Reserve Banks and the Board, the legally required dividend payments (currently 6% on the paid-in capital stock), while maintaining a limited balance in a surplus fund. The Bank of Japan is partly privately owned; its stock is traded over the counter and has a stock number. The Bank of England is a joint stock company owned 100% by the UK Treasury.

The Intertemporal Budget Constraint of the State and the Lure of Monetary Financing

From the budget constraint of the state, we can obtain the intertemporal budget constraint or solvency constraint of the state if we assume (1) that, in the long run, the effective real interest rate on the public debt, r, exceeds the growth rate of real GDP, g, and (2) that Ponzi finance is not possible: the non-monetary public debt cannot grow faster than GDP forever (see Buiter, 2021a). The intertemporal budget constraint (IBC) of the state asserts that the outstanding stock of non-monetary public debt as a share of GDP must be less than or equal to the sum of two present discounted value terms. The first is the present discounted value of current and future primary surpluses of the state as a share of GDP, s, where the primary surplus equals non-interest revenues minus non-interest expenditures; the second is the present discounted value of current and future seigniorage as a share of GDP, σ, where seigniorage is the change in the monetary base minus any interest paid on the outstanding stock of base money. The discount rate used for the present discounted value calculations is $r - g$.

The budget constraint and the IBC of the state highlight the cause of the tensions that are likely to arise between the government and a central bank targeting price stability if the public debt is growing in an unsustainable manner because of large primary deficits and because the interest rate on the public debt exceeds the growth rate of GDP. For the state to remain solvent, the outstanding stock of non-monetary public debt has to be "serviced" either, painfully, by the present discounted value of current and future primary surpluses (s, i.e., higher taxes and/or lower public expenditures) or, apparently painlessly, by the present discounted value of current and future seigniorage (σ, i.e., printing money).

Excessive issuance of central bank money will, sooner or later lead to excessive inflation. Even the Bank of Japan is at last experiencing (modestly) above-target core inflation. The monetary base numbers for Japan, the US, the Eurozone, and the UK shown in Table 2 are supportive of the inflationary impulses coming from adverse supply shocks and the massive fiscal stimulus prompted by the Covid pandemic (see also Yardeni and Quintana (2022)). The consolidated assets of the central banks and their holdings of sovereign debt closely track the monetary base.

At the end of 2021, BoJ holdings of Japanese government bonds amounted to Yen 521 trillion, or 96% of GDP, out of a total General Government Gross Debt of Yen 1426 trillion or 263% of GDP.

Table 2 Monetary base (% of GDP, end-of-period)

(% of GDP, end-of-period)	*2007*	*2019*	*2021*
BoJ currency	16.0	23	23
Deposits	0.5	63	104
Monetary base	16.5	96	127
Fed currency	5.7	8.4	9.7
Deposits	0.3	7.2	17.6
Monetary base	6.0	15.6	27.3
ECB currency	7.2	10.8	12.6
Deposits	1.8	15.8	37.1
Monetary base	9.0	26.6	49.7
BoE currency	3.1	3.7	4.1
Deposits	1.5	21.2	41.9
Monetary base	4.6	24.9	46.0

Source: BoJ, Fed, ECB, BoE, and National Accounts Statistics

Could There Be a Painless $R < G$ Solution to the Public Debt Sustainability Conundrum?

The intertemporal budget constraint of the state is only binding—only exists—if, in the long run, the effective interest rate on the public debt exceeds the growth rate of GDP, $r > g$, and thus of the fiscal resources of the state. If the interest rate on the public debt is forever below the growth rate of GDP, Ponzi Finance is feasible. A growing stock of outstanding debt can be financed without the need for primary budget surpluses, s, or seigniorage revenues, σ. I will focus on the risk-free real interest here. For most borrowers (including sovereigns), the default risk premium is large enough to ensure that the $r > g$ condition is satisfied. We have been in a more than 30-year long episode of extremely low risk-free real interest rates, and there is evidence that the world may have experienced eight centuries of "suprasecular" decline in the real rate of interest (see Schmelzing (2020)). I believe that, globally, the low real interest rate era is coming to an end. A significant driver will be reduced household saving rates as a result of demographic changes. Economies with ageing and, soon in many AEs and China, old and shrinking populations, are likely generate less household saving. Governments are unlikely to save more, and neither is the corporate sector. Weaker planned saving will have to be reconciled with robust planned capital expenditure, driven by demographics (ageing and shrinking labour forces) and by technical change, including automation, artificial intelligence, robotics, and the digital revolution. The likely outcome will by a higher risk-free (neutral) real interest rate. The intertemporal budget constraint of the state will continue to be a binding constraint.

Central Bank Responses to the Public Debt and Deficit Overhang

The arithmetic of public debt dynamics is clear: a reduction in the ratio to GDP of the non-monetary debt of the state requires some combination of a larger primary budget surplus, higher real GDP growth, higher inflation (if it is unexpected and there is a significant amount of fixed rate nominally denominated debt outstanding), lower interest rates on the public debt or increased issuance of base money. Real GDP growth is only very partially under the control of the state. Unexpected inflation is not a reliable policy instrument. The risk-free interest rate is not a policy variable, and the sovereign risk premium can only be addressed effectively by the Treasury through increased current and future primary surpluses which are politically unpopular. That leaves monetary financing as a natural outcome when the state is confronted with a material increase in the debt service burden or in the primary deficit. And it is what we have been witnessing, to varying degrees, all over the world.

Does the massive public debt overhang in many countries effectively make the central bank a captive of the fiscal funding needs of the sovereign?

When the political priorities of the government are in material conflict with the mandate of an operationally independent central bank, central bank independence will all but surely be the loser. The government will get its way either by the incumbent leadership of the central bank giving in to government pressure, or by the government replacing the incumbent leadership with persons likely to do its bidding or, if all else fails, by the government using legislative or administrative procedures to change the legal and institutional framework, including the mandate of the central bank. The government will, unless it is extremely frail, be able to force the central bank to follow its instructions. There may have been an exception to this rule with the German Bundesbank, whose independence was reinforced by collective memories of the hyperinflation of 1922–1923.

There are many instances in EMDEs where central bank independence was effectively destroyed by the government forcing the central bank to engage in highly inflationary monetary financing of the government deficit. Two recent examples are Argentina and Sri Lanka.

In Argentina, monetary financing of the fiscal deficit was 7.4% of GDP in 2020, clearly inconsistent with low and stable inflation.[4] From October 2018, the central bank had abandoned its 5% inflation target for 2020. CPI inflation in Q4 2020 was 36% YoY. It reached 79% (and rising) in August 2022. The ample monetary financing of the fiscal deficit could not resolve Argentina's problems servicing its foreign-currency-denominated sovereign debt. The ninth external sovereign default occurred in May 2020.

Sri Lanka since 2019 is another textbook example of fiscal dominance.[5] The central bank's inflation target range of 4–6% was undermined by it being forced to monetize the fiscal deficits resulting from large and fiscally unsustainable tax cuts in 2019. CPI inflation was 64.3% YoY in August 2022. Here too, monetary financing could not ensure the servicing of foreign-currency-denominated sovereign debt and Sri Lanka defaulted on its external debt obligations in April 2022.

Fiscal Dominance and Central Bank Independence? The Case of the ECB

As regards the Fed, the ECB, and the BoE, it is possible that the serious overshooting of the inflation target starting in Q2, 2021 can be explained fully by the unexpected nature of the Covid and Ukraine invasion shocks and persistent errors of judgement and analysis. An alternative interpretation is that these central banks knowingly engaged in interest rate and asset purchase policies to support the expansionary fiscal policies adopted by their governments, even though it was highly likely that this would result in a violation of the price stability mandate. This second interpretation is particularly convincing for the ECB, which has to deal with a number of national sovereigns whose debt sustainability is questionable at best. Greece, Italy, Portugal, and Spain belong to the fiscally fragile category of countries that could be faced with sovereign funding problems when the next cyclical downturn hits, the inflation rate comes down, risk-free interest rates continue to normalize, and sovereign risk is priced more realistically.

[4] See IMF (2022a) and Ferreira Lima and Marsh (2022).

[5] See IMF (2022b).

The concern of the ECB with potential sovereign deficit funding problems for fiscally weak member states is apparent from its announcement, on March 24, 2022, that it would continue to accept Greek government bonds as collateral until at least the end of 2024, despite the fact that they do not meet the ECB's minimum credit quality requirement because they are rated sub-investment grade. Under the PEPP, initiated in March 2020, the ECB/Eurosystem had bought Greek sovereign debt for the first time in almost a decade, despite its sub-investment grade rating. When the Governing Council of the ECB decided, on December 16, 2021, to discontinue net asset purchases under the PEPP at the end of March 2022, it also decided to reinvest maturing principal payments until at least the end of 2024. The Governing Council also made clear in March 2022, that it could continue to buy the debt of other member state governments and accept them as collateral even if they were downgraded below investment grade.

Eurosystem holdings under the €1850 envelope PEPP at the end of March 2022 were €1696 bn of which €1644 bn were public sector securities—13.4% of 2021-euro area GDP. Cumulative net purchases of Greek sovereign debt under the PEPP at the end of March 2022 were €38.5 bn or 21.1% of Greece's 2021 GDP. For Portugal, the corresponding figure is 16.4% of GDP, for Italy 16.0% of GDP and for Spain 15.7% of GDP. In 2020 and 2021, the Eurosystem bought more than 120% of net euro area sovereign debt issuance. Further additions to the stock of public sector debt held by the Eurosystem were made since November 2019 through the Public Sector Purchase Programme (PSPP), which does not purchase sub-investment grade debt. I expect that either the PSPP eligibility rules will be changed to allow the purchase of sub-investment grade debt, or that the new facility created in July 2022, the Transmission Protection Instrument (TPI) will, like the PEPP, allow the purchase of sub-investment grade debt.

Early in 2022, the ECB was said to be working on a "new instrument" to support euro area member states as it raises its policy rates (see also Lagarde (2022)). The official rationale is a form of MMLR: the prevention or mitigation of sovereign debt market fragmentation and the wider financial fragmentation this engenders. The avowed objective is the protection of the effective functioning of the monetary transmission mechanism across national boundaries in the monetary union—the preservation of the singleness of the Eurozone's monetary policy.

Sovereign yield spreads on risky euro area sovereign debt are rising again. Italy's 10-year yield spread versus Germany reached 253 bps on September 28, 2022; it was 18.5 bps on June 13, 2007, and peaked at 557.2 bps on November 9, 2011. Continued large net debt issuance is planned by many vulnerable sovereigns. Italy is targeting a general government budget deficit for 2022 of 5.6% of GDP, down from the 7.2% of GDP deficit in 2021, but still likely to pose funding challenges. The fiscal plans of the new Meloni administration are unknown.

The "new instrument" was introduced on July 21, 2022, as the TPI. It is an-easy-on-the-beneficiary-government alternative to the Outright Monetary Transactions (OMT). It is unclear whether the TPI will be able to purchase sub-investment grade debt, but I expect it will be. Unlike the OMT, the TPI does not require its asset purchases to be sterilized. Instead, the somewhat vague commitment is made that "Purchases under the TPI would be conducted such that they cause no persistent impact on the overall Eurosystem balance sheet and hence on the monetary policy stance." The OMT imposes budgetary and other conditionality (including IMF involvement) on beneficiary member states that is perceived as so onerous that it has never been activated since its inception as successor to the Securities Markets Programme (SMP) in 2012.[6]

I believe that the available evidence since the start of the Covid pandemic on Eurosystem purchases of sovereign debt, on the monetary financing of these purchases and on the Eurosystem's collateral policy, supports the view that the ECB has become the de facto captive of the fiscally weak euro area sovereigns: it will purchase and, if necessary, monetize vulnerable public debt even if this poses a clear threat to the price stability mandate.

I expect that, although the ECB is, at last, raising its policy rates towards the neutral level, it will continue purchasing the debt of fiscally fragile member states. Its purpose is to support sovereigns or corporates facing a sharp increase in borrowing costs (or at risk of being frozen out of the market) when policy rates are raised. Such asset purchases can have MMLR overtones as they may occur during disorderly market conditions. But the fact that the Eurosystem will probably be a long-term holder of the vulnerable sovereign debt it acquires (after market liquidity has been restored)

[6]The fact that the OMT has not been activated can also be viewed as evidence of the credibility of the ECB's commitment to do whatever it takes to safeguard the monetary union (as per Mario Draghi's famous words on July 26, 2012).

can turn these sovereign debt purchases into fiscal support operations and at times fiscal rescue operations. This manifestation of fiscal dominance in the eurozone may be voluntary or "self-inflicted"—no-one is telling the Governing Council what to do—but "internalized" fiscal dominance it is.

Operational independence in the pursuit of price stability or of a dual mandate depends on the social and political equilibrium in the political entity spanned by the central bank. There has to be widespread and effectively expressed political support for central bank operational independence in the pursuit of price stability. The polity has to be aware of the eventual impact of large-scale monetization of public sector deficits on inflation; it has to dislike higher inflation more than higher taxes or cuts in public spending and it has to be able to compel or induce policy makers to act in accordance with these views and preferences.

It is clear that the central banks of Argentina and Sri Lanka did not have meaningful operational independence and were subject to fiscal dominance and indeed fiscal capture. The case of the ECB is less clear-cut, but there is mounting evidence of "internalized" fiscal dominance.

Conclusion

Central bankers have their work cut out for them in 2022 and beyond. Many, including the decision makers at the Fed, the ECB, and the BoE, have to relearn inflation control. There have also been vivid reminders of the simple truth that the central bank can be operationally independent in the pursuit of price stability only if it can effectively resist government pressure for monetary funding of its expenditures whenever, in the opinion of the central bank, doing so would pose a threat to price stability. This capacity to say "no" is a scarce commodity indeed.

References

Bernanke, B. S. (2015). *The Taylor rule: A benchmark for monetary policy?* Brookings Institution.

Buiter, W. H. (2021a). *Central banks as fiscal players; the drivers of fiscal and monetary policy space.* Cambridge University Press.

Buiter, W. H. (2021b, November 14). The fed must abandon average inflation targeting. *Financial Times.*

Buiter, W. H. (2021c, December 29). Why the fed must tighten. *Jackson Hole Economics.* https://jheconomics.com/why-the-fed-must-tighten/

Ferreira Lima, K. P., & Marsh, C. (2022, January 10). *The IMF's 2018 stand-by arrangement with Argentina: An Ultra Vires Act?* Available also at SSRN.

Fleming, M., & Ruela, F. (2020, April 17). Treasury market liquidity during the Covid-19 crisis. *Liberty Street Economics*. Federal Reserve Bank of New York.

Garbade, K. D., & Keane, F. M. (2020, August 20). Market purchases by the Federal Reserve. *Liberty Street Economics*. Federal Reserve Bank of New York.

Goodhart, C. (2022, February 8). The real cause of inflation. *IAI News*.

Goodhart, C., & Pradhan, M. (2020). *The great demographic reversal: Ageing societies, waning inequality, and an inflation revival*. Palgrave Macmillan, (April 4 version).

International Monetary Fund. (2022a, March). Argentina; Staff Report for the 2022 Article IV Consultation and Request for an Extended Arrangement under the Extended Fund Facility – Press Release; Staff Report; and Staff Supplements.

International Monetary Fund. (2022b, March, 1). Sri Lanka, 2021 Article IV Consultation-Press Release; Staff Report; and Statement by the Executive Director for Sri Lanka.

Lagarde, C. (2022). *Monetary policy in an uncertain world*. Speech at "The ECB and Its Watchers XXII" conference, Frankfurt am Main, 17 March.

Schmelzing, P. (2020). *Eight centuries of global real interest rates, R-G, and the 'suprasecular' decline, 1311-2018*. Bank of England Staff Working Paper No. 845, 03 January.

Taylor, J. B. (1993). *Discretion versus policy rules in practice*. Carnegie-Rochester Conference Series on Public Policy, no 39, pp. 195–214.

Taylor, J. B. (1999). Introduction to "monetary policy rules". In J. B. Taylor (Ed.), *Monetary policy rules*. University of Chicago Press.

Taylor, J. B. (2021, August 12). The Fed's state of exception. *Project Syndicate*.

Yardeni, E., & Quintana, M. (2022, April 22). *Central banks: Monthly balance sheets*. Yardeni Research, Inc. https://www.yardeni.com/pub/peacock-fedecbassets.pdf

How the Flows Change When Interest Rates Are Normalized: Risk to Economic and Financial Stability

Sigridur Benediktsdottir

Introduction

Central banks in major economies are normalizing interest rates after a long period of accommodative monetary policy. The main motivation for the interest rate normalization is to combat the sharp increase in inflation in the last few decades. In some instances, policy rates have already, or are expected to, go beyond the long run equilibrium monetary policy rates for the first time since the Global Financial Crisis. The last time Central Banks of major economies had to increase interest rates to fight high inflation was in the late 1970s and early 1980s. Multiple financial crises followed, most notably in Latin America, in what has been called the Latin American Debt crisis. Many lessons can be learned, from that period and from the latest research about systemic risk emanating from capital flows, to gauge

S. Benediktsdottir (✉)
Yale University, New Haven, CT, USA
e-mail: sigridur.benediktsdottir@yale.edu

R. Z. Aliber et al. (eds.), *Fault Lines After COVID-19*,
https://doi.org/10.1007/978-3-031-26482-5_13

where and to what extent financial instability may materialize in the next few years.

Financial flows increased noticeably in the run up to the Global Financial crisis. These were both increases in purchases of foreign assets and in borrowing from abroad. There was a sharp reversal in these flows at the onset of the GFC in the form of both retrenchments of foreign assets and sudden stops to foreign lending. Forbes and Warnock (2012) conclude that 78% of countries experienced a sudden stop in foreign lending during the global financial crisis.[1] The sudden stop was sharp but short lived. As major economies maintained accommodative monetary policy to counter the economic downturn, investors sought higher yield in non-major economies. Cross-border capital flows rose quickly back to levels seen in the run up to the GFC and has remained elevated for over a decade now. In a sample of 126 countries, all but 19 countries increased the total external liabilities in the five years leading up to the Covid health crisis (Benediktsdottir and Ahmed 2023). This build-up of systemic risk threatens to materialize now as interest rates rise worldwide. For countries where external liability is high, debt service costs will increase and refinancing will become, in some cases, prohibitively expensive. Exchange rate movements threaten to amplify the risk, as the dollar strengthens due to higher interest rates in the US and flight to safety as debt sustainability becomes the focus of international investors.

This chapter will bring together the lessons learned from the steep increase in major economies' policy rates in early 1980s and the ensuing debt and financial crises in a number of economies and recent literature on risks emanating from extreme capital flows. The chapter will start with discussion about financial crises in the 1980s. The focus will be on the Latin American Debt crisis. Then a short overview of recent research on external imbalances, foreign borrowing, and risks associated with it. The chapter will conclude with some indicators, informed by recent literature, of external imbalances and systemic risk.

Lessons from the 1980s

In the early 1980s multiple Latin American countries experienced a severe economic and financial crisis, often called the Latin American Debt Crisis. During the 1970s capital inflow into Latin America rose sharply in the

[1] Their sample includes 97% of global financial inflows during the GFC.

Table 1 Latin American debt crisis

Country	*Start*	*Output loss (% of GDP)*	*Gross fiscal costs (% GDP)*	*Increase in public debt (% GDP)*
Argentina	1980	58.2	55.1	33.1
Chile	1981	8.6	42.9	87.9
Colombia	1982	47.0	5.0	16.6
Mexico	1981	26.6	...	22.6
Peru	1983	55.2	...	14.3
Uruguay	1981	38.1	31.2	83.3

Source: Laeven and Valencia (2013)

form of both sovereign lending and lending to banks. As major economies increased interest rates sharply to fight the exuberant inflation in the early 1980s these flows came to a sudden stop and servicing the debt became prohibitively expensive. The resulting crises were costly, see Table 1. Output loss was over 50% of gross domestic product in Argentina and Peru over a five-year period. Gross fiscal cost was over 40% for Chile, where public debt almost doubled, see Table 1.

During the inflation years of the 1970s the Mexican Peso real exchange rate appreciated a lot and external debt grew fast. Foreign public debt grew in the double digits, and even over 30% per year in 1974–1976. At the end of the 1970s the stock of foreign public debt in Mexico had grown fivefold (Ortiz and Serra-Puche 1986), although this only refers to public debt. Simultaneously, there was a sharp increase in external borrowing by Mexican banks (van Wijnbergen & Oks, 1994). Private creditors borrowing increased tenfold, from around half a billion dollars in the early 1970s to over $5 billion in 1975 and 1976 and remained elevated to the end of that decade. As monetary policy in major economies was tightened to fight high inflation, private capital reversed out of Mexico. Initially, the government reacted to this by increasing public debt in defense of the peso, further exacerbating the looming debt crisis. The increase in debt and interest rates in the early 1980s almost doubled the ratio of interest payments of public debt to current account income to 29%. The cost of these crises proved to be substantial, or almost 27% of gross domestic product in the five-year period 1981–1986.

Other countries in Latin America experienced similar crises. Argentina experienced a sharp increase in external liabilities throughout the 1970s. The crisis in Argentina erupted in early 1981 with a failure of a major commercial bank which resulted in a widespread bank run. By 1983 almost 70 banks had failed and Argentina defaulted on its external debt as the debt service of external debt became double its exports income (Sachs and Williamson 1985). This was the highest external debt servicing ratio in Latin America at the time. Output loss in Argentina in the first half of the 1980s reached a staggering 58% of GDP and the gross fiscal cost was of similar magnitude.

Capital Flows and Systemic Risk

Systemic risk from capital inflows accumulated in a number of emerging markets throughout the 1970s and materialized in 1980s with considerable real costs. At the time the risks associated with those flows were hard to evaluate, mainly due to the quality of data that was available about those flows (Cuddington 1986). The current account was used as the main indicator of external imbalance. Recent research concludes that other, more focused indicators may be better indicators of external imbalances. Goldfajn and Valdés (1997) show that foreign lending to the financial sector is amplified through their increased lending into the domestic economy. A sudden outflow may then be triggered by international interest rates shocks. The sudden stop to foreign lending to the financial sector can then end in bank runs, which further amplifies the financial cycle, similar to what Argentina and Mexico experienced. Calvo in 1998 uses a simple theoretical model to connect cyclical movement in foreign capital flows with asset price bubbles and bursts in non-tradable assets, including housing. High leverage in real estate amplifies these cycles and the effects on other sectors of the economy. Calvo also concludes that these amplification cycles may occur irrespective of the current account.

More recent research has focused on which aspects of capital flows may be the best indicators of accumulation of systemic risk and increased likelihood of severe financial crisis. Prolonged periods of ***extreme capital inflows,*** or capital inflow bonanza's increase the likelihood of banking, sovereign debt, and currency crisis (Reinhart and Reinhart, 2009). The risks are amplified further if the surge in capital flows coincides with a ***boom in domestic private leverage*** (Caballero, 2016). The result is that the odds of a banking crisis increase about 3.7 times, to 15.5%, following a capital inflow bonanza. If in addition there is a simultaneous lending boom in the economy, then the odds of a banking crisis rise to over 33%. Net capital flows are all capital outflows minus all capital inflows. Capital inflows can be either foreigners acquiring a domestic asset or a domestic entity selling a foreign asset. Both are labeled as capital inflows, but are likely motivated very differently by economic shocks and changes in risk perception.

Motivated by that Forbes and Warnock (2012) identified separately ***foreign liability flows and domestic asset flows.*** They find that foreign driven extreme liability flow episodes have historically been driven by global factors, in particular global risk perception. Additionally, they found that a sudden stop in liability flows may not be detectable in net capital flow data as sudden stops are frequently accompanied by domestic investor's retrenchments of assets from abroad. Still, the negative effects of a stop and reversal in liability flows may be widespread in markets that foreigners are pulling money out of, including securities markets. Lastly, the ***composition and term structure*** of the assets foreigners invest in also matters when considering systemic risk originating from liability flows. Rodrik and Velasco (1999) find that countries with short-term external liabilities over three times their reserves are more likely to experience a sudden stop followed by a prolonged and severe crisis. For the composition of flows, booms in foreign direct investment have not been linked with increased likelihood of a crisis; however, both a boom in portfolio equity inflows and debt inflows increase the probability of a crisis considerably (Caballero, 2016). The boom in inflow will increase risks through an increase in domestic leverage like Goldfajn and Valdés (1997) describe and unsustainable increases in asset prices, akin to what Calvo's (1998) model describes. Both are unsustainable in the long run and will end in a debt overhang and an asset price burst as the flows reverse.

Connected with this literature is research on the effects of US monetary policy on capital flows to emerging market economies. Banerjee et al. (2016) find that a "US contractionary monetary policy shock leads to a retrenchment in EME capital flows, a fall in EME GDP, and an exchange rate depreciation." Their theoretical DSGE model even indicates that responses of asset prices and interest rate spreads in peripheral countries can be larger than in the center country that implements the contractionary policy. This is in line with Calvo et al. where policy rate increases in the US in 1994 are said to have translated quickly into changes in cross-border capital flows.

This research indicates that a current account deficit may not be the best measure of external imbalances which are likely to result in economic and financial crisis. It is necessary to look beyond that to how the current account deficit is funded. It has to be assessed whether it is through stable foreign direct investment or for example short-term lending to the financial sector which then amplifies the risk through increased lending into the domestic economy. External imbalances and risks may even accumulate irrespective of the current account if external debt is fueling unsustainable increase in domestic leverage and asset price bubbles.

External Imbalances and Systemic Risk

New data, motivated by the above research, is now available to improve assessment of external imbalances and potential risks associated with increases in monetary policy rates in major economies.

Robin Koepke and Simon Paetzold (2020) put together a dataset of monthly ***debt and equity flows*** to a number of countries. This is hence net capital flows, excluding foreign direct investment. Looking at seven EMEs it is clear that debt and equity flows have increased a lot in the past decade. According to their dataset net debt and equity inflows were more than double on average each month in the five years leading up to the Covid health crisis than they were in the run up to the Global Financial Crisis. Debt and equity flows were in particular high and persistently positive in the aftermath of the GFC up until major economies announced they would start to taper their quantitative easing in 2014–2015. A noticeable pattern is that net debt and equity inflows are persistently positive over a long period while reversals are more extreme but short lived.

When looking at individual countries this becomes even more apparent. Brazil and Chile experienced substantial debt and equity inflows in the run up to the GFC. The capital reversal was sharp but lasted only a few months. As soon as late 2009 capital started to flow into both countries, which experienced a capital inflow bonanza in 2009–2014. The inflows in that period far exceeded previously capital inflow periods. This occurred even though Brazil employed a number of capital inflow measures, including a tax on portfolio equity and fixed income inflows, to try to dampen the flows (Chamon and Garcia 2016). Net equity and debt flows have reversed, out of Brazil in the past five years. It is not clear from this dataset if this reversal is driven by foreigners lending less to Brazil (reversal of liability flows) or Brazilians acquiring more equity and debt abroad (asset flows). Brazilian external debt has declined by a third 2015–2020, indicating that the main factor is less borrowing from abroad. Chile has had volatile but mostly positive inflows into debt and equity in the last five years. Is this retrenchment of foreign debt and equity (asset flows) or is this borrowing from abroad (liability flows)? Chile's external debt has increased 15% 2015–2020, indicating these flows are liability flows.[2]

A new dataset splits flows into liability and asset flows (Avdjiev et al., 2022). In 21 countries from 1996 to 2020 liability flows to these countries increased significantly in the run up to the GFC when they reversed sharply. By 2010, liability flows were again similar to what they were in the run up to the GFC and they remained elevated until major central banks signaled they would start tapering their asset purchases in 2014. In the last five years, liability flows have still remained considerably higher than they were at the turn of the century. This has led to historically high external debt, which will be discussed below. First, however, it is notable that the liability flow reversal at the onset of the Covid health crisis is barely noticeable, compared to the sharp reversal in net debt and equity flows. This indicates that the capital flow reversals were more in the form of domestic capital flight then a foreign sudden stop.

Comparing capital flows for India from both data sets supports this. In the first quarter of 2020 net debt and equity outflow was almost $15 billion. In this same quarter the only liability flows that turn negative are corporate portfolio flows, other liability flows remain positive. This indicates a large amount of domestic capital flight in the first quarter of 2020. This is very different from the GFC where liability flows turn very negative—that is foreigners divesting from India, while net debt and equity flows turn negative, but not to the same extent. The sudden stop in 2008 was partially buffered by domestic retrenchment. These results may be crisis specific, or it may indicate that liability flows now are more stable than they were in the run up to the GFC.

The liability flows since the GFC have resulted in record high external debt around the world. The World Bank IDS dataset confirms that in the five years leading up to the Covid health crisis 109 of 126 increased their external debt. Nine of those countries more than double their external debt. They are, in alphabetical order, Angola, Bangladesh, Egypt, Laos, Mongolia, Montenegro, Nigeria, Qatar, and Uzbekistan (Benediktsdottir and Ahmed 2023). It is notable that most, if not all, of these countries have increased their external borrowing from China. Of the 24 countries which increased their external debt 70% or more in 2015–2020, 13 have liability data available. There is a sharp increase in liability flows in 2006

[2] World bank IDS data set and authors calculations.

and 2007 followed by a sudden stop and reversal in 2008. Foreign lending increased again in 2010 and then more noticeably in 2016 and on. Again there is little, if any, reversal of liability flows during the Covid crisis.

The sharp increase in liability flows to these 13 countries in 2016 coincides with the push from China to fund infrastructure projects around the world. Around a third of China lending to Africa in 2000–2019 went to Angola. There was a sudden stop to this lending in 2020. In early 2021 Angola signed a debt relief agreement with China, which gave it a three-year moratorium on debt payments.[3] Kenya's liability flows have remained elevated since 2011. Most of the liability flows have been to the general government from China, who now account for a third of Kenya's external debt.[4] The liability flows continued in 2020, despite the onset of the Covid health crisis. In October 2022, the Kenyan government official said that they needed to renegotiate a large loan from China, or else they may default.

Conclusions

A prolonged period of low interest rates in major economies has resulted in high systemic risk in many economies. This systemic risk threatens to materialize as interest rates are hiked in an effort to combat inflation. The Latin America debt crisis transpired following a sharp interest rate rise following a decade of increased external borrowing by governments and banks in Latin America.

Recent research indicates that the current account is not the best indicator of systemic risk emanating from external imbalances. First, foreign direct investment flows have not been linked to increased risks of financial crisis. Data from Koepke and Paetzold (2020) for net debt and equity flows shows that these flows have been positive and elevated into non-major economies in the past decade. This indicates increased external imbalances. Liability flow data from Avdjiev, Kalemli-Özcan, and Servén (2022) supports this further. Foreign lending to non-major economies was very high from the end of the GFC to the onset of the taper of asset purchases by major central banks. This has resulted in high external debt,

[3] Reuters January 11, 2021, "Angola gets breathing space from Chinese creditors, says finance minister."

[4] VOA news October 19, 2022. "Kenya Wants to Renegotiate Loans for Chinese-Built Railway."

which may not be sustainable. Some of this can be attributed to China's push for infrastructure financing. There is some indication, though, that this persistent foreign capital inflow in the last decade is not as unstable as the capital inflow bonanza in the run up to the GFC. At the onset of the Covid health crisis net equity and debt flows turned negative fast, but liability flows did not.

Research indicates that in addition to focusing on debt and equity liability flows the term structure of external liabilities is important. Good data on that is still not available and may be hard to get. In addition to term structure of debt other runnable liabilities are also important, including foreign-owned deposits and foreign ownership in liquid securities.

The conclusion based on liability flows and external debt of non-major economies is that systemic risk is elevated and it threatens to materialize as dollar interest rates are increased. Better knowledge of how reversible the liability flows are would be helpful for the assessment of overall risk for individual countries.

References

Avdjiev, S., Hardy, B., Kalemli-Özcan, Ş., & Servén, L. (2022). Gross capital flows by banks, corporates, and sovereigns. *Journal of the European Economic Association, 20*(5), 2098–2135.

Banerjee, R., Devereux, M. B., & Lombardo, G. (2016). Self-oriented monetary policy, global financial markets and excess volatility of international capital flows. *Journal of International Money and Finance, 68*, 275–297.

Benediktsdottir, S., & Ahmed, S. (2023). Interest rate normalization in a world with high indebtedness. *Atlantic Economic Journal, 51*, 39–63.

Caballero, J. A. (2016). Do surges in international capital inflows influence the likelihood of banking crises? *The Economic Journal, 126*(591), 281–316.

Calvo, G. A. (1998). Capital flows and capital-market crises: the simple economics of sudden stops. *Journal of Applied Economics, 1*(1), 35–54.

Chamon, M., & Garcia, M. (2016). Capital controls in Brazil: effective? *Journal of International Money and Finance, 61*, 163–187.

Cuddington, J. T. (1986). *Capital flight: Estimates, issues, and explanations* (Vol. 58, p. 1986). International Finance Section, Department of Economics, Princeton University.

Forbes, K. J., & Warnock, F. E. (2012). Capital flow waves: Surges, stops, flight, and retrenchment. *Journal of International Economics, 88*(2), 235–251.

Goldfajn, I., & Valdés, R. O. (1997). *Capital flows and the twin crises: The role of liquidity*. IMF Working Papers 087.

Koepke, R., & Paetzold, S. (2020). *Capital flow data–A guide for empirical analysis and real-time tracking*. IMF Working Paper 171.

Laeven, L., & Valencia, F. (2013). Systemic banking crises database. *IMF Economic Review, 61*(2), 225–270.

Ortiz, G., & Serra-Puche, J. (1986). A note on the burden of the Mexican foreign debt. *Journal of Development Economics, 21*(1), 111–129.

Reinhart, C. M., & Reinhart, V. R. (2009). Capital flow bonanzas: An encompassing view of the past and present. *NBER international seminar on macroeconomics, 5*(1). Chicago, IL: The University of Chicago Press.

Rodrik, D., & Velasco, A. (1999). *Short-term capital flows*. National Bureau of Economic Research Working Paper No. 7364.

Sachs, J. D., & Williamson, J. (1985). External debt and macroeconomic performance in Latin America and East Asia. *Brookings Papers on Economic Activity, 2*, 523–573.

van Wijnbergen, S., & Oks, D. (1994). *Mexico after the debt crisis: Is growth sustainable?* (No. 1378). The World Bank.

Policy Responses in Small Economies to Stability Challenges from Cross-Border Financial Integration

Már Gudmundsson

Introduction

There has been a significant shift in views on the nature and size of the challenges faced by small, open economies (SOEs) due to cross-border financial integration. This has been associated with a reassessment of the appropriate use of policy tools aimed at preserving macroeconomic and financial stability in these economies. The potential benefits from cross-border financial integration continue to be recognised, but there is a better understanding that for these economies cross-border financial integration also comes with significant risks and can give rise to difficult trade-offs that call for the use of more policy tools than was deemed

Governor of the Central Bank of Iceland 2009–2019. The views expressed are mine and do not necessarily reflect the views of the institutions that I have been associated with.

M. Gudmundsson (✉)
Institute of International Affairs, University of Iceland, Reykjavík, Iceland
e-mail: margud@hi.is

R. Z. Aliber et al. (eds.), *Fault Lines After COVID-19*,
https://doi.org/10.1007/978-3-031-26482-5_14

appropriate by the former prevailing orthodoxy. This shift was underpinned by analytical advances on how to deal with volatile capital flows in emerging market economies (EMEs) and a better recognition that heterodox policy responses that had been used by many of them had some merits.[1]

The main aim of this chapter is to contribute from a former policymaker's perspective to the ongoing discussion about improved frameworks for preserving macroeconomic and financial stability in what I call small, open and financially integrated economies (SOFIEs).[2] Not all SOEs are financially integrated as they have relatively closed capital accounts and underdeveloped financial markets. It is, however, not necessary for economies to qualify as a SOFIE to have a completely open capital account, only that it is sufficiently open so that global financial conditions, shaped by a few big countries, have a significant influence on financial conditions in the relevant economy. This definition of SOFIEs will include both advanced economies (AEs) and EMEs, but there are differences between them regarding the degree of cross-border financial integration and its effects on the domestic economy that have relevance when it comes to policy responses as will be discussed further in the main sections of the chapter.

The rest of the chapter is organised as follows. The next section analyses the effects of cross-border financial integration on SOFIEs with a special focus on those aspects that might call for policy responses. Section "Policy Responses" examines potential and actual policy responses. It includes a discussion of multilateral constraints on some policy tools and the advice of international organisations. Section "Developing an Integrated Policy Framework" discusses the development of an integrated policy framework around policy tools that belong to central banks and financial supervisors in SOFIEs that have a flexible exchange rate and the aspiration to operate an independent monetary policy. Section "Concluding Remarks" concludes.

[1] Research by IMF staff played an important role in this reassessment. Gosh et al. (2017) provide an extensive overview.

[2] The chapter is motivated and informed by my role as the governor of the Central Bank of Iceland 2009–2019, my work on these issues at the BIS during the build-up and break-out of the Great Financial Crisis (GFC) and my recent involvement with the SEACEN project on challenges and options in managing capital flows. This chapter is to a significant degree based on longer paper of mine that was prepared as a part of that workstream; see Guðmundsson (forthcoming in Guðmundsson, 2023a). For other key publications of mine in this field, see Gudmundsson (2008) and (2017).

Stability Challenges from Cross-Border Financial Integration

Full financial integration implies that expected risk-adjusted real returns on similar types of financial assets will be equal in any two or more fully integrated markets. To draw out the implication of this for SOFIEs let us assume a world of one big economy that shapes global financial conditions (core rate-setter) and several SOFIEs that have one and each no influence on global financial conditions. Let us further assume that both the inflation differential and the risk premiums on financial assets in each SOFIE are constant vis-à-vis those in the big economy. Then we get the result that nominal returns on financial assets are pegged to those in the big country. Their levels can vary, but the correlation of changes in nominal returns will be one. This, of course, is an "unrealistic" theoretical simplification, but it gives a starting point for the analysis.[3]

In the case of a significant, but not full, cross-border financial integration, the link between the expected real returns on financial assets in SOFIEs with those of the big economy will depend on the degree of cross-border financial integration. This will in turn be translated into correlations in changes of nominal returns to a degree that depends on the fluctuations of inflation differentials and risk premiums. These correlations will be stronger at the longer end of the maturity spectrum.

SOFIEs that have their own currency and flexible exchange rate regimes can still have independent monetary policies of a sort even if changes in their long-term nominal interest rates are mostly determined by conditions in the big economy. They can choose their own inflation targets and set their own short-term interest rates that would affect economic activity in the short run and inflation in the long run. More intensive cross-border financial integration will in SOFIEs shift the transmission of monetary policy from the interest rate channel to the exchange rate channel as the effects of the policy rate on longer-term interest rates become more limited. If the exchange rate is "well behaved" in the sense that it moves smoothly in line with underlying economic conditions, then monetary transmission through the exchange rate channel can work reasonably well. It is here, however, where the problem arises as there is a significant body of empirical evidence to suggest that exchange rates are often far from

[3] The content of this and next three paragraphs are based on Gudmundsson (2017) and references therein.

being smooth reflections of underlying fundamentals, with foreign exchange markets exhibiting excess volatility and exchange rates diverging from fundamentals for protracted periods. The existence of carry trade can be seen as evidence of this, as it involves betting that interest rate differentials are not fully compensated by exchange rate movements over the investment horizon. This is supported by the result of several empirical studies that uncovered interest rate parity does not hold, except at long horizons, and then often through sharp and disorderly corrections.[4]

This potentially disorderly exchange rate dynamics gives rise to two concerns. The first is the detrimental effects that exchange rate excess volatility and misaligned exchange rates can have on the traded goods sector. The second is the potential adverse interaction with financial stability due to the presence of domestic financial vulnerabilities like currency and foreign exchange (FX) maturity mismatches in domestic balance sheets and income flows. In the case of a significant depreciation such vulnerabilities will increase the FX debt burden in terms of domestic currency. That can in turn undermine the stability of domestic financial institutions to the degree that they play a role in the intermediation of FX credit debt to unhedged entities.

The close correlation of changes in long-term interest rates in SOFIEs with those of the big core rate setters does not in itself pose a stability challenge. What it does is that the transmission of monetary policy has to rely more on exchange rate adjustment than in the case of less cross-border financial integration, and the likelihood that this adjustment will involve excessive volatility and potentially protracted under- or overshooting of the equilibrium exchange rate. This scenario carries economic costs compared to the case of an orderly exchange rate adjustment and poses risks to financial stability as explained above.

Prices and quantities are generally duals in economics and so it is also in this field where the relevant quantities are capital flows and external balance sheets. Shifting the focus to these reveals further stability challenges due to at times large swings in capital flows that can significantly affect financial conditions in SOFIEs, sometimes in the opposite direction of what is needed for domestic economic stability. That in turn can contribute to economic and financial imbalances that pose risks to financial stability.

[4] See, for instance, Plantin and Shin (2006) and Breedon et al. (2012).

It is useful to make a distinction between what are called push and pull factors when analysing the effects of capital flows. Push factors are those that are external to the economies receiving the flows, primarily global financial conditions. Pull factors are those that are internal to individual economies receiving capital flows, such as their business environment and investment opportunities. Push factor flows are generally seen to have a bigger potential to adversely affect macroeconomic and financial stability in SOFIEs, whereas pull factor flows can be more benign as they are more likely to contribute to growth in economic potential in the receiving economies.

Recent studies have provided rather convincing evidence of a global financial cycle with US financial conditions as its main driver. This cycle creates synchronised swings in capital flows to SOFIEs, which are to a significant degree unrelated to their domestic conditions.[5]

It is generally positive that financial markets differentiate based on economic fundamentals when they invest in individual economies and capital flows driven by pull factors can come with substantial benefits. These are, however, not always problem free. One example of this is when the economic cycle in a SOFIE is out of sync with its major trading partners and there is a need to tighten monetary policy to keep inflation on target. Higher policy rate will increase the interest rate differential vis-à-vis the rest of the world. This can induce carry trade flows that divert monetary transmission towards the exchange rate channel and result in the accumulation of stocks that could exit in a disorderly manner when perceptions of the SOFIE change. This is then a case where cross-border financial integration reduces the scope for independent monetary policy. Another, but related, example is when foreign investors become over-optimistic about an individual SOFIE. This can result in the build-up of economic and financial imbalances during the inflow phase such as an unsustainable current account deficit, strong credit growth and over-indebtedness. That in turn can lead to financial instability when foreign investors abruptly change their views and leave in a disorderly manner.

The degree to which cross-border financial integration creates challenges to macroeconomic and financial stability in individual SOFIEs depends on the one hand on the level of that integration and on the other hand on the level of development of its financial markets, the content of

[5] For some key contributions to the global financial cycle and discussion of its implications, see Rey (2013), and Obstfeld (2015) and (2021).

financial regulations, the quality of financial supervision and the soundness of systemic financial institutions. In general, we would expect AE SOFIEs to be more financially integrated with the rest of the world than EME SOFIEs. Because of the higher level of financial market development and institutional strength of AEs, we also expect them to be more able to absorb capital flows and deal with other negative effects of cross-border financial integration. How the degree of cross-border financial integration and absorptive capacity counteract each other has relevance for the design of policy responses. This will vary between AEs and EMEs and individual economies within these groups. The first step in making this evaluation is to assess the level of cross-border financial integration in individual economies and look at its distribution within and between AEs and EMEs.

Table 1 provides two indicators of the level of cross-border financial integration for fifteen SOEs, thereof seven AEs and eight EMEs.[6] The first indicator is correlations of monthly changes in nominal long-term government bond rates with corresponding US rates for eight years before the Great Financial Crisis (GFC) (2000–2007) and eleven years after (2009–2019). The second indicator is the sum of gross external assets and liabilities relative to GDP (gross IIP) in 2007 and 2019. Most of the SOEs have highly significant rate correlations in the post-GFC period, which is consistent with a relatively high degree of cross-border financial integration. The same was mostly the case in the period before the GFC. The gross IIP positions are more difficult to interpret as there is no clear benchmark as in the case of rate correlations.[7] Higher gross IIP is though expected to be associated with higher degree of cross-border financial integration and country ranking is instructive.

The numbers in Table 1 indicate that the differences between AEs and EMEs are indeed significant. However, although the differences between AEs and EMEs SOFIEs as groups are on average highly significant for the rate correlations, there is no clear demarcation line between them as can be seen from the result that the rate correlations 2009–2019 are almost the same for the highest EME as for the lowest AE. This partly explains significant variations in policy responses within the groups.

[6]The selection of countries in Table 1 might seem arbitrary, but they are those of a group of governors from SOEs that meets regularly at BIS bi-monthly meetings with the addition of the missing ASEAN-5 countries (Indonesia, Malaysia and Thailand).

[7]These correlations need to be positive and significantly different from zero to indicate cross-border financial integration and the closer to the limit of one the higher the degree of the integration is likely to be.

Table 1 Correlations of long-term government bond rates with US rates and gross external assets and liabilities (international investment positions) relative to GDP

	Rate correlations		*Gross IIP/GDP*	
	2000–2007	*2009–2019*	*2007*	*2019*
Chile[a]	N/A	0.44**	1.9	3.1
Colombia[a]	N/A	0.36**	0.8	1.7
Croatia[a]	N/A	-0.03	2.0	1.8
Czech Republic[a]	0.46**	0.46**	1.6	2.7
Denmark	0.80**	0.69**	4.5	6.4
Iceland	0.24**	0.06	10.8	2.4
Indonesia[a]	N/A	-0.01	0.7	1.0
Israel	0.07	0.61**	2.2	2.1
Malaysia[a]	0.39**	0.49**	2.2	2.4
New Zealand	0.83**	0.76**	2.2	2.4
Norway	0.77**	0.81**	4.5	6.9
Peru[a,b]	N/A	0.28**	1.2	1.5
Philippines[a]	0.02	0.37**	1.0	1.1
Singapore	0.49**	0.55**	18.9	20.2
Thailand[a]	0.39**	0.37**	1.3	2.0

Notes: Bond rates: Correlation between monthly changes in ten-year government bond rates. ** = 95% significance. All other correlations are below 90% significance. N/A where data points are too few to meaningfully measure correlation with US rates. Gross international investment positions are here the sum of total assets and liabilities recorded in the IIP in USD relative to current price GDP in USD

Sources: Bond rates: Central Reserve Bank of Peru (Peru), Global economy (Croatia), Investing.com (Indonesia, Malaysia, Philippines, Thailand), OECD (Chile, Colombia, Czech Republic, Denmark, Iceland, Israel, New Zealand, Norway, US), Monetary Authority of Singapore (Singapore). International investment positions: IMF WEO data base, April 2021, and International Investment Position by Country – IMF Data, https://data.imf.org/regular.aspx?key=62805744, accessed 13 April 2021

[a]Starting point of the data set for bond rates is after December 1999: Chile: August 2004, Colombia: February 2003, Croatia: January 2006, Czech Republic: May 2000, Indonesia: September 2004, Malaysia: December 2001, Peru: June 2006, Philippines: August 2000, Thailand: March 2001

[b]2006 data instead of 2007

Looking at several indicators, the big picture seems to be that cross-border financial integration peaked around the globe just prior to the GFC. It then reversed somewhat as capital flows turned back to big rate-setting economies, cross-border banking partly retreated to home base and restrictions on capital movements were in some cases reintroduced. It is, however, a mixed picture and varies between AEs and EMEs. As an example, capital account openness increased strongly among AEs in the

1990s and has since stayed mostly flat in spite of the GFC. Among EMEs, however, it continued to increase during the 2000s to reach a peak in 2008, although at a substantially lower level than in AEs. It then fell back and remained at a lower level than before the GFC.[8] World gross capital flows also peaked before the GFC. They have since remained at a significantly lower level but have been more volatile (Obstfeld, 2021).

There is some evidence indicating that the effects of the global financial cycle on SOFIEs have become stronger after the GFC. This seems to be partly attributable to the increase in the role of market-based finance in capital flows to EMEs. EME fundamentals have, however, improved since before the GFC. It is against this background that Mark Carney wrote in 2019 that "fast reforming EMEs could be running to stand still in their quest for higher sustainable capital flows" (Carney, 2019).

Policy Responses

The optimal policy response to the stability challenges explored in this chapter will vary between economies depending on the depth and level of development of their financial markets and on the degree of the relevant financial vulnerabilities. The optimal policy response will therefore vary between AE and EME SOFIEs and within these groups. For most EME and at least some AE SOFIEs, this does, however, not undermine the validity of the statement that with completely free capital movements and a freely floating exchange rate it is not sufficient for preserving macroeconomic and financial stability to put your own house in order and only use "old orthodoxy" (pre-GFC) instruments. An adequate response to these challenges will therefore have to involve a departure from inflation-targeting monetary policy with the policy interest rate as the almost only tool, micro-supervision and "let the markets do the rest". Furthermore, a floating exchange rate is not sufficient for "safe" monetary policy independence. This implies that more instruments and reformed policy frameworks are needed compared to the pre-GFC orthodoxy for economies to be better placed to deal with the shocks, the complexities and the difficult trade-offs involved.

It is useful in this connection to distinguish between three types of policy responses. The first is structural reforms and other measures aimed

[8] This is based on Chinn and Ito (2006) *de jure* index reported by Obstfeld (2021) for industrial, emerging market and less developed countries 1970–2018.

at increasing resilience to shocks, reducing domestic financial vulnerabilities and increasing the capacity of economies to absorb capital flows without the need for short-term action by economic and financial authorities. The second is exchange rate arrangements. The third is the addition of tools and better use of existing tools for shorter-term management of macroeconomic and financial stability. The time dimensions of these three types of policy responses are different. Building resilience and absorptive capacity are longer-term measures, both because they take time to implement and because their effect is long lasting. Exchange rate arrangements are usually not changed frequently. Macroeconomic stabilisation tools, however, operate in a cyclical or higher frequency domain. These three types of policy responses are discussed in turn in the next three sub-sections.

Structural Reforms and Resilience

Various measures fall into this category, including developing financial markets, accumulation of adequate buffers (e.g. FX, bank capital and liquidity), management of policy space, hard-wired prudential rules that, for instance, limit currency mismatches and maturity mismatches in FX, good financial regulations and sound financial supervision. Improvements in these areas should make economies better able to live with capital flow and exchange rate volatility without putting financial stability at risk.

There was a significant progress on structural reforms and the building of resilience among EMEs after their crises of the 1990s and again after the GFC. However, structural reforms often take time to implement and deliver their benefits. Furthermore, EMEs cannot change themselves into AEs overnight, and there are limits to how deep FX and other financial markets can be in small economies. The need to use additional macroeconomic and financial stability tools will therefore not easily disappear due to such reforms. There will still be a need for a multitude of higher frequency instruments and the development of policy frameworks around them.

Exchange Rate Arrangements

Capital account liberalisation in the decades leading up to the GFC made it more difficult to maintain pegged exchange rates. As a result, there was a shift away from such pegs, mostly towards flexible exchange rates, but among EU countries towards a monetary union. The stability challenges from cross-border financial integration that are discussed in this chapter give, however, a cause to revisit this issue. It is at least clear that a freely floating exchange rate might not be the best option for SOFIEs. A good case can be made that a better option, at least for most EMEs and some of the smaller and more vulnerable AE SOFIEs, would be a managed float where various policy tools are used with the aim to keep the exchange rate aligned with fundamentals and avoid it turning into a shock amplifier. The optimal degree of exchange rate management will vary from time to time and between economies, depending among other things on their size and the level of financial market development.

There are in principle alternative exchange arrangements for SOFIEs other than a flexible exchange rate in the free or managed form. These include an entry into a monetary union, unilateral adoption of another economy's currency or pegging to such a currency.

From the vantage point of the risks associated with cross-border financial integration, monetary union is a better option than a peg due to its multilateral nature, common safety nets and higher probability of durability. There are after all several examples in relatively recent history where broken exchange rate pegs have been the trigger of a severe financial crisis. For a SOFIE that enters a monetary union that is at the same time its biggest trading partner, excess exchange rate volatility and currency mismatches will become much less critical. Monetary union has, however, wider pros and cons that will not be entered into here. Furthermore, apart from SOFIEs on the periphery of the euro area, most SOFIEs around the world do not currently have this as a realistic option within a reasonable time horizon.

Stabilisation Tools

The tools considered here are those used for shorter-term stabilisation of the macroeconomy by minimising deviations of actual output from potential and inflation from target and by minimising deviations from external equilibrium (exchange rate aligned with fundamentals and sustainable current and capital accounts of the balance of payments), those aimed at keeping deviations from financial stability at bay, and those that affect capital flows or the exchange rate more directly. These tools are those of fiscal policy, monetary policy and macroprudential policy, along with the use of foreign exchange reserves and capital flow management measures (CFM). The first three are usually assigned to specified goals such as balanced growth with sustainable full employment in the case of fiscal policy, price stability in the case of monetary policy and financial stability in the case of macroprudential policy. The use of foreign exchange reserves and CFM can, depending on context, both be used for macroeconomic stabilisation and financial stability. In relation to the topic of this chapter, what matters is to what degree these tools could and should be used to deal with the stability challenges created by cross-border financial integration. We would generally expect that the best contribution of individual tools is to deliver on their primary goals. In special situations and/or due to the interactions of the tools that might not always be the case. This in turn gives rise to the possibility of temporary diversions of tools from their primary goals in situations where there are expected net benefits from doing so and other tools are not available that can be used without putting important goals at risk.

Both fiscal policy and monetary policy play key roles in macroeconomic stabilisation, each on their own and in their interaction. The mix of these two policies can as such have important effects on capital flows and macroeconomic stability, and it matters whether these two arms of macroeconomic management are pulling in the same direction or are in conflict. An extreme example of a conflict is when fiscal policy is loosened at the same time as inflation above target and overheating are calling for lower aggregate demand. Monetary policy will then have to do more than otherwise, which can suck in more capital flows through carry trade with the associated risks further down the road.

History has repeatedly shown that conflicts between fiscal and monetary policy can be risky. The problem is, however, that fiscal and monetary policies are, largely for good reasons, managed by separate governance mechanisms. It is therefore difficult to include fiscal policy in an integrated policy framework (IPF) where the use of all the relevant instruments is decided jointly. The stakes are, however, so high that it is important to try to avoid policy conflicts involving fiscal policy. That requires at least information sharing and policy dialogue.

Macroprudential policy is one of the additional instruments if compared with the pre-GFC prevailing orthodoxy. Several of its tools have, however, been around for much longer and have been used in EMEs and further back by AEs. Good macroprudential policy will mitigate the risks from volatile capital flows and disorderly exchange rate dynamics by leaning against the financial cycle and the accumulation of financial vulnerabilities. Examples of that are the use of macroprudential tools that indirectly reduce capital inflows and the tightening of variable prudential limits during a capital inflow surge.

The use of foreign exchange reserves and CFMs are like macroprudential policy also part of the additional instruments when compared to the pre-GFC prevailing orthodoxy and have also a long history of being used by EMEs and before by AEs. As the use of foreign exchange reserves and CFMs are not strongly assigned to particular goals and can be used in an on-off manner, they can be used to support other tools that have a primary assignment, mitigating the effect of policy conflicts and the unavailability of other instruments to deal directly with capital flow surges and bad exchange rate dynamics.

The use of foreign exchange rate reserves includes the buying and selling in the FX market and operations with financial institutions that bypass the market in the first round. The former is traditional sterilised foreign intervention (FXI) done to affect the exchange rate or address disorderly market conditions. The second can take various forms and is more likely to be done for financial stability reasons. An example of that is FX lending by central banks to domestic banks that are in a crisis and unable to roll over their short-term FX liabilities. FXI can be used to mitigate the effects of temporary balance of payments shocks, whereas the rule is to adjust to long-lasting ones. FXI can mitigate the effects of capital flows on domestic financial conditions. Views on the use of FXI have shifted considerably in recent decades, and it seems to have become widely accepted that it is one of the potential tools for managing the stability challenges from cross-border financial integration in SOFIEs.

CFMs are in this chapter defined as measures that directly affect the volume of capital flows, either through outright restrictions of particular flows or through influencing the expected payoff to investors in the case of inflows (e.g. taxes or non-remunerated reserve requirements). CFMs can certainly be rather forceful interventions, especially on the outflow side. Inflow CFMs can, however, be designed in a relatively market-friendly way that make them far removed from full-scale capital controls. Some would still argue that there will be economic costs associated with such interventions. That is in principle correct and the same applies to this as to any other public action that it should not be undertaken except if the expected benefits outweigh the expected costs. However, like in the cases of the alleged net benefits of capital account liberalisation or the cost of capital controls, it has proven difficult to substantiate in empirical studies that these costs are always substantial. More work is needed in this area, but in the meantime, policymakers should not shy away from using such tools in situations where the case for net benefits is good, but at the same time be careful of making such tools not more intrusive than necessary.

What Options Have Been Chosen?

Most economies expanded their toolkit for preserving macroeconomic and financial stability after the GFC. The most significant part of that was due to the international effort to improve prudential regulation of the financial sector and develop macroprudential policies, which was driven by the need to heed the lessons of the financial crisis regarding how to regulate the banking system and manage the domestic financial cycle. At least indirectly these reforms help to deal with the stability challenges arising from cross-border financial integration by building resilience and containing systemic risk. Furthermore, economies that are more exposed to capital flows and FX risks have under the umbrella of these reforms introduced specific regulations pertaining to them (e.g. liquidity cover ratios and net stable funding ratios in FX, and limits on FX lending to unhedged borrowers).

The big picture of how individual economies deal with the stability challenges arising from cross-border financial integration varies in ways that are broadly consistent with their structural characteristics. Big AEs and several AE SOFIEs have opted to live with them by sticking mostly to freely floating exchange rates and abstaining from using CFMs. Some AE SOFIEs have, however, used FXI more actively in the recent period, but in some cases at least that was intended to deliver their preferred monetary stance (e.g. Czech Republic and Switzerland) rather than due to concerns about the financial stability risks of large and volatile capital flows. EMEs have been more active in using FXI and CFMs.[9]

Multilateral Constraints and Policy Advice

Economies might be restricted in using CFMs due to international or regional obligations that they have undergone. An example of this is the free movement of capital rule in the European Union single market, which extends to a few other European countries through the Treaty of the European Economic Area and the OECD Code for Liberalisation of

[9] See, for instance, ASEAN (2019), BIS (2020) and (2021).

Capital Movements (OECD, 2022). Multilateral treaties that aim at free movements of capital tend to have escape clauses that allow derogations from the rule under certain conditions, such as a balance of payment crisis.[10]

The IMF plays an important role as an economic adviser to its member countries. Free movement of capital is, however, not part of its Articles of Agreement (IMF, 2020a) and the members are therefore not under obligation to follow its advice in that area.[11] The exemption to that is if the use of CFMs is deemed to be in breach of other Articles that bind the members, such as on the unfair manipulation of exchange rates.[12] CFMs should, however, not be special in this regard as the same should apply to other tools that individually or in combination are used for such manipulation.

The policy advice of the IMF regarding the management of capital flows is guided by its institutional view on the liberalisation and management of capital flows that was first adopted in 2012 (IV1- see IMF 2022) and revised in 2022 (IV2 - see IMF 2012). The IV1 partly reflected analytical advances in this area, many of which were made by IMF staff, but came under criticism to be too inflexible and to be incompatible with a truly integrated policy framework. Furthermore, IMF and OECD advice in this area were in some cases in conflict.[13] The IV2 is certainly an improvement, for instance, in accepting preventive CFMs under certain conditions, but the issue about its compatibility with a fully fledged IPF seems to remain.

[10] Usually, these derogations require the formal approval of the other partners to the treaty. The OECD Code (OECD, 2022) is a partial exemption as certain measures relating mainly to short-term capital movements can be taken immediately by the country involved but are required to be subject to a peer dialogue that provides transparency and accountability.

[11] Article VI (3) states: “Members may exercise such controls as are necessary to regulate international capital movements”.

[12] Article IV (1) states that “each member shall … avoid manipulating exchange rates or the international monetary system in order to prevent effective balance of payments adjustment or to gain unfair competitive advantage over other members”.

[13] Guðmundsson (forthcoming in 2023b) analyses the case where the IMF and OECD had almost an opposed view on Iceland’s special reserve requirement on certain capital inflows 2016–2019.

Developing an Integrated Policy Framework

The development of an integrated policy framework (IPF) around an enhanced toolset remains a work in progress. This section provides some of the key elements of such a framework for SOFIEs where the exchange rate regime is managed float and there is an aspiration to have some degree of an independent monetary policy. This framework will not be relevant for the bigger AE SOFIEs that rarely use FXI and CFMs.

The tools considered are those that are assigned to central banks and financial regulators and supervisors as it is difficult to mix fiscal policy in where the tools are used as if they were in the hands of a single policymaker that attempts to combine them in an optimal way. In this case the goals are, arguably, financial stability and monetary stability rather than overall macroeconomic stability that would require the help of fiscal policy. The tools are then those of monetary policy (policy interest rate, the use of the domestic currency part of central bank balance sheets and reserve requirements that are not CFMs), macroprudential measures (MPMs), FXI and CFMs.

In a fully integrated policy framework, there are no prior restrictions on the use of individual tools. Calibration and combination of tools depends on the context that is revealed by careful analysis of the concrete situation and the assessed efficacy, side effects and interaction of tools. There is in principle a contradiction between this approach and that of the IMF IV that restricts the use of CFMs to predetermined conditions.

Accumulated experience and research will inform such decisions, but we are still far from having the knowledge to be able to formulate robust policy rules for the multitude of tools that we can cover all contingencies. This might argue for an institutional solution where goals are set, tools are assigned, policy committees are set up and analytical support is provided. Then there would be a learning curve to climb with dynamic interactions between domestic policymakers, international organisations and academia.

The IMF has done valuable analytical work in recent years to support the development of an IPF around the toolset listed above. The main conclusions are summarised in IMF (2020b). The most relevant ones from the standpoint of this chapter are the following:

- Optimal policy combinations depend on the nature of shocks (e.g. real versus financial and temporary versus permanent); country characteristics such as currency mismatches and the depth of FX markets; and initial conditions such as the composition and level of debt.

- There are no prior restrictions on the use of individual tools and their combinations.
- Policy combinations can, depending on conditions, be more effective than using a single tool.
- The appropriate use of MPMs, FXI and CFMs can create a greater room for monetary policy to focus on price stability.
- MPMs and inflow CFMs used during normal times can prevent the build-up of risky liability structures.
- Precautionary CFMs on capital inflows can lower risks to financial stability in economies that are vulnerable to sudden stops.
- In a risk-off situation economies with shallow FX markets should use FXI, CFMs and MPMs in a temporary fashion to stabilise interest rate premia.
- There is some evidence that FXI can encourage the build-up of unhedged FX liabilities.
- The models do not provide rationale for the use of FXI and CFMs in AEs with deep FX markets and continuous market access.

The results of the IMF research amount to a strong case for the use of FXI and CFMs as a part of IPF in EMEs and possibly also in smaller AEs with relatively shallow FX markets. There are, however, also several words of warning against inappropriate use and negative side-effects of such tools in IMF (2022). They should not be substitute for warranted macroeconomic adjustment or support a misaligned exchange rate. There is a risk that CMFs become unnecessarily sticky. Communication becomes more complicated, which can negatively affect credibility. It might be easier to build and maintain central bank reputation and credibility when following a relatively simple and transparent approach.

These points are as such correct but in the context somewhat misleading as they apply to any tool, not only these. Monetary and fiscal policies should, for example, not be used as substitutes for warranted macroeconomic adjustment, and no tool should be used to support a misaligned exchange rate. The whole point about the use of these additional tools in the context of preserving macroeconomic and financial stability is to try to avoid misaligned exchange rates and their turn into shock amplifiers. The communication challenges are a real issue that needs to be given a serious consideration. A simpler framework that ignores the real-world complexities and difficult trade-offs involved is, however, not the solution as an inappropriate shying away from using additional instruments when conditions require can, as history has shown, contribute to serious financial instability further down the road with long-lasting negative consequences for central bank reputation and credibility.

Even if the principle of the IPF is that there is no a priori assignment of individual tools to particular goals, it might still make sense to do so in practice. Some tools have more effect on particular goals than others, and for this reason it is likely that the outcome of an unconstrained optimisation in normal times will be close to a more traditional assignment, where monetary policy is assigned to price stability, MPMs to financial stability and FXI and CFMs to external stability, which in turn feeds into price stability of financial stability. Furthermore, although the restrictions on the use CFMs in the IV2 are not fully consistent with an IPF approach, they might in many cases not be binding in normal times. This will make communication somewhat easier than otherwise. The remaining challenges will have to be faced head on which means that central banks and other relevant authorities need to try to explain the rationale of their actions, the uncertainties and complexities they face.

Concluding Remarks

Cross-border financial integration comes with significant benefits, but also with risks to macroeconomic and financial stability in SOFIEs. These risks have two related sources. First, the interaction of a weakened transmission of monetary policy through the interest rate channel, a potentially disorderly exchange rate dynamic and financial vulnerabilities. Second, large and volatile capital flows are driven by the global financial cycle and shaped by big reserve currency economies (mainly the US). There is some evidence that these challenges have increased since the GFC, but EME fundamentals have at the same time improved.

The optimal policy response to the stability challenges created by cross-border financial integration will vary between economies depending on the depth and level of development of their financial markets and the nature and size of their financial vulnerabilities. The optimal policy response will therefore vary between AE and EME SOFIEs and within these groups. For most EME and at least some AE SOFIEs, this does, however, not undermine the validity of the statement that with completely free capital movements and a freely floating exchange rate it is not sufficient for preserving macroeconomic and financial stability to put your own house in order and only use "old orthodoxy" (pre-GFC) instruments. This implies that more instruments and reformed policy frameworks are needed compared to the pre-GFC orthodoxy for economies to be better placed to deal with the shocks, the complexities and the difficult trade-offs involved.

Most economies expanded their toolkit for preserving macroeconomic and financial stability after the GFC that varies in ways that are broadly consistent with their structural characteristics. Big AEs and several AE SOFIEs have opted to live with them by sticking mostly to freely floating exchange rates and abstaining from using CFMs. EMEs have been more active in using FXI and CFMs.

The IMF's work on IPF and its revision of the IV are welcome steps in the right direction. It is, however, not clear to what degree the revised IV is consistent with a fully fledged IPF. The development of an IPF by the IMF and the authorities in individual economies remains a work in progress. Furthermore, we are still far from being able to formulate robust policy rules for multiple tools that can cover all contingencies. This might argue for an institutional solution where goals are set, tools are assigned, policy committees are set up and analytical support is provided. Then there would be a learning curve to climb with dynamic interactions between domestic policymakers, international organisations and academia.

References

ASEAN Working Committee on Capital Account Liberalisation. (2019). *Capital account safeguard measures in the ASEAN context*. https://www.bsp.gov.ph/Media_and_Research/Primers%20Faqs/ASEAN_theroleofsafeguardmeasuresinASEAN.pdf

Bank for International Settlements. (2020). *Capital flows, exchange rates and policy frameworks in emerging Asia*. A report by a Working Group established by the Asian Consultative Council of the BIS, November. https://www.bis.org/publ/othp34.htm

Bank for International Settlements. (2021, April). *Capital flows, exchange rates and monetary policy frameworks in Latin America and other economies*. A report by a group of central banks including members of the Consultative Council for the Americas and the central banks of South Africa and Turkey. https://www.bis.org/publ/othp37.htm

Breedon, F., Pétursson, T., & Rose, A. K. (2012). Exchange rate policy in small rich economies. *Open Economies Review, 23*, 421–445. https://papers.ssrn.com/sol3/papers.cfm?abstract_id=2092877

Carney, M. (2019). *Pull, push, pipes: Sustainable capital flows for a New World Order*. Group of Thirty Occasional Paper no. 96. Group of Thirty, Washington, DC. https://group30.org/publications/detail/4625

Chinn, M. D., & Ito, H. (2006). What matters for financial development? Capital controls, institutions and interactions. *Journal of Development Economics, 81*, 162–192. https://www.ssc.wisc.edu/~mchinn/Chinn_Ito_JDE.pdf

Gosh, A. R., Ostry, J. D., & Qureshi, M. S. (2017). *Taming the tide of capital flows*. MIT Press.

Gudmundsson, M. (2008, April). *Financial globalisation: Key trends and implications for the transmissions mechanism of monetary policy*. BIS papers no. 39. http://www.bis.org/publ/bppdf/bispap39c.pdf

Gudmundsson, M. (2017). Global financial integration and central bank policies in small, open economies. *Singapore Economic Review, 62*(01), 135–146. https://www.worldscientific.com/doi/abs/10.1142/S0217590817400069

Guðmundsson, M. (forthcoming in 2023a). *Preserving macroeconomic and financial stability in small, open and financially integrated economies*. SEACEN.

Guðmundsson, M. (forthcoming in 2023b). *Special reserve requirement on capital inflows into interest-bearing financial assets in Iceland 2016–2019.*

International Monetary Fund. (2012). *The liberalization and management of capital flows: An institutional view*. Available at https://www.imf.org/en/News/Articles/2015/09/28/04/53/pn12137

International Monetary Fund. (2020a). *Articles of Agreement*. https://www.imf.org/external/pubs/ft/aa/index.htm

International Monetary Fund. (2020b, October). *Towards an integrated policy framework*. IMF Policy Paper. https://www.imf.org/en/Publications/Policy-Papers/Issues/2020/10/08/Toward-an-Integrated-Policy-Framework-49813

International Monetary Fund (2022). *Review of the institutional view on the liberalisation and management of capital flows*. IMF Policy Paper. https://www.imf.org/en/Publications/Policy-Papers/Issues/2022/03/29/Review-of-The-Institutional-View-on-The-Liberalization-and-Management-of-Capital-Flows-515883

Obstfeld, M. (2015). *Trilemmas and trade-offs: Living with financial globalisation*. BIS working papers 480. https://www.bis.org/publ/work480.htm

Obstfeld, M. (2021). The global capital market reconsidered. *Oxford Review of Economic Policy, 37*(4), 690–706. https://static1.squarespace.com/static/5d0ed7795d764000017ccc00/t/618ac359f54f31395f6f202a/1636483929432/Oxrep_Obstfeld.pdf

OECD. (2022). *OECD code of liberalisation of capital movements*. www.oecd.org/investment/codes.htm.

Plantin, G., & Shin, H. (2006). Carry trades and speculative dynamics. *SSRN Electronic Journal*. https://doi.org/10.2139/ssrn.898412. https://papers.ssrn.com/sol3/papers.cfm?abstract_id=898412

Rey, H. (2013). *Dilemma not trilemma: The global financial cycle and monetary policy independence*. Paper presented at the Jackson Hole Symposium, August 2013. Available at http://www.kansascityfed.org/publications/research/escp/escp-2013.cfm

PART V

The International Monetary and Financial System

The Fed's Swap Lines: Narrow Circle, Broad Effect?

Joshua Aizenman

FED's Networks of Bilateral Swap Line During the Global Financial Crisis

This paper takes stock of the growing networks of Central Banks' bilateral swap lines (BSLs) in the past 20 years. Going back to the first decade of the twenty-first century, US dollar dominance morphed the US financial crisis of 2007–2008 into the "Global Financial Crisis," GFC. The resultant flight to safety led to the $ appreciation and to a liquidity crunch, inducing global recessionary forces. Concerns that the GFC would result in the Great Depression of the twenty-first century induced the FED to act as the dollar lender of last resort, extending unprecedented selective swap lines. At the peak of the GFC, the FED provided elastic BSLs to four major Central Banks (ECB, BoE, BoJ, and SNB); BSLs of $30 billion to three OECD countries and four EMs, and $15 billion to three smaller OECD countries. FED policies during the GFC and its aftermath supported the international role of the dollar, and the safe haven status of the

J. Aizenman (✉)
University of Southern California, Los Angeles, CA, USA
e-mail: aizenman@usc.edu

R. Z. Aliber et al. (eds.), *Fault Lines After COVID-19*,
https://doi.org/10.1007/978-3-031-26482-5_15

US Treasuries. The GFC also induced the ECB to extend modest BSLs to six European countries; while China provided swap lines to 23 EMs. The selectivity of BSLs during the GFC indicates that countries with significant trade, financial and geopolitical linkages can expect access to ad-hoc swap arrangements on a case-by-case basis, in ways that fit the priorities of major central banks.

Remarkably, with the exception of the ECB, BoE, BoJ, and SNB during first year of the GFC, the usage of the Federal Reserve's dollar swaps during the GFC, December 2007 to December 2009, has been limited (see Aizenman et al., 2011). Since the announcements of dollar swap liquidity,[1] the amounts outstanding have declined across the swap receivers. Canada, Brazil, Singapore, and New Zealand have never used the dollar swaps, and the total dollar swap liquidity extended had dropped to US $57 billion as of September 30, 2009. These swap lines were originally authorized through February 1, 2010, but were rescheduled to October 30, 2009. Notably, the Bank of Korea-Fed swap agreement came into effect on October 30, 2008, and was part of a network of $30 billion agreements that the Fed simultaneously signed with the central banks of four emerging markets—Brazil, Korea, Mexico, and Singapore (Fig. 1).

In November 30, 2011, the FED took stock of these bold policies, signaling its commitment for stabilizing the global financial system through unprecedented BSLs extended to systemic central banks of the US, announcing:

Coordinated Central Bank Action to Address Pressures in Global Money Markets
The Bank of Canada, the Bank of England, the Bank of Japan, the European Central Bank, the Federal Reserve, and the Swiss National Bank are today announcing coordinated actions to enhance their capacity to provide liquidity support to the global financial system. The purpose of these actions is to ease strains in financial markets and thereby mitigate the effects of such strains on the supply of credit to households and businesses and so help foster economic activity.

These central banks have agreed to lower the pricing on the existing temporary US dollar liquidity swap arrangements by 50 basis points so

[1] December 12, 2007 for the ECB and the Swiss National Bank, and 29 October 2008 for the other central banks, except the Bank of England and the Bank of Japan, where the dollar swaps are implicitly always in place.

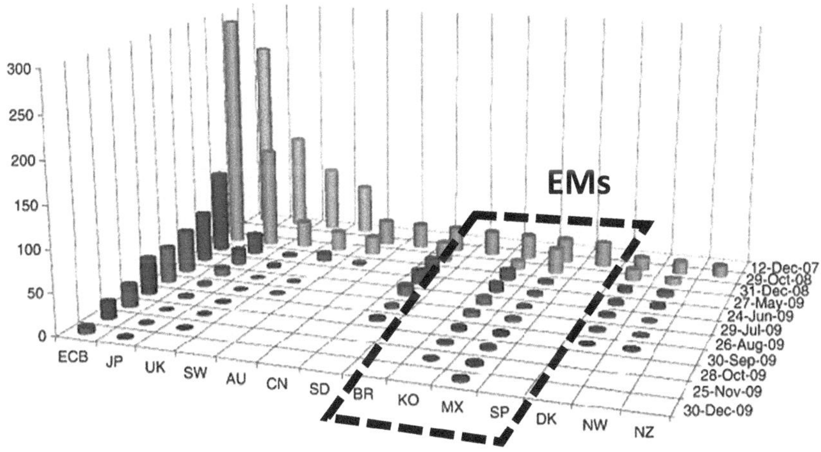

Fig. 1 FEDs swap lines, December 2007–December 2009. (Source: Aizenman et al., 2011)

that the new rate will be the US dollar overnight index swap (OIS) rate plus 50 basis points. This pricing will be applied to all operations conducted from December 5, 2011. The authorization of these swap arrangements has been extended to February 1, 2013. In addition, the Bank of England, the Bank of Japan, the European Central Bank, and the Swiss National Bank will continue to offer three-month tenders until further notice.

As a contingency measure, these central banks have also agreed to establish temporary bilateral liquidity swap arrangements so that liquidity can be provided in each jurisdiction in any of their currencies should market conditions so warrant. At present, there is no need to offer liquidity in non-domestic currencies other than the US dollar, but the central banks judge it prudent to make the necessary arrangements so that liquidity support operations could be put into place quickly should the need arise. These swap lines are authorized through February 1, 2013.

Federal Reserve Actions

The Federal Open Market Committee has authorized an extension of the existing temporary US dollar liquidity swap arrangements with the Bank of Canada, the Bank of England, the Bank of Japan, the European Central

Bank, and the Swiss National Bank through February 1, 2013. The rate on these swap arrangements has been reduced from the US dollar OIS rate plus 100 basis points to the OIS rate plus 50 basis points.

US financial institutions currently do not face difficulty obtaining liquidity in short-term funding markets. However, were conditions to deteriorate, the Federal Reserve has a range of tools available to provide an effective liquidity backstop for such institutions and is prepared to use these tools as needed to support financial stability and to promote the extension of credit to US households and businesses.[2]

These steps solidified the notion that the FED is committed to defend the global stability of the US dollar network, in line with Gourinchas and Rey (2007) interpretation of the US dollar dominance. The division of backstop services reflects a balancing act—the foreign central banks acted as the lender of last resort in their jurisdiction. This arrangement reflects Foreign Central Banks presumed better ability to monitor and assess the balance sheet of local financial institutions, and the FED's desire to minimize its balance sheet exposure to moral hazard concerns in foreign jurisdictions. *Thereby, the FED* de-facto *functions as the Central Bank of selected foreign Central Banks, at backstop interest rates determined by the FED. The FED's balancing acts reflected also its practice of minimizing US congressional and political criticism.*[3]

Yet, the highly selective nature of swap recipients means that a majority of developing countries will not have access to swap facilities. While BSLs can contribute to the global public good of global financial stability, large central banks provide liquidity support only when it is in the self-interest of their respective countries to do so. For example, during the GFC, exposure of US banks was the single most important explanation for why the US entered into swap deals with Brazil, Korea, Mexico, and Singapore. Large central banks tend to enter into swap agreements with their counterparts in countries which are important export markets and countries with large exposure of US banks (Aizenman & Pasricha, 2010). For these countries, swap lines may provide insurance services substituting hoarding

[2] Source: https://www.federalreserve.gov/newsevents/pressreleases/monetary20111130a.htm

[3] See Bordo et al. (2015) for historical perspective of FEDs BSLs, showing how swaps exposed the Federal Reserve to fears that they bypassed the Congressional appropriations process.

International reserves, at a possible political "stigma cost" of relaying on the good will of the US.[4]

FED's Networks of Bilateral Swap Line During the COVID-19 Crisis

The COVID-19 crisis turned out to test the robustness of the dollar dominance at a time when the US, EU, and China converged to similar global GDP shares, each of about 20%, PPP adjusted, yet the dollar retained its overwhelming supremacy.[5] The COVID-19 crisis saw the emergence of acute strains in the offshore dollar funding markets in March 2020. These strains manifested as deviations from neo-classical arbitrage conditions, including deviations from Covered Interest Parity (CIP), see Aizenman et al. (2022).[6] As during the Global Financial Crisis (GFC) of 2008, the US Federal Reserve (Fed) took several actions to provide US dollar liquidity to global financial markets through foreign central banks. It reduced the pricing of swap operations, extended the maturity, and increased the frequency of swap operations with the five central banks with which it has standing swap lines. It also reactivated swap lines with nine other central banks with which it had established the lines during the GFC (Fig. 2).

Furthermore, for the first time, on March 31, 2020, the Fed announced the establishment of a temporary repurchase agreement facility for foreign and international monetary authorities (FIMA). With this facility, the Fed allowed existing FIMA account holders at the New York Federal Reserve (NY FED) to borrow dollars against US Treasuries held in these accounts. The US dollars obtained by the central banks could then be used for onward lending to institutions in their jurisdictions, thus mitigating the

[4] Obstfeld et al. (2009) showed that a country's reserves holdings just before the current crisis, relative to their predicted holdings based on financial motives, can significantly predict exchange rate movements of both emerging and advanced countries in 2008. Countries with large war chests did not depreciate—and some appreciated. See also McCauley and Schenk (2020) for central bank swaps and dollar liquidity in the 1960s and now.

[5] Carney's (2019) remarks at the Jackson Hole Symposium outlined the challenges associated with the dollar dominance during the COVID times when the US share of global nominal GDP was about 15%, countries making 70% of global GDP use the dollar as anchor currency; two-thirds of global securities issuance, of official foreign currency reserves, and of Emerging Market external debt were dollar denominated; and half of global trade is invoiced in the dollar.

[6] See Du et al. (2018) and Liao and Zhang (2020) for linking these deviations to countries' net foreign asset positions and the hedging channel of exchange rate determination.

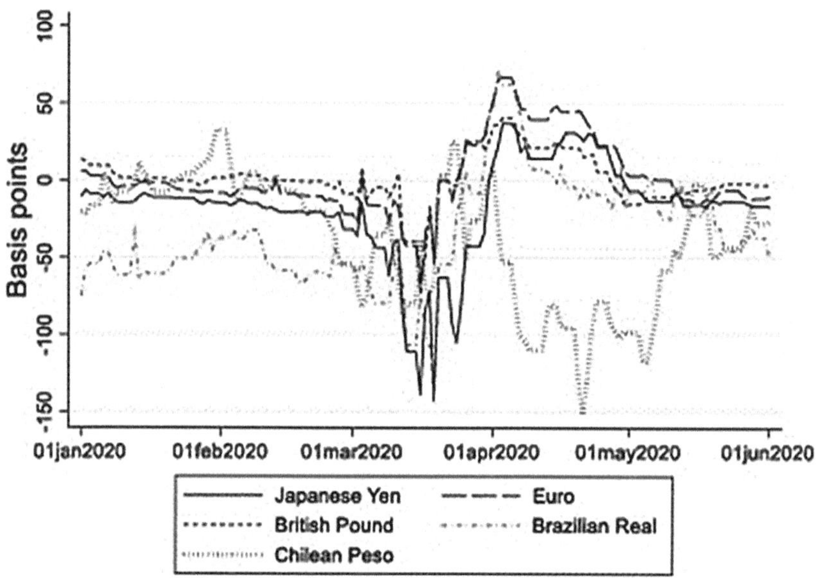

Fig. 2 Cross-currency basis (3-month swaps, basis points) widened during the COVID-19 crisis. (Source: Aizenman et al., 2011)

US dollar liquidity shortage in these jurisdictions. FIMA participants had the option to temporarily exchange their US Treasury securities held with the FED for US dollars. *This facility provided, at a backstop rate, an alternative temporary source of US dollars for foreign official holders of Treasury securities other than the sales of securities in the open market.*[7]

The FIMA facility has ambivalent characteristics from the perspective of other economies. On the one hand, it is egalitarian. Because the facility is accessible not only to economies with standing swap lines or bilateral repo arrangements with the Fed, but also to economies which do not have any such agreements, or whose banks do not have direct access to the Fed's lending window through their US subsidiaries or branches. It allows

[7] To obtain US dollar liquidity through this facility, FIMA account holders had to apply for the use of the facility, and once approved, they could enter into repo agreements with the Fed. The Hong Kong Monetary Authority announced on April 22, 2020, the launch of a US dollar liquidity facility based on US dollars obtained via FIMA. In addition, central banks of Colombia, Chile, and Indonesia announced on April 20, April 8, and June 24, respectively, that they had gained access to the FIMA facility.

central banks to provide dollar liquidity to their markets without necessarily reporting a decline in FX reserves and potentially increasing risk perceptions for their currency.[8] On the other hand, liquidity through FIMA is not equally accessible. It is more easily available for those economies which already hold a large volume of US Treasuries.

US dollar liquidity was actively provided to local markets through US dollar auctions by several central banks. The dates and terms of these auctions were pre-announced, including for those conducted by central banks other than major central banks. *The auctions by the four major central banks—ECB, BOJ, SNB, and BOE—peaked in mid-March at about US $112 billion per day and were the orders of magnitude larger than those by all other central banks.*[9] The auctions by the other 13 central banks that published data on these auctions, used either US dollars obtained via swap lines with the Fed or their own foreign exchange reserves. Assuming that countries used only dollars obtained via the Fed for all auctions after they gained access to Fed liquidity facilities, we find that nine central banks auctioned up to US $8 billion a day using Fed facilities, peaking at the end of March 2020. Some of these nine central banks conducted US dollar auctions prior to gaining access to Fed facilities, while other central banks (e.g., India, Georgia) conducted auctions without access to Fed facilities. These auctions peaked in mid-March, at about US $23 billion per day.

[8] The treatment of these repo transactions in BOPS involves the following considerations: First, FIMA is an overnight repo facility, that is, the transaction is settled every day (and may be rolled over immediately after that). Second, FIMA repo is a collateralized loan. The foreign central bank sees an increase in cash and a reclassification of securities (as the US treasury securities are collateralized at the FED and frozen, they would ideally be reclassified to central banks' other portfolio assets rather than remain in reserve assets), with a counter entry of cash liability in other investment. However, some central banks may not reclassify the collateralized securities and decide to leave them in reserve assets, resulting in an increase in reserve assets, along with the liability in other investment.

[9] Auctions by major central banks are those conducted by BoE, BoJ, ECB, SNB; reaching more than US $100 billion during the first months of activating the COVID-19 BSLs. Auctions by other Central Banks with Fed facilities are those conducted by Australia, Denmark, Hong Kong (China), Indonesia, Korea, Mexico, Norway, Singapore, Sweden after the announcement of the Fed swap line or announcement of approval of access to these economies under FIMA; reaching less than US $10 billion during the first months of activating the COVID-19 BSLs. Auctions by other Central Banks without Fed facilities include those conducted by central banks of Chile, Colombia, Georgia, India, and Indonesia (prior to approval of FIMA access if relevant); reaching less than US $2.5 billion during the first months of activating the COVID-19 BSLs. See Aizenman et al. (2022) for further details.

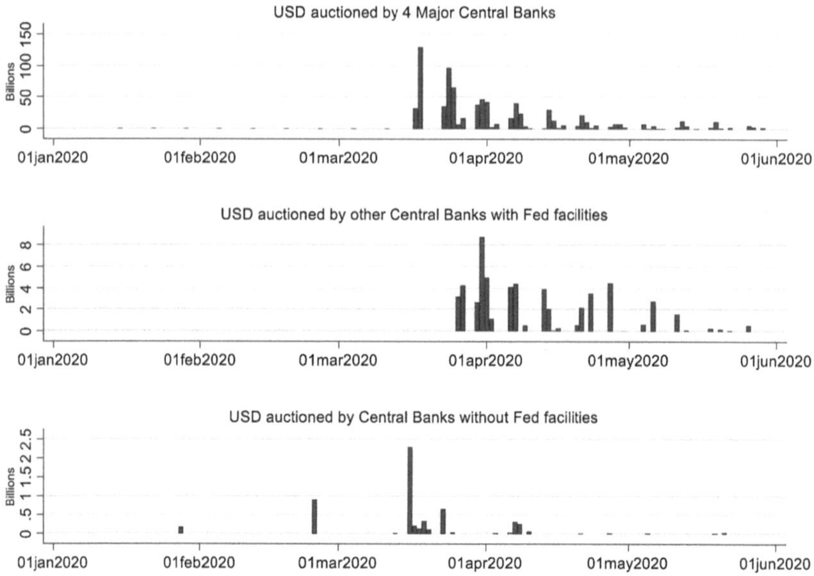

Fig. 3 Many advanced and emerging-market central banks auctioned US dollars during the COVID-19 crisis. (Source: Aizenman et al., 2022). Note: Auctions by major central banks are those conducted by BoE, BoJ, ECB, SNB. Auctions by other CBs with Fed facilities are those conducted by Australia, Denmark, Hong Kong (China), Indonesia, Korea, Mexico, Norway, Singapore, Sweden after the announcement of the Fed swap line or announcement of approval of access to these economies under FIMA. Auctions by other CBs without Fed facilities include those conducted by central banks of Chile, Colombia, Georgia, India, and Indonesia (prior to approval of FIMA access if relevant)

The US dollar shortage was mitigated by late June, so was the demand for US dollar liquidity from major central banks (Fig. 3).

Investigating the proliferation of the FED's BSLs and Repo arrangements, Aizenman et al. (2022) finds that access to Fed liquidity was driven by close financial and trade ties with the US. An economy's share in US trade and a military alliance with the US were positive factors associated with access to a Fed swap agreement. Economies with high levels of banking and financial exposure to the US, and stronger trade ties with the US tended to have greater access to Fed liquidity, via swap lines or

FIMA. Economies with a large share of global trade, regardless of whether they were major trading partners of the US, also had greater access to US dollar liquidity via the Fed. Economies that faced appreciation pressures against the US dollar and whose local currency exchange rate became more volatile were more likely to auction greater amounts of US dollar in their domestic market. Swap-related announcements led to the appreciation of the currencies against the US dollar and reduced these currency deviations from CIP.

Dollar auctions by major central banks (BoE, ECB, BoJ, and SNB) generated positive spillovers: They led to a temporary appreciation of other currencies against the US dollar, to reduced CIP deviations, and to persistently reduced sovereign bond yields of other economies. The impact of major central bank auctions was the same for economies with different financial and trade links with the US, or for economies with different balance sheet currency exposures.

Notably, under the FIMA repo facility, the Fed supplies overnight US dollar liquidity in exchange for existing US Treasuries held by these institutions, and the transaction can be rolled over. The FIMA facility was expected to reduce the need for the sale of US Treasuries and mitigate pressure in this market. As a facility collateralized by US treasures (rather than foreign currency as in the case of swap lines), FIMA does not expose the US Fed to credit risk from the foreign central bank. The facilities have been successful in limiting the sale of US Treasuries—economies with access to Fed facilities on average saw significantly smaller percentage declines in holdings of US treasuries between February and April 2020. (Fig. 4)[10]

Concluding Remarks

Noteworthy results of FED BSLs and FIMA arrangements during the COVID-19 crisis were that major central bank auctions benefitted even the more vulnerable economies. The impact of major central bank auctions was the same for economies with different financial and trade links with the US, or for economies with different balance sheet currency

[10] The economies with Fed facilities include the 14 economies with Fed swap lines as well as Hong Kong (China), Indonesia, Chile, and Colombia. Economies without Fed facilities are the 84 other economies on which data is available. See Aizenman et al. (2022) for further details.

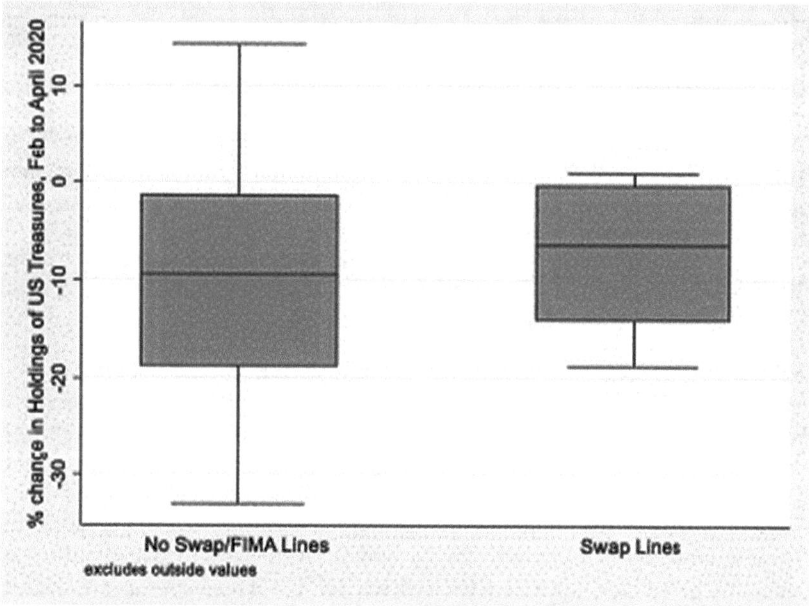

Fig. 4 Economies with access to Fed liquidity lines saw smaller decline in US treasury holdings between February and April 2020. (Source: Aizenman et al., 2022)

exposures. These features confirm the "*Narrow circle, broad effect*" of the US FED swap lines and Repo facilities during recent crises.

A buoyant interpretation of the FED's experience with bilateral swap lines and FIMA is "mission accomplished"—the FED acted successfully in stabilizing the global financial system, by providing elastic supply of liquidity to systemic financial centers and to close US allies, at backstop rates, encouraging them to provide dollar liquidity to their systemic institutions. The timing and magnitude of these innervations was adequate, triggered by the heightened global instability and "flight to the safety of the dollar."[11] FED emergency credit lines provided the global backstop that prevented the panic equilibrium induced by the attempts to liquidate dollar exposure in fire sales, where the "flight to safety" in the abases of the lender of last resort ends with a self-fulfilling financial crisis (Diamond & Dybvig, 1983).

[11] See Goldberg et al. (2022) for a detailed overview of FED's accomplishments and challenges during the COVID-19 crisis.

One may hope that by now the FED established credibility of its policies, and the blueprint of emergency BSLs will be enacted in the future at times of heightened instability triggering global risk-off and flight to quality. Yet, there is no reason to presume that the future will resemble the past. Future challenges to the US dollar standard may dilute the effectiveness or willingness of the FED to provide the global backstop services. We close this chapter with an outline of open questions and possible developments that would weaken the US dollar dominance, developments that may restrain FED's policy space and weaken the credibility of FED's backstop global services. Thus, chances are that the dollar standard would be tested again, possibly in a more challenging environment, where FED policies would possibly be less successful:

1. Will the closer alliance between the US and the EU survive beyond the Biden administration? During the GFC and the Covid crisis the FED and the ECB cooperated by invoking similar policy stance, providing positive spillovers. The possible return of a future US administration that will apply "American First" isolationist policies may raise questions on the credibility and the depth of US FED backstop dollar policies.
2. Will the deepening of sovereign € bonds and the greater ECB and EU commitment to backstop these bonds, mitigate $ dominance? These trends may strengthen the € global position by increasing the size, liquidity, and the safe haven status of sovereign € bonds issued by Euro Zone states.
3. Will weaponizing the $ dominance, and the greater geopolitical tension between the West (OECD countries) and the East (China, Russia, and their allies) induce growing fragmentation of trade and local barter and credit arrangements, mitigating over time the $ dominance?
4. Will the exit from QE and low interest policies triggered by adverse stagflationary shocks, constrain the future application of BSLs and destabilize the $ dominance?
5. Are we heading from the era of illusive stabilizing "irreversible globalization" into a fragmentation period that would rhyme with the first half of the twentieth century, this time with the destructive capabilities of modern technologies, modern global warming and climate volatility, and more than doubled global population?

Addressing these challenges with greater cooperation among the US, EU, and China is essential for future global stability.

References

Aizenman, J., & Pasricha, G. K. (2010). Selective swap arrangements and the global financial crisis: Analysis and interpretation. *International Review of Economics & Finance, 19*(3), 353–365.

Aizenman, J., Jinjarak, Y., & Park, H. (2011). International reserves and swap lines: Substitutes or complements? *International Review of Economics & Finance, 20*(1), 5–18.

Aizenman, J., Ito, H., & Pasricha, G. K. (2022). Central bank swap arrangements in the covid-19 crisis. *Journal of International Money and Finance, 122*, 102555.

Bordo, M. D., Humpage, O. F., & Schwartz, J. (2015). The evolution of the Federal Reserve swap lines since 1962. *IMF Economic Review, 63*(2), 353–372.

Carney, M. (2019, August). The growing challenges for monetary policy in the current international monetary and financial system. In *Remarks at the Jackson Hole Symposium* (Vol. 23).

Diamond, D. W., & Dybvig, P. H. (1983). Bank runs, deposit insurance, and liquidity. *Journal of Political Economy, 91*(3), 401–419.

Du, W., Tepper, A., & Verdelhan, A. (2018). Deviations from covered interest rate parity. *Journal of Finance, 73*(3), 915–957.

Goldberg, L. S., Lerman, R., and Reichgott, D. (2022). *The US Dollar's Global Roles: Revisiting Where Things Stand* (No. 20220705a). Federal Reserve Bank of New York.

Gourinchas, P. O., & Rey, H. (2007). From world banker to world venture capitalist: US external adjustment and the exorbitant privilege. In R. H. Clarida (Ed.), *G7 current account imbalances: Sustainability and adjustment*. University of Chicago Press.

Liao, G., & Zhang, T. (2020). *The hedging channel of exchange rate determination* (FRB International Finance Discussion Paper (1283)).

McCauley, R.N. and Schenk, C.R. (2020). *Central bank swaps then and now: swaps and dollar liquidity in the 1960s* (BIS Working Paper No. 851).

Obstfeld, M., Shambaugh, J. C., & Taylor, A. M. (2009). Financial instability, reserves, and central bank swap lines in the panic of 2008. *American Economic Review, 99*(2), 480–486.

Bond Market Crises and the International Lender of Last Resort

Robert N. McCauley

The shift in private credit markets from bank intermediation to intermediation through other financial intermediaries poses challenges to the central bank's ability to stabilise markets hit by crisis. In a bank-dominated financial system, the central bank can respond to runs on banks as a last resort lender against the collateral of bank assets. How should a central bank respond to a run on securities firms, money market funds (MMFs) or bond mutual funds? What is the central bank to do if the commercial paper market, the repo market or the bond market seizes up? What should be done if a shock to leveraged positions at pension funds lead to a vicious circle of margin calls and sales of government bonds? How do these responses play out in global markets in which much dollar intermediation takes place outside the United States?

Runs on non-banks and seized-up markets can threaten monetary and financial stability as much as a run on banks. Higher yields, closed markets, unavailable credit and fire sales can all crimp economic activity.

R. N. McCauley (✉)
Boston University, Boston, MA, USA

University of Oxford, Oxford, UK

R. Z. Aliber et al. (eds.), *Fault Lines After COVID-19*,
https://doi.org/10.1007/978-3-031-26482-5_16

Central banks have risen to the challenge. They have adapted their last resort operations to securities markets by serving as buyers of last resort of securities when crises have hit money and bond markets (although the role is frequently mislabelled dealer of last resort or market maker of last resort). Buying of last resort seeks to keep markets open and bond prices from spiralling downward.

So far, central banks have carried out strictly solo last resort operations in securities markets. By contrast, central banks have cooperated in last resort lending to banks, to accommodate the widespread use of the dollar by non-US banks abroad. In 2008 and 2020 runs on the dollar liabilities of non-US banks overwhelmed the Fed's domestic lender of last resort and threatened US monetary and financial stability. The Fed swapped dollars to key central banks which in turn extended Fed credit to non-US banks abroad against local collateral. To backstop global dollar banking, central banks cooperated with swaps.

Events could demonstrate that to backstop the bond market, central banks would have to cooperate. The global dollar bond market also has a large foreign component that could render Fed operations in the domestic bond market insufficient to preserve US monetary and financial stability. This is particularly true for dollar bonds not issued by the US Treasury or its agencies that embody varying degrees of credit risk (so-called spread product). To stop runs on dollar bond mutual funds, it might be necessary to buy dollar bonds issued by firms and other borrowers headquartered outside the United States.

This chapter looks to central bank cooperation to match the cosmopolitan nature of the dollar bond market with a cosmopolitan buyer of last resort. The Fed could extend its credit through central bank swaps to its key central bank counterparts abroad to fund their purchases of dollar bonds issued by their nationals. Just as the swaps have served to stabilise global dollar banking, so too swaps could serve to stabilise the global dollar bond market.

The rest of this chapter is in three parts. The first provides a typology of last resort operations in securities markets, citing examples mostly from 2008, 2020 and 2022. The second profiles the fortunate result of the Fed's last resort buying of domestic bonds in March 2020 that stabilised not only the domestic but also the foreign component of the global dollar bond market. The third suggests that such good luck should not be taken for granted and proposes that central bank swaps could fund a cooperative international buyer of last resort operation.

Last Resort Operations in Securities Markets: A Typology[1]

When banks dominate financial intermediation, the central bank can **adapt the traditional lender of last resort to backstop a seized-up securities market**. In particular, the central bank can open its discount window to banks that can in turn extend credit to firms that cannot roll over maturing securities. This was the Fed's approach to the seizing up of the US commercial paper market in 1970 after the surprising bankruptcy of Penn Central, a major railroad. The Fed temporarily reversed its moral suasion against banks' use of the discount window to encourage banks to lend to firms unable to sell commercial paper. Corporate loans of the big banks could expand by 3% in order to offset a rapid 10% decline in commercial paper. Ultimately, the major banks were large enough to accommodate a one-third shrinkage of the commercial paper market on their balance sheets. That was then.

In a system dominated by non-bank intermediation, the same approach may require the central bank to operate against a wider range of securities. Facing disruptions to the long end of the UK bond market associated with margin calls on leveraged pension funds in October 2022, the Bank of England first stepped in as buyer of last resort (see below) but then widened its collateral policy at its repo facility to encourage banks to lend to pension funds.[2] For one month, the Bank would repo cash against corporate bonds, including those denominated in the dollar. The aim was to encourage banks to provide credit against such collateral to pension funds to meet margin calls without fire sales of securities.[3]

When securities market bulk large in overall financial intermediation, such an indirect approach through the banks may not be up to the task. The central bank can backstop securities markets in two more ways. First, it can **lend as a last resort** to non-bank financial institutions and even non-financial firms. Second, it can step into the role of non-bank financial

[1] See McCauley (2020a) for references for this section.

[2] The first response of the Bank of England was to buy long UK Treasury bonds; see below.

[3] Bank of England, *Temporary Expanded Collateral Repo Facility – Market Notice 10 October 2022*, https://www.bankofengland.co.uk/markets/market-notices/2022/october/temporary-expanded-collateral-repo-facility-market-notice-10-october-2022, accessed 15 October 2022. Initial reporting suggested little interest in the one-month facility, priced at 15 basis points above the bank rate.

firms as **market maker of last resort** in securities or even **buyer of last resort** of them.

A **lender of last resort** takes a big step when it extends the who's who of counterparties from banks to securities firms, insurance companies, mutual funds or pension funds. Their asset holdings may require a widening of the central bank's acceptable collateral. For instance, in 2008 and 2020 the Fed invoked emergency powers in effect to extend its discount window to its primary dealers, that is, its recognised market makers in Treasury securities. It took corporate bonds as collateral, which are not eligible for the regular discount window. The 2008 Fed loan to AIG, an insurance company, was collateralised with the firm's equity in its insurance subsidiaries, also ineligible at the discount window. In addition to the issue of collateral, lending to such financial firms generally poses the problem of the central bank's lending to intermediaries over which it does not exercise supervisory powers or from which it receives no reports of financial condition. The moral hazard, the danger that prudence is undermined by the prospect of central bank help, argues against acting predictably in such circumstances.

When sharply higher energy prices in 2022 led to margin calls on energy derivatives entered into by energy firms, the UK Treasury and the Bank of England took the unusual step of announcing that the Bank would provide up to £40 billion in credit to such firms.[4] After undergoing solvency checks, firms operating in the UK wholesale gas and electricity markets could borrow from commercial banks with a 100% central bank guarantee. Pricing is intended to ensure the last resort use of the facility. Presumably, the UK Treasury bears the risk of this facility; governments and state development banks have borne such risks elsewhere in Europe.

This author is unaware of any last resort lending to a mutual fund by an advanced country central bank. The closest was the US Treasury's guarantee of the par value of money market mutual funds in 2008.[5] It would be risky to preclude such lending in the future.

[4] Bank of England, *Update on the Energy Markets Financing Scheme*, 23 September 2022, https://www.bankofengland.co.uk/news/2022/september/energy-markets-financing-scheme, accessed 15 October 2022.

[5] Using banks as above, in April 2020 the Reserve Bank of India set up a Special Liquidity Facility for Mutual Funds after Franklin Templeton's Indian affiliate halted redemptions from six high-risk bond funds, freezing $3 billion. Banks could borrow at the RBI's policy repo rate to extend credit to mutual funds or to buy assets from them. See Sankar (2020).

Going beyond lending to non-bank financial firms, the central bank can step into their role as **market maker of last resort** or buyer of last resort (Mehrling, 2010). Thus, a market maker of last resort posts a narrower bid-ask spread than obtains in a dysfunctional market, but a wider one than obtains in a normal market (Tucker, 2018). With the central bank bid as backstop, a dealer can offer to buy a security without running the risk that no dealer is answering the phone when it comes time to sell the position. In essence, the market maker of last resort seeks to buy and to sell in order to encourage others to do likewise.

The Bank of England played the role of market maker of last resort in the sterling corporate bond market in 2009, not only buying but also selling. It counted its success in narrower bid-ask spreads and ultimately a revived primary market. The market liquidity added by the Bank of England operations ultimately helped to raise corporate bond prices, but that was not the immediate goal.

The **buyer of last resort** (Kaminska, 2020; McCauley, 2020a, 2020b, August; Hauser, 2021) is often mislabelled a dealer or market maker of last resort, but the differences in modus operandi and goals are striking. The buyer of last resort seeks to ensure that there is a bid in a dysfunctional market and that the price is not so low as to amount to a fire sale. The goal is the functioning of the market itself and the breaking of a downward price spiral.

For instance, in response to the ongoing one-sided pension fund sales and crash of the prices of long-term government bonds, the Bank of England initially announced on 28 September 2022 a limited period of gilt purchases 'to restore orderly market conditions… on whatever scale is necessary'.[6] The subsequent market notice put maximum daily purchases of £5 billion for 13 days.[7] Purchases would be unwound in the indefinite future, after orderly market conditions had been restored. UK government bond prices rose after the intervention, but bid-ask prices remained wide. Targeted and temporary it may have been, but this was a buyer of last resort operation.

[6] Bank of England, Bank of England announces gilt market operation, 28 September 2022 https://www.bankofengland.co.uk/news/2022/september/bank-of-england-announces-gilt-market-operation, accessed 15 October 2022.

[7] Bank of England, Gilt Market Operations - Market Notice 28 September 2022 https://www.bankofengland.co.uk/markets/market-notices/2022/september/market-notice-28-september-2022-gilt-market-operations, accessed 15 October 2022.

The precedents for the Fed as security buyer of last resort date to 2008, when the Fed both in effect bought commercial paper outright and underwrote roll-overs of maturing paper. When Lehman Brothers defaulted in September 2008, the oldest money market fund (MMF) repriced its shares at less than $1 par value. This set off a run first on similar MMFs that buy private corporate and bank debts and then on the underlying commercial paper and bank deposit markets in which such funds invest. By in effect buying asset-backed commercial paper, the Fed helped to provide funding to MMFs and to break the run on them. And by underwriting commercial paper, the Fed helped to limit the shrinkage of the commercial paper market, where non-financial firms finance inventories and non-bank financial firms do much funding.

Whether a central bank does last resort lending beyond banks or acts as buyer of last resort, Hauser and Logan (2022) emphasise that they should respect the 'backstop principle'. This principle means not only appropriate regulation and supervision to limit distortions to markets and incentives. In addition, pricing should be unattractive except in the case of severe market dysfunction, and the duration of intervention should not outlast the dysfunction.

The Bond Market Crisis of 2020[8]

The response to the financial crisis that hit the US money and bond markets with the pandemic in March 2020 proved four things. First, the Fed was prepared again to offer unlimited swaps to key central banks in order to stabilise the global dollar money market. Second, the Fed was again prepared to serve as buyer of last resort in the commercial paper market. Third, the Fed was prepared to stabilise the US Treasury market as unlimited buyer of last resort. And fourth, the Fed was prepared to buy US corporate bonds and this served to stabilise the global dollar bond market. What follows elaborates on these four points.

When in March 2020 market participants began to understand the challenge of the Covid pandemic, they responded in a dash for cash. Firms worried that revenues would crash to zero, leaving cash flows deeply negative. The 'cash' resources of the corporate treasury, often invested more for yield than immediate availability, suddenly needed to be really liquid. And firms drew down credit lines with banks to bulk up on bank deposits.

[8] This section draws on Chap 13 of Aliber et al. (2023).

Banks did not suffer runs, as in 2008, but they prepared for large cash calls on committed lines of credit.

As in 2008, the riskier MMFs suffered runs. Investing in bank and corporate IOUs, 'prime' MMFs experienced redemptions of $125 billion in March 2020, 11% of their assets (IOSCO, 2020, p. 13). This was a smaller liquidation than in 2008, when this segment of MMFs was larger. This time none broke the buck (repriced shares at less than $1) or impeded redemptions. Still, as MMFs paid out to redeem shares, remaining shareholders worried that dwindling liquid assets would trigger 'gates'—constraints on redemptions mandated by regulators after 2008. A reform to deal with liquidity strains on MMFs turned out to accelerate runs (FSB, 2021).

As in 2008, the run on MMFs had knock-on effects on other markets. It threatened to close the commercial paper market, a key source of short-term financing for firms. And, as in 2008, the run on MMFs left non-US banks scrambling for dollars. Onshore and offshore MMF funding of non-US banks dropped by $200 billion in February–March 2020 (Aldasoro et al., 2021, p. 33).

The dash for cash did not just disrupt money markets, however. It also led to massive selling of US dollar bonds. This selling not only destabilised the global benchmark bond market—the US Treasury bond market—but also the US corporate bond market, where US firms do most of their funding.

As background, US corporate bonds outstanding had grown very considerably since the Great Financial Crisis (GFC) of 2008, in part as an *intended* consequence of the Fed's repeated rounds of bond-buying. The Fed encouraged US corporations to issue bonds by buying Treasury and agency securities, reducing the so-called term premium demanded for locking in funding for years at a fixed rate. As an *unintended* consequence of the same Fed bond-buying, firms and governments outside the United States had also issued dollar bonds in size. Instability in the dollar bond market put at risk the access to credit of a global swath of borrowers.

In March 2020, hedge funds, foreign officials and bond mutual funds all heavily sold bonds at once. First, hedge funds dumped US Treasuries. Highly leveraged so-called relative value funds held relatively cheap Treasury bonds (financed in the repo market) against short positions in Treasury bond futures. The normally modest spread between these two—certain cash bonds could be periodically delivered into maturing bond futures, linking their prices—widened amid rising volatility, increasing margins and impaired liquidity. This 'wrong-way' move cost the highly leveraged funds dearly on their long positions in cash bonds. Losses in turn forced them to deleverage by selling Treasuries in the hundreds of billions of dollars in March. Other hedge fund strategies magnified the moves (Schrimpf et al., 2020). Lots of leverage among holders could make even a safe asset risky by making its price volatile and its trading difficult. The data are partial, given the incorporation of some US hedge funds offshore, but something well over $200 billion in hedge fund selling is a reasonable estimate (Vissing-Jørgensen, 2021).

Second, foreign central banks also dumped Treasuries. Anticipating pressure on their dollar-borrowing banks and firms as in 2008, and in many cases intervening to support their currencies by selling dollars, they sought to turn Treasury holdings into immediately useful bank deposits. Treasury data show $244 billion in US Treasury bond sales, or 3.3% of holdings, by foreign officials in March–May 2020 (Weiss, 2022).

Third, responding to and magnifying these sales, households staged the largest and sharpest liquidation of bond mutual funds in memory, and the run forced fund managers to sell bonds in the market. Since the GFC, low interest rates had encouraged US households to reach for yield by buying bond mutual funds. US bond fund holdings as a share of the corporate bond market rose from less than a tenth to almost a fifth. Facing the uncertainties of pandemic and turmoil in the bond market, households liquidated an unprecedented 5.6% of bond fund assets in March (Vissing-Jørgensen, 2021, Table 5). One interpretation is that households originally viewed this investment as almost as safe as a bank deposit but in March 2020 suddenly viewed it as risky (ibid.). Another interpretation is that given the hedge fund and foreign selling of Treasury bonds and their resultant yield spike in early to mid-March 2020, bond fund holders redeemed about what one would expect in response to recently experienced price declines (Collins, 2021). In any case, bond fund managers had little choice but to pass on the selling pressure to the bond market, if not amplify them by adding to liquidity buffers. The easiest bonds to sell were US Treasuries, and funds sold by a disputed estimate of $260 billion in the first quarter of 2020 (Vissing-Jørgensen, 2021; Ma et al., 2022; Antoniewicz and Collins 2022).

Stepping back, then, the Fed faced big runs on MMFs and bond mutual funds, as well as widespread dumping of US bonds. Holders of the riskier MMFs sought out, pulling dollars out of non-US banks. The Fed had dealt with such a money market crisis in 2008. But what to do in the face of large selling of US Treasury securities and an incipient run on bond mutual funds? This required a new playbook. At risk was the main source of funding for US corporations—and for non-bank dollar borrowers outside the United States as well.

The Fed responded with a combination of old and new policies. It dealt with the disruption of the money markets along the lines of its response in 2008, but innovated in its response to the disruption of the bond markets. To calm bond markets, the Fed became the buyer of last resort in a manner that had profound international implications. To underscore: the Fed did not target foreign holdings of US bonds or foreign-issued dollar bonds in particular. Nevertheless, the effect of the Fed bond-buying on foreign holdings of US bonds and foreign-issued dollar bonds amounted to an extension of its international lender of last resort operations.

The Fed quickly consulted its playbook from 2008 to stabilise MMFs and thereby to stabilise their funding of non-US banks. The Fed rolled out facilities to inject its credit into the commercial paper market as buyer of last resort. In order to increase the confidence of MMF investors, on 17 March it revived a programme to underwrite new issues of commercial paper, reassuring investors that maturing paper could be rolled over. On 18 March, it revived a 2008 facility to allow the Federal Reserve Bank of Boston in effect to buy outstanding commercial paper (not just asset-backed commercial paper as in 2008) held by MMFs (technically lending on a non-recourse basis to banks to buy the paper).

To enable non-US banks to access dollars and thereby to replace the loss of funding from MMFs, the Fed reactivated the swap lines. In 2007–2008, the Fed had taken a year to widen access to larger amounts for more central banks, for longer maturities, in more frequent operations. Playbook in hand, the Fed took these steps in days in March 2020.

Once again, as non-US banks scrambled for dollars, Libor began lifting off from the Fed's policy interest rate. Even as the Fed lowered its federal fund policy rate, as reflected in the expected overnight rate (the overnight index swap or OIS), the key three-month Libor rate began to rise on 12 March.

Swiftly, the Fed acted to keep the transmission of its interest rate policy to the real economy from breaking down. The very next day, the Fed eased its interest rate on central bank swaps from OIS+50 basis points to OIS+25 basis points for five core central banks with standing swaps; it also offered 84-day swaps. Libor fell but then began to rise again and the Fed extended the swaps to the other nine central banks on 19 March and started daily operations. The start of daily swap operations on 23 March marked the local maximum of Libor, which fell to within 25 basis points of OIS by early May. With these swift moves, Fed credit extended to central banks through swaps rose much more sharply in 2020 than in 2008 but peaked at a lower level at less than $500 billion. The Fed succeeded in preventing the cost of floating rate dollar financing from rising for US households with variable-rate mortgages and for firms all over the world with floating rate dollar loans. Thus, the swaps not only served financial stability (responding to runs on non-US banks) but also monetary stability (ensuring the transmission of Fed policy rates to benchmark private rates).

The political reaction to the use of swaps in 2020 confounded widespread fears that de facto the Fed faced a high political hurdle to mobilise the swaps. In 2008 and after, the Fed had fielded sharp questions from Congress regarding the central bank swaps (Broz, 2015). In the end, the new banking legislation known as the Dodd-Frank Act did not restrict the legal ability of the Fed to extend its credit to other central banks through swaps. This absence of constraint stood in contrast to new constraints on the Fed's emergency lending powers, which proscribed deals for individual firms (as with Bear Stearns in March 2008 and AIG in September 2008) and required Treasury assent. Still, there was a practical political question about the use of swaps. In the event, heavy use of central bank swaps in 2020 stirred little controversy.

In response to Treasury bond selling and the spike in Treasury rates, the Fed entered the market as a determined, rapid and heavy buyer. The operating instruction to the open market desk at the New York Fed charged it with buying Treasury and agency securities 'in the amounts needed' to restore the proper functioning of the market (Logan, 2020). In the three weeks between 11 March and 2 April the Fed bought no less than $900 billion of Treasury and agency securities.[9] Thus, Fed more than offset the domestic and foreign official selling of US Treasuries of as much as $800 billion over a longer period. From the standpoint of the foreign official holders of US Treasury securities, the Fed purchases allowed them to turn securities with suddenly wildly fluctuating prices set in surprisingly illiquid markets into bank deposits or secured placements with the New York Fed (repos).

[9] Federal Reserve, H.4.1 Release-Factors Affecting Reserve Balances, 12 March, 2 April 2020.

Watching central banks selling US Treasuries, only to see them sit on much of the cash at the New York Fed, led the Fed at the end of March to offer overnight advances to central banks using US Treasuries as collateral at a rate above private repo rates. This little-used facility, dubbed the Foreign and International Monetary Authorities (FIMA) Repo Facility, is discussed below.

Dislocations were evident in the corporate bond market as well and the Fed responded speedily. As mutual funds sold corporate bonds, these went to big discounts to levels implied by credit derivatives. Such market dynamics threatened to cut off US firms' major source of financing of investment and hiring, and even to cause defaults if maturing bonds could not be refinanced. On 17 March the Fed announced that it would use its emergency powers to lend to its primary dealers, i.e. its bond market counterparties, as it had in 2008. This gave them an assurance of funding that would allow them to make markets and to arbitrage cash and derivatives markets. On 20 March, when the Fed extended the first loans to the primary dealers using these emergency powers, the primary dealers offered corporate bonds as collateral for the Fed advances. Fed credit was flowing through the dealers into the corporate bond market.

The Fed then took an unprecedented step as corporate bond buyer of last resort. On 23 March, it announced that it would invoke emergency powers to buy investment grade US corporate bonds. The principle of the Fed buying corporate commercial paper at money-market tenors had been set in 2008 and reinforced earlier in the month with the revival of the commercial paper buying programme. What was unprecedented was the Fed going beyond the money market, the usual focus of its operations. But given that US firms rely on corporate bonds more than any other source of external financing, arguably the Fed's powers to buy bonds should be widened to allow it to backstop the corporate bond market (McCauley, 2020b).

The Fed's terms for the corporate bond purchases showed a sensitivity to the political hazard of being seen to help firms without a direct stake in the US economy. Issuers of bonds could be foreign owned but had to be incorporated in the United States, have significant US operations and a majority of its employees based in the United States.[10] This targeted

[10] Federal Reserve Bank of New York, 'Secondary Market Corporate Credit Facility: Program Terms and Conditions', 28 July 2020 https://www.newyorkfed.org/markets/secondary-market-corporate-credit-facility/secondary-market-corporate-credit-facility-terms-and-conditions, accessed 6 April 2022.

intention, however, did not preclude that the programme would indirectly lift the prices of dollar bonds by foreign firms that did not meet these criteria.

More surprising was the announcement on 9 April that the Fed would buy junk bonds, the low-rated bonds of more leveraged and more risky firms. After all, the Fed as bank regulator had been warning banks not to lend to firms that private equity firms were loading up with debt, both bank loans and junk bonds. Indeed, ultimately the Fed bought mutual funds designed to hold the whole gamut of junk bonds, including bonds that had been issued by firms that the Fed had cautioned banks not to lend to (McCauley, 2020a).

In any case, one can imagine that the corporate bond purchases could affect non-Treasury dollar bond prices in one of two ways. The Fed buying could be a thumb on the scale of just those bonds purchased. There was certainly evidence for such: the Fed's announcement highlighted its intention to lower yields on short- to medium-term bonds, and their yields fell more markedly, for instance.

Alternatively, the effect of the Fed buying could diffuse from those bonds purchased across the spectrum of dollar bonds embodying credit risk. This diffusion could work through portfolio substitution by investors, as they sold into the prospective Fed bid for US corporate bonds and bought cheaper bonds not targeted by the Fed. Consider both prices and flows to choose between these two alternative possibilities.

The prices of the biggest exchange-traded funds (ETFs) for investment grade US corporate bonds, junk US corporate bonds and emerging market dollar bonds broadly support the second view. Prices for ETFs for investment grade bonds (LQD) and emerging market bonds (EMB) had both bottomed between the Fed announcement of its lending to the primary dealers late on 17 March and its doing so on 20 March (Fig. 1). This timing points to funding liquidity rather than credit concerns, reinforcing the impression conveyed by the gap between US corporate cash bond prices and those of the corresponding credit derivatives. When the Fed announced the buying of investment grade bonds, the price of LQD rose for three days. With a one-day lag, both the junk bond and emerging market bond ETF prices rose for three days as well. When the Fed announced that it would buy junk bonds on 9 April and upped its overall maximum of corporate bond purchases, the prices of all three ETFs jumped the same day. By mid-June 2020, the prices of all three ETFs had recovered substantially. Though the Fed bought corporate bonds and did not buy any

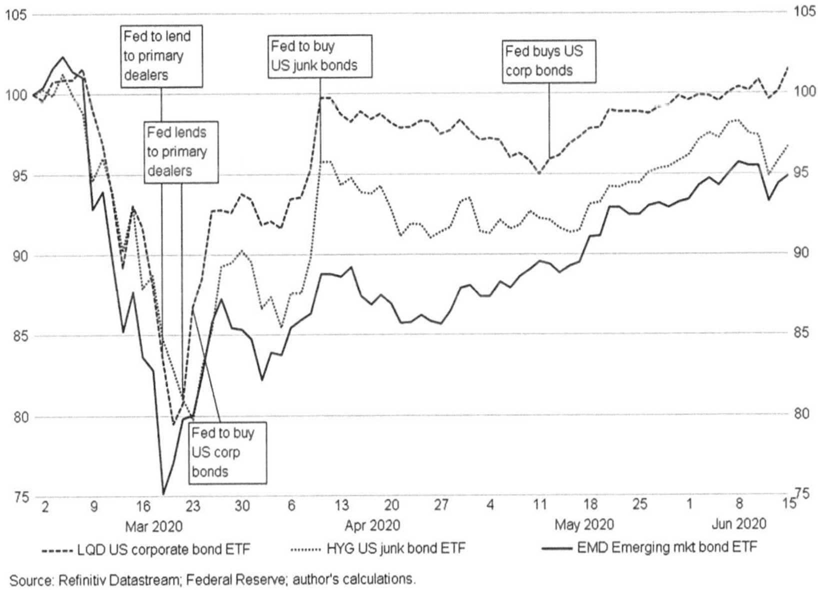

Fig. 1 Emerging market bond prices rise as Fed buys US corporate bonds

of the emerging market dollar bonds, their price performance did not differ much. The effect of the Fed corporate bond purchases diffused widely.

The Fed's promise to purchase corporate bonds also turned around flows into what the Investment Company Institute calls global bond funds. Outflows from global bond funds seemed to respond more quickly to the Fed announcement than did outflows from investment grade bond funds (Fig. 2). But broadly flows into global bond funds that did not benefit from Fed purchases tracked flows into the corporate bond funds that did benefit from Fed buying. With the flows, as with the prices, the effect of the Fed announcement seemed to diffuse beyond US corporate bonds to dollar bonds from issuers in the rest of the world.

In sum, in March 2020 the combination of the Fed's lending of last resort to securities dealers and its buying of last resort of US corporate bonds had an unintended consequence. Not only US corporate bonds but also emerging market dollar bonds bottomed in price between the announcement of the primary dealer lending and the first loans. One can interpret this observation as suggesting that Fed credit allowed the

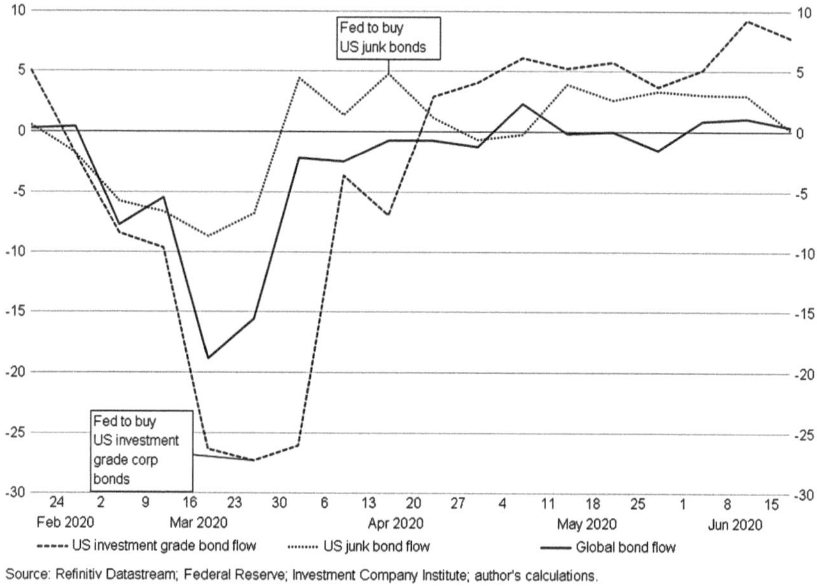

Fig. 2 Flows into global bond funds recover as Fed buys US corporate bonds

primary dealers to make markets in all sorts of dollar bonds embodying credit risk, both domestic and foreign. And the subsequently similar price movements in the US corporate and emerging market bonds point to investors' treating domestic and foreign dollar bonds as close substitutes in their credit portfolios. Lending to bond dealers and buying bonds domestically, the Fed halted an incipient run on funds holding dollar bonds issued by non-US obligors. This in turn prevented fire-sales of dollar bonds issued by borrowers outside the United States and a closure of the market for new issues that would bring a wave of defaults. In effect, if not in intention, the Fed backstopped the global dollar bond market.

Bond-Buyer of Last Resort and Central Bank Swaps

The Fed has found it necessary to extend its credit to banks outside the United States through swaps with key central banks because dollar money markets have become so global. Non-US banks have $12.5 trillion in dollar funding, and less than a quarter comes from deposits in the United

States (Aldasoro et al., 2021, Graph 1, p. 33). Disrupted dollar intermediation outside the United States threatens higher interest rates to borrowers in the United States; difficulty in borrowing dollars on the part of either foreign banks or foreign institutional investors threatens fire sales of US assets or disruptive dollar purchases. The dollar lender of last resort to banks needs a global reach.

By contrast, in 2020, the Fed stabilised the global dollar bond market by buying just domestic bonds: Treasuries and agencies in huge volume and corporate bonds in relatively limited amounts. But there is reason to consider this a fortunate, even serendipitous, outcome, rather than one that policy-makers should count on. Scale matters. Dollar borrowers outside the United States have shifted from bank loans to bonds, and their stock of bonds has become a substantial part of the global dollar bond market.

Since the GFC, the stock of dollar bonds issued by borrowers outside the United States has grown more rapidly than the stock of bank loans. Indeed, non-banks outside the United States now have a larger outstanding dollar debt in bonds than in bank loans.[11]

Outstanding international bonds denominated in the dollar have reached $13 trillion, more than half of the US corporate bond market. It would be a stretch for the Fed to buy any of these save those issued by US residents at $1.5 trillion, or US-headquartered firms, at $3.3 trillion.[12]

In the event that a broad disruption of the global dollar bond market occurred, other central banks could join the Fed as buyer of last resort. Each participating central bank could buy dollar bonds issued by its residents or nationals. The motivation would be to keep open this source of finance to its own borrowers and to reduce spillovers to its own domestic credit market. It might happen that Fed cash available through the FIMA facility against the collateral of Treasury securities would be enough to fund such purchases. But a sizeable operation could require funding on such a scale that participating central banks would need access to Fed credit made available through central bank swaps.

The distribution of risk in such an operation would be analogous to that in the swaps that allow key central banks to advance dollars to banks in their jurisdictions. The partner central banks would bear the price and

[11] https://www.bis.org/statistics/gli2207.htm, accessed 18 October 2022.

[12] See https://www.bis.org/statistics/about_securities_stats.htm?m=1033 and https://stats.bis.org/statx/srs/table/c3?c=US&p=20222, accessed 19 October 2022.

credit risk of holding the dollar bonds issued by borrowers outside the United States. The Fed's exposure would be confined to its claim on its central bank partner (secured by its currency).

To stabilise a global dollar bond market may require a global buyer of last resort. Central bank swaps could make that possible.

References

Aliber, R., Kindleberger, C. & McCauley, R. (2023). *Manias, Panics, and Crashes.* Palgrave Macmillan.

Aldasoro, I., Eren, E. & and Huang, W. (2021, March). Dollar funding of non-US banks through Covid-19. BIS Quarterly Review, 31-40.

Antoniewicz, S. & Collins, S. (2022, March 24). Policymakers say bond mutual funds contributed significantly to Treasury market stress but... Investment Company Institute *Viewpoint.*

Broz, J. L. (2015, August). The politics of rescuing the World's financial system: The Federal Reserve as a global lender of last resort. *The Korean Journal of International Studies, 13*(2), 323–351.

Collins, S. (2021, March 4). Bond mutual fund outflows: A measured investor response to a massive shock. Investment Company Institute *Viewpoint.*

Financial Stability Board (FSB). (2021, October). *Policy proposals to enhance money market fund resilience* (Final Report).

Hauser, A. (2021, 7 January) [Bank of England executive director of markets]. *Why central banks need new tools for dealing with market dysfunction*, speech given at Thomson Reuters newsmaker, https://www.bankofengland.co.uk/speech/2021/january/andrew-hauser-speech-at-thomson-reuters-newsmaker. Accessed 6 April 2022.

Hauser, A. and Logan, L. (2022, May 11*). Market dysfunction and Central Bank Tools: Insights from a Markets Committee Working Group.* Bank for International Settlements.

International Organization of Securities Commissions. (2020, November). *Money market funds during the March–April episode: Thematic note.* The Board of the International Organization of Securities Commissions.

Kaminska, I. (2020, 26 March). When Central Banks take over bond markets, *Financial Times* Alphaville.https://ftalphaville.ft.com/2020/03/25/1585143723000/When-central-banks-take-over-securities-markets/, accessed 6 April 2022.

Logan, L. (2020, October 23). *Treasury market liquidity and early lessons from the pandemic shock.* Remarks at Brookings-Chicago Booth Task Force on Financial Stability (TFFS).

Ma, Y., Xiao, K. & Zeng, Y. (2022). Mutual fund liquidity transformation and reverse flight to liquidity. The Review of Financial Studies, 35(10), 4674–4711.

McCauley, R. (2020a, August 7). *The Fed in the corporate bond market, 2020* (CEGI Working Paper 41). Global Development Policy Center, Boston University.

McCauley, R. (2020b, August 26). *The federal reserve needs the power to buy corporate bonds.* VoxEU.

Mehrling, P. (2010). *The new Lombard street: How the Fed became the dealer of last resort.* Princeton University Press.

Sankar, P. (2020, 20 May). *India extends special liquidity facility to mutual funds.* Yale School of Management, Program on Financial Stability, https://som.yale.edu/blog/india-extends-special-liquidity-facility-to-mutual-funds, accessed 15 October 2022.

Schrimpf, A., Shin, H. S. & Sushko, V. (2020, 2 April). *Leverage and margin spirals in fixed income markets during the Covid-19 Crisis* (BIS Bulletin No 2).

Tucker, P. (2018). *Unelected power: The quest for legitimacy in central banking and the regulatory state.* Princeton University Press.

Vissing-Jørgensen, V. (2021, October). *The treasury market in spring 2020 and the response of the Federal Reserve* (BIS Working Papers, No 966).

Weiss, C. (2022, January 28). *Foreign demand for U.S. treasury securities during the pandemic* (FEDS Notes, 2022).

Telegraph to Tether: Challenges in the Global Payments System and the Struggle between Private and Public Interests

Catherine R. Schenk

In March 2022, the governments of the US and Europe decided on various sanctions in response to the Russian invasion of Ukraine, including asking for Russian banks to be excluded from the global payment system Society for Worldwide Interbank Financial Telecommunications (SWIFT).[1]

Research was funded by the 'Global Correspondent Banking 1870–2000' project which has received funding from the European Research Council (ERC) under the European Union's Horizon 2020 research and innovation programme (Grant Agreement No 883758). I'm grateful for research assistance from Thibaud Giddey.

[1] SWIFT also disconnected Belarusian entities.

C. R. Schenk (✉)
University of Oxford, Oxford, UK
e-mail: catherine.schenk@history.ox.ac.uk

R. Z. Aliber et al. (eds.), *Fault Lines After COVID-19*,
https://doi.org/10.1007/978-3-031-26482-5_17

That this sanction relied on cooperation from a private sector institution drew public attention to an otherwise obscure but fundamental aspect of globalisation: namely, the way funds move across borders. While most of the public was unaware of how their foreign goods and services were paid for, governments and multilateral agencies were already investigating the vulnerabilities in the underlying plumbing of global payments. In order to support global trade and commerce, the system needs to be fast, efficient, inclusive and transparent but these characteristics have been challenged by long transaction chains, fragmentation and complexity, legacy technology, weak competition and limited operating hours.[2] Improving the way that cross-border payments are made has been a key focus of the G20 and the Financial Stability Board since 2015.[3]

A key concern is that the correspondent banking system has been contracting over the past ten years.[4] Figure 1 shows the decline in active pairs of correspondent banks since 2011 while the value and volume of SWIFT messages has increased (including a surge in value and fall in volume at the start of the pandemic in March 2020).

The fall in the number of active bilateral bank relationships on the SWIFT messaging service is particularly stark for some regions compared to others, likely due to the increased costs of checking that counterparties conform to rules to stop money laundering and the finance of terrorism (see Fig. 2). But some regions may be excluded from the benefits of efficient cross-border payments. Or, customers might have to divert their payments through less reliable routes.

The time taken to settle payments also varies widely from 12 minutes for payments to the United States to over 22 hours for some countries in North Africa and South Asia using SWIFT's new streamlined service.[5] Understanding how the global payments system developed can deliver important insights into how it might be reformed. How did this obscure but essential system develop over time? Why is it primarily in private ownership rather than public control? What are its weaknesses and how might digital currencies disrupt the system?

[2] CPMI (2020), 'Stage 2 Report to the G20 – Technical Background Report', July.

[3] FSB (2015) 'Report to the G20 on actions taken to assess and address the decline in correspondent banking', 6 November.

[4] Rice et al. (2020) and Erbenova et al. (2016).

[5] Nilsson et al. (2022).

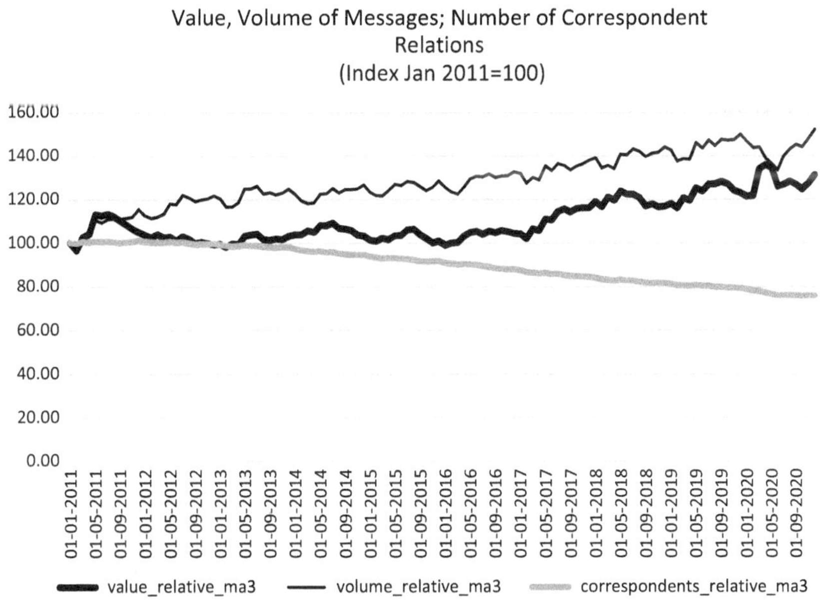

Fig. 1 Value, volume of message; number of correspondent relations (Index Jan 2011=100)

The challenges posed by time and distance are as old as international trade itself. For centuries traders went to their banks to borrow funds to cover them for the time it took for their goods to travel over distances before they were paid by their customers.[6] Access to credit shrank time and distance, but settlement ultimately required a debit in the account of the buyer's bank in one country and a credit to the seller's bank in another, and therefore relied on a communication system, such as letters posted between banks to adjust their accounts. The speed and efficiency of this correspondence was hugely enhanced by the spread of undersea and coastal telegraph in the second half of the nineteenth century.[7] These cables, heroically unwound across vast ocean floors, are still the fundamental framework of telecommunications today. Most internet

[6] These credit instruments were known as Bills of Exchange. For a long view of finance, see W.N. Goetzmann (2016).

[7] Ejrnaes and Persson (2010) and Lin et al. (2021).

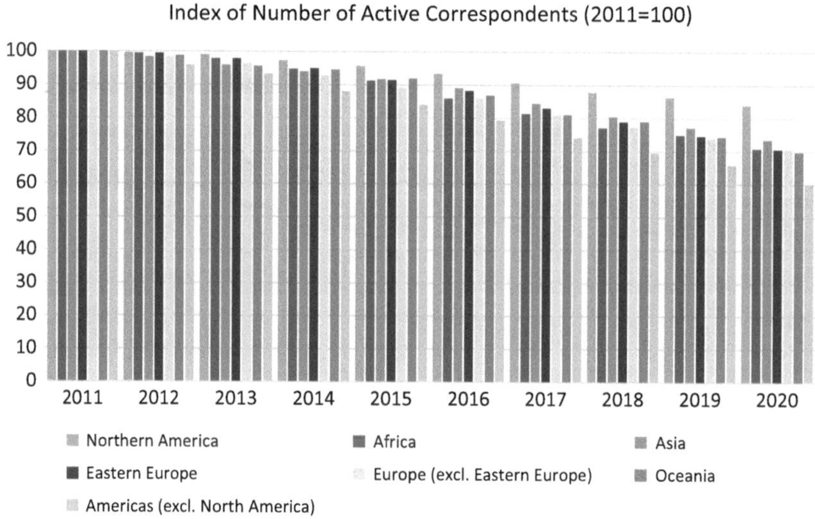

Fig. 2 Index of number of active correspondents (2011=100)

traffic still relies on undersea cables that closely follow the networks laid before 1914.

Late nineteenth-century globalisation was an era of intense flows of people, goods and capital. With telegraph cables in place, the network of banks expanded quickly so that traders could transact with buyers anywhere in the world through banks in London or other regional centres. The importance of communication is evident in the name for this relationship formed between banks for the purpose of settling accounts, which became known as correspondent banking. Instructions between banks to credit/debit customer accounts were sent in complex code to shorten the messages and thereby reduce costs. Processing was labour intensive and costly requiring complex and error-prone coding and decoding of instructions and confirmations. The Bank of England, for example, used a 5-letter code for all verbal telegrams, which consisted of 582 code words and 388 pages of English phrases in 1939.[8] Nevertheless, cables remained the standard messaging system well into the twentieth century when telex began to be adopted. Developed in the 1920s, Telex machines were more automated and reduced spending on staff, albeit with higher upfront costs to

[8] Memorandum, 31 March 1939. Bank of England Archives (hereafter BoE) C6/49.

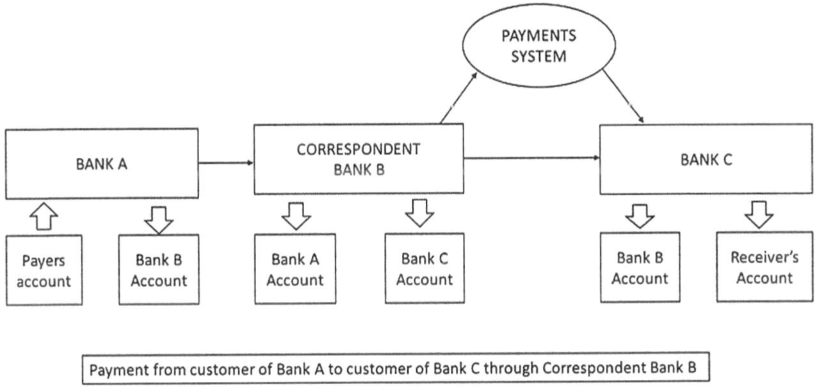

Fig. 3 Global payment system. (Note: Payment may or may not go through a national payments system)

purchase the machine and slightly higher message fees. Coding was no longer necessary since fees were charged by time rather than by length of the message itself. Although the platforms and technology changed, the correspondent banking system of mirrored account debits and credits remains the fundamental framework of global payments despite the dramatic transformation of global trade and finance over the past 150 years. A simplified diagram is shown in Fig. 3.

After the telegraph and Telex, the most important payments innovation was the computer, which helped a large volume of transactions to be settled among a complex network of correspondent banks, but introducing this technology was challenging. In the 1970s, two important private sector initiatives introduced computer technology for cross-border payments; Clearing House Interbank Payments System in New York (CHIPS) formed in 1970, and the Society for Worldwide Interbank Financial Telecommunications (SWIFT) activated in 1977 in Europe. CHIPS is a clearing and settlement system for global USD payments while SWIFT is a messaging system to communicate payments instructions between banks. These initiatives emerged in an era of intensifying cross-border banking and set the norm for cross-currency payments infrastructures to be controlled and governed in the private sector.[9]

[9] Domestic payments systems were more closely supervised and have been in a mixture of public and private sector control. In 2017, for example, the operations of the British large value sterling payments system, Clearing House Automated Payments System (CHAPS), were taken over by the Bank of England to enhance systemic stability. In the US, Fedwire, in contrast, has always been in the control of the US Federal Reserve System.

Origins of Clearing House Interbank Payments System (CHIPS) and Settlement Risk

The most recent era of globalisation is usually dated from the end of the Cold War in 1989, when there was a burst of ICT innovation and the volume of financial flows swept ahead of the growth of international trade or production, but the basis for the great financialisation of the international economy was set in previous decades. The innovation of the Eurodollar market from the end of the 1950s led to exponential growth in international dollar balances in the later part of the 1960s.[10] The opportunities presented by this innovation, the acceleration of US multinational companies (MNCs) moving abroad and the prospect of European integration all encouraged banks into a new phase of internationalisation.[11] American banks surged into the City of London to take advantage of the dollar money markets there, outside the jurisdiction of their home regulators.[12] As British and European banks confronted this competition for their staff and customers, they sought to maintain their market share by expanding abroad. The float of the pound sterling exchange rate in June 1972, followed by the US dollar in March 1973 created new foreign exchange trading business for banks, but also new market risk from less predictable currency rates.

CHIPS was prompted by the urgent need to expand capacity once capital controls became less effective and the volume of international payments increased.[13] Until April 1970, international payments in New York were settled by cheques issued by correspondent banks—a paper-based system. Foreign banks did not keep large balances with their New York correspondents while they moved money through their accounts and daily turnover was many times the capital of the banks themselves, which created liquidity and operational risks.[14] First, the process involved several steps, each of which introduced the risk of clerical error. Foreign banks cabled or telexed their New York correspondents to debit their account to

[10] Schenk (1998), Aliber (1973).
[11] Altamura (2016), Battilossi (2002).
[12] Sylla (2002).
[13] For more detail see C.R. Schenk (2021).
[14] For a review of foreign exchange risks see Rambure and Nacamuli (2008).

make payments on behalf of customers. This required careful checking of the messages and balances available and then printing, typing and physically delivering official bank cheques to the Clearing House in New York. Using bank cheques (not corporate cheques drawn directly on the customer) meant that settlement was an obligation of a bank, not of the individual customer, so the New York correspondent had to make sure of the creditworthiness of its counterparty, ensure the telex was authentic, that either the foreign bank had sufficient funds in its account or that the correspondent New York bank was willing to extend credit for the amount of the payment, and that the cheque was filled out correctly and properly delivered to the Clearing House by one of an army of bank messengers. Bankers tended to wait until the last of the five daily clearings to submit most of their cheques to try to ensure that funds had already arrived to cover them, and this caused congestion at the end of the day.[15]

By the late 1960s, the volume of transactions made this system excessively cumbersome. Large numbers of staff had to be employed to undertake the clerical tasks, mainly young and with minimal training. In 1974 Robert J. Crowley, Vice President at the Federal Reserve Bank of New York (FRBNY), reported that 'one New York bank had its payments staff drop from an average of 22 years in the bank to an average of 8 months in a two-year span'.[16] This staff constraint made back-office operations more prone to clerical errors.[17] Cost was another issue: Crowley observed that 'Two banks told me they estimated their processing cost per official check to be between $5 and $7'.[18] The size of the business challenged the back-office resources even of large banks.

CHIPS allowed banks to make coded entries through computer terminals during the day, with a final netting out at the end of the day at the hub computer in the New York Clearing House. Each member had 30 minutes to meet any overall deficit, with final payment through accounts with the FRBNY. The value of transactions through the system surged but the

[15] *CHIPS; the computerized communications network used by the New York Clearing House Association for interbank payments*, revised June 1976. Included in evidence to US Senate Committee 1976.

[16] Memo by Robert J. Crowley to Governor Wallich, 'CHIPS/PEPS System', 5 July 1974. Archives of the Federal Reserve Bank of New York [hereafter FRBNY] 555225 Box 1, Central Records 1. Franklin-Herstatt Failure 1963–75 Coombs.

[17] *CHIPS; the computerized communications network* (1976).

[18] Crowley to Wallich, 'CHIPS/PEPS System', 5 July 1974. FRBNY 555225 Box 1, Central Records 1.

perils of time and distance had not been overcome. Several issues quickly emerged and some persisted until the mid-1980s. Access was restricted to banks in New York who were members of the Clearing House and so excluded branches and subsidiaries of foreign banks as well as most US banks directly. Banks that were not members of the Clearing House had to access the system indirectly through a member. Secondly, Clearing House funds were traditionally only freely available to payees on the business day after payment to allow time for clerical work to reconcile payments among the New York banks. Thus, dollars deposited at correspondent banks in exchange for foreign currency were available for use the following day, but the foreign exchange could be used immediately. This left banks exposed to counterparty credit and liquidity risk. A further implication was that Friday funds were not available until Monday, so there was an incentive to book on Friday and hold over of the funds to put into money markets over the weekend, creating more congestion. Thirdly, turnover during the day for each bank was many times greater than the deposits they held for their respondent banks. These 'Daylight Overdrafts' could become extremely large while the interbank deposits covered only a tiny proportion of turnover. More fundamentally for an international system, the final clearing in New York took place hours after European and Asian banks had closed so the system supported billions of dollars of unsecured credit between banks over the course of the day until payments were finally cleared and settled. As Crowley noted, 'it is a business in which trust and confidence is essential'.[19] This trust was soon tested.

In July 1974 the collapse of the Herstatt Bank in Germany almost brought down the USD payments system when it exposed the risks in correspondent banking.[20] The fraudulent Herstatt Bank was closed by the German authorities while its New York correspondent, Chase Manhattan Bank, was still waiting for inflows to release funds to Herstatt's counterparties in New York. Trust evaporated and CHIPS payments froze. Banks only agreed to resume making payments under pressure from the Federal Reserve, and even then, they insisted on waiting for funds to arrive before paying out to customers, causing a lag that could last up to several days in the world's main dollar settlement system. The episode was so striking

[19] Crowley to Wallich, 'CHIPS/PEPS System', 5 July 1974. FRBNY 555225 Box 1, Central Records 1.

[20] Schenk (2014), Mourlon-Druol (2015).

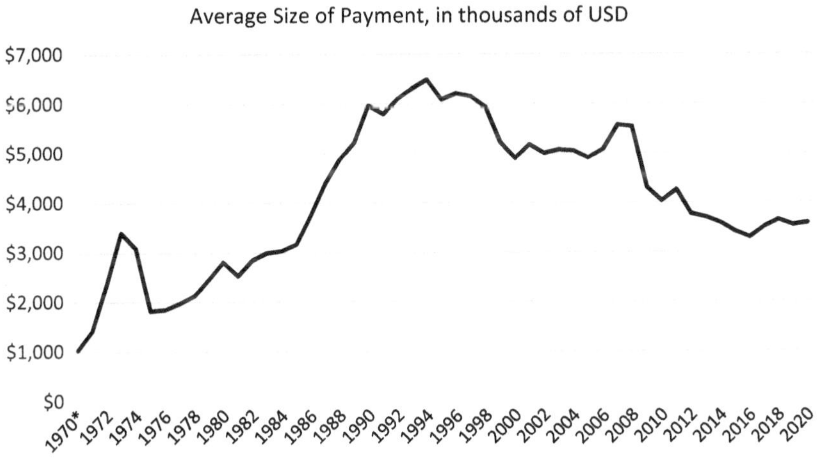

Fig. 4 Average size of payment, in thousands of USD

that cross-border settlement risk posed by the potential collapse of one counterparty is still known as Herstatt Risk.

When the Herstatt crisis struck, public authorities were drawn in to get the market going again and to pressure this private sector institution to reform. The Fed encouraged the CHIPS banks to introduce more safeguards over the next ten years including minimum size of participant banks, letters of comfort from parent banks for subsidiaries, speeding up settlement and limits on intraday credits. As an indicator of the erosion of trust, Fig. 4 shows that it took 12 years for the average size of transactions through the system to recover to the level of 1974—and that was *nominal* value during a period of rapid inflation and global trade growth.

Part of this decline in the average size of transactions may have come from greater netting of payments before they went through CHIPS, but netting was not widely practised until the 1990s as will be shown below. In a rare survey in 1989, intraday credit in CHIPS was measured at almost $54 billion.[21] In 2000 CHIPS finally moved from end of day (deferred net settlement) to intra-day final settlement by requiring participants to deposit funds upfront at a special account at the FRBNY. The liquidity of the system was further enhanced in mid-2008 by the ability of banks to

[21] This was the peak average amount, recorded at 11:30 am in February 1989 in a survey conducted by the Federal Reserve Bank of Dallas. Clair (1989).

add Supplemental Funding to clear payments. The Fed's injection of bank liquidity in the wake of the crisis of September–October 2008 increased the resources for banks to provide Supplemental Funding to keep the system functioning, although payments left unresolved by 5 pm did increase in the short term.[22]

Beyond CHIPS, settlement risk continued to challenge the resilience of global payments into the 2000s. While central banks remained concerned about systemic risks arising from cross-currency payments, they did not seek to replace private sector initiatives and restricted themselves mainly to encourage and inform and latterly to provide some form of oversight that fell short of supervision. A key method they promoted to reduce bank exposure was through schemes that net payments on a continuous basis so that a smaller value needs final settlement at the end of the day. After a range of private sector netting proposals emerged, the G10 central bank governors set up an ad hoc Committee on Interbank Netting Schemes in 1989 to review the issues and then established a more permanent Committee on Payment and Settlement Systems (CPSS) in 1990. It quickly aimed to set the terms for central bank oversight.[23] While recognising each nation's sovereignty over its own national payments system, the report encouraged communication among central banks for cross-border payments to promote systemic stability and harmonisation. Nevertheless, '[T]he primary responsibility for ensuring that netting and settlement systems have adequate credit, liquidity, and operational safeguards rests with the [private sector] participants'.[24] Central banks did not want to take responsibility. During the 1990s a series of ripples in the market caused by the failures of counterparties (such as Bank of Credit and Commerce International (BCCI) in 1991) drew central bankers back into discussion about whether the private sector was best placed to reinforce the framework's scaffolding. In 1996 the CPSS 'call[ed] upon individual banks and industry groups alike to improve current practices and devise safe mechanisms for addressing settlement risk'.[25] The market response was mixed; a survey two years later found that 'over 60% of the banks in

[22] McAndrews and Vartin (2022).

[23] This exercise was analogous to the 1983 Basel Concordat setting out responsibilities for supervising international bank entities.

[24] Report of the Committee on Interbank Netting Schemes of the Central Banks of the Group of Ten Countries, November 1990, BIS, Basel. Known as the Lamfalussy Report.

[25] Settlement Risk in Foreign Exchange Transactions, CPSS Allsop Report, BIS, Basel, 1996.

the surveys are still underestimating their exposures'.[26] At this point the CPSS acknowledged that the 1990s strategy 'founded on the belief that the private sector, with the active support of the public sector, had the power to contain the risk that first came into focus at the time of the 1974 failure of Bankhaus Herstatt' had not produced robust solutions. This time they sought to push banks further by threatening to increase regulatory capital for foreign exchange exposure.[27] In 1997 seven banks launched CLS (continuous linked settlement) in London as a cross-border netting scheme for foreign exchange transactions on a payment-versus-payment basis so that payments were not released unless there were funds available to clear them. It took a further seven years to become operational, initially for a limited group of 39 banks and seven currencies.[28] Thirty-eight years after Herstatt collapsed, this private sector solution did finally reduce counterparty risk. In September 2008, CLS was able to clear almost all of Lehman Brothers' trades via Citibank, its primary cash dealer.[29] The private sector system proved its resilience, albeit with the support from central banks to restore global liquidity in the weeks that followed.

Origins of SWIFT and Messaging

When CHIPS launched in 1970, European banks had already spent a year planning for a standardised messaging system to underpin international payments. The aim was to save time translating from one system to another and hopefully prompt fewer errors while making global payments more

[26] Ibid.

[27] Reducing Foreign Exchange Settlement Risk: a progress report, CPSS, BIS, Basel, 1998.

[28] By 2022 CLS included 18 currencies and had more than 70 members. https://www.cls-group.com/about/ (accessed 28 October 2022). Globally the share of PvP settlement in foreign exchange markets fell since 2013 because many EME currencies do not have access to PvP schemes. CPMI (2022) Facilitating increased adoption of payment versus payment (PVP), BIS Consultative Report. https://www.bis.org/cpmi/publ/d207.pdf (accessed 1 November 2022).

[29] L. Oliver, 'CLS Bank: CLS passes the test', *Euromoney*, 8 October 2008. Lehman had $7 billion in credit lines with Citi in June 2008 of which $3 billion was for CLS and a further $2 billion in other FX. Lehman Bros Citibank Clearing and Intraday Credit, LBHI_SEC07940_7 45595. https://web.stanford.edu/~jbulow/Lehmandocs/docs/DEBTORS/LBHI_SEC07940_745595-745602.pdf (accessed 2 November 2022). Benos et al. (2014) show that domestic payments systems also slowed in the wake of the crisis. E. Benos, R.J. Garratt and P. Zimmerman, 'The role of counterparty risk in CHAPS following the collapse of Lehman Brothers', *International Journal of Central Banking*, 2014, pp. 143–171.

efficient. But unlike the case of CHIPS, which was based in a single national clearing house, agreement at a multilateral level proved challenging. SWIFT is a non-profit cooperative among member banks, headquartered in Brussels, and is the dominant global messaging standard. But there were moments when central banks challenged whether it should be a private sector initiative. As in the case of settlement and clearing, there is a public interest in the stability and resilience of the messaging system that instructs correspondent banking transactions. Archive evidence shows that in 1969–1971 technicians from the central banks of major industrialised economies tried to take part in the design of SWIFT and to secure a place in its governance, but they were rebuffed by the commercial banks leading the planning. Commercial banks had better technical knowledge about the new-fangled computer systems and collectively had the capital to invest in the technology required. Most central banks were behind the curve technologically and in the end merely joined as members alongside the world's commercial banks.

For Scott and Zachariadis, the 'galvanising' event that hastened SWIFT was the launch of First National City Bank's own proprietary messaging standard, MARRTI (Machine Readable Telegraphic Input), developed in 1973 and implemented in 1974/1975.[30] FNCB tried to use its market power to enforce the use of its standard, giving fresh impetus to the European-led, cooperative framework of SWIFT. But new archival evidence shows that the initiative rested with European bankers who were anticipating the integration of European banking systems. During the late 1960s groups of banks from the key markets in Western Europe formed clubs and consortia to confront competition from larger American banks in their home markets and to prepare for European financial and monetary integration. These started out as loose agreements, but sometimes led to distinctly incorporated institutions that often included a US bank. For the most part, these were non-competition agreements, but they also offered the opportunity for more practical cooperation.[31] The international payments system became one of the areas of cooperation.

In 1969 three plans were underway in Europe to develop cross-border inter-bank communication networks.[32] Societe Financiere Européenne

[30] Scott and Zachariadis (2014). See also Scott and Zachariadis (2012).

[31] Alexis Drach (2022).

[32] 17 March 1971 memo to Mr. Graham 'Automation Group – EAC' by T.H.E.C. Midland Bank Archives [hereafter MBA] UK 0200/0838.

(SFE) was a consortium of Barclays Bank, Algemene, Banca del Lavoro, Bank of America, Banque Nationale de Paris (BNP) and Dresdner Bank. Members of SFE met at the end of 1969 to set up a Steering Group representing all the countries that made up the consortium plus Switzerland, Sweden and Belgium. In January 1970 Barclays and BNP wrote a feasibility report for an International Inter-Bank Message Switching System and it was circulated to other banks both within and beyond the SFE. Meanwhile another set of bankers were brought together by the Bilderberg Group chaired by Prince Bernhard of the Netherlands. A third system was developed separately by Societe Generale de Banque, which was at an advanced stage and ready to become operational to link Brussels, London and New York in 1971.[33] It was clear that competing systems made no sense given the importance of network externalities to achieve the gains from a messaging system, so the European banking consortia eventually fell in behind the SFE proposal. It was more inclusive than SGB's scheme albeit less well advanced.

Evidence from the archives of central banks, commercial banks and the Bank for International Settlements (BIS) shows that central bankers did worry about the dominance of the private sector in the design of cross-border payments. At the end of January 1969 the BIS convened its first meeting of experts on the use of computers in central banking.[34] At this point there was a range of take up of new technology among central banks; the Swiss National Bank had no computer and did not see that its operations would require one for the next five years,[35] Canada rented computer time rather than having its own and the Bank of England used computing for a range of administrative purposes including registration of government debt, clearing cheques and giro payments with commercial banks.[36] The Banca d'Italia had the widest use for all large government receipts and

[33] SGB was part of the EBIC consortium but did not develop its plan in cooperation with its partners—in the end this was likely a reason why it was not adopted over the more collective SFE scheme, although it was further advanced at the time.

[34] Letter Gabriel Ferras to L.K. O'Brien, 3 December 1968. BoE 7A386/1. The initiative was not rushed—it was first discussed at the 17 November 1968 governors' meeting. Central banks represented from Belgium, Canada, FRBNY, Fed, Bank of England, Italy, Switzerland, Japan, Germany, Netherlands, Sweden and France.

[35] Appendix to report on meeting 27–28 January 1969. 25 February 1969. BoE 7A386/1.

[36] The Use of Computers at the Bank of England, circulated at the BIS meeting, filed 24 January 1969. BoE 7A386/1.

payments as well as its own research purposes.[37] A key obstacle was the difficulty in attracting and retaining skilled computing staff due to the relatively low salaries on offer at central banks. Given the mixed levels of engagement and expertise in computerisation, it is perhaps not surprising that the initiative for computerised cross-border messaging came from the private sector. Nevertheless, this central bank computing committee became a main conduit between MSP/SWIFT and the BIS and G10 central banks as they came to consider the computerisation of international payments.

John J. Clarke, Vice President and Special Legal Adviser at Federal Reserve Bank of New York (FRBNY) was particularly concerned about the absence of central bank influence over the Message Switching Project (MSP). He wanted G10 central bank representatives meeting at the UN Commission on International Trade Law (UNCITRAL) in December 1970 to seek a consensus that 'central banks interest themselves in proposals now being pursued by sectors of the commercial banking communities in several countries looking toward an international payments mechanism that would be computerized on a multilateral basis'.[38] Clarke worried about the proliferation of incompatible standards and believed it was 'natural that the central banks should be the leaders' even if such a system was a long way off 'and may take a form now undreamed of'.[39] Despite a lack of support from most central bank participants in the UNCITRAL meeting, Clarke tabled his paper, but he faced resistance from, for example, Bank of England representatives.[40] As the central bank governing the world's largest foreign exchange market at the time, the Bank of England was hugely influential.

In New York, Clarke's position had hardened. At the start of 1971, three years before the Herstatt Bank collapse, he argued that 'one of the most serious problems facing international banking today is that of promoting and maintaining efficiency in effecting international transfers of funds' and suggested that the central banks at Basle set up 'possibly with commercial bank participation' an organisation to establish 'a computerized multilateral payments mechanism, harmonized standards for

[37] Memo for Governor O'Brien on BIS meeting, 6 February 1969. BoE 7A386/1.

[38] Letter from J.J. Clarke to Henri Guisan, Legal Adviser BIS, 23 October 1970. BoE 7A386-2. UNCITRAL efforts to standardise the international bill of exchange in cooperation with the International Chamber of Commerce.

[39] Ibid.

[40] Memo by D.C. Keys 31 March 1971 and Bennett 22 March 1971. BoE 7A386-2.

negotiable instruments'.[41] He noted that European commercial banks were seeking to create their own message switching system for the international flow of payment orders 'as well as a clearing house type operations' without any central bank representation.[42] Clarke believed, 'The central banks, it seems, have the prestige and the resources to be of assistance to the international banking community in regard to this matter of common interest and concern'.[43] It is not clear what level of support Clarke had at the FRBNY for his views, which were firmly couched in personal terms, but he was not a lone voice.

The Banque de France contributed a paper from January 1971 on 'The Use of Computers in International Transfers of Funds' between correspondent banks. Echoing Clarke's views, the paper emphasised the problem of incompatible standards emerging.[44] Given the momentum of proposals it was 'of some importance for the central banks to take up a position in this matter'. The report concluded that 'in view of the development of private projects, we believe that the central banks should rapidly come to an agreement to set up a permanent body to study the automated transmission of data concerning international payments' and recommended that the G10 central bank governors take a position on whether to pursue this or not.[45] The National Bank of Belgium also pushed its peers to give more consideration to automated international payments.[46] Like others, they pointed out the risks of incompatible networks and the benefits of standardising codes etc. but they also emphasised the special needs of the EEC as it moved towards monetary union. Clearly there were several straws in the wind when the topic was due to be discussed at the May 1971 BIS Meeting of Experts on Computing.[47] At this point, BIS staff also sought views on whether the BIS itself could 'establish a multilateral mechanism for effecting international payments, transfers and clearings on a computerised basis in an off-line or on-line mode, both for

[41] J.J. Clarke FRBNY, Establishment of an International Payments Mechanism and Related Matters, 26 February 1971. BoE 7A386-2.

[42] Ibid. At this point the scheme was known as 'Banks International Telecommunications System' (BITS) – a precursor to MSP and signalling a wider scope.

[43] Ibid.

[44] Banque de France paper 27 January 1971. BoE 7A386-2.

[45] Ibid.

[46] National Bank of Belgium, 'Summary Note on the European System of International Payments', 4 March 1971. BoE 7A386-2.

[47] This process of how the Group became involved with SWIFT is from the summary report of the 9th Meeting of Experts on 4 September 1972. BoE 7A386-3.

central and commercial banks'.[48] There was no general enthusiasm among central banks for the BIS to expand its role in this way.

Meanwhile commercial banks continued their planning, setting up national working groups of local banks to broaden the scope of engagement.[49] At this point, the scheme was to be as 'widespread as possible with the stress on clean payments; the study of a clearing should not be excluded'.[50] A clearing system was still an ambition of the group and this drew in central bankers at the highest level.

At the meeting of Governors at the BIS in September 1971, the central banks of the G10 agreed formally that the Computing Experts Meeting should 'study the possibility of using a communications system for effecting international payments similar to the one which was being studied at that time by the Central banks of the EEC' and that the Meeting should contact commercial banks that were 'considering establishing alternative networks with the aim of discouraging the development of a series of possibly incompatible telecommunications facilities'.[51] This proved too late for the MSP discussions, which by December 1971 had already moved to feasibility studies. Rather than creating their own system, central banks tried to make a direct contribution to the design of the commercial banks' scheme.

A month later, the chair of the BIS Meeting of Experts wrote to the commercial banks' MSP Steering Committee to ask about the possibility of central banks and the BIS joining the project. The Steering Committee considered this at its meeting in Rome in March 1972, but the outcome was not what central bankers had hoped for. The banks decided only to invite central banks to participate as individual members 'in the same position as the participating commercial banks'. Each Steering Committee member agreed to contact their national central bank to discuss the project, and to invite them to join through their national working group, but central banks were excluded from the Steering Committee itself. The banks also proposed to take advice from their national central banks on

[48] Memo by BIS for the May 1971 meeting, 5 April 1971. BoE 7A386-2.

[49] Extract from the Report on the Meeting of the MSP Steering Committee 15-16 June 1971. BoE 7A386-3.

[50] Ibid.

[51] Note for Governor of Bank of England for Meeting of Governors September 1972, 6 September 1972. BoE 7A386-3.

how the BIS should be involved rather than respond directly.[52] The preference by the Steering Committee at this stage was for the BIS to join merely as part of the Swiss national working group.[53]

A BIS Meeting of Experts was quickly convened in April 1972 in Basle to discuss this outcome. Central bankers were urged to pay the fee and join the MSP 'in order to obtain the full documentation presented to the existing membership'.[54] For most central banks, the MSP scheme itself offered few practical benefits because their own correspondent traffic was relatively small but they needed to know what was going on and try to introduce their own views as market supervisors. The computing experts still hoped that the BIS could represent central banks on the Steering Committee, separate from the national committees. By this time the clearing facility, which had been part of the original vision, was dropped 'largely because of the troublesome political and jurisdictional problems it was likely to generate'.[55] Technically and constitutionally, though, the banks were designing the system so that 'a clearing facility could be grafted on without drastic changes to the basic structure'.[56]

Shelving the payments element reduced the impetus for central bank involvement. As agreed, the chair of the Experts Group requested that the BIS should join the MSP as a 'separate entity' in the Steering Committee because of its status as an international organisation but this request was turned down.[57] The MSP Steering Committee's view was that 'it is the only object of the project to forward messages relating to international payments by means of a message switching system. As such, the system will not affect actual banking activities and it was therefore that the members of the Steering Committee could not see why a special position would be taken by the central banks'.[58] Since payments were not being settled or cleared through the system, the MSP Steering Committee saw no special role for central banks.

[52] At this point the US Federal Reserve was not a formal member of the Governing Board of the BIS.

[53] K. Weber, Secretary Steering Committee MSP to d'Aroma BIS, 21 March 1972. BoE 7A386-3.

[54] Memorandum on BIS International Inter-Bank Message Switching Project, R.S. Bennett 19 April 1972. BoE 7A386-3.

[55] Note for the Record by Bennett of a meeting at the Bank of England on 10 April 1972. BoE 7A386-3.

[56] Ibid.

[57] D'Aroma to K. Weber, 21 April 1972. Weber to d'Aroma 15 May 1972. BoE 7A386-3.

[58] Weber to d'Aroma 15 May 1972. BoE 7A386-3.

Opinion among central bankers was mixed. The Bank of England viewed the scheme mainly as a communications channel between banks, with no processing or settlement features, at least so far.[59] Participant banks would still be subject to each country's exchange control for the payments entered through the network so that the scheme was not 'fundamentally different from the present system'. The impact on central banks themselves would not be great because of the low level of their own correspondent business. Most other G10 central banks 'had reservations as to the further evolution of the proposed network, with a number of participants feeling that it was as a mechanism for effecting clearing and settlement transactions that the MSP would in fact be of most value to the network users' and therefore was a likely outcome.[60] The MSP was also likely to be expensive in terms of hardware and subscriptions compared to direct telex costs.[61] Nevertheless, by July the Dutch, Italian, UK, Swedish, German and Canadian central banks had joined their national working groups and paid the $3200 fee to get access to the MSP documentation. The Federal Reserve's position in their national working group was complicated because it was led by the American Bankers' Association, which had difficult relations with the Fed.[62] The French and Swiss were waiting for the outcome of the July Experts Meeting and the National Bank of Belgium had not paid 'but professed to be fully informed'.[63] The drawbacks to joining were mainly the cost and ambiguity in the proposed bylaws. On the positive side, there were several advantages that central banks could get from joining[64]:

[59] Memo GHW Bennett to R.T.P Hall (who minutes his agreement with the memo's position, as does George Blunden), 29 June 1972. BoE 7A386-3

[60] Bennett reported to his colleagues in London that 'the Belgian-led campaign to the effect that SWIFT in some way (which is far from clear) threatens the interest of central banks did not make any headway. The bogey that commercial banks were in the process of setting up a new international clearing and settlement mechanism appears to have been dispelled'. Bennett report on the 12 July 1972 Meeting of Experts at the BIS, 2 August 1972. BoE 7A386-3.

[61] Summary Report of the 8th Meeting of Experts to Study Problems Concerning the Use of Computers in Central Banks, 12 July 1972, 20 July 1972. BoE 7A386-3

[62] This is mentioned a few times within the Bank of England, including by Bennett, brief for Morse on SWIFT 6 September 1972. BoE 7A386-3.

[63] Bennett report on the 12 July 1972 Meeting of Experts at the BIS, 2 August 1972. He described the meeting as 'slow and rambling'. BoE 7A386-3.

[64] Summary Report of the 8th Meeting of Experts to Study Problems Concerning the Use of Computers in Central Banks, 12 July 1972, 20 July 1972. BoE 7A386-3

- protecting the interests of small banks and non-commercial credit institutions
- establishing a link with national clearing systems
- ensuring compatibility of standards
- possible facilities for collecting relevant statistics
- central banks' responsibilities as monetary authorities

By September all G10 central banks had joined except for the Swiss National Bank (for constitutional reasons) the FRBNY (because of issues with the ABA), the Bank of Japan and the National Bank of Belgium. Given that the organisation was due to be based in Brussels, the position of the National Bank of Belgium was intriguingly negative. They agreed that it was useful to maintain informal contact with SWIFT developments but believed that central banks would not be able to influence it from inside or use it to get access to data to fulfil their supervisory responsibilities.[65] In the end, however, the Governor of the National Bank of Belgium did not oppose the general view that in principle the G10 central banks should join SWIFT.[66] Still, the potential for SWIFT to pose both challenges and opportunities for central bank supervisors meant central bank governors continued to worry about whether they should be more active participants in the design of the system.

In early 1974, the BIS Group of Computer Experts advised the Governors of the BIS of their concerns about the security and reliability of the newly founded SWIFT cooperative. As a result, the G10 central bank governors approved a proposal to set up a Working Party on Electronic Systems for International Payments that included representatives from the Bank of Italy, the FRBNY and the Bank of England to determine whether central banks should take further action in regard to SWIFT before it became operational.[67] After three years of deliberations, as SWIFT was due to be launched in 1977, they concluded it was unlikely that helpful regulatory information could be collected by central banks from the proposed system. By this time, it was clear that SWIFT was set to remain merely a messaging system rather than morph into a settlement or

[65] Note for Governor of Bank of England for Meeting of Governors September 1972, 6 September 1972. BoE 7A386-3.

[66] Morse minute 10 September 1972 on the G10 Governors' meeting at the BIS of that day. BoE7A386-3.

[67] Summary Report from the Working Party on ESIP to the Group of Computer Experts, 16 March 1977. BIS Archives (hereafter BISA) BoE 7.31.1.2 File 19.

payments system per se. As a result, the Working Party recommended that central banks did not have a direct interest in SWIFT. Instead, the BIS and central banks should merely join the system and 'monitor developments'. They continued to have concerns over the decades that followed but the chance to be in on the design of the system had been rejected.

These sometimes tortuous discussions demonstrate the gulf in expertise between the commercial banks and central banks but also highlight that the private sector ownership and control was contested by several central banks.[68] Moreover, the pace of developments among commercial banks was faster than the ability of the public authorities to arrive at a consensus for action. With the Bank of England, in particular, keen to leave it to the commercial banks there was little basis for the FRBNY, Banque de France or the Bank of Belgium representatives to hold sway.

SWIFT had a rocky start with computer glitches, high costs (to join, to buy terminals, to pay fees), and an evolving rulebook that caused uncertainty and legal ambiguity. Once it started in 1977, however, SWIFT quickly gathered volume and members but it was a very European organisation with only 8% of shares owned by US banks in 1979. Figure 5

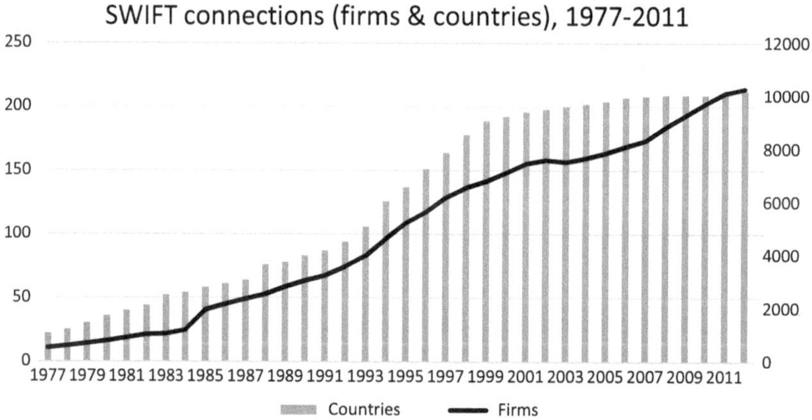

Fig. 5 SWIFT connections (firms and countries), 1977–2011. (Source: Scott & Zachariadis, 2014: 113)

[68] The legal foundations for cross-border electronic payments continued to attract the interest of the United Nations Commission on International Trade Law, which set conventions on bills of exchange and letters of credit in 1987–1992. https://uncitral.un.org/en/texts/payments (accessed 28 October 2022).

shows the number of users and the number of countries they came from. Opening to securities firms and national clearers in 1987 and to fund managers in 1992 increased the scope of members and the benefits of network externalities. In 1998, 20 years after it started operating, the G10 central banks began to engage in 'cooperative oversight' of SWIFT because so many critical payments systems depend on it. As noted on the SWIFT website, in the absence of formal regulation, 'the main instrument for oversight of SWIFT is moral suasion'.[69] The details of transactions through SWIFT remain confidential.

Conclusions and Prospects

Technological change in the late nineteenth century made the network of global payments more efficient and facilitated globalisation. The framework of bilateral or nested correspondent bank relationships based on the telegraph that developed in this era persists as the fundamental method of final settlement for a significant proportion of global payments. In the nineteenth and early twentieth centuries, commercial banks developed this network themselves in response to customer needs and commercial interests. By the late twentieth century, when computers began to transform international communications, commercial banks cooperated to apply this new technology to enhance the existing network of correspondent bank relationships. Public sector actors such as central banks and the United Nations sought oversight of these developments but the system remained in private sector control even as the volume of cross-border transactions surged and the potential for systemic crisis was exposed. By the 1990s, international institutions like the BIS were concerned about the stability of the cross-currency settlement system but continued to encourage private sector solutions. As the correspondent banking system entered a new phase in the 2010s, with a contraction in the network, public sector interest has re-emerged in the form of an ambitious programme of research commissioned by the G20. Geopolitics has also drawn in public sector influence. In March 2012 the EU passed specific law to prohibit messaging services being provided to Iran, which required SWIFT to disconnect Iranian banks (until 2016). In 2022 this was followed by similar regulations prohibiting SWIFT's services to Russian and Belarusian

[69] https://www.swift.com/about-us/organisation-governance/swift-oversight (accessed 31 October 2022)

entities. The global payments system thus becomes part of geopolitical action.

Political and technological frictions have prompted new thinking about how finally to replace the 150-year-old system of correspondent banking through new digital technologies. Like the telegraph and the computer in the past, digital currencies and block-chain may be the next disruptive technology for the global payments system. The use of smart contracts in distributed ledgers could make cross-border payments much faster and final than the current system, but there are challenges also in this solution.

The prospects for cryptocurrencies have not been rosy since 2020, exemplified by the collapse in value of the flagship Bitcoin in 2022. A new generation of crypto-currencies with more transparent foundations sparked considerable optimism, but in 2022 the stability of so-called stable coins has also been questioned. Tether was subject to Securities and Exchange Commission fines for misleading the public about the extent of its US dollar backing in October 2021 and then dropped below its $1 peg in May 2022. Another stable coin, Terra/Luna, which operated with an algorithmic base, collapsed entirely in the same month. Nevertheless, the block-chain technology that emerged with cryptocurrencies might offer a cheaper and faster means of payment, especially through smart contracts.[70] The medium could be stable coins (which are anonymous and make supervision difficult) or central bank digital currencies (CBDC).

Central banks have trialled a bewildering range of regional experiments in different forms of cross-border CBDC since 2019 but obstacles to governance, harmonisation and supervision as well as technical challenges remain.[71] The new inflationary environment and higher interest rates may also complicate these initiatives. Nevertheless, this may be the moment for public agencies to take over the governance and security of the global payments system from the private sector. On the other hand, history shows that the pace of change has not been fast in global payments and that public authorities have not led innovation. Correspondent banking relationships persisted over the past 150 years through two waves of globalisation, dramatic information and communications innovations and many geopolitical disruptions. They may yet survive a bit longer.

[70] Zetzsche et al. (2021).

[71] BIS, IMF, World Bank (2022) Options for access to and interoperability of CBDCs for cross-border payments, Report to the G20, July. https://www.bis.org/publ/othp52.pdf (accessed 28 October 2022).

References

Aliber, R. Z. (1973). *The international money game* (1st ed.). Palgrave.

Altamura, C. E. (2016). *European banks and the rise of international finance: The post-Bretton Woods era*. Routledge.

Battilossi, S. (2002). Banking with multinationals: British clearing banks and the Euromarket challenge, 1958–1974. In S. Battilossi & Y. Cassis (Eds.), *European banks and the American challenge: Cooperation and competition in international banking under Bretton Woods*. Oxford University Press.

Clair, R. T. (1989). *The clearing house interbank payments system: A description of its operation and risk management* (Research paper no. 8910). Federal Reserve Bank of Dallas, June.

Drach, A. (2022). An early form of European champions? Banking clubs between European integration and global banking (1960s–1990s). *Business History.*

Ejrnaes, M., & Persson, J. G. (2010). The gains from improved market efficiency: Trade before and after the transatlantic telegraph. *European Review of Economic History, 14*(3), 361–381.

Erbenova, M., Liu, Y., Kyriakos-Saad, N., Lopez Mejia, A., Gasha, J. G., Mathias, E., Norat, M., Fernando, F. and Almeida, Y. (2016). The Withdrawal of Correspondent Banking Relationships: A Case for Policy Action, International Monetary Fund Staff Discussion Note.

Goetzmann, W. N. (2016). *Money changes everything; how finance made civilization possible*. Princeton University Press.

Lin, C., Ma, C., Sun, Y., & Xu, Y. (2021). The telegraph and modern banking development, 1881–1936. *Journal of Financial Economics, 141*(2), 730–749.

McAndrews, J., & Vartin, D. (2022). *The use of liquidity in CHIPS*. The Clearing House. https://mc-e3a82812-8e7a-44d9-956f-8910-cdn-endpoint.azureedge.net/-/media/New/TCH/Documents/Payment-systems/CHIPS_Liquidity_Algorithm_April_2022.pdf?rev=4b5d1cc768ac4de38fcca14de63263d1&hash=5F76D821581C74E0F95FB76D5B0E845D [accessed 30 October 2022].

Mourlon-Druol, E. (2015). "Trust is good, control is better": The 1974 Herstatt Bank Crisis and its Implications for International Regulatory Reform. *Business History, 57*(2), 311–334.

Nilsson, T., Bouther, R., Acoleyen, M., Cohen, L. (2022). SWIFT gpi data indicate drivers of fast cross-border payments. CPMI, BIS, 8 February [accessed 31 October 2022].

Rambure, D., & Nacamuli, A. (2008). *Payment systems: From the salt mines to the board room*. Palgrave Macmillan.

Rice, R., von Peter, G. and Boar, C. (2020). On the global retreat of correspondent banks. BIS Quarterly Review, March.

Schenk, C. R. (1998). Origins of the Eurodollar market in London: 1955-63. *Explorations in Economic History, 35*(2), 221–238.

Schenk, C. R. (2014). Summer in the city: Banking failures of 1974 and the development of international banking supervision. *English Historical Review, 129*(540), 1129–1156.

Schenk, C.R. (2021). The development of international correspondent banking in the USA 1970-89. GloCoBank working paper series 1(1). https://glocobank.web.ox.ac.UK/working-papers (accessed 2 November 2022].

Scott, S. V. and Zachariadis, M. (2014). *The Society for Worldwide Interbank Financial Telecommunications (SWIFT)*. Routledge.

Scott, S. V., & Zachariadis, M. (2012). The origins and development of SWIFT 1973-2009. *Business History, 54*(3), 462–482.

Sylla, R. (2002). United States banks and Europe: Strategy and attitudes. In S. Battilossi & Y. Cassis (Eds.), *European banks and the American challenge: Competition and cooperation in international banking under Bretton Woods*. Oxford University Press.

Zetzsche, D. A., Anker-Sørensen, L., Passador, M. A., & Wehrli, A. (2021). DLT-based enhancement of cross-border payment efficiency – A legal and regulatory perspective. *Law and Financial Markets Review, 15*(1–2), 70–115.

Stablecoins

Anne C. Sibert

Decentralized finance, or DeFi, is a recent innovation that uses cryptocurrency's decentralized ledger blockchain technology to eliminate financial intermediaries and allow peer-to-peer financial transactions. DeFi is designed to use cryptocurrencies for transactions. However, it requires cryptocurrencies that provide a stable base value, and the original cryptocurrencies are too volatile for this role. For example, the price of bitcoin had an average daily volatility of about 4 percent in 2021.[1] It rose from about $1000 in March 2017 to about $64,000 in November 2021 before falling below $22,000 in July 2022.[2] A result is the innovation of *stablecoins*: digital assets on the same blockchain networks that support

I am grateful to Willem Buiter, Nicolaes Tollenaar, Tony McLaughlin, and Robert McCauley for helpful conversations.

[1] Martin Armstrong, "The Varying Volatility of Cryptocurrencies." *Statista* (https://www.statista.com/chart/27577/cryptocurrency-volatility-dmo: 7 June 2022).

[2] "BTC Price," chart, "Markets: Prices," *The Block*. (https://www.theblock.co/data/crypto-markets/prices: accessed 27 October 2022).

A. C. Sibert (✉)
Birkbeck, University of London, London, UK
e-mail: a.sibert@bbk.ac.uk

R. Z. Aliber et al. (eds.), *Fault Lines After COVID-19*,
https://doi.org/10.1007/978-3-031-26482-5_18

cryptocurrency pegged to a reference asset or basket of assets. This chapter describes the market for stablecoins and some of their different forms. It explains the EU regulatory response. Finally, it discusses some of the regulatory challenges and issues associated with stablecoins.

The Stablecoin Market

Stablecoins were launched in 2014 when Tether introduced its stablecoin, USDT. By the start of 2017, the supply of USDT—still the only stablecoin—was under $10 million. In October 2022, there were over 50 actively traded stablecoins, although five had the lion's share of the market, and the total supply was about $141 billion.[3] In addition to facilitating DeFi, these new coins are an appealing medium of exchange for the real economy. With low fees and rapid execution, they are used for small foreign exchange transactions, sending remittances, and as a hedge against an inflation-induced depreciation of the domestic currency.[4] They come in many forms, depending on what they are pegged to, how the peg is maintained, how decentralized they are, and the issuer's business model. Rather than attempting a taxonomy, four important examples are described: USDT, a stablecoin pegged to the dollar and ostensibly backed by fiat reserves; Dai, a decentralized stablecoin backed by cryptocurrency; TerraUSD, the algorithmic stablecoin whose crash began the crypto winter of 2022; Libra, the stablecoin that never was.

Tether

Stablecoins pegged to a fiat currency and backed by fiat currency reserves make up about 93 percent of the stablecoin supply and almost all this supply is dollar-backed.[5] Within this class it appears many business models are possible.

[3] "Total Stable Coin Supply," chart, "Defi: Stablecoins," *The Block* (https://www.theblock.co/data/decentralized-finance/stablecoins: accessed 27 October 2022). Kara J. Bruce, Christopher K. Odinet, and Andrea Tosato. "The Private Law of Stable Coins," *Arizona State Law Journal*, forthcoming 2023, specifically p. 21. Online at https://papers.ssrn.com/sol3/papers.cfm?abstract_id=4191646

[4] "Bruce et al., "The Private Law of Stable Coins," specifically p. 25.

[5] "Total Fiat-Backed Stable Coin Supply" and "Share of Fiat Stablecoin Supply (in USD) by Currency," charts, "Defi: Stablecoins." Data for 17 October 2022. The dollar share of the supply of fiat stablecoins is 99.4 percent.

The most widely used fiat currency backed stablecoin is USDT, issued by the Hong Kong Company, Tether, owned by iFinex, a company registered in the British Virgin Islands. It makes up about 48 percent of the total supply of stablecoins.[6] The USDT is pegged one to-one to the dollar, and Tether claims it is fully backed by reserves. However, these reserves are about 80 percent cash, cash equivalents, other short-term deposits, and commercial paper. The rest are corporate bonds, funds, precious metals, secured loans, and "other investments." Only about 8 percent of reserves are cash.[7]

The fine print on Tether's webpage reveals that redemptions are subject to a $100,000 minimum and a fee equal to the maximum of $1000 or 0.1 percent. They are limited to account holders; residents of the United States and those who do business in New York are not eligible. Payment can be in reserve assets rather than currency. If there is reserve illiquidity or losses, Tether reserves the right to delay.[8] In the event of bankruptcy, token holders are unsecured creditors with no proprietary claim on the reserves. Rather than audits, up until July, Tether relied on "attestations" from a Cayman Islands accounting firm.[9] While Tether does charge fees, its business model is not that of a custodian broker-dealer but the potentially far more profitable one of traditional fractional reserve banks.

Dai

Some stablecoins are backed by cryptocurrency assets rather than fiat currency. A prominent example is Dai, the fourth most important stablecoin, accounting for about 4 percent of the total supply.[10] The Maker Protocol—designed by a disparate group of software developers—is a DeFi protocol on the Ethereum blockchain intended to enable peer-to-peer borrowing and lending. It creates and governs Dai, which is soft-pegged one-to-one with the dollar and intended to give its loans a stable

[6] "Total Stable Coin Supply," chart "Defi: Stablecoins." Data for 27 October 2022.

[7] "Transparency: Reports & Reserves," *Tether* (https://tether.to/en/transparency/#reports: accessed 27 October 2022).

[8] "Fees," *Tether* (https://tether.to/en/fees) and "Legal Terms," *Tether* (https://tether.to/en/legal). Both accessed 27 October 2022.

[9] Vicky Gee Huang, "Biggest Stablecoin Issuer, Tether, Switches Accounting Firm to BDO Italia," *Wall Street Journal* (https://www.wsj.com/articles/biggest-stablecoin-issuer-tether-switches-accounting-firm-to-bdo-italia-11660795062?mod=article_inline: 18 August 2022).

[10] Total Stable Coin Supply, "Defi: Stablecoins." Data for 23 October 2022.

value. The software is available to the public, who use it at their own risk. There are no formal agreements and no legal recourse if things go wrong.[11]

Dai is supplied when users post excess crypto-asset collateral and borrow Dai up to a fixed collateral-to-loan ratio. Access to the collateral is lost until the loan is repaid. Borrowed Dai can be invested in a smart contract that pays interest; outstanding Dai accrue a "stability fee" paid when the loan is repaid. Penalties are charged, and the loan is liquidated if the value of the collateral dips below the required amount. The value of Dai is maintained by adjusting the interest rate and stability fee, and with a mechanism that sells Dai if its value exceeds a dollar and buys it if it falls below. Another cryptocurrency, the MKR, holds this *decentralized autonomous organization* (DAO) together. MKR holders make rules about collateral and set interest, stability, and penalty rates. In good times, surpluses are auctioned for MKR, which is burned, appreciating its value; in bad times, MKR is used to recapitalize the system, depreciating its value.

TerraUSD

The notorious stablecoin TerraUSD (UST) was issued by Terraform Labs (TFL), the developer of the Terra blockchain with native cryptocurrency LUNA. TFL operates Mirror Protocol, an associated DeFi protocol that creates and offers synthetic assets, and UST was meant to denominate trades on Mirror. It was soft pegged, one UST to one dollar's worth of LUNA. Unlike Maker's DAO, where there is a reserve of crypto-assets larger than the face value of Dai, TFL operated a purely algorithmic stablecoin (although it did hold some bitcoin reserves). Possibly a Ponzi scheme, although perhaps meant as a loss leader, TFL's Anchor protocol offered those who invested UST nearly 20 percent interest. Investors flocked in, and the UST became the third-largest stablecoin. An unexpected withdrawal of $84 million UST from Anchor sparked a run on the protocol, leading to a collapse of both UST and its sister currency, LUNA. The value of the UST went from a dollar in May 2022 to less than a penny in June.[12]

[11] The Maker Protocol: MakerDAO's Multi-Collateral Dai (MCD) System," MakerDAO (https://makerdao.com/en/whitepaper#introduction). Bruce et al., "The Private Law of Stable Coins," specifically p. 15.

[12] Muyao Shen, "How 60 Billion in Terra Coins Went Up in Algorithmic Smoke," online article, *Bloomberg* (https://Bhttps://www.bloomberg.com/graphics/2022-crypto-luna-terra-stablecoin-explainer/loomberg.com: 21 May 2022).

Libra

On 18 June 2019, Facebook announced a project called Libra. In brief, the plan was for a governing entity, the Libra Association, to issue a token pegged to a basket of fiat currencies. The Libra Association would sell tokens to selected Crypto Exchanges called authorized resellers (ARs) in return for an equal value of currency or highly liquid government bonds. A custodian would hold these reserve assets. The Libra Association would intervene to maintain the peg by buying and selling tokens with the ARs. The ARs would sell tokens to customers on a secondary market. Retail customers would probably have been required to have a Libra account, and transactions were to be recorded on a permissioned blockchain.[13]

To policymakers, this setup must have looked like a rival central bank with its own financial system and currency. Appalled at the scale of the project, their response was immediate. The G-7 said it would set up a high-level working group to consider the risk to the financial system. Mark Carney, the governor of the Bank of England, said that "it would instantly become systemic and will have to be subject to the highest standards of regulation."[14] In July 2019, the US Senate's Banking Committee summoned the head of the project to a hearing. Following pressure from the EU and, especially, US policymakers, the endeavor was abandoned.[15]

EU Regulation

Unfortunately, EU policymakers have responded to stablecoins with the European Commission's proposed Markets in Crypto-assets (MiCA) regulation for EU crypto-assets and service providers, expected to come

[13] Dirk A. Zetzsche, Ross P. Buckley, and Douglas W. Arner, "Regulating Libra," *Oxford Journal of Legal Studies* 41 (Spring 2021): 80–113. Online at https://doi.org/10.1093/ojls/gqaa036. Luciano Somoza and Tammaro Terracciano, "Stabilising Stablecoins: A Pragmatic Regulatory Approach," *VoxEU* (https://cepr.org/voxeu/columns/stabilising-stablecoins-pragmatic-regulatory-approach: 3 December 2019).

[14] Caroline Binham, Chris Giles, and David Keohane, "Facebook's Libra Currency Draws Instant Response from Regulators—G7 Countries Establish Group to Examine Risk to Financial System from 'Stable Coins'," *Financial Times* (https://www.ft.com/content/5535fb3a-91ea-11e9-b7ea-60e35ef678d2: 18 June 2019).

[15] Viki Auslender, "The Scientist who Almost Made Mark Zuckerberg President of the World Bank," *CTECH* (https://www.calcalistech.com/ctechnews/article/e7m09zgfe: 23 September 2022).

into force in 2024.[16] Much of the MiCA regulation of stablecoins focuses on those pegged to a commodity or a basket of commodities, a cryptocurrency or a basket of cryptocurrencies, or a basket of fiat currencies. Fears that these stablecoins might become sufficiently important that they could pose risks to financial stability and monetary sovereignty mean that their issuers are subject to especially stringent requirements. There are no significant stablecoins of this variety, however, and it is unclear why stablecoins pegged to a basket of fiat currencies should be treated separately from those pegged to a single fiat currency. The regulation must be a response to the proposed Libra.[17]

The regulation also addresses *e-money tokens* or stablecoins, the "main purpose of which is to be used as a medium of exchange and that purports to maintain a stable value by referring to the value of a fiat currency that is legal tender." The recital makes it clear that the definition is meant to be as encompassing as possible to avoid circumvention of the law. The legislation provides some needed standards of transparency and disclosure. Unfortunately, it also mandates a single business model. Tokens must be issued and redeemable on demand at par. Reserve assets must be sequestered from the issuer's assets and can only be invested in highly liquid and minimally risky investments denominated in the relevant fiat currency. It proscribes issuers and crypto-asset service providers from paying interest on e-money tokens. Unless the issuer is a custodial broker-dealer making money from transaction fees or the operator of an exchange who acts as a market-maker and profits from the bid-ask spreads, its business will be unsustainable when interest rates deviate significantly from zero.[18]

The apparent intent of MiCA is to end the issuance of most current stablecoins and their associated crypto-asset services in the EU. Of the five

[16] Proposal COM (2020) 593 Final of the European Parliament and of the Council 24 September 2020 on Markets in Crypto-Assets, and Amending Directive (EU) 2019/1937 (https://data.consilium.europa.eu/doc/document/ST-11053-2020-INIT/en/pdf).

[17] Some stablecoins are those pegged to a commodity, typically gold. They have a niche use, and none have a market capitalization sufficiently large enough to be subject to the regulation's harsher requirements. See "Today's Cryptocurrency Prices by Market Cap," *CoinMarketCap* (https://coinmarketcap.com: accessed 27 October 2022).

[18] See Willem Buiter, Anne Sibert, and Nicolaes Tollenaar, "E-Money Tokens, Tokenised Money-Market Shares, and Tokenised Bank Deposits," *VoxEU* (https://cepr.org/voxeu/columns/e-money-tokens-tokenised-money-market-shares-and-tokenised-bank-deposits: 18 August 2022).

most significant stablecoins, USDT, Dai, and Abracadabra's crypto-asset-backed Magic Internet Money (MIM) seem hopelessly incompatible with the MiCA's requirements. Presumably, while EU residents will be able to buy and sell MIM and USDT in the secondary market, they will no longer have access to Abracadabra's loans or the possibility of transacting with Tether on EU platforms.

Challenges and Issues in Regulating Stablecoins

Regulation for Consumer Protection Is Necessary

The EU is suitably worried about consumer protection. Policymakers have a legitimate interest in preventing wrongdoing and misrepresentation. In a study of seven leading stablecoins, Bruce et al. find that what is boldly stated on a stablecoin provider's website is qualified in the fine print of their (not always easily findable) terms-of-service documents agreed to by account holders. The ability to exchange a stablecoin for fiat currency can be limited; reserves are not necessarily held in safe and liquid funds; in the event of bankruptcy, stablecoin holders can have limited protection.[19]

Good accounting and auditing standards should be developed, and it is reasonable to insist that companies be more transparent. Both providers and investors can benefit from this as it increases investor confidence. Private law solutions may develop as well—say, contractual provisions that give investors a proprietary right in reserve assets.[20] Governments should also go after the wrongdoers. If TFL ran a Ponzi scheme or Tether used its reserves to refinance iFinex's BitFinex exchange, then civil and criminal penalties should be imposed on those responsible.

Effective Regulation May Be Difficult

Without coordinated multinational regulation—something that seems hard to achieve—it is challenging to regulate the providers of purely digital assets. Tether might state it will not directly transact with EU residents and continue business as usual. EU residents can earn interest on stablecoins on non-EU platforms. Singapore-based Crypto.com is offering 14 percent for one-month USDC stablecoin deposits over $40,000;

[19] "Bruce et al., "The Private Law of Stable Coins," specifically p. 25.

[20] Ibid.

MyConstant—with headquarters in California—offers 12.5 percent on USDC and USDT for one-month deposits up to $5000 and 8 percent on additional balances.[21] Even if global coordination of regulation were possible, the algorithmic stablecoin Dai has no issuer to regulate.

Regulation May Be an Attempt to Kill Off Competition

The legislation is at least *consistent* with a political economy theory of regulation. George Stigler states, "We propose the general hypothesis: every industry or occupation that has enough political power to utilize the state will seek to control entry. … Crudely put, the butter producers wish to suppress margarine."[22] Issuers of regulated liabilities see unregulated stablecoins as unwelcome competition. To the extent that the framers of MiCA shared a worldview with, or were influenced by, the issuers of regulated liabilities, it is conceivable that some of the rush to regulate stablecoins might stem from conflicts of interest rather than legitimate concerns.

Maudos and Vives and Carletti and Vives suggest that the EU would benefit from more competition in retail banking markets.[23] In the United States, 15 percent of adults in the bottom 40 percent of the income distribution do not have bank accounts. Low-income account holders pay over $12 monthly for basic access to the financial system.[24] Banking services are non-existent or expensive in some emerging markets. Competition between bank deposit coins and stablecoins would likely increase access and lower costs, improving consumer welfare. It would be unfortunate if anti-competitive legislation anywhere in the world kept this from happening.

[21] "Best USDC Interest Rates," *Benzinga* (https://www.benzinga.com/money/best-usdc-interest-rates). "Lend Crypto," *MyConstant* (https://www.myconstant.com/lending-to-earn?v=c&r=IG3CUIXDHM). Both accessed 27 October 2022.

[22] George J. Stigler, "The Theory of Economic Regulation," *The Bell Journal of Economics and Management Science* 2 (1971): 3–21, specifically 5–6.

[23] Joaquín Maudos and Xavier Vives, "Competition Policy in Banking in the European Union," *Review of Industrial Organization* 55 (2019): 27–46. Carletti, Elena, and Xavier Vives. "10 Regulation and Competition Policy in the Banking Sector." In Xavier Vives, ed. *Competition Policy in the EU: Fifty Years on From the Treaty of Rome*. Oxford: Oxford Academic, 2009. Online edition. https://doi.org/10.1093/acprof:oso/9780199566358.003.0010

[24] Christian Catalini and Jai Massari, "Stablecoins and the Future of Money," *Harvard Business Review* (https://hbr.org/2021/08/stablecoins-and-the-future-of-money: 10 August 2021).

Regulation Might Lead to Regulatory Arbitrage, and It Might Kill Off Innovation

If MiCA's ban on interest rates curtails stablecoin issuers, issuers of regulated liabilities may take advantage of this and tokenize their liabilities. Retail money market funds might issue shares as tokens pegged to a unit of fiat currency on a public blockchain under EU money market law. Outside MiCA's purview, they would be free to charge whatever interest they wished. Alternatively, commercial banks might offer the possibility of on-chain deposits. They would administer them in the distributed database of a public blockchain rather than their usual database. As bank deposits are also exempt from MiCA, they could pay interest. A benefit of this is that the decentralized ledger blockchain technology could be used for both assets and liabilities in an "always on" global network.[25] A cost is that it might kill off potential innovation and competition.

The regulated sector, with its lender of last resort, will continue to exist for those who want it. However, allowing stablecoins to exist in a relatively unregulated environment might spur innovation.

MiCA legislates that all reserves must be safe and highly liquid. However, Routledge and Zetlin-Jones demonstrate that speculative attacks may be eliminated and stability maintained with less than 100 percent reserves with a dynamic mechanism that adjusts in response to conversion demands. While the competing objectives of the issuers of fiat currency mean that it is unlikely that they could credibly commit to such a plan, it might be credibly implemented by issuers of stablecoins in a smart contract blockchain environment.[26]

Diamond and Dybvig demonstrate that fractional reserve banks can provide efficient risk sharing. However, they can also produce runs, providing a rationale for deposit insurance, lender of last resort activity, and regulation. Green and Lin, however, demonstrate that if banks can specify the amount a person can withdraw as a function of the timing of the withdrawal and the history of withdrawals up to that point, then the socially optimal outcome is the unique plausible outcome. Runs are not

[25] See Tony McLaughlin, "The Regulated Internet of Value," *Citi Treasury and Trade Solutions* (https://www.citibank.com/tts/insights/articles/article191.html: June 2021).

[26] Bryan Routledge and Ariel Zetlin-Jones, "Currency Stability Using Blockchain Technology," *Journal of Economic Dynamics and Control* 142 (September 2022) 104155.

possible.[27] Critics of Green and Lin claim these contracts are too complicated to be feasible or are not credible for banks. However, it may be possible to credibly implement them in a smart contract blockchain environment.

Some private-sector innovations may not prove to be beneficial. If, say, purely algorithmic stablecoins are unsuccessful, they will die off on their own without government assistance.

Regulation Might Kill Off DeFi

The depreciation of the local currency makes survival in Venezuela difficult, and there is a heavy dependence on remittances. Venezuelans in Colombia can send remittances to family and friends in Venezuela using Valiu, a US-based digital remittance platform. They deposit Colombian pesos onto the platform, and Valiu buys bitcoin using peer-to-peer platforms. The recipient can exchange bitcoin for Venezuelan bolivars as needed, which can be deposited into a Venezuelan bank account.[28]

In Sub-Saharan Africa, only 3 percent of smallholding farmers have crop insurance. Traditional insurance is expensive, and there is a lack of data to verify claims. Parametric crop insurance on a decentralized blockchain that is inexpensive to provide, fair, and transparent is being developed. Weather conditions determine contractual payouts. An independent network of oracles provides weather data, and extreme events automatically trigger policies.[29]

Stablecoins are a vital component of DeFi. If regulation kills them, it will likely end opportunities like the above.

[27] Douglas W. Diamond and Philip H. Dybvig. "Bank Runs, Deposit Insurance, and Liquidity," *Journal of Political Economy* 91 (1983): 401–419. Edward J. Green and Ping Lin, "Implementing Efficient Allocations in a Model of Financial Intermediation," *Journal of Economic Theory* 109 (2003): 1–23.

[28] Chainalysis, The 2021Geography of Cryptocurrency Report: Analysis of Geographic Trends in Cryptocurrency Adoption and Usage (https://go.chainalysis.com/rs/503-FAP-074/images/Geography-of-Cryptocurrency-2021.pdf: October 2021), 42.

[29] "Etherisc Teams up with Chainlink to Deliver Crop Insurance in Kenya," Etherisc Blog (https://blog.etherisc.com/etherisc-teams-up-with-chainlink-to-deliver-crop-insurance-in-kenya-137e433c29dc: 14 November 2020).

References

Armstrong, M. (2022, June 7). The varying volatility of cryptocurrencies. *Statista.* https://www.statista.com/chart/27577/cryptocurrency-volatility-dmo/

Auslender, V. (2022, September 23). The scientist who almost made mark Zuckerberg President of the World Bank. *CTECH.* https://www.calcalistech.com/ctechnews/article/e7m09zgfe

Best USDC Interest Rates. *Benzinga.* https://www.benzinga.com/money/best-usdc-interest-rates. Accessed 27 October 2022.

Binham, C., Giles, C., & Keohane, D. (2019, June 18). Facebook's Libra currency draws instant response from regulators—G7 countries establish group to examine risk to financial system from 'stable coins'. *Financial Times.* https://www.ft.com/content/5535fb3a-91ea-11e9-b7ea-60e35ef678d2

Bruce, K. J., Odinet, C. K., & Tosato, A. (2023). The private law of stable coins. *Arizona State Law Journal,* forthcoming. Online version. https://papers.ssrn.com/sol3/papers.cfm?abstract_id=4191646

Buiter, W., Sibert, A., & Tollenaar, N. (2022, August 18). E-money tokens, tokenised money-market shares, and tokenised bank deposits. *VoxEU.* https://cepr.org/voxeu/columns/e-money-tokens-tokenised-money-market-shares-and-tokenised-bank-deposits

Carletti, E., & Vives, X. (2009). 10 regulation and competition policy in the banking sector. In X. Vives (Ed.), *Competition policy in the EU: Fifty years on from the treaty of Rome.* Oxford Academic. Online edition. https://doi.org/10.1093/acprof:oso/9780199566358.003.0010

Catalini, C., & Massari, J. (2021, August 10). Stablecoins and the future of money. *Harvard Business Review.* https://hbr.org/2021/08/stablecoins-and-the-future-of-money

Chainalysis. (2021). *The 2021 geography of cryptocurrency report: Analysis of geographic trends in cryptocurrency adoption and usage.* https://go.chainalysis.com/rs/503-FAP-074/images/Geography-of-Cryptocurrency-2021.pdf

"Defi: Stablecoins." *The Block.* https://www.theblock.co/data/decentralized-finance/stablecoins. Accessed 27 October 2022.

Diamond, D. W., & Dybvig, P. H. (1983). Bank runs, deposit insurance, and liquidity. *Journal of Political Economy, 91,* 401–419.

Etherisc Teams up with Chainlink to Deliver Crop Insurance in Kenya. *Etherisc Blog.* https://blog.etherisc.com/etherisc-teams-up-with-chainlink-to-deliver-crop-insurance-in-kenya-137e433c29dc, 14 November 2020.

Fees. *Tether.* https://tether.to/en/fees. Accessed 27 October 2022.

Green, E. J., & Lin, P. (2003). Implementing efficient allocations in a model of financial intermediation. *Journal of Economic Theory, 109,* 1–23.

Huang, V. G. (2022, August 18). Biggest stablecoin issuer, Tether, switches accounting firm to BDO Italia. *Wall Street Journal.* https://www.wsj.com/articles/biggest-stablecoin-issuer-tether-switches-accounting-firm-to-bdo-italia-11660795062?mod=article_inline

Legal Terms. *Tether.* https://tether.to/en/legal. Accessed 27 October 2022.

Lend Crypto. *MyConstant.* https://www.myconstant.com/lend-crypto-to-earn-interest. Accessed 27 October 2022.

Markets: Prices. *The Block.* https://www.theblock.co/data/crypto-markets/prices. Accessed 27 October 2022.

Maudos, J., & Vives, X. (2019). Competition policy in banking in the European Union. *Review of Industrial Organization, 55*, 27–46.

McLaughlin, T. (2021, June). The regulated internet of value. *Citi Treasury and Trade Solutions.* https://www.citibank.com/tts/insights/articles/article191.html

Proposal COM. (2020). 593 Final of the European Parliament and of the Council 24 September 2020 on Markets in Crypto-Assets, and Amending Directive (EU) 2019/1937. https://data.consilium.europa.eu/doc/document/ST-11053-2020-INIT/en/pdf

Routledge, B., & Zetlin-Jones, A. (2022). Currency stability using blockchain technology. *Journal of Economic Dynamics and Control, 142*(September 2022), 104155.

Shen, M. (2022, May 21). How 60 billion in Terra coins went up in algorithmic smoke. Online article. *Bloomberg.* https://Bhttps://www.bloomberg.com/graphics/2022-crypto-luna-terra-stablecoin-explainer/loomberg.com

Somoza, L., & Terracciano, T. (2019, December 3). Stabilising stablecoins: A pragmatic regulatory approach. *VoxEU.* https://cepr.org/voxeu/columns/stabilising-stablecoins-pragmatic-regulatory-approach

Stigler, G. J. (1971). The theory of economic regulation. *The Bell Journal of Economics and Management Science, 2*, 3–21.

The Maker Protocol: MakerDAO's Multi-Collateral Dai (MCD) System. *MakerDAO.* https://makerdao.com/en/whitepaper#introduction

Today's Cryptocurrency Prices by Market Cap. *CoinMarketCap.* https://coinmarketcap.com. Accessed 27 October 2022.

Transparency: Reports & Reserves. *Tether.* https://tether.to/en/transparency/#reports. Accessed 27 October 2022.

Zetzsche, D. A., Buckley, R. P., & Arner, D. W. (2021). Regulating Libra. *Oxford Journal of Legal Studies, 41*(Spring 2021), 80–113. https://doi.org/10.1093/ojls/gqaa036

PART VI

Global Warming

The Yellow Brick Road to a Decarbonized World Economy

Brynhildur Davídsdóttir

Introduction

Anthropogenic climate change, caused by emissions of greenhouse gases, is the largest global environmental threat the world is facing today. The consequences in addition to increased temperatures include ocean acidification, sea-level rise, the melting of glaciers and polar icecaps, the disappearance of sea-ice, increased frequency of intense storms, landslides and drought. These changes in the physical environment translate to ecological changes, including changes in growing seasons and agricultural growth potentials, changes in species habitats and habitability and derived changes in biodiversity. The physical and biological changes translate to implications for societies worldwide with associated social and economic costs, threatening future prosperity, well-being and the fulfilment of the Sustainable Development Goals (SDGs) (IPCC, 2022a).

For a while, climate change seemed a distant threat, yet evidence supports that climate change is taking place and is already having significant

B. Davídsdóttir (✉)
University of Iceland, Reykjavik, Iceland
e-mail: bdavids@hi.is

R. Z. Aliber et al. (eds.), *Fault Lines After COVID-19*,
https://doi.org/10.1007/978-3-031-26482-5_19

social and economic consequences with escalating threats into the future. Intergovernmental Panel on Climate Change's (IPCC, 2022a) Working Group 2, sixth assessment report (IPCC, 2022a), confirms that climate change has already led to increases in "frequency and intensity of climate and weather extremes", including droughts, raging wildfires, more intense precipitation events and increased heat-related human mortality. Climate change is affecting food and water security with already observed implications in the Arctic, small island developing states and communities in Asia, Africa and South and Central America (IPCC, 2022a).

Despite a few reported cases of positive economic implications of climate change, such as those related to "last chance tourism", extended growing seasons or migration of new harvestable species, the negative economic impact is expected to be significant for example through the impact on climate vulnerable economic sectors, international supply chains, human settlements and infrastructures and the looming humanitarian crisis. Losses from tropical cyclones already have increased due to sea-level rise and increased storm intensity which has translated directly into economic loss. For example, Collier et al. (2021) illustrate that insured and economic losses in 2018 linked to disasters were 148% and 77% higher than the 10-year average, respectively. Albeit this increase is not all derived from weather-related events it is an indication of what is to come (IPCC, 2022a). The near-term consequences (to 2040) of climate change are likely to be most felt in least developed countries, coastal areas, small island developing states and where species exist close to their habitable temperature boundaries, such as in the Arctic. The long-term consequences will be felt worldwide and the risk escalates with each degree increase in average temperatures (IPCC, 2022a).

The world community has responded to the climate change threat through international agreements, most notably the United Nations Framework Convention on Climate Change (UNFCCC) in 1992, the Kyoto Protocol (1997) and the Paris Agreement (2015). The UNFCCC acknowledged the threat of climate change and the need to limit greenhouse gas (GHG) emissions without setting numerical targets. The Kyoto Protocol of 1997 set mitigation targets but only to a limited number of developed countries that aimed for a collective reduction of GHG emissions by 5.2% below 1990 levels by 2008–2012. The targets were deepened in the second budget period of the Kyoto Protocol to 20% below 1990 levels by 2020, again only by developed countries. The successor of the Kyoto Protocol, the 2015 Paris Agreement approached the issue differently and aims to limit the increase in average global temperatures below 2 °C and as close to 1.5 °C as possible by 2100. To fulfil this aim all nations have mitigation targets, global carbon neutrality should be reached by 2050 and to remain under 2 °C increase or as close to 1.5 °C as possible, peak global emissions should be reached by 2027 or 2025, respectively, and rapidly decline thereafter (IPCC, 2022b).

The narrow window of time to reach peak emissions is due to the very long-lifetime of carbon dioxide in the atmosphere. This means that as carbon dioxide continues to be emitted its concentration in the atmosphere and thereby global temperatures continue to increase. The relationship between emissions, the increasing concentration due to long lifetimes and the temperature goal of the Paris Agreement creates what can be considered a global carbon budget defined as: "the maximum amount of cumulative net global anthropogenic carbon dioxide (CO_2) emissions that would result in limiting global warming to a given level with a given probability, taking into account the effect of other anthropogenic climate forcers" (IPCC, 2018). When the global carbon budget has been exhausted the increase in global temperatures is likely to exceed 2 °C and thereby increase the likelihood of catastrophic climate change.

The planetary boundaries concept clearly articulates this point (Rockstrom et al., 2009). Planetary boundaries depict earth system limitations or boundaries in which humanity can continue to operate, defining the "safe operating space for humanity". The planetary boundaries concept defines the safe operating space for climate change to be anything below a concentration of carbon dioxide of 350 ppm with the upper bound of 450 ppm indicating that any increase in concentration beyond 450 ppm is considered to evoke high risk of serious climate impacts (Steffen et al., 2015). This closely mirrors the warnings of the IPCC (2022).

Given the physically defined upper limits of the concentration of carbon dioxide to prevent catastrophic climate change and the rapidly declining world carbon budget the world economy must quickly become decarbonized. This requires drastic reduction in greenhouse gas emissions worldwide and an enhancement of carbon sinks, effectively creating a low-carbon world economy while maintaining well-being and prosperity. This chapter addresses the following questions:

How are GHG emissions developing worldwide in the context of decarbonization?

How are mitigation efforts leading to decarbonization?

What are key issues to address going forward to realize a decarbonized world economy?

The Development in GHG Emissions over Time. Towards a Decarbonized Economy?

Decarbonization and Decoupling

A successfully decarbonized economy is an economy that has permanently net zero emissions for each unit of economic production and is able to maintain or enhance economic prosperity at the same time. The road to a decarbonized economy therefore necessitates a permanent reduction of GHG emissions per unit of economic production which is a process called decoupling. Decoupling can be either absolute or relative. Relative decoupling takes place when variables change in the same direction but at different speeds. This means in the context of decarbonizing an economy that economic growth increases faster than GHG emissions, and thereby reducing slowly the ratio of GDP and GHG emissions. Relative decoupling is normally associated with an increase in total emissions, except in the case of recession. Absolute decoupling takes place when the variables in question develop in different directions. In the context of decarbonizing an economy, if economic growth increases and GHG emissions decrease permanently, strong absolute decoupling has taken place and the ratio of GDP and GHG emissions has declined significantly. Absolute decoupling is a prerequisite for green or low-carbon growth to be realized, as without an absolute, rapid and permanent reduction in GHG emissions the aim of the Paris Agreement is beyond reach.

The emphasis on reducing GHG emissions in absolute terms, rather than simply achieving incremental reduction per unit of production is in line with the aims of the Paris Agreement and the Planetary boundaries concept. Given the long lifetime of carbon dioxide in the atmosphere, any emissions of carbon dioxide will add to the amount and thereby concentration of carbon dioxide. Absolute and significant reduction must therefore be achieved to remain within "planetary boundaries" that ensure a safe space for human development (Hickel & Kallis, 2019; Rockstrom et al., 2009).

Is Decoupling and Decarbonization Taking Place?

Despite stated international commitments and warnings of the IPCC, GHG emissions continue to increase worldwide. Since 1990, the base year of the UNFCCC and its associated Protocols and Agreements, global GHG emissions have kept increasing and in 2019 emissions were 54% higher than emissions in 1990, the highest they had ever been. Emissions increased on average 0.7% per year from 1990 to 2000, 2.1% per year from 2000 to 2010 and 1.3% per year from 2010 to 2019 (IPCC, 2022b).

As a result, the global concentration of carbon dioxide continues to increase and in 2020 was 413 parts per million (ppm) and rose in 2021 to close to 415 ppm (Friedlingstein et al., 2021). The increase in worldwide emissions contributed to the steady increase in the concentration of carbon dioxide, which will continue to increase until net zero emissions are reached as we continue to exhaust the global carbon budget. According to Friedlingstein et al. (2021), if humanity continues to emit at the same rate as in 2021, the remaining global carbon budget will be exhausted in 2033 or 2054 to fulfil the 1.5 or 2.0 °C temperature targets of the Paris Agreement, respectively, or in 11 and 32 years.

Empirical studies illustrate a non-disrupted statistically significant positive association between economic growth and GHG emissions within nations and regions at all levels of development (IPCC, 2022b; Onofrei et al., 2022; Azam et al., 2016). This positive relationship illustrates that absolute decoupling has not yet emerged. It therefore was not surprising that global fossil-based carbon dioxide emissions declined by 5.4% as the world economy slowed down due to Covid-19 (Friedlingstein et al., 2021). Nations worldwide engaged in Covid-19 stimulus spending and pledged to prioritize spending towards green initiatives (IPCC, 2022b). This could have facilitated a continued decline in GHG emissions as economic growth rose again and thereby absolute decoupling. Actions however did not fulfil this promise as worldwide Covid-19-related stimulus spending that directly and indirectly stimulated activities that led to increased use of fossil fuels was six times larger than the spending that enhanced the transition towards low-carbon energy (REN21 2021). By 2021 fossil carbon dioxide emissions increased worldwide by 4.8% nearly back to 2019 levels (UNEP, 2022).

Despite the lack of empirical evidence for absolute decoupling the evidence grows for a steady global trend towards *relative* decoupling of carbon dioxide emissions especially among numerous high-income countries in the twenty-first century (Hickel & Kallis, 2019; Haberl et al., 2020). The empirical examples of absolute decoupling largely are based on a narrow scope of domestic GHG emissions and in the context of very high levels of emissions in highly developed economies (IPCC, 2022b; Wu et al., 2018; Haberl et al., 2020). The rebounding of emissions after Covid-19, illustrates this as emissions in China and India increased by 5.9% and 3.2%, respectively, in 2021 compared to 2019 levels while emissions in the EU, the USA remained 4.2% and 5.3%, respectively, below 2019 levels (UNEP, 2022). But does this confirm absolute decoupling, or have emissions related to imports simply been shifted elsewhere?

Mitigation Efforts

The empirical evidence of relative decoupling for highly developed economies follows the theory behind the Environmental Kuznets Curve (EKC). The EKC describes the phenomenon that as a national economy develops it continues to increase environmental pressures per unit of economic production until it reaches a turning point at which time environmental pressures per unit of production decline, creating an inverted U-shaped curve. As the turning point is reached, hard and soft infrastructures have been built and social systems developed, enabling increased concern for the environment. This results in a reduction of environmental impact through mitigation as well as possibly by shifting impact to other countries through imports.

Mitigation efforts under the UNFCCC, the Kyoto Protocol and the Paris Agreement seem to have been designed to follow the EKC, despite the understanding that this would not result in absolute reduction in GHG emissions. Only developed countries had mitigation commitments under the Kyoto Protocol, and despite that all nations under the Paris Agreement have mitigation commitments, these commitments are non-binding, focus on domestic emissions and enable peak emissions by developing countries not to be reached until 2030 or thereafter.

Looking within national boundaries, mitigation efforts have largely applied to emissions that take place within national geographical boundaries, so-called domestic emissions. These normally are allocated to predefined sectors, including energy production and energy use, industry, waste, agriculture and land-based emissions and sequestration. In 2020 the energy supply sector accounted for 37% of total emissions, industry 26% and transport 14%. Agriculture and land use contributed 18% of total emissions (UNEP, 2022). Globally, since 1990 the largest growth in GHG emissions has been from energy-related sectors, energy supply and transport, in addition to process-based emissions from industry but emissions have continued to increase across all sectors and subsectors (IPCC, 2022b).

Given the focus on domestic emissions, the emissions that do not fall under that criteria have received little attention by national decision-makers. These include emissions associated with international transport, travel or shipping. As a result, minimal evidence is available of mitigation efforts from international transport, including aviation and marine shipping. This means that changes are needed in how emissions from these sectors are accounted for as well as governed (IPCC, 2022b). The same applies to emissions embedded in imports, the so-called consumption-based emissions. As expected, and described by the EKC, developed nations have in part outsourced emissions from their GHG budget to other countries, largely to developing nations. In fact, according to the IPCC developed countries currently are net emissions importers and developing countries tend to be net emission exporters (IPCC, 2022b). Thus, even if emissions seem to decrease in developed nations, total emissions increase from these same nations when including all emissions associated with domestic consumptive activity. On top of this, domestic emissions from developing countries continue to increase as they seek to increase their standard of living and economic production and consumption increases (IPCC, 2022b).

The Future

Future national mitigation targets under the Paris Agreement are as before allocated to domestic emissions, excluding emissions from international transport and shipping and emissions embedded in imports. The Paris Agreement as stated before aims to keep the increase in average global temperatures under 2 °C and as close to 1.5 °C as possible. To collectively meet this aim, each nation subject to the Agreement has submitted updated nationally determined contributions (NDCs), which illustrate the voluntary mitigation target to be reached by each country by 2030.

The UNEP and the IPCC have evaluated the revised NDCs and both confirm that mitigation commitments are far from sufficient to reach the aims of the Paris Agreement (IPCC, 2022b; UNEP, 2022). The 1.5 °C target seems to be already beyond reach and reaching the 2 °C target will require radical acceleration in mitigation efforts after 2030 if the mitigation pathway capturing current pledges is followed. In addition, nations seem not to be implementing the stated efforts in the NDCs and therefore an *implementation gap* is apparent as implemented policies are not expected to enable the stated mitigation reduction in the NDCs UNEP, 2022) The NDCs however, if realized, do indicate a slight decline in GHG emissions to 2030. This means that there are weak hints to the beginning of absolute global decoupling between GHG emissions and economic growth in the stated NDCs but only relative decoupling globally when pathways that capture implemented policies are examined. If the world is serious in staying within planetary boundaries and preventing catastrophic climate change, rapid and absolute decoupling has to take place as illustrated by the mitigation pathways needed to fulfil the aim of the Paris Agreement (see e.g. IPCC, 2022b Summary for policymakers fig. 4). The most recent COP, COP27 in November 2022 did not deliver such commitment and in fact weakened the language on the global commitment to mitigating GHG emissions.

Hickel and Kallis (2019) reviewed the literature on global decoupling of GDP and GHG emissions and confirmed that a global decoupling of GDP and GHG emissions and thereby a transition to low-carbon economy is possible. Albeit it is very unlikely to take place at the speed needed. Energy, transport and agricultural systems must become decarbonized, buildings to become net-zero and industries engage in carbon capture and storage to enable immediate reduction in emissions. Material and waste management needs to become circular as material needs for the transition in part are fulfilled by scarce metals that already have exhibited volatile price paths (IEA, 2022). Consumers will need to change their consumptive habits, transform their diets and alter their travel demand. National and regional/municipal governments must create enabling conditions for the transition through policies and planning, and public finance and international finance flows be aligned with national and international climate goals. Given the timeframe the task ahead may seem unsurmountable but significant technical, economic and behavioural opportunities already exist to change course. According to Fouquet and Person (2012) the prerequisites for a transition to take place was that the service derived had to be competitive in price. Fortunately, for example, levelized cost of electricity generated from renewable energy sources such as from photovoltaics or offshore wind has significantly declined during the last decade or by 85% and 54%, respectively (REN21, 2022).

But time is running out as the carbon budget is close to exhausted and transformations are not realized overnight. For example, in the energy sector an examination of past transitions illustrated that it took at least 40 years from the time a technology had been commercialized until it reached market dominance (Fouquet & Pearson, 2012). Thus, despite the available technical and economic opportunities it is unlikely that the realized future speed of absolute decoupling is sufficient to reach the goals of the Paris Agreement. This means that to be able to reduce absolute emissions of GHG within the timeframe allowed (peak emissions the latest in 2027) may require almost immediately a steady or a declining GDP in developed countries, a contraction, akin to what was witnessed worldwide during the Covid-19 pandemic. Following the principle of common but differentiated responsibility, developing countries would have a short window of economic growth and associated increase in emissions, but in the medium term as well reach a steady state in their GDP or possibly a contraction as well until their economies have been decarbonized.

As the ultimate responsibility of a national planner is to ensure national well-being, a consideration of the impact of an immediate contraction in GDP and emissions in developed countries and a convergence by all in the medium term to net zero needs to be considered. This necessitates that each national planner realizes how to achieve a just transition of the economy such that basic needs are fulfilled for all yet remaining within planetary boundaries (Raworth, 2017). We may, possibly forced by our past inaction on climate change, be entering an era where we need to transition away from a growth-oriented economy to an economy that centres on well-being and equity subject to the global carbon budget.

Three Challenges to Policymakers—How to Move Forward?

Move from Relative to Absolute Emission Reductions, from Sector to Systems Perspectives

Given current trends illustrate that despite stated intensions, GHG emissions continue to increase and current national mitigation pledges are far from fulfilling the aims of the Paris Agreement. To change this, the focus within each nation must be to reach absolute emission reduction in all sectors simultaneously, prevent shifting emissions between sectors and systematically look at relationships between sectors, consumers and enablers. As described earlier, national mitigation efforts have in the past been geared towards specific sectors, frequently without considering larger system-related impacts such as relationships between sectors or the reactions of consumers and thereby ignoring the possibility of rebounding (Freire-González, 2017; Galvin et al., 2021).

Mitigation planning, for example, in transportation sectors needs to consider strategies that simultaneously aim to reduce the need for transport, shift to low carbon energy such as electricity or e-fuels, enhance active mode of transport and improve efficiency without rebounding. This means that mitigation actions in the transport sector require cooperation with municipal and regional planners to create the enabling conditions needed to enable shifts to active modes of travel and enhanced use of public transport in addition to shifting to e.g. e-transport. Shifting to e-transport requires coordination with utilities and electricity producers as grids need to be able to support additional demand and the electricity for electric vehicles or the production of e-fuels must be derived from renewable energy resources. The focus therefore cannot only be on transport by vehicles and a transformation to e-transport, but requires an assessment of the entire transport system, and its users and the impact on and needs from other sectors as well. This calls for a close coordination and collaboration between national and municipal leaders, the business community and the public across sectors. The same applies to other sectors, such as, for example, the agricultural sector which must shift from the use of fossil fuels in their farming activities and to transition to low-GHG intensity products. This means a reduction in the production of animal products such as beef and an increase in plant-based production, but this requires consumers to be onboard and a change in diets. The scale of the required transition necessitates a radical systems-level transformation instead of the incremental sector-focused change currently pursued. Such radical economy-wide transformation can only be realized if policy- and decision-makers lift themselves above conventional silo- and sector-focused approaches and realize that a systems change is needed.

Looking Beyond National Borders and Across the Life Cycle

As alluded to before, national emissions and emissions reductions only tell part of the mitigation story. According to UNFCCC GHG accounting rules, only domestic emissions are included in each country GHG budget, excluding emissions associated with the production of imported goods and raw materials (consumption-based emissions). The invisibility of consumption-based emissions has led to the illusion that domestic emissions, for example, in developed countries are declining when in fact emissions have partly been outsourced to other countries. Since you "manage what you measure", actions leading to emission reductions largely have focused on domestic emissions, ignoring the impact of consumption and import demand.

Empirical evidence confirms that when accounting for consumption-based emissions, for example, related to fossil fuels-based emissions, emissions in developed countries increase and decline in developing countries. For example, if consumption-based emissions are accounted for, emissions in the EU increase by 6% and the USA by 14% but decline by 9 and 10% in China and India, respectively (Friedlingstein et al., 2021). When examining consumption-based emissions by income it is revealed that the bottom 50% of households ranked by income, emit approximately 12% of total emissions whereas the top 1% emit 17% of the total (UNEP, 2022). This indicates that more affluent nations have outsourced their emissions to developing nations in the global south.

Another related issue is the lack of inclusion of life cycle–related emissions associated with both consumption and domestic focused accounting. Life cycle–related emissions are emissions that take place over the entire life cycle of goods or services. For an electric vehicle, for example, the life cycle–related emissions include emissions associated with vehicle production (including raw materials extraction, processing, equipment manufacturing), vehicle use (operation and maintenance) and end-of-life. Results of LCA studies illustrate that emissions related to the production of electric vehicles are higher than the emissions associated with the production of comparable internal combustion vehicles (Dillman et al., 2020). Including life cycle–related emissions also requires the inclusion of emissions associated with the production of the energy required for the use of vehicles, both conventional vehicles and hybrid or electric vehicles. This becomes particularly important when electricity used to charge electric vehicles is produced using fossil fuels. A study by Dillman et al. (2020) illustrated that to overcome higher production emissions, an electric vehicle that runs on electricity derived from low-carbon renewable energy would have to be driven 17,000–31,000 km. However, if the electricity is produced from coal, life cycle emissions of the electric vehicle could be higher over the lifetime of the electric vehicle, assuming average lifetime. This illustrates the importance of assessing life cycle system-based emissions in order to support appropriate mitigation strategies.

A New Narrative Is Needed

The commonly known double dividend is defined as the notion that environmental taxes can both reduce pollution (the first dividend) and reduce the overall economic costs associated with the tax system by using the revenue generated to displace other distortionary taxes that slow economic growth at the same time (the second dividend).

However, climate action, if done correctly may have significant positive implications across all sustainability dimensions, economic, social and environmental in addition to the reduction of GHG emissions. Quoting Sr Nicolas Stern in his report to the 2021 G7 meeting: "The transition to a zero-emissions and climate-resilient world provides the greatest economic, business, and commercial opportunity of our time". Policies pushing for climate action therefore not only can deliver the classic double dividend but in fact can be considered to deliver multiple dividends. For example, a shift to use of renewable energy to produce electricity will not only reduce GHG emissions but also for example have positive implications for reduced air pollution and thereby public health, and if systems level implications are properly addressed will help stabilize energy prices and enhance energy security. Electrification of transport, enhanced use of public transport and increased use of active transport can improve public health, provide employment and enhance equity. More sustainable and climate-friendly agricultural practices may in addition to reducing GHG emissions enhance food security and address land degradation (IPCC, 2022b). Accelerated climate action can if done correctly have positive impact on well-being and the attainment of the Sustainable development goals (SDGs).

To enhance the support of the public and the business community to mitigation actions and to entice action, a new collaborative win-win narrative is needed where the implications of mitigation actions are framed in the context not only of the cost of actions, but also of the multiple co-benefits of being more climate responsible. The new narrative of course cannot be naive, but it needs to redirect the focus from cost, cost effectiveness and impact on GDP, to include the impact on multi-dimensional well-being. In a world where an absolute reduction in GHG emissions is needed and the pathway to fulfil the aims of the Paris Agreement may become towards a decarbonized post growth economy, this becomes even more important.

Conclusion

To prevent catastrophic climate change and ensure that temperature increase remains as close to 1.5 °C as possible requires close to immediate decarbonization of the world economy as the global carbon budget is close to exhausted. Despite efforts since 1992 global greenhouse gas emissions continue to increase. Absolute decoupling between GHG emissions and economic growth is rare, and the empirical evidence of relative decarbonization is limited.

Updated NDCs illustrate expected minor declines in GHG emissions while maintaining economic growth—but the reduction in emissions is insufficient to limit temperature increases in line with the intent of the Paris Agreement. Nations engage in creative carbon accounting, where GHG emissions are shifted between sectors and shifted abroad to other nations as neither life cycle emissions nor emissions embedded in imports are acknowledged. Emissions due to international travel and shipping are largely excluded from mitigation efforts as well.

A rapid decarbonization requires immediate decoupling of GDP and economic growth, a radical change in GHG accounting, scope of efforts and economic thinking. This includes lifting mitigation actions above/beyond national boundaries and applying a life cycle systems thinking with much broader societal engagement. Decoupling is possible. However, the radical energy and agricultural transitions that are needed will take time, time that we have lost due to hesitation to act. This hesitation, and the derived increase in GHG emissions has resulted in the need for drastic mitigation measures that may necessitate economic contraction if absolute decoupling is not quickly realized. Yet climate action can have significant co-benefits, and a new narrative is needed that focuses on win-win efforts and the multiple co-benefits in the context of mitigation and well-being. This requires a new way of economic thinking and planning, where the focus is on making sure that all can fulfil their basic needs for a good life and wellbeing is secured without exceeding the carbon budget and other planetary boundaries (Raworth, 2017).

References

Azam, M., Khan, A. Q., Abdullah, H. B., & Qureshi, M. E. (2016). The impact of CO_2 emissions on economic growth: Evidence from selected higher CO_2 emissions economies. *Environmental Science and Pollution Research, 23*(7), 6376–6389. https://doi.org/10.1007/s11356-015-5817-4

Collier, S. J., Elliott, R., & Lehtonen, T.-K. (2021). Climate change and insurance. *Economies et Societes, 50*(2), 158–172. https://doi.org/10.1080/03085147.2021.1903771

Dillman, K. J., Árnadóttir, Á., Heinonen, J., Czepkiewicz, M., & Davíðsdóttir, B. (2020). Review and meta-analysis of EVs: Embodied emissions and environmental breakeven. *Sustainability, 12*(22), 9390. https://doi.org/10.3390/su12229390

Freire-Gonzalez, J. (2017). Evidence of direct and indirect rebound effect in households in EU-27 countries. *Energy Policy, 102*, 270–276. https://doi.org/10.1016/j.enpol.2016.12.002

Fouquet, R., & Pearson, P. J. G. (2012). Past and prospective energy transitions; insights from history. *Energy Policy, 50*, 1–7. https://doi.org/10.1016/j.enpol.2012.08.014

Friedlingstein, P., Jones, M. W., O'Sullivan, M., Andrew, R. M., Bakker, D. C. E., Hauck, J., Le Quéré, C., Peters, G. P., Peters, W., Pongratz, J., Sitch, S., Canadell, J. G., Ciais, P., Jackson, R. B., Alin, S. R., Anthoni, P., Bates, N. R., Becker, M., Bellouin, N., Bopp, L., Chau, T. T. T., Chevallier, F., Chini, L. P., Cronin, M., Currie, K. I., Decharme, B., Djeutchouang, L. M., Dou, X., Evans, W., Feely, R. A., Feng, L., Gasser, T., Gilfillan, D., Gkritzalis, T., Grassi, G., Gregor, L., Gruber, N., Gürses, Ö., Harris, I., Houghton, R. A., Hurtt, G. C., Iida, Y., Ilyina, T., Luijkx, I. T., Jain, A., Jones, S. D., Kato, E., Kennedy, D., Klein Goldewijk, K., Knauer, J., Korsbakken, J. I., Körtzinger, A., Landschützer, P., Lauvset, S. K., Lefèvre, N., Lienert, S., Liu, J., Marland, G., McGuire, P. C., Melton, J. R., Munro, D. R., Nabel, J. E. M. S., Nakaoka, S.-I., Niwa, Y., Ono, T., Pierrot, D., Poulter, B., Rehder, G., Resplandy, L., Robertson, E., Rödenbeck, C., Rosan, T. M., Schwinger, J., Schwingshackl, C., Séférian, R., Sutton, A. J., Sweeney, C., Tanhua, T., Tans, P. P., Tian, H., Tilbrook, B., Tubiello, F., van der Werf, G. R., Vuichard, N., Wada, C., Wanninkhof, R., Watson, A. J., Willis, D., Wiltshire, A. J., Yuan, W., Yue, C., Yue, X., Zaehle, S., & Zeng, J. (2021). Global carbon budget. *Earth System Science Data, 14*, 1917–2005.

Galvin, R., Dutschke, E., & Wieb, J. (2021). A conceptual framework for understanding rebound effects with renewable electricity: A new challenge for decarbonizing the electricity sector. *Energy, 176*, 423–432.

Haberl, H., Wiedenhofer, D., Virág, D., Kalt, G., Plank, B., Paul Brockway, P., Tomer Fishman, T., Hausknost, D., Krausmann, F., Leon-Gruchalski, B.,

Mayer, A., Melanie Pichler, M., Schaffartzik, A., Sousa, T., Streeck, J., & Creutzig, F. (2020). A systematic review of the evidence on decoupling of GDP, resource use and GHG emissions, part II: Synthesizing the insights. *Environmental Research Letters, 15*(6), 065003. https://doi.org/10.1088/1748-9326/ab842a

Hickel, J., & Kallis, G. (2019). Is green growth possible? *New Political Economy, 25*(4), 1–18.

Intergovernmental Panel on Climate Change (IPCC). (2018). Summary for policymakers. In: *Global Warming of 1.5 °C. An IPCC Special Report on the impacts of global warming of 1.5 °C above pre-industrial levels and related global greenhouse gas emission pathways, in the context of strengthening the global response to the threat of climate change, sustainable development, and efforts to eradicate poverty* [Masson-Delmotte, V., Zhai, P., Pörtner, H.-O., Roberts, D., Skea, J., Shukla, P. R., Pirani, A., Moufouma-Okia, W., Péan, C., Pidcock, R., Connors, S., Matthews, J. B. R., Chen, Y., Zhou, X., Gomis, M. I., Lonnoy, E., Maycock, T., Tignor, M., & Waterfield T. (eds.)]. Cambridge University Press, Cambridge, UK, and New York, NY, USA, pp. 3–24, https://doi.org/10.1017/9781009157940.001.

Intergovernmental Panel on Climate Change (IPCC). (2022a). *Climate change 2022: Impacts, adaptation, and vulnerability.* Contribution of Working Group II to the Sixth Assessment Report of the Intergovernmental Panel on Climate Change [H.-O. Pörtner, D. C. Roberts, M. Tignor, E. S. Poloczanska, K. Mintenbeck, A. Alegría, M. Craig, S. Langsdorf, S. Löschke, V. Möller, A. Okem, & B. Rama (Eds.)]. Cambridge University Press, Cambridge, UK and New York, NY, USA, 3056 pp., https://doi.org/10.1017/9781009325844.

Intergovernmental Panel on Climate Change (IPCC). (2022b) *Climate Change 2022: Mitigation of Climate Change. Contribution of Working Group III to the Sixth Assessment Report of the Intergovernmental Panel on Climate Change* [P.R. Shukla, J. Skea, R. Slade, A. Al Khourdajie, R. van Diemen, D. McCollum, M. Pathak, S. Some, P. Vyas, R. Fradera, M. Belkacemi, A. Hasija, G. Lisboa, S. Luz, J. Malley, (eds.)]. Cambridge University Press, Cambridge, UK, and New York, NY, USA. https://doi.org/10.1017/9781009157926.

International Energy Agency (IEA). (2022). *World energy outlook.* IEA. https://iea.blob.core.windows.net/assets/830fe099-5530-48f2-a7c1-11f35d510983/WorldEnergyOutlook2022.pdf

Onofrei, M., Vatamanu, A. F., & Cigu, E. (2022). The relationship between economic growth and CO_2 emissions in EU countries: A cointegration analysis. *Frontiers in Environmental Science.* https://doi.org/10.3389/fenvs.2022.934885

Raworth, K. (2017). *Doughnut economics: Seven ways to think like a 21st century economist.* Oxford University Press.

REN21. (2021). *Renewables 2021: Global Status Report.* Paris REN21 Secretariat. https://www.ren21.net/wp-content/uploads/2019/05/GSR2021_Full_Report.pdf

REN21. (2022). *Renewables 2022: Global status report,* Paris: REN21 Secretariat. https://www.ren21.net/wp-content/uploads/2019/05/GSR2022_Full_Report.pdf.

Rockstrom, J., Steffen, W., Noone, K., Persson, A., Chapin, F. S., III, Lambin, E., Lenton, T. M., Scheffer, M., Folke, C., Schellnhuber, H., Nykvist, B., De Wit, C. A., Hughes, T., van der Leeuw, S., Rodhe, H., Sorlin, S., Snyder, P. K., Costanza, R., Svedin, U., Falkenmark, M., Karlberg, L., Corell, R. W., Fabry, V. J., Hansen, J., Walker, B., Liverman, D., Richardson, K., Crutzen, P., & Foley, J. (2009). Planetary boundaries: Exploring the safe operating space for humanity. *Ecology and Society, 14*(2), 32. http://www.ecologyandsociety.org/vol14/iss2/art32/.

Steffen, W., Richardson, K., Rockström, J., Cornell, S. E., et al. (2015). Planetary boundaries: Guiding human development on a changing planet. *Science, 347*(736), 1259855.

United Nations Environmental Programme (UNEP). (2022). *The closing window: Emissions gap report 2022.* UNEP Copenhagen Center. https://www.unep.org/resources/emissions-gap-report-2022

Wu, Y., Zhu, Q., & Zhu, B. (2018). Comparisons of decoupling trends of global economic growth and energy consumption between developed and developing countries. *Energy Policy, 116*(2018), 30–38. https://doi.org/10.1016/j.enpol.2018.01.047

PART VII

Consequences of the Economic Slowdown

The Need for Growth

Hian Teck Hoon, Edmund Phelps, and Gylfi Zoega

Many of the problems discussed in this volume stem from the slowdown of economic growth in the West over the past half a century. Debt would be less of a problem were it not for the anaemic growth in the US, Japan and Europe. With higher growth, wages would grow more rapidly, social cohesion would be greater and there would be greater political stability.

There are differences in average growth rates across countries and also between epochs. The European golden age was followed by stagnant economies and high unemployment. The promise of "Japan number 1" was followed by three decades of slow growth. As argued in earlier chapters, China's growth may now be coming to an end, or slowing, at any rate. Italy has not had any growth to speak of for more than 20 years. The

The original version of the chapter has been revised. A correction to this chapter can be found at https://doi.org/10.1007/978-3-031-26482-5_21

H. T. Hoon
Singapore Management University, Singapore, Singapore

E. Phelps
Center on Capitalism and Society, Columbia University, New York, NY, USA

G. Zoega (✉)
University of Iceland, Reykjavik, Iceland

Birkbeck, University of London, London, UK
e-mail: gz@hi.is

R. Z. Aliber et al. (eds.), *Fault Lines After COVID-19*,
https://doi.org/10.1007/978-3-031-26482-5_20

epochs of high and low growth are reflected in differences in investment and in asset prices. In a growing economy, stock prices and investment are higher, usually employment too. We have called such booms structural and the lengthy lagunas of high unemployment, low investment and low growth structural slumps. The growth of China after 1990, Japan from 1950 to 1990 and Europe until the 1980s are structural using our terminology because this growth was propelled by imported technology, primarily from the US, and high investment.

The economic history of Singapore is a case in point. This former British colony, established by Stamford Raffles as a trading post of the British Empire, has grown rapidly in the past decades and currently has the highest GDP per capita in the world. The key to its growth was free trade, export orientation and foreign direct investment. The authorities used foreign direct investment to import technology and close its technology gap with the rest of the world. As a result, Singapore ranks highly in terms of education, healthcare, and housing and has a high home-ownership rate.

After reviewing the literature on the sources of growth we identify growth epochs, then discuss some of the consequences of the growth slowdown in the West before ending on an optimistic note by spelling out some of the policies needed to revive growth.

The Sources of Growth

While the Solow growth model treats productivity growth as exogenous, endogenous growth models have firms investing in innovations with a known probability of success. These firms face risk and not Knightian uncertainty. Another view on innovation has been formulated in papers and books published by members of the Center on Capitalism and Society at Columbia University since its founding in 2001. These models are not Schumpeterian in that the role of entrepreneurs is not confined to designing marketable goods based on recent technological innovations. Instead, productivity growth emanates from indigenous innovations at the firm level—from the grassroots on up—made by both managers and workers in solving problems, exercising creativity, and devising new products and new methods of production. A dynamic economy—one that is rich with people possessing outsized appetite and the capacity to innovate—also needs a financial system that can weed out bad ideas and provide funding for good ideas.[1] Finally, consumers and firms have to be venturesome using the terminology of Amar Bhidé (2009). Successful businesses such as Apple and Boeing use components produced all over the world; they are venturesome in the use of these inputs and in design of products, but they do not do all of the innovating themselves. Similarly, both companies rely on venturesome customers who take chances by buying the latest models.[2] Long lines form in front of Apple stores when a new generation of iPhones arrives on the scene.

The capitalist economy is a system of free markets and private ownnership that is open to the adoption and implementation of new commercial ideas—which can take the form of new inputs, new products, or new methods of production—and by a decentralized financial system for selecting ideas and financing them. While utilitarianism has led policy makers to introduce welfare states that in essence amounts to publicly run and compulsory insurance against unemployment, ill health and poverty, many European states have extended the domain of the state so as to directly or indirectly impede the functioning of the capitalist system. Starting with the economic policies of Mussolini in the 1920s, European economies have had to a varying degree corporatist features.

Corporatism consists of a government working with the social partners, unions and employer associations, to coordinate the economy, reconcile different interests, preserve the unity of the nation and prevent conflict from arising. As such it was presented as both an alternative to unbridled capitalism and to communism. In spite of the failure of corporatism in Italy, Germany and Juan Peron's Argentina in the 1940s, many corporatist institutions exist in Europe to this day and especially in South America. Many of these institutions hinder innovation. Employment protection legislation makes it difficult for firms to reorganize and trim their workforce. It therefore obstructs innovation by acting as a tax on setting up new firms, hiring new workers and expanding their operations. Employment protection also reduces mobility between declining and emerging industries. Excessive regulation, intended to protect the stakeholders' interest also stifles innovation. There is a lot of red tape in

[1] See Phelps (2006).

[2] Amar Bhidé and Edmund Phelps (2005) use this model to explain persistent Chinese trade surpluses in the 1990s and early 2000s. Their explanation is that China did not have a sufficient number of venturesome consumers and firms to be able to import and adopt sophisticated US exports. Instead, they accumulated trade surpluses that helped buy US technology.

corporatist economies. Labour unions have a detrimental effect on innovations for a similar reason as red tape. Finally, tariffs while protecting domestic industries lower the volume of trade and have an adverse effect on innovation.

Economic culture—societal attitudes towards work and risk taking—also differs between countries.[3] Such cultural differences may explain why apparently similar or even identical institutions function well in one country and badly in another. Thus the institutions of corporatism function better in the Nordic countries in Europe and worse in Italy and other countries in the south of Europe. Even the word corporatism has a positive connotation in Denmark and Sweden and a more negative one in Italy. To take a simple example: An increase of public investment in a northern country increases aggregate demand and generates better infrastructure, while in a southern country it may be a tool to enrich particular firms or industries. Such differences even exist within countries. Banfield (1958) and Putnam (1993) attribute differences in economic and social behaviour between northern and southern Italy to differences in past history and traditions. Tabellini (2008) finds an effect of past political institutions on current individual values and a correlation between the diffusion of generalized morality and the quality of institutions. Tabellini (2010) measures culture by indicators of values and beliefs, such as trust, respect for others and confidence in individual self-determination. Using data on the literacy rate at the end of the nineteenth century and past political institutions as instruments, he finds a strong correlation with current regional economic development. In our recently published book *Dynamism*, published in 2020, we found that productivity growth, job satisfaction, employment and labour force participation are positively related across countries to values that parents instil in their children. In countries where parents teach children to be obedient to authorities, the economy performs worse than in countries where they teach them to be independent. We find that the well-performing countries include the US; the Nordic countries of Denmark, Finland and Sweden; and then Ireland, the UK and Australia. Thereafter we have the large continental economies of France, Germany, Italy and Spain that lag in terms of performance and values. Arnorsson and Zoega (2016), published in *Capitalism and Society*, use data from European (Nomenclature of Territorial Units for Statistics (NUTS1)) regions to show that unemployment, labour force participation and hours of work were statistically correlated with survey data showing

[3] See Phelps (2013).

differences in attitudes towards the importance of work, job security, job initiative and achievement as well as whether parents teach children to be independent, imaginative and tolerant in contrast to being obedient. The regions of northern Europe came out at the top and the regions of Eastern Europe at the bottom of the list.

So what explains the slowdown of growth in the West over the past decades? One explanation is that the Schumpeterian entrepreneurs have managed to bring the production possibility frontier close to the one that is feasible given existing technologies.[4] The opportunities provided in the second industrial revolution petered out in the 1970s and the opportunities provided by the third industrial revolution, mostly based on personal computers, have by now been exhausted. We are currently in the fourth industrial revolution, but the effects on productivity are difficult to discern. The rapid growth of output in Europe over the 1950s, 1960s and 1970s, and in Japan over the 1980s can be explained by a technology catch-up in the spirit of Nelson and Phelps (1966). These countries had sufficient human capital and experience of a market economy to be able to learn about, choose between, and adopt American ways of producing developed in the 1920s, 1930s and the 1940s. But the pool of technology and business ideas was gradually exhausted making these countries have to rely on domestic innovations and novel ways of importing and combining foreign innovations.

Growth Epochs

In Table 1 we show average growth rates of output and total factor productivity (TFP) during the twentieth century and the first two decades of this century. Growth rates of 2% or higher are shown in bold. We use the historical data base of Jorda, Schularick and Taylor (2019) (JST) for GDP per capita, data from the Bank of France for output per hour worked, and total factor productivity growth (see Bergeaud, 2022) to identify growth epochs. Note the cluster of bold numbers in all three tables just after the middle of the twentieth century. This is the golden age of growth in Europe. There is also a parallel golden age in Japan and Canada. Growth falls in the 1970s in the US, in the 1980s in Europe and in the 1990s in Japan and the UK.

[4] See Gordon (2016) on the rise and fall of American growth.

Table 1 Growth of output, productivity and TFP by decade

Growth of real GDP per capita							
	Canada	France	Germany	Italy	Japan	UK	US
1900–09	**3.4**	1.2	0.9	-0.1	1.9	1.4	**2.3**
1910–19	0.7	-2.1	-0.6	0.9	-0.2	**3.6**	1.4
1920–29	**2.6**	**5.0**	**5.5**	1.3	**2.9**	1.1	**2.0**
1930–39	-0.2	**3.1**	0.3	1.3	0.8	**3.5**	-0.1
1940–49	**4.2**	-2.3	1.9	1.2	1.0	-2.5	**3.9**
1950–59	**2.1**	**8.2**	**3.5**	1.7	**5.7**	**7.1**	**2.4**
1960–69	**3.2**	**3.8**	**4.5**	**2.5**	**5.6**	**9.6**	**3.1**
1970–79	**3.1**	**3.0**	**3.0**	**2.3**	**3.5**	**4.1**	**2.2**
1980–89	1.7	1.7	1.7	**2.3**	**2.5**	**3.2**	**2.1**
1990–99	1.2	1.1	1.4	**2.2**	1.3	1.1	1.9
2000–09	1.2	0.8	0.7	1.5	0.1	0.5	0.7
2010–19	1.1	1.6	1.0	1.2	0.2	1.4	1.6
Growth of output per hour worked							
	Canada	France	Germany	Italy	Japan	UK	US
1900–09	**3.1**	1.6	1.7	**2.1**	**2.5**	0.4	1.1
1910–19	**2.6**	-1.2	-1.1	**2.6**	**4.5**	0.1	**4.5**
1920–29	**2.6**	**8.8**	**2.7**	**2.9**	**2.0**	**2.8**	1.7
1930–39	-0.1	1.5	**2.8**	1.3	**3.6**	0.4	**3.3**
1940–49	**5.3**	0.8	1.5	**3.1**	-0.3	**2.6**	**2.7**
1950–59	**3.9**	**5.4**	**6.2**	**6.4**	**5.6**	**2.3**	**3.1**
1960–69	**3.0**	**6.0**	**5.6**	**7.6**	**9.1**	**3.9**	**2.7**
1970–79	1.4	**4.5**	**4.5**	**4.7**	**5.0**	**3.3**	1.3
1980–89	1.0	**3.1**	**2.4**	**2.0**	**3.4**	**2.3**	1.3
1990–99	1.4	1.5	**2.6**	1.6	**2.3**	**2.5**	1.9
2000–09	1.0	1.1	0.7	0.1	1.3	1.4	1.9
2010–19	1.1	1.0	1.1	0.3	1.1	0.5	1.0
Growth of TFP							
	Canada	France	Germany	Italy	Japan	UK	US
1900–09	**2.0**	1.1	1.0	1.5	1.0	-0.1	0.7
1910–19	0.7	-1.4	-2.3	1.3	**2.9**	0.3	**3.2**
1920–29	**2.4**	**7.6**	**2.8**	**2.5**	1.1	1.8	1.2
1930–39	0.0	0.3	**3.1**	0.3	**2.3**	0.3	**2.2**
1940–49	**4.8**	**2.1**	1.2	**2.3**	-0.9	**2.3**	**3.2**
1950–59	**2.4**	**4.5**	**5.2**	**4.6**	**4.4**	1.2	**2.5**
1960–69	**2.1**	**4.6**	**3.4**	**4.8**	**5.8**	**2.2**	**2.1**
1970–79	0.8	**2.9**	**2.7**	**2.6**	**2.1**	1.9	0.9
1980–89	0.2	**2.0**	1.5	1.1	**2.1**	1.6	1.0
1990–99	0.8	1.0	1.7	0.8	0.8	1.5	1.6
2000–09	0.3	0.5	0.2	-0.4	0.6	0.7	1.0
2010–19	0.6	0.6	1.0	0.1	1.0	0.4	0.9

Source: Jorda, Schularick and Taylor (2019) and Bergeaud (2022). Growth rates of 2% and higher are in bold.

Since 2000 there has been almost no growth of output per capita or output per hour worked in Italy and slow growth in the other countries. The era of slow growth starts earlier, in the 1980s, in Canada, France, Germany and in the 1970s in the US. Figure 1 shows output per hour worked and total factor productivity (TFP) for the countries that currently belong to the eurozone, Japan and the US. Several remarks can be made on the figure.

First, output per hour was higher in the US than in Europe until around 1980, the gap grew in the 1920s and the 1930s and during World War II (WWII), thereafter Europe grew more rapidly until 1980. Second, output growth was higher in Europe in the post-war period, while its output per hour was lower than that in the US, Europe was catching up with the US. Third the slope of the US plot flattens in the mid-1970s, becomes slightly steeper in the mid-1990s and then flattens again. The path for Europe flattens around the 1980s and becomes flatter than that of the US showing that the US is now growing more rapidly than Europe. Fourth, output per hour was lower in Japan throughout this period, it fell more than in Europe after WWII and then narrowed the gap with the US. Fifth, output growth fell in the late 1970s in Japan, a few years earlier than in Europe. Sixth, output per hour is lower in Japan than in Europe and the US. The pattern is similar for TFP except that US TFP is not higher than Europe in the first 15 years of the twentieth century.

The Consequences of the Growth Slowdown

The low and falling rates of productivity growth in the past four to five decades have had several important consequences as discussed in our book *The Great Economic Slowdown*, see Phelps et al. (2023). First, there is the fall in the equilibrium real rate of interest. The very low equilibrium real rate has made monetary policy more difficult, causing expansionary policy to hit the zero lower bound. In Keynesian circles this problem has led some to propose abolishing cash altogether so as to make negative nominal rates possible.[5] Another consequence is high asset prices, both house prices and stock prices, around the world. The booming, and probably

[5] See Rogoff (2014).

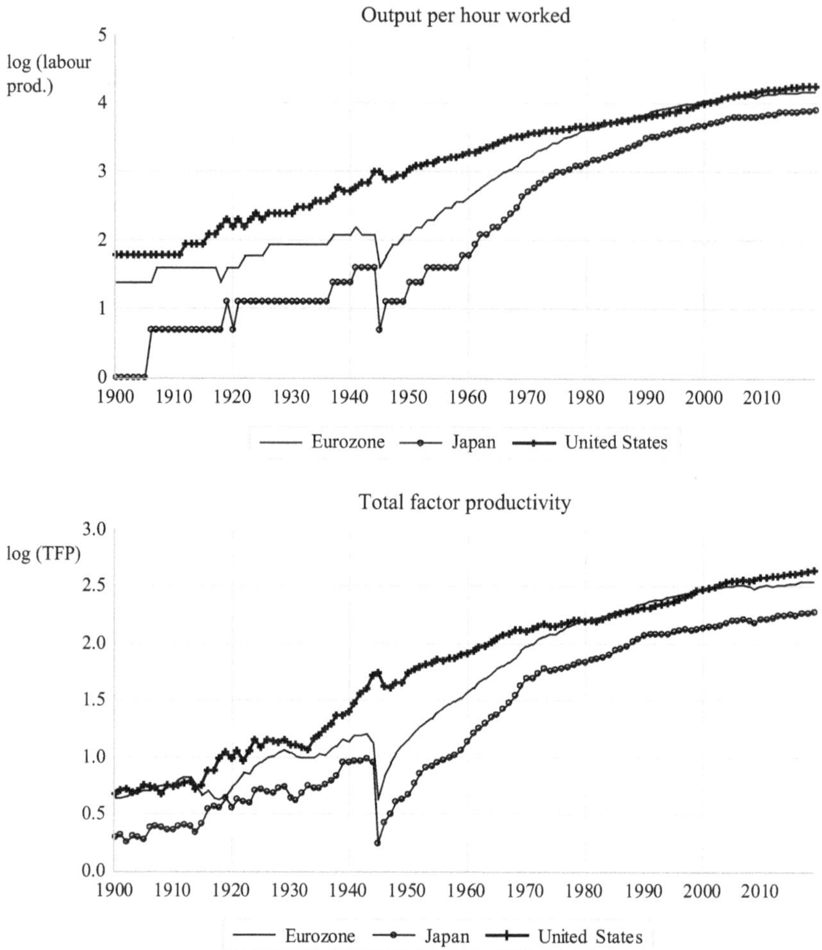

Fig. 1 Output per hour and TFP in the current eurozone and the US, 1900–2019. (US dollars 2010 ppp based. Source: Bergeaud et al. (2016), updated.)

overpriced, stock markets have made the distribution of wealth more unequal, which along with stagnant real wages has a destabilizing effect on politics. A fourth consequence, which also has a destabilizing effect, is lower job satisfaction, which to some extent stems from the stagnant real wages but also from changes in the nature of jobs. A fifth consequence is that when growth in the leading economies stalls, growth rates in the developing countries will eventually fall.

There are also geopolitical ramifications. Lower growth in the West has allowed other countries to catch up, in particular the size of the economy of China has come to rival that of the US. The convergence between GDP in the two countries has put them on a collusion path, reminiscent of the rivalry between an ascending Germany and Britain at the beginning of the twentieth century.

It is ironic that productivity and wages have stagnated at a time when our lives are being transformed by new technologies, from smartphones to the internet, from electric cars and social media to rapidly emerging artificial intelligence. Jobs and professions are being abolished and there is uncertainty where and what kind of jobs will exist in the future. But these developments do not show up in the productivity statistics nor in wage growth. Some of the new technology makes some jobs obsolete while other types increase the productivity of other jobs.[6] The new technologies have unfortunately helped saw social discord.

A Return of Growth

A return to the growth rates of productivity seen in the middle of the last century would help resolve many of the problems described in this book. There would be less need for governments to pay back the debts they have accumulated in recent years and inflation tax would no longer be needed to satisfy their intertemporal budget constraint. A relaxation of that budget constraint would free up monetary policy to curb inflation. Equilibrium real interest rates would be higher, creating an incentive to save, and the required return to capital would also become higher. Stock prices would be brought down and normalized.

Higher productivity would generate more output for a given use of inputs so as not to increase global warming. Rising output and growing wages would make it easier to reduce greenhouse gas emissions. Innovations in the area of green technologies would make it even easier. Geopolitical tensions would be eased and political stability in the West increased. Populism would no longer be as appealing and trust in politics would increase.

[6] See Teck Hoon (2020).

What can countries in the West do to increase innovation and growth? First, they can eliminate, or at least reduce, impediments to growth such as rules and regulations that protect stakeholders and entrenched interests such as mandatory redundancy payments, tariffs, red tape, subsidies and state contracts awarded on the basis of political connections—corporatism in all its gory manifestations.

For growth, an economy needs institutions that encourage innovation instead of rent seeking, a financial system that rewards innovators and is able to separate those with good ideas from others with ideas that would not generate profits. A healthy financial system is the heart of capitalism as is a set of modern values that emphasize self-reliance, independence, good work ethics and integrity in business. It goes without saying that the rule of law and the protection of property rights is also needed. Exposure to ideas and innovations in other countries is important. The closer a country moves towards the technology frontier, the more important education becomes—not just education in technology but also in business and the humanities (see Churchwell, 2018). Teaching students to imagine and think of something new makes good economic sense, but so does weaning the population off feelings of entitlement and materialism.

It is to be hoped that the new technologies will spur innovations thus increasing productivity growth and making the world a better place, at least one with fewer problems, at any rate.

References

Arnorsson, A., & Zoega, G. (2016). Social capital and the labor market. *Capitalism & Society, 11*(1), 1–29.

Banfield, E. C. (1958). *The moral basis of a backward society.* The Free Press.

Bergeaud, A., Cette, G., & Lecat, R. (2016). Productivity trends in advanced countries between 1890 and 2012. *Review of Income and Wealth, 62*(3), 420–444.

Bergaud, A., Cette, G., & Lecat, R. (2022). The long-term productivity database. Prod. Bank of France. Paris, November 24. http://www.longtermproductivity.com/about.html.

Bhidé, A. (2009). The venturesome economy: How innovation sustains prosperity in a more connected world. *Journal of Applied Corporate Finance, 21*(1), 8.

Bhide, A., & Phelps, E. S. (2005). *A dynamic theory of China-U.S. trade: Making sense of the imbalances.* Manuscript Columbia University. https://papers.ssrn.com/sol3/papers.cfm?abstract_id=763284

Churchwell, S. (2018, January 25). If you want to run the world, study a "useless" subject. *Financial Times*.
Gordon, R. J. (2016). *The rise and fall of American growth*. Princeton University Press.
Jorda, O., Knoll, K., Kuvshinov, D. S., & Taylor, A. M. (2019). The rate of return to everything. *Quarterly Journal of Economics, 134*(3), 1225–1298.
Nelson, R. R., & Phelps, E. S. (1966). Investment in humans, technological diffusion, and economic growth. *The American Economic Review, 56*(1/2), 69–75.
Phelps, E. S. (2006). *Toward a model of innovation and performance along the lines of Knight, Keynes, Hayek and M. Polanyi*. Center on Capitalism and Society, Columbia University. https://academiccommons.columbia.edu/doi/10.7916/D8XS66WR
Phelps, E. S. (2013). *Mass flourishing: How grassroots innovation created jobs, challenge, and change*. Princeton University Press.
Phelps, E., Bojilov, R., Teck Hoon, H., & Zoega, G. (2020). *Dynamism: The values that drive innovation, job satisfaction, and economic growth*. Harvard University Press.
Phelps, E. S., Hoon, H. T., & Zoega, G. (2023). *The great slowdown: How narrowed technical progress brought static wages, sky-high wealth, and much discontent*. Palgrave Macmillan.
Putnam, R. D. (1993). *Making democracy work: Civic traditions in modern Italy*. Princeton University Press.
Rogoff, K. (2014). Costs and benefits to phasing out paper currency. *NBER Macroeconomics Annual*, 445–456.
Tabellini, G. (2008). Institutions and culture. *Journal of the European Economic Association, 6*, 255–294. https://academic.oup.com/jeea/article/6/2-3/255/2295755.
Tabellini, G. (2010). Culture and institutions: Economic development in the regions of Europe. *Journal of the European Economic Association, 4*(1), 677–716.
Teck Hoon, H. (2020). Wage effects of additive and multiplicative robots alongside factory buildings and physical structures. In Í. E. S. Phelps, R. Bojilov, H. T. Hoon, & G. Zoega (Eds.), *Dynamism: The values that drive innovation, job satisfaction and economic growth*. Harvard University Press.

Correction to: The Need for Growth

Hian Teck Hoon, Edmund Phelps, and Gylfi Zoega

Correction to:

Chapter 20 in: R. Z. Aliber et al. (eds.), *Fault Lines After COVID-19*, https://doi.org/10.1007/978-3-031-26482-5_20

The original version of the chapter "The Need for Growth" was inadvertently published with incorrect values in the Table 1. The table has now been corrected in this chapter.

The updated version of this chapter can be found at
https://doi.org/10.1007/978-3-031-26482-5_20

R. Z. Aliber et al. (eds.), *Fault Lines After COVID-19*,
https://doi.org/10.1007/978-3-031-26482-5_21

Index[1]

A

Abkhazia, 186, 187, 189–191, 190n17, 193, 195
Absolute decoupling, 320, 321, 324, 325, 329
Acemoglu, Daron, 43, 44, 48
Acheson, Dean, 143
Acquis Communautaire, 179
Ahtisaari, Martti, 187
AIG, 264, 270
Alaska, 75
Albania, 192
Albright, Madelaine, 25, 25n45
Andy Warhol Theory of Economic Growth, 65
Angell, Norman, 138
Annual Report of Freedom House, 27
Anti-Oligarch law, 156
Apple, 337
Arctic, 318
Argentina, 6, 212, 215, 219, 220, 337
Aristotle, 26, 26n46
Armenia, 187
Artificial intelligence, 3, 9, 85–87, 211, 343
Australia, 63, 64, 115, 144, 338
Autocratic authorities, 3, 106
The Avoidable War, 63
Azerbaijan, 187

B

Bagehot, Walter, 42
Balcerowicz, Leszek, 150, 170
Balkans hostilities, 136
Baltics, 165, 168
Banca d'Italia, 291
Banfield, Edward C., 338
Bangladesh, 64, 223
Bank cheques, 285
Bank for International Settlements, 291
Bank of Belgium, 298

[1] Note: Page numbers followed by 'n' refer to notes.

R. Z. Aliber et al. (eds.), *Fault Lines After COVID-19*, https://doi.org/10.1007/978-3-031-26482-5

Bank of England, 20–21, 204, 206, 207, 208n3, 250, 250n1, 251, 282, 307
Bank of Japan, 202, 250, 250n1, 251
Bank of Korea, 110, 250
Banque de France, 298
Barclays, 291
Bear Stearns, 270
Belarus, 144, 152, 165, 191
Belt and Road Initiative, 72, 79, 90, 117, 119, 146
Bergemann, Patrick, 98
Berlin Wall, 40
Bhidé, Amar, 337, 337n2
Bilateral swap lines, 7
Bildeberg Group, 291
BIS, 114
BIS Group of Computer Experts, 297
Bismarck, Otto von, 166
Bitcoin, 303
BitFinex, 309
BNP, 291
Boeing, 337
Bolshevik revolution, 167
Bolsonaro, Jair, 27, 41
Bond market, 7, 120, 129
The bond market crisis of 2020, 266–274
Bond mutual funds, 261
Boom in domestic private leverage, 220
Brazil, 41, 222, 250, 252
Bretton Woods Systems, 141
Brexit, 28n54, 138, 205
Bucharest summit, 190
Buffers, 235
The Bulletin of the Atomic Scientists Doomsday Clock, 137
Buyer of last resort, 264, 265

C
Calvo, Guillermo, 220
Canada, 64, 122, 126, 160, 162, 250, 251, 339–341
Capital flow management, 7, 236
Capital flows, 6, 217, 218, 220–223, 228, 228n2, 230–240, 243
Carney, Mark, 234, 307
Center on Capitalism and Society, 336
Central bank, 5, 6, 18n23, 29n62, 30n65, 113, 126, 129, 150, 151, 160, 181, 201, 206–209, 211–215, 241–243, 307
Central Bank of Iceland, 6, 228n2
Central Bank of Russia, 160
Chase Manhattan Bank, 286
Cheney, Richard B., 138
Cheney, Dick, 138
Chernyhiv, 153
Chiang Mai Initiative, 127–128
Chiang Mai Initiative Multilateralization, 127
Chile, 6, 219, 222, 233
China, 1–4, 21–23, 26, 28n55, 37–39, 41, 46–48, 50, 55, 63–93, 98, 99, 104–106, 109–130, 114n2, 118n9, 118n10, 119n11, 121n13, 123n18, 135, 136, 142, 145, 146, 174, 202, 210, 223–225, 322, 327, 335, 337n2, 343
China Development Bank, 117
China Evergrande, 120
Chinese Communist Party, 3, 82, 92
CHIPS, *see* Clearing House Interbank Payments System in New York
Citibank, 289
Clarke, John J., 292
Clearing House Interbank Payments System in New York (CHIPS), 283–290

Climate change, 8, 14, 17, 21, 22, 24, 28, 135, 202, 203, 317–319, 324, 325, 329
Committee on Interbank Netting Schemes, 288
Communal apartments, 104
Complex adaptive system, 14
Computer, 89, 93
Constitutional Court of Ukraine, 156
Contempt for the rule of law, 41
Corporate bond market, 267, 271
Corporate debt, 15
Corporatism, 337
Correspondent banking, 282
Correspondent banking system, 280, 283, 299
Corruption, 5, 49n12, 54, 73, 83, 84, 93, 151, 156, 161–163, 178, 179, 179n12, 182
Covid/ COVID-19, 1, 2, 7, 13–32, 39, 98, 104, 112, 138, 160, 201–215, 218, 222–225, 253, 258n11, 259, 322
Crash in China's real estate market, 65
Creative destruction, 173
Crimea, 5, 54, 152, 153, 173, 186, 186n5, 192, 192n22, 193, 193n25, 195
Crimean intervention, 193
Croatia, 165, 188n10, 233
Cross border capital flows, 218
Cross-border financial integration, 6, 227–244, 232n7
Cross-border payments, 280
Crowley, Robert J., 285
Crypto.com, 309
Cryptocurrency, 303
Crypto Exchanges, 307
Cuban missile crisis, 39
Cult of the personality, 41
Cultural Revolution, 81, 90
Cybercrime, 17
Cyber dictatorship, 88–90
Cyprus, 136, 196
Czech Republic, 233, 239

D

Dai, 304–306, 306n11, 309, 310
Darwin, Charles, 42–44, 50, 51, 54, 55
Daylight Overdrafts, 286
Debt and equity flows, 222
Debt-deflation, 23
Decentralized finance, 303
Deep and Comprehensive Free Trade Area (DCFTA), 155
Deep Historical Roots, 44, 46, 52
Deng Xiaoping/Deng Xiao Peng, 77, 81
Denunciations, 3, 98–107
The Descent of Man, 42, 50
Despotism, 49
Diamond, Douglas, 258, 311, 312n27
Dictator's dilemma, 83
Dixit, Avinash, 48
Dodd-Frank Act, 270
Dollar funding, 4, 109, 110, 112–116, 119, 120, 122, 124–127, 129
Dollar intermediation, 261
Dollar swap liquidity, 250
Dollar swaps, 250, 250n1
Domestic asset flows, 221
Donbass region, 152
Donetsk, 152, 153, 186, 193–195, 193n26
Donetsk oblast, 152
Dugin, Alexander, 55
Dybvig, Philip H., 258, 311, 312n27
Dynamism, 338

E
The Economic Consequences of the Peace, 141
Economic freedom, 3, 5, 177
Egypt, 46, 223
E-money tokens, 308
Employment protection legislation, 337
Enlai, Zhou, 54
Environmental Kuznets Curve, 322
Equilibrium real rate of interest, 8
Era of the Strongman, 39
Erdogan, Recep T., 2, 41
Estonia, 163, 165
Eurasian Economic Union, 191
Euro area (eurozone), 18
Eurodollar market, 284
European Bank for Reconstruction and Development, 150–151
European Central Bank, 75, 204, 250–252
European Economic Area, 239
European Union (EU), 5, 8, 121, 136, 141, 144, 149–164, 155n6, 156n7, 156n8, 159n13, 162n20, 166, 168, 172, 172n4, 174, 175, 178, 179n12, 181, 182, 191, 196, 235, 239, 253, 259, 304, 307–311, 308n16, 310n23, 322, 327
Eurozone, 6, 139, 215, 341, 342
Evergrande, 69, 78, 118, 120, 120n12
Everything bubble, 16
Excessive regulation, 337
Exchange-traded funds, 272
Extreme capital inflows, 220

F
Federal Funds target rate, 205
Federalist Papers, 25
Federal Open Market Committee, 251
Federal Reserve, 7, 16–19, 110, 113, 124, 126, 129, 136, 208, 208n3, 250–253, 252n3, 285
Fed liquidity facilities, 255
Ferdinand, Franz, 140
Fergusson, Niall, 159
FIMA, 124, 126, 128, 129, 253, 254, 254n7, 255n8, 255n9, 257, 258
FIMA Repo Facility, 124, 126, 128
Financial Action Task Force, 156
Financial buffers, 6
Financial Cold War, 63
Financial crisis, 2, 6, 7, 15, 39, 40, 138n4, 145, 218, 220, 221, 224, 236, 239, 249, 258
Financial instability, 17, 109
Financial regulations, 6, 232, 235
Financial Stability Board, 280
Financial supervision, 6, 232, 235
Findlay, Ronald, 142
FinTech firms, 17
Fiscal dominance, 6, 29, 29n62, 30, 201, 207–208, 212, 215
Fiscal policy, 171, 173, 180–181, 236, 237, 241
Fitzroy, Robert, 42
Floating exchange rates, 4, 39, 141, 239, 244
Fok, J. A., 63
Foreign exchange intervention, 7
Foreign exchange reserves, 121, 123–125, 127, 141, 236, 238
Foreign liability flows, 221
France, 339
Friedman, Milton, 39
Fukuyama, Francis, 42–46, 49, 51, 55

G
GATT, 38, 39
Gazeta Wyborcza, 179
Geeley, 79

Geopolitical shocks, 4, 135, 136, 139
Geopolitical tensions, 1, 4, 8, 23, 135, 138–140, 203, 343
Georgia, 5, 138, 165, 186, 187, 189–193, 255, 255n9
German Bundesbank, 211
German Democratic Republic, 98
Glasnost, 57
Global Financial Crisis, 113, 217, 222, 249–253
Global financial cycle, 6
Global Polycrisis, 24n41
Global tensions, 135–139
Goodhart, Charles, 22, 203, 204
Gorbachev, Michail, 2, 53n16, 56–58
Great Depression, 7, 23n38, 25, 40
Greater fool theory, 68
Great Financial Crisis, 204, 228n2
Great Firewall, 85
The Great Illusion, 138
The Great Leap Forward, 81
Greece, 6, 136, 196, 212, 213
Greek sovereign debt, 213
Greenhouse gases, 8, 14, 24, 317

H
Hayek, Friedrich, 3, 24, 24n43
Herstatt Risk, 287
High speed railroads, 79
Hitler, Adolf, 27
Hong Kong, 110, 121n13, 122, 128, 254n7, 255n9, 257n10, 305
Hong Kong Monetary Authority, 128
Hoon, Hian Teck, 341n5
Huawei electronics, 142
Huntington, Samuel P., 43
Huxley, Thomas Henry, 42

I
iFinex, 305, 309
India, 2, 27n51, 41, 136, 223, 255, 255n9, 322, 327
Inflation, 2, 5, 6, 18, 19, 19n25, 21–24, 29, 30, 30n64, 32, 39, 40, 139, 143, 146, 151, 159, 160, 162, 180, 180n14, 181, 201–215, 217, 219, 224, 229, 231, 234, 236, 237, 304, 343
Inflation control, 201
Institute for New Economic Thinking (INET), 29n59
Interest rate normalization, 217
International Court of Justice, 192, 192n24
International Monetary Fund (IMF), 15, 17n18, 38, 39, 113, 115n6, 122n15, 123n16, 124, 125, 127n24, 128, 144, 146, 150, 181, 212n4, 212n5, 214, 228n1, 233, 240–242, 240n13, 244
Internet Engineering Technical Forum, 144
Islamic insurgency, 136
Italy, 6, 89, 138, 212–214, 335, 337, 338, 340, 341

J
Japan, 3, 22, 64–66, 68, 69, 71, 72, 75–77, 112, 121, 122, 124, 126, 127, 137, 162, 203–205, 208n3, 209, 335, 339–341
Jim Crow laws, 27n51
Job satisfaction, 338, 342
Johnson, Boris, 41
Jorda, 339, 340

K
Kennedy, John F., 32n68, 145
Keynes, John M., 28n56, 39n4, 140, 141

Keynesian economics, 40
Keynesian era, 39
KGB agents, 150
Kherson, 152, 186, 194, 194n30, 195
Kindleberger, Charles, 142, 145
Korea, 22, 28n55, 66, 72, 91, 92, 110, 136
Kosovo, 5, 136, 185–196, 186n5, 187n6, 187n7, 188n11, 188n12, 189n13, 190n16, 192n22, 192n23, 192n24, 193n27
Kyiv, 149, 158n12, 159n14, 159n15
Kyiv School of Economics, 152
Kyoto Protocol, 318, 322

L
Labor unions, 338
Late 19th century globalization, 282
Latin America, 217–219, 224
Latin American Debt crisis, 217, 218
Latvia, 163, 165
Leader for life, 75
Lehman Brothers, 289
Lender of last resort, 262
Lenin, Vladimir, 83, 90
Libra, 304
Libya, 136, 153, 186, 195
Life cycle related emissions, 327
Liquidity crunch, 126, 249
Lithuania, 163, 165
Long transaction chains, 280
Lucas, Robert, 39
Luhansk, 152, 153, 186, 193–195
Luhansk oblast, 152, 153
LUNA, 306

M
Ma, Jack, 73
Macroprudential policy, 7, 236, 237
Madison, James, 25, 27
Magic Internet Money, 309
Managed float, 236, 241
Mandela, Nelson, 339
Mao Zedong/Mao Zedung, 41, 81, 90
Mariupol, 153
Market-maker of last resort, 264, 265
Markets in Crypto-assets (MiCA) regulation, 307
MARRTI, 290
Marshall Plan for Ukraine, 161
Marx, Karl, 83
McKinsey Global Institute, 16, 16n10
Medvedev, Dmitry, 189
Message Switching Project, 292, 295n54
Mexico, 6, 41, 42, 122, 219, 220
Middle East, 89
Milosevic, Slobodan, 188
Minimum wages, 31
Minsky, Hyman, 40
Modi, Narendra, 27, 41
Moldova, 187, 196
Monetary policy, 6, 15, 16, 19, 21, 30, 142, 181, 204, 206, 207, 213, 214, 217–219, 221, 222, 228–231, 234, 236, 237, 241–243, 341, 343
Monetary union, 213, 214n6, 235, 236
Money market funds, 261
Mussolini, Benito, 27, 337
MyConstant, 310, 310n21

N
Narrow Corridor, 48
The Narrow Corridor, 43, 48, 50n14
National Bank of Ukraine, 162
National Socialist, 24

NATO, 5, 18, 38, 39, 42, 46, 48, 52, 144, 151, 154, 174, 182, 185, 187, 188, 190
Navalny, Alexei, 41
Nazi Germany, 98, 103, 105, 167
Neo-liberal era, 39
New Generation Artificial Intelligence Development Plan, 87
New World Order, 37–56
New Zealand, 233, 250
Nixon, Richard, 141, 143
Non-cooperative game theory, 48–50
North, Douglass, 88
Nostalgic nationalism, 42
Nunn-Lugar Act, 144

O
OECD, 16n12, 29, 29n59, 29n61, 83, 91, 121, 173, 233, 239, 240, 240n10, 240n13
Olson, Mancur, 90, 145, 179
One-child policy, 64, 66, 67, 91
Orban, Viktor, 27, 41
O'Rourke, K. H., 142
Output gap, 143, 205
Outright Monetary Transactions (OMT), 214

P
Pakistan, 136
Paris Agreement, 318–325, 329
Pegged exchange rates, 235
People's Bank of China, 74, 76, 123
Perestroika, 57
A perfect storm, 64, 76
Peron, Juan, 337
Peru, 219
Phelps, Edmund, 8, 337n1, 337n2, 338n3, 339, 341n5
Philips curves, 19
Poland, 4, 5, 41, 149–151, 154, 163, 165–182, 172n4, 177n11, 180n14
Ponzi, 40, 69, 78, 209, 210, 306, 309
Popper, Karl, 27
Populism, 39, 42, 343
Portugal, 46, 212, 213
Post-Soviet space, 186
Power and Plenty, 142
Power Law, 14
Pradhan, Dharmendra, 22, 203
Press freedom, 5, 177–179
Price stability, 201, 207–209, 212, 214, 215, 237, 242, 243
Private sector debt, 23
Productivity, 16, 339
Productivity growth, 8, 23n36, 82, 87, 88, 92, 336, 338, 339, 341, 344
Property rights, 9, 46, 82, 84, 156, 161, 162, 171, 344
Prudential rules, 235
Przeworski, Adam, 53
Public sector debt, 23, 213
Puri, Samir, 47, 51
Putin, Vladimir, 2, 5, 38, 39, 41, 42, 47, 51–58, 53n16, 140, 151, 151n2, 152, 160, 185n2, 186n3, 191, 191n19, 193, 193n27, 194, 194n29
Putnam, Robert D., 89, 338

Q
QE asset purchases, 207
Quantitative Easing, 18, 18n22, 30, 41

R
Rachman, Gideon, 38, 47
Reagan, Ronald, 40, 143

Real estate market, 67–70
Real rate of interest, 2, 205, 210
Real wages, 2, 8, 22, 202, 342
Reconstruction, 161
Reich, Robert, 39, 40
Reserve currency, 75
Richardson, Lewis Fry, 137
The Rise and Fall of the Great Powers, 145
Risk-free (neutral) real interest rate, 211
The Road to Serfdom, 24
Robinson, James, 43, 44
Roland, Gerard, 43, 44, 46–48
Roman, Emmanuel, 64
Romania, 136, 163, 196
Ruble zone, 170
Rudd, Kevin, 63, 66
Rule of law, 2, 9, 55, 75, 82, 155, 162, 163, 167, 170, 177–179, 344
Russia, 18
Russian banks, 279
Russian-Ukrainian war, 21

S
Sachs, Jeffrey, 168
St Petersburg, 46
Salazar, Antonio de, 46n9
Samuelson, Paul, 40
Schularick, M., 339, 340
Schumpeter, Joseph, 23n38, 88
Securities Markets Programme, 214
Serbia, 140, 185
Shanghai, 63, 78, 98, 104
Shultz, George, 143
Singapore, 64, 122, 233, 250, 252, 255n9, 309, 336
Slovakia, 136, 196
Slowdown in China, 75
Small, open and financially integrated economies (SOFIEs), 228
Small, open economies, 227
Smart courts, 86
Social capital, 5, 167, 179
Social credit, 85, 86, 89
Societe Financiere Europeéenne, 290
Societe Generale de Banque, 291
Society for Worldwide Interbank Financial Telecommunications (SWIFT), 283
Solidarity, 172, 179
Solow, Robert, 40, 336
Soros, George, 29n59
South Korea, 90, 92
South Ossetia, 186, 187, 189–191, 190n16, 193, 195
Soviet state regulation, 150
Spain, 6, 136, 196, 212, 213, 338
Sri Lanka, 146, 212, 215
Stablecoins, 8, 303–305, 304n3, 304n5, 307–312, 308n17, 310n24
Stalin, Joseph, 104
Stanley, Jason, 25
Stigler, George, 310
Stock prices, 2, 8, 65, 77, 336, 341
Structural reforms, 235
Structural slumps, 336
Sudden outflow, 220
Sustainable Development Goals, 317
Svyrydenko, Yuliya, 163
Swap lines, 7, 112, 126–127, 127n23, 129, 249–259, 257n10
Sweden Democrats, 27n53
SWIFT, 7, 141, 279
Swiss National Bank, 250–252, 250n1, 297
Switzerland, 126, 192n22, 239
Systemic risk, 220

T

Tabellini, Guido, 338
Taiwan, 4, 83, 90–92, 121n13, 135, 136
Tariffs, 9, 338, 344
Taylor, John, 339, 340
Taylor rule, 6, 143, 204–206
Technology frontier, 3, 344
Telegraph, 281
Telex machines, 282
TerraUSD, 304, 306
Terrorism, 136
Tether, 7, 304–305, 305n7, 305n8, 305n9, 309
Thatcher, Margaret, 39, 40, 44
The Thucydides Challenge, 63
Thucydides's Trap, 145
Tinbergen, Jan, 170
Tooze, Adam, 24n41
Total factor productivity, 82, 339, 341
Trade disputes, 76
Treasury bonds, 7
Trump, Donald J., 2, 27, 32n67, 41, 42, 75
Tucker, Paul, 17
Turkey, 2, 41, 66, 136, 160

U

UK, 2, 6, 7, 20, 21, 26, 27, 28n54, 30n64, 32n67, 39–41, 139, 141, 145, 177n11, 203–206, 209, 338–340
Ukraine, 1, 2, 4, 5, 7, 18, 39, 48, 52, 54, 55, 83, 135–139, 141n6, 144, 149–182, 151n1, 152n4, 153n5, 155n6, 156n7, 156n8, 157n9, 157n10, 158n11, 159n13, 160n16, 160n17, 161n18, 161n19, 162n20, 177n11, 179n12, 180n14, 185, 186, 190–196, 201, 202, 205, 207, 212
Ukraine Recovery Conference, 157
UNCTAD, 15, 175
UN General Assembly, 144
United Nations, 38, 299
United Nations Framework Convention on Climate change (UNFCCC), 318
United States, 2, 4–8, 15n7, 17–20, 19n27, 23, 25–27, 26n48, 27n51, 28n55, 32n67, 39–41, 63–65, 72, 73, 75, 76, 78–79, 82, 83, 91, 92, 106, 109, 110, 112–129, 120n12, 125n20, 136, 141–145, 141n6, 151, 158, 159, 160n17, 162, 177n11, 190, 202–206, 208n3, 218, 221, 231–233, 243, 305, 310, 335, 336, 338–343
UN Security Council, 5, 185, 187n6, 192
Uppsala Conflict Data Program, 137
US bond market, 7
US dollar funding, 109
USDT, 304, 305, 309, 310
US Treasuries, 17, 20, 120, 121, 124–126, 253, 255, 257

V

Venturesome customers, 337
Vietnam, 4, 64, 141
Volcker, Paul, 202
Volvo, 79

W

Wilberforce, Samuel, 42
World Bank, 38, 39, 118n8, 150, 153, 153n5, 168, 169, 174, 176–180, 177n10, 177n11, 307n15

World Health Organization, 121
World in Depression 1929-1939, 142
World Trade Organization, 66, 82
World Values Survey, 180, 180n13
World War I, 4, 138, 139, 167
World War II, 2, 39n4, 40, 77, 143–145, 167
Wuhan, 63

X

Xi Jinping, 3, 83
Xi Jinping Thought on Socialism with Chinese Characteristics for a New Era, 84

Y

Yeltsin, Boris, 2, 53n16, 56–58

Z

Zaporizhe oblast, 152
Zaporizhzhia, 186, 194, 195
Zero lower bound, 341
Zoega, Gylfi, 341n5

Kolibri 360 GmbH
Ferdinand-Jühlke-Straße 7
99095 Erfurt, Deutschland
produktsicherheit@kolibri360.de